P.T.T. HISTORY

AT A GLANCE

The obvious and natural symbols S, D, ~~are~~
significant. S means that the motion req~~uires a second;~~
A, it is Amendable; M means Majority ~~vote; 2/3,~~
two-thirds vote to pass; R, it can be Recon~~sidered;~~
the symbols are not subject to these rules.

The general rules are given here. For exce~~ptions~~, see their pages.

DEMETER'S MANUAL OF PARLIAMENTARY LAW AND PROCEDURE

DEMETER'S MANUAL OF PARLIAMENTARY LAW AND PROCEDURE

For the Legal Conduct of Business in All Deliberative Assemblies

BLUE BOOK EDITION
Revised, Expanded and Updated

by GEORGE DEMETER, A.B., M.A., LL.B.

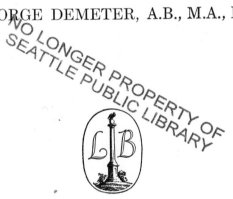

LITTLE, BROWN AND COMPANY
34 Beacon Street, Boston, Mass. 02106

LITTLE, BROWN AND COMPANY (CANADA) LIMITED
Toronto

HISTORY

LIBRARY OF CONGRESS CATALOG CARD NO. 69-15061

Revised Edition

*Published simultaneously in Canada
by Little, Brown & Company (Canada) Limited*

PRINTED IN THE UNITED STATES OF AMERICA

Δικαιοσύνη καὶ Ἰσονομία
(Justice and Isonomy)

CONTENTS

DEMETER'S MANUAL OF
PARLIAMENTARY LAW
AND PROCEDURE

NOTE ON THIS EDITION

This new edition, the Blue Book Edition, successor now to all my previous editions, has been revised throughout, brought up to date and expanded from 256 pages to 375 pages, thus making it still more useful to individuals and to thousands of clubs and organizations that have adopted it as their parliamentary authority.

It embodies more law and more proceedings, and it supersedes my previous editions. In the event of conflict with any rule in a previous edition, the rule contained in this updated revision supersedes a previous rule.

It abounds in drills, illustrations and frequent repetition of parliamentary rules and their authentic forms for quick mastery and proficient application. It contains many new viewpoints and many new parliamentary aspects — features not found in any other book.

All the serviceable and popular features of previous editions of this book, first published twenty years ago, have not only been retained but also broadened, thus rendering this volume one of continuing great force, prominence and influence in deliberative assemblies.

In the interest of orderly procedure, and of self-education in the rules of order in a great democratic nation which abounds in organizations and societies, a parliamentary law book which is authoritative and easy to comprehend and apply at meetings and conventions should be in every club member's home.

Moreover, this Manual will be found exceptionally suitable for adoption as parliamentary authority for organizations, municipalities, and other assemblies using parliamentary law.

This book will enable you and your organization, club or society to overcome parliamentary perplexities and difficulties. It was painstakingly designed not only to render the subject of parliamentary law plain, easy and immediately acquirable, but also to make it rich in cultural values.

In a word, *Demeter's Manual* serves four notable objectives: (1) it is a reliable *reference* authority; (2) an effective *self-instruction* book; (3) a unique *textbook* as a teaching manual; (4) its five hundred *court citations* affecting essential rights of members will help minimize, or avoid altogether, costly law suits and vexatious litigation against the organization by dissentious members or its antagonistic factions.

I wish at this time to express my profound gratitude to the men and women throughout the United States who have written to me in appreciation of the usefulness of my book, and to the organizations that have adopted it as their parliamentary authority.

Boston, Massachusetts   GEORGE DEMETER

Chapter 1
INTRODUCTION

Definition of parliamentary law. Courts have defined parliamentary law as "the rules and usages of Parliament or of deliberative bodies, which takes its name from the British Parliament and on the practice of which it mainly originated, with such changes and modifications in American deliberative assemblies as have been necessary to adapt it to the usages of this country."

In other words, the term *parliamentary law* refers to the rules, laws or regulations of organizations, governing the orderly, expeditious and efficient transaction of business at meetings and conventions. Without rules there would be injustice and confusion. Hence, it is as necessary to follow the rules of parliamentary law as it is to follow the rules of a ball game or a card game.

Origin of parliamentary law as a science. The rules of parliamentary law as a science originated in England in the British Parliament of the thirteenth century. They then spread rapidly to other parts of the world, with each nation modifying them to suit its own system of parliamentary practice.

Parliamentary law was introduced in the United States by the American colonists, and was used in their town meetings, colonial legislatures, and other assemblies both public and private.

Parliamentary law in ancient times. Parliamentary law, by which is meant orderly deliberation and action by an assembly of persons or a body of citizens, was nonexistent before 750 B.C.

Prior to 750 B.C. all gatherings of the people were held under the strict authority of the father of the family (paterfamilias) or under the despotic rule of kings and viceroys. Gatherings then were convened only for deity worship or for war and defense measures. They were never convened to discuss affairs of government, or to deliberate and to vote on public questions. The people had no share in government, and no voice or vote in it.

About 750 B.C. the idea of self-government, with the right to deliberate in assembly and to speak and vote on public questions, was conceived in Greece, the "cradle of liberty."

The Greeks instituted the Athenian *Agora* or general assembly, equivalent to the American town meeting, consisting then of the whole body of male citizens above eighteen years of age. The general assembly met forty times each year on the Acropolis, the famous hill in Athens where any citizen could address the meeting from a stone platform called *Bema* and vote on questions before the assembly.

This novel and ingenious Grecian concept of self-government gradually captured the fancy of the Romans, who, some three hundred years later (c. 450 B.C.), adopted it and expanded it with the institution of the Roman Forum, or meeting place of the people, where Roman orators addressed the general assembly from the Rostra (a stone platform) on the Palatine-Capitoline hills in Rome. The people afterward voted on pending questions.

From such beginnings did parliamentary and democratic processes of self-government begin to evolve. They were conceived in Athens c. 750 B.C., expanded by Rome in 450 B.C., then systematized by the British Parliament some two thousand years after the institution of the Greek *Agora*, and, since 1789, broadened and perfected by the U. S. House of Representatives into a system that ranks second to none. The House's rules of parliamentary law today are "perhaps the most finely adjusted, scientifically balanced, and highly technical rules of any parliamentary body in the world. Under them a majority may work its will at all times in the face of the most determined and vigorous opposition of a minority" (*Lewis Deschler*, U. S. House *Rules and Manual*, p. vi).

Other names for parliamentary law. Parliamentary law is known by several other names: parliamentary law and procedure, parliamentary practice, parliamentary law and practice, rules of order, etc.

Derivation of the word parliamentary. The word "parliamentary" is derived from the French *parler* (to speak, discuss, or deliberate), and obviously refers to the body or code of rules, regulations or laws and practices of deliberative bodies.

The object of parliamentary law. This author adjudges the object of parliamentary law to be *to transact the assembly's business legally and to control the conduct of its members.*

Other authors conceive its object to be as follows:

JEFFERSON: "To attain accuracy in business, economy of time, order, uniformity and impartiality."

CUSHING: "To subserve the will of the assembly rather than to restrain it; to facilitate, and not to obstruct its deliberate sense."

ROBERT: "To enable an assembly, with the least possible friction, to deliberate upon questions in which it is interested, and to ascertain and express its deliberate sense or will on these questions."

Notes on the above authors: Thomas Jefferson, third President of the United States, was born in 1743. He was a civil engineer. He attended the College of William and Mary, and studied law in a law firm in Williamsburg. He was the author of *Jefferson's Manual*. Luther S. Cushing, born in 1803, served in the Massachusetts Legislature. A lawyer, he taught law at Harvard. He was the author of *Cushing's Manual*. Henry M. Robert was born in 1837. He was a graduate of the U. S. Military Academy at West Point and a superintendent of the Academy. He was a U. S. Army engineer and a general. He was the author of *Robert's Rules of Order*. George Demeter, lawyer, Massachusetts legislator, and author of *Demeter's Manual*, was born in 1900.

Foundations of parliamentary law. There are five great principles underlying the rules of parliamentary law, namely:

(1) *Order.* That is, there must be orderly procedure. (2) *Equality.* That is, all members are equal before the rule or law. (3) *Justice.* That is, "justice for all." (4) Right of the *minority* to be heard on questions; (5) Right of the *majority* to rule the organization.

Purpose of rules. Rules are necessary because it is dangerous to rely on the inspiration of the moment for standards of action or conduct. Hence, rules are set up for three necessary purposes:

(1) For orderly procedure. Without it, the meeting would result in utter confusion, chaos and disorder — just as would be the case in a ball game or a card game if there were no rules to go by and each player did as he pleased.

(2) For the protection and liberty of the minority. That is why, for instance, parliamentary law provides that "Every member shall have the right to debate main motions," and "Debate cannot be shut off except by a $\frac{2}{3}$ vote of the body," thus affording the minority freedom of speech and liberty from constraint.

(3) For the expression of the will of the majority. It is axiomatic that an assembly functions best when the majority rules. Hence, democratic self-government implies that the minority, however convinced of its own wisdom, consents to be ruled by the majority, until in orderly process it can make itself the majority.

"Unwritten" duties of members. The basic or unwritten duties of a member are as follows:

(1) To attend meetings, thus acquiring experience, talent and the attributes of leadership, not only for the good of the order, but also for the community, state and nation. Meetings of organizations offer tremendous educational as well as social advantages.

(2) To participate in the proceedings and deliberations, thus acquiring proficiency in the rules of parliamentary practice and in debate, decorum and discipline.

(3) To accept the final decision of the majority without animosity or violence — just as one accepts the will of the people in a political election or the final decision of a judge, umpire or referee. One must demonstrate sportsmanship in the forum of a deliberative body (lodge, chapter, council, local, unit or other body) as much as in the field of sports.

(4) To obey the rules of the organization and to pay his dues and other assessments promptly, thus helping to maintain the organization's dignity and integrity.

(5) To bring in or recommend new members, and thus help to promote the organization's growth and extend its influence.

Duty of presiding officer to know parliamentary law. It is the duty of the presiding officer to know the rules of parliamentary law and basic parliamentary practice. There is nothing more pitiable than one who is ignorant of parliamentary law trying to preside over an assembly; the more intelligent the assembly, the sadder the spectacle.

Taking the initiative and exercising leadership. Those who aspire to leadership and who would exert power and influence in organizations should not only know the rules of parliamentary procedure, but should also train themselves to take the initiative in proposing appropriate action to meet situations as they arise.

Examples of initiative and leadership:

(1) If you are elected a delegate to a convention or conference, for instance, think of some needful or desirable motion or resolution which you can present for adoption and that will benefit your organization, community, state or nation, as the case may be.

(2) If the bylaws of your organization are outmoded, imperfect or deficient, take the initiative and propose their amendment or revision. Write your amendment, read it, and give it to the Chair.

(3) If prices for goods, wares or merchandise are high and it is in line with your organization's scope and purposes to concern itself with prices, take the initiative and propose suitable action to combat the situation by appropriate motion or resolution.

(4) If the head of an organization dies, or the president or king of a nation, governor, major, fellow-member, classmate, etc., passes on, and the duty or concern of the organization for the deceased warrants expression of sympathy or a memorial, take the initiative and propose an appropriate motion or resolution.

(5) If the regular presiding officer is incompetent or arrogant or a member is frequently obnoxious or obstructive to the organization's progress, before resorting to removal proceedings or suspension, take the initiative and propose censure (see Censure, the "voice of warning" of suspension, removal from office, or expulsion, p. 260).

(6) In like manner, learn to cope with countless other important situations or events — whether they be world or national affairs, politics, sports, births, marriages, promotions, decorations, etc. As situations arise, reflect what steps should be taken, if any. Then propose suitable action, arranging beforehand to have your motion seconded and your supporters at the meeting. Train yourself to exercise initiative and leadership ahead of others.

Note: Meetings of deliberative bodies — fraternal orders, women's clubs, labor organizations, veterans' associations, and all other useful clubs and societies — offer tremendous educational advantages and many opportunities for leadership.

Exhortation

To presiding officers: Avoid debating motions with the members while presiding. You may not be aware of it, but when you take sides in debate you are usurping rights that more properly belong to the members, who often resent it since they are as jealous of their exclusive rights as you are of your own prerogatives.

Astute presiding officers appear impartial when presiding, and they never reveal their feelings or assert their partisanship from the chair; instead, they have their prechosen "lieutenants" do it for them when need be, or they surrender the chair and then debate.

Avoid being dictatorial — which usually arises from being ignorant of the rules of parliamentary law and practice. Study and know procedure so that you will not deny to members their proper rights or exclude their legitimate motions or entertain improper ones.

Use correct parliamentary forms and language, as urged in this manual — any others used in their place are bound to be impure, incomplete or confusing.

To vice presidents: Know procedure and the duties of the president and when you succeed him put into practice only the best, most constructive and efficient precedents set by him. Attend all meetings. Observe all proceedings.

To new members: New members with no previous experience in organizations and who may be shy (but who will constitute tomorrow's officers and leaders) can acquire proficiency and confidence in three easy ways: (1) by attending meetings regularly; (2) by merely, at first, for a meeting or two, seconding motions — sensible ones; and (3) by rising and discussing, very briefly at first, only questions or motions which appear certain to pass or be defeated.

After you have thus acquired poise and the technique of debate, you can then enter into plenary participation. Remember: practice makes perfect — and those speakers who appear to debate questions with amazing eloquence and persuasiveness have acquired that skill mostly through just such practice. You can do the same.

Prepare yourself early for top leadership. Look over often pages A and B (inside front cover); but study page C and rehearse frequently page D (inside back cover) and pp. 10 and 11.

To all members: As fellow-members, be just always and helpful whenever you can; you are all allied in the same cause. Ask to see your bylaws, and check: (1) how your bylaws may be amended; (2) by what vote officers are elected; and (3) your quorum. You will thus be enabled to prevent unconstitutional amendments, illegal elections and quorumless meetings.

DO YOU WISH TO KNOW IMMEDIATELY...?

CLASS, RULES, AND RANK OF CERTAIN IMPORTANT MOTIONS

Mastery of the contents of pages 10 and 11 will give you at once a 50 percent skeleton knowledge of basic parliamentary law and practice.

Read the following to yourself or to a group:

Observe that three classes of familiar motions are listed below: first, *privileged;* second, *subsidiary;* and third, *main,* or principal, motions. The word *subsidiary* means helping or assisting motions.

The privileged and subsidiary motions supersede the main motion. In practice this means that any of them can be proposed upon a pending main motion. These motions, especially the subsidiary, are the most frequently used motions at meetings and conventions. Hence, learn their rules.

Their rules. The symbols S, D, A, M, ⅔, and R alongside each motion reveal their rules and give you on-the-spot information; thus: S means the motion requires a Second; D, it is Debatable; A means that it is Amendable; M, it requires a Majority vote to adopt it; and ⅔, a Two-thirds vote is necessary; R means that the motion can be Reconsidered. Here they are:

Privileged Motions

1. Fix a day to which to adjourn (S, A, M, R)...... page 119
2. Adjourn (S, M).................................... 113
3. Recess (S, A, M)................................. 112
4. Raise a question of privilege (no symbols).......... 106
5. Call for the orders of the day (no symbols).......... 104

Subsidiary Motions

1. Lay on the table (S, M)........................ page 98
2. Previous question (S, ⅔, R)..................... 92
3. Limit or extend debate (S, A, ⅔, R)............... 90
4. Postpone to a definite time (S, D, A, M, R)........ 88
5. Refer to a committee (S, D, A, M, R)............. 82
6. Amend the main motion (S, D, A, M, R)........... 68
7. Postpone indefinitely (S, D, M, R)................ 66

Main (or Principal) Motions

Main motions or resolutions (S, D, A, M, R)...... page 50

Their rank. Each motion is listed according to its rank. Each one in the above scale from top to bottom is of higher rank than every motion listed below it, and of lower rank than every motion listed above it. This means that a motion of *higher* rank is always in order when a motion of *lower* rank is pending, and a motion of *lower* rank is out of order if proposed while a motion of *higher* rank is before the assembly — just like bids at an auction sale. (See also page 11.)

The symbols S, D, A, M, ⅔, R, in that logical order, are easy to fix in the mind. A motion without any of these symbols is, as the case may be, unsecondable, undebatable, unamendable, unvotable, or unreconsiderable. Fix in mind the *subsidiary* motions by their first letters: L, P; L, P; R, A, P.

HOW TO TRANSACT MOTIONS BY RANK

Transacting motions according to their rank as shown in the scale on pp. 46–49 is as simple as transacting bids in an auction sale — higher motions, like higher bids, being always in order; and lower motions, like lower bids, being always out of order.

To illustrate their operation, assume the following main motion pending before the body (and assume all motions are duly seconded):

MAIN MOTION: "To build a new clubhouse."

MEMBER A: "Mr. Chairman, I move to *table* the main motion." (To table is a subsidiary motion of higher rank than a main motion, and the Chair entertains it; he has to know its *rank;* thus:)

CHAIR: "It is moved and seconded to lay the motion on the table."

MEMBER B: "Mr. Chairman, I move to *refer* the main motion to the House Committee, with instructions to report back at the next meeting."

CHAIR: "The motion to refer [note the language used] is not in order now; it is of lower rank than the pending motion to table."

MEMBER C: "Mr. Chairman, I move to *amend* the main motion by adding at the end thereof the words 'at a cost not to exceed $250,000.' "

CHAIR: "The amendment is not in order at present; it is of lower rank than the pending subsidiary motion to table."

MEMBER D: "Mr. Chairman, I move to *postpone* the main motion."

CHAIR: "The motion to postpone is not in order at the present time; it is of lower rank than the pending motion to table."

MEMBER E: "Mr. Chairman, I move we *recess* for five minutes." (The privileged motion to recess is in order; it outranks to table.)

CHAIR: "It is moved and seconded to recess for five minutes."

MEMBER F: "Mr. Chairman, I move we *adjourn*." (The privileged motion to adjourn outranks to recess and to table. The Chair says:)

CHAIR: "It is moved and seconded to adjourn."

MEMBER G: "Mr. Chairman, I move that we buy a new desk."

CHAIR: "The *main* motion just proposed is presently not in order, as only one *main* motion at a time may be considered."

MEMBER H: "Mr. Chairman, how many motions are now properly pending?"

CHAIR: "Four: to *adjourn, recess, table* and the *main* motion to build a new clubhouse." (Only one *main motion* is pending; the other three are mere parliamentary *forms,* which outrank it.)

Taking the vote on many pending motions. When more than one motion is pending, as above, the *highest* motion in rank is voted on first, then each *next highest,* for example:

CHAIR: "The first vote is on the motion to adjourn. Those in favor will say aye; those opposed will say no; the *noes* have it. Next, the motion to recess. Those in favor will say aye; those opposed will say no; the *noes* have it. Now, the motion to lay on the table. Those in favor will say aye; those opposed will say no; the *ayes* have it, and the main motion to build a new clubhouse has been *tabled.*" (Then he asks:) "Is there further new business?"

Other sets are similarly transacted. Master pages 10 and 11.

Note: Presiding officers are expected to know the *rank* of the motions shown here and on pp. 46–49, otherwise they have no business presiding.

PARLIAMENTARY VOCABULARY
Definitions

Accept: adopt, approve, agree to, concur in, assent.
Amend: change, alter, modify, correct, improve, substitute.
Apply: adhere to, attach, go with, implicate.
Assembly: body, meeting, members present, gathering.
Aye (pronounced "I"): yes, as in "the ayes have it"; voice vote.
Business: motion, resolution, etc.; topic, subject, order.
Bylaws, constitution: rules, regulations, canon (canon law).
Chair: presiding officer (whatever be his title).
General consent: silent majority consent.
Immediately pending motion: the last stated motion or question.
Laws: charter, articles of incorporation, constitution, bylaws.
Main motion: resolution, order, recommendation, topic, subject.
Majority: more than half of the votes actually cast.
Meeting: session, sitting.
Orders of the day: program, order of business, agenda.
Pending: any matter(s) actually and properly before the body.
Plurality: the most votes without regard to majority.
Postpone indefinitely: suppress, rid of, "kill" (the motion).
Precedence: priority, supersedence, order of rank of a motion.
Present: those actually physically present; must be counted.
Present and voting: those who cast a vote (ignoring all blanks).
Previous question: stop the debate, "I move the previous question."
Principal motions: main motion, resolution, recommendation, topic.
Question: any motion, resolution, subject, topic, resolve, order.
Rank: precedence, priority, order, supersedence.
Recommendation: main motion, resolution, town article.
Society: organization, club.
Secondary motions: all motions *not* main.
Subsidiary motions: "helping," "aiding," or "assisting" motions.
Table: the secretary's file or records, secretarial custody.
Unanimous consent: unanimous vote required, no one dissenting.
Voting: those actually casting a vote (blanks are not votes).
Yeas and nays: yeses and noes, roll-call vote.
Yield: give way to, concede to, superseded by, outranked by.

Derivative Terms

Act, actable, unactable. **Amend,** amendable, unamendable, amendability, unamendability. **Debate,** debatable, undebatable, debatability, undebatability. **Entertain,** entertainable, unentertainable. **Reconsider,** reconsiderable, unreconsiderable, reconsideration. **Rescind,** rescindable (rescissible), unrescindable (unrescissible), rescission. **Restore,** restorable, unrestorable. **Second,** secondable, unsecondable. **Substitute,** substitutable, unsubstitutable. **Table,** tablable, untablable. **Transact,** transactable, untransactable. **Vote,** votable, unvotable.

Chapter 2
ESSENTIALS OF MEETINGS

I. REGULAR, SPECIAL, AND ADJOURNED MEETINGS

How convened. Regular and special meetings are convened in the manner prescribed in the bylaws; if there is no provision therein and no special rule or prevailing custom, meetings can be called by the president or by the president and secretary jointly. A regular meeting can convene a special meeting, but a special meeting cannot convene a regular meeting. A special meeting may not be scheduled to a time beyond the next regular meeting under normal parliamentary practice.

What business transacted in regular meetings. If the organization has no established order of business for its regular meetings, any business can be transacted that comes within the scope and purposes of the organization, except such as requires previous notice (as amendments to bylaws). If it has an established order, follow it.

What business transacted in special meetings. If the bylaws do not require the business of a special meeting to be specified in the call, such meeting is but an extra regular meeting, and there is no difference between it and any other regular meeting; hence, it is treated as a quasi-regular meeting. If the call embraces a permissive clause such as "and such other business as may properly [or, legally] come before it," then in addition to the business announced in the call, any other business falling within the scope of the organization can be acted on except such as requires previous notice. If the bylaws prescribe that "no business shall be transacted in a special meeting except that specified in the call," then no other business can properly be transacted therein.

In special meetings the organization's regular order of business is not followed. All that need be done therein is to (*a*) conduct the usual opening formalities (if any), (*b*) read the call for the meeting, and (*c*) transact the business for which the special meeting was called, and (*d*) adjourn.

What business transacted at adjourned-regular and adjourned-special meetings. Continued meetings of a regular or special meeting, technically known respectively as adjourned-regular and adjourned-special meetings, perform or complete the business contemplated in the call of the original regular or special session because it is a continued meeting. Nothing can be considered at an adjourned-special meeting unless it could have been considered at the special meeting it was adjourned from.

Notice of regular or special meetings. Notice of a proposed meeting, whether regular or special, must be mailed or communicated to all members. Notice of all meetings must be given as prescribed in the bylaws. In some cases a week's notice or more, especially when the membership is scattered, is adequate notice; in others, three days, more or less, may be reasonable. In the final analysis, the assembly can best judge this for itself. If your bylaws do not specify notice, incorporate a bylaw dealing with this; lacking which, three to five days constitutes good local notice.

Members transacting business where the required notice has not been given do so at their own risk; but they can move to ratify the action at the next or any future meeting.

Notice of adjourned meetings (regular or special). Members are bound to take notice of the time of an adjourned meeting, regular or special, and to be present at the time and place of adjournment without further notice, since such meeting is a continued meeting of the original one of which they already have had notice; but where advisable, additional notice may be sent to remind the members and to convene as many as possible. Such notice does not have to be sent; if it is sent, it must not convey prejudice for or against any proceeding or member; such notice should merely state that an adjourned meeting of the previous meeting will be held on the designated date.

Minutes. Minutes of a regular meeting are not read in a special meeting, but the minutes of a special meeting are read at the next regular meeting. When minutes come into competition, those of a regular meeting are read and acted on ahead of the special meeting's minutes.

II. THE ORDER OF BUSINESS

All proceedings of deliberative bodies are divided into three parts as shown in the standard order of business that follows. This recognized order of business may be adopted by organizations which do not already have one. It is easy to remember the business part by initial letters: R, R, R, S, U, N, G.

The Opening
Prayer, anthem, pledge, password, paid-up dues cards, etc.

The Business
Reading of the minutes of the last meeting
Reports of (1) officers, (2) boards, and (3) standing committees
Reports of special (temporary) committees
Special orders (specially scheduled business)
Unfinished business
New business
Good of the order

The Closing
Saluting the colors, secret sign, hymn, announcements, etc., prayer

Note: Prayer is always first and last in an order of business.

There is no standard rule for including in any particular order such topics as roll call of officers, bills, correspondence, initiation, etc. Each organization decides for itself what its order of business shall comprise and where to insert the headings. See the examples of the order of business of six organizations at the end of this chapter.

How the Chair Transacts the Order of Business

Chair keeps assembly informed. In the interest of orderly procedure, the Chair, when about to take up a subject, should prepare the assembly for it and keep the members constantly informed; thus: "The first business in order is the reading of the minutes of the last meeting"; or, "The next business in order is [naming it]"; or "Unfinished business is the business in order"; or "New business is the next business in order"; or "The question before the house is on [thus-and-so]," etc.

Vocabulary. "Order of business" is known by several other names: orders of the day, schedule of business, program, agenda, calendar of business, etc.

The phrase "the next *business in order*" is correct; the phrase "the next *order of business*" is incorrect.

Note: To say "the first *order* of business," or "the next [or, the third] *order* of business," is like saying "the first *week* of the day," or "the next [or, the third] *year* of the month," or "the next [or, the third] ball game of the inning," etc. The assembly has but one order of business — the various categories or items of business as *listed* under an order of business are to be acted on in that scheduled business order. Hence say: "the first *business in order*," "the next business in order," "the last business in order," and not "the first *order of business*," or "the second order of business," etc. It is a gross error to say "the first order of business" and the like.

How transacted. The following drill illustrates how to transact the standard order of business. As previously stated, the order of business consists of three essential parts: (1) the opening part, (2) the business part, and (3) the closing part. (In other words, if we could have a bird's-eye view of the millions of meetings that are at this moment now in session throughout the world, we would see them conducting either the opening part, or the business part, or the closing part.)

Note: Act the Chair's part, below. Repeat aloud the proceedings.

The Opening

Calling meeting to order.

CHAIR (striking once with gavel): "The meeting will come to order. The Chaplain will now make the invocation." (Assembly rises.)

Prayer may be memorized, or use your own words.

CHAPLAIN: "Almighty God, we thank Thee for bringing us together this day. Help us to achieve worthwhile accomplishments. We pray Thee to bless and protect our nation and to so guide and inspire us that we may live in unity and peace. Amen." (Assembly is seated.)

The Business

Reading of the minutes.

CHAIR: "The first business in order is the reading of the minutes. The secretary will please read the minutes of the last meeting." (Reading completed.) "Are there any corrections to the minutes? There being no corrections, the minutes are approved as read."

Reports of officers, boards, and standing committees (in that order)

CHAIR (continuing): "The next business in order [keep using this form for announcing each successive piece of business] is reports of officers. Brother Titus, treasurer." (Reports of the treasurer are given at meetings for information purposes only; no vote is taken, or need be taken, to adopt or accept them, as this would be certifying to their correctness without proper audit.)

TREASURER: "Total receipts from all sources, since our last meeting $290; total disbursements, $140; total amount in the Tenth Federal Bank as of tonight, $1,234.56." (The members have a right to inquire into any item, and can ask questions thereon.)

Report of boards

CHAIR: "The next business in order is the report of the executive board [or executive committee]. Brother Foreman, chairman."

FOREMAN: "Mr. President, the executive committee at its last meeting voted to recommend the construction of a new clubhouse, which I shall bring up under new business."

Note: Such proposal is properly actable under *new* business and not under "Reports" here, because the proposal originated in committee. But if the clubhouse question had been previously *referred* to the committee by the body, it would properly be actable here under Reports.

Reports of standing committees

CHAIR: "The next business in order is reports of standing committees. First, the House Committee; Brother Green, chairman."

Note: As each officer or member makes his report, the Chair *may* (but he is not required to) say "Thank you!"

GREEN: "Mr. President, as authorized by the assembly, the House Committee ordered a new coat rack for the checkroom."

Note: No motion to accept is necessary; but if it is done, it is harmless. Act on it, thus exercising assembly participation.

CHAIR: "Thank you. The next standing committee is Visitation and Relief; Brother Brown, chairman."

BROWN: "Mr. President, your committee visited Brothers A and B at the X Hospital. Both are coming along nicely. They asked your committee to thank the members for the fruit and candy sent them."

Note: No motion to accept is needed; but if it is done, it injects parliamentary interest; it is a pat on the committee back.

Reports of special committees

CHAIR: "Thank you. The next business in order under reports is reports of special committees; and first, the Chair recognizes the chairman of the committee on the Spring Dance, Miss Joy."

JOY: "Mr. President, the committee to whom was referred the motion to hold a Spring Dance met three times since our last meeting and voted unanimously to recommend the adoption of that motion." This has to be acted on here because it was *referred* to the committee by the body at the previous meeting; and the Chair transacts it thus:

CHAIR: "You have heard the committee's recommendation. The question before the body is on the motion 'to hold a Spring Dance.' Is there any debate on the question?" (After debate, if any, it is put to vote, and the result announced accordingly.) "Next," (the Chair continues,) "is the report of [such-and-such] other special committees," naming the chairman in each case.

Special orders (specially scheduled business)

CHAIR: "The next business in order is special orders." (He turns to the secretary and asks:) "Are there any special orders?" (meaning any business or motions postponed from the last meeting and made a *special* order for a particular hour at this meeting).

SECRETARY: "There are no special orders."

Unfinished business

CHAIR: "There being no special orders, unfinished business is the next business in order." He turns to the secretary and asks: "Is there any unfinished business?"

SECRETARY: "Yes. A motion to organize a glee club was postponed to this meeting from the last meeting."

CHAIR (informing the body): "Under unfinished business, there was postponed to this meeting from the last meeting the motion to organize a glee club. The question is now before you. Is there any discussion on the question?" (After discussion, if any, it is put to vote and the result announced. The Chair continues:) "Is there any further unfinished business?"

SECRETARY: "No."

New business

CHAIR: "New business is now in order [or, the next business in order is new business]."

MEMBER A: "Mr. President, I move that we invite the mayor to speak to us at the next meeting." (Seconded, debated and voted on.)

CHAIR: "Is there further new business?"

MEMBER B: "Mr. President, I move that our second meeting next month be held jointly with the Ladies Auxiliary." (Voted on.)

Here also, under new business, are properly actable any and all proposals or recommendations which originate in committee, such as Mr. Foreman's proposal, under "Reports of Boards."

Good of the order (if so scheduled)

CHAIR (continues): "Is there further new business? (Silence.) There being none, the next business in order is the good of the order." ·

MEMBER C: "Mr. President, our meetings have not been commencing on time, although a quorum was always present. I thought that under the good of the order I might make a constructive suggestion. I move that it be the sense of this body that all meetings in the future begin on time when a quorum is present." (Seconded, stated, and put to vote.) It is allowable to introduce main motions under the heading of "good of the order," if, as here, they concern that topic.

Helpful distinction. New business allows generally any new question. "Good of the order" allows specific suggestions, constructive comments, criticism, or even compliments, to achieve which they can be proposed as main motions. This makes it unnecessary to revert back to the category of new business in order to act on them.

But no tabled, postponed, referred, defeated or otherwise disposed of motion acted on by the body can be reintroduced under the good of the order, as this would circumvent the assembly's previous action thereon.

The Closing

CHAIR: "Is there anything further under the good of the order?" (Silence.) "There being nothing further, we shall proceed to adjourn [or, a motion to adjourn is in order]."

MEMBER D: "Mr. President, I move we adjourn." (Put to vote.)

Analysis of the Standard Order of Business

Reading of the minutes. Read the minutes of the last meeting. But if two or more sets remain unread from previous meetings, the minutes of the meeting farthest back are read and approved first, then those of the next farthest. When finished, take up reports.

Restoratory motions: when they may be made. Motions to reconsider, rescind, ratify, and take from table can be taken up and be acted on at any stage of the proceedings following the reading of the minutes up to adjournment, provided no other motion is actually pending before the assembly at the time, or when their *category* (or business of their own *class*) is reached.

Note: Motions to reconsider, rescind, ratify and take from the table can also be acted on under two other categories, unfinished business or new business, if they were previously overlooked.

Reports of officers, boards and standing committees. Take up first the reports of officers in the order designated in the bylaws, if any other officers besides the treasurer customarily report; then the report of the executive board; then, standing committees. When finished, take up reports of special committees.

Reports of special (temporary) committees. They report in the order they were elected or appointed. When finished, take up the next subject — special orders, if any.

Methods of accepting committee reports. (All are good forms.) (1) "I move to accept the report of the Committee as read." This is equivalent to adopting and approving the report fully as rendered, including any and all recommendations, unless the above motion is phrased to except or exclude all or some of the contents or recommendations. (2) "I move that the report of the committee be accepted as one of progress." (3) "I move that the report of the committee be accepted and the committee be discharged with thanks" or "and be given a rising vote of thanks," etc.

Some assemblies are in the habit of voting to accept any and every kind of report. Ordinarily, however, unless a committee reports a motion, resolution or recommendation, no action is taken on the report; the mere submission is sufficient. If it is done, there is no harm.

Action on committee recommendations. Recommendations or resolutions of committees on matters previously referred to them by the body are properly actable under reports; but recommendations on matters originating with or initiated by committees themselves are properly actable under new business, because they are new questions.

Special orders. Special orders (the technical name for special business or motions, specially postponed and made a "special order" at a previous meeting to be acted on at a particular hour at the subsequent meeting) are taken up at the designated hour. If there are no special orders, pass on to the next heading—unfinished business.

Unfinished business. First, take up the business, if any, that was actually pending before the body when it was voted to adjourn at the last meeting (as in conventions, annual meetings, or other groups meeting daily); then, the business, if any, which was scheduled to be acted on but was left untransacted because of the adjournment; and, finally, the motions or business, if any, postponed to this meeting from the last meeting (but not motions postponed indefinitely).

Amendments to the bylaws or their revision, which were previously duly proposed, also come up under unfinished business, including any other proposals or questions for which previous notice is required and such notice was duly given. When finished, take up new business.

New business. First take up such new business, if any, as necessarily arises out of mandates, orders or official communications from a superior body or higher authority, and from advantageous general correspondence; then such motions or recommendations, if any, as arise out of reports of officers, boards, and committees (standing and special); and finally any and all new business usually proposed by the members. When there is no further new business, pass on to the good of the order, or proceed to adjourn.

Good of the order. Take up or point out any constructive suggestion or criticism deemed beneficial to the welfare of the members or the general good of the organization (in a very liberal and broad sense).

What You Can Do to an Order of Business

After the body completes its opening exercises and it reaches the business part, its fixed order of business and all categories and items of business thereunder are in the body's control, and the body can do with them as it likes if the required *vote* is obtained for the purpose (just as a person who goes to a restaurant to eat has the bill of fare at his command and can order from it any item if he has the money to pay for it).

Hence the body can skip any items of business, under any category; or it can vote to adopt or defeat any item; or it can apply on it any *subsidiary* motion (p. 62), and thus amend it, or postpone it, refer it, or table it, etc.; or the body can recess or adjourn while any item of business is before the body, or make use of any other *privileged* motion (p. 102), or any pertinent *incidental* motion (p. 120).

Note: The reason subsidiary, privileged, and incidental motions can be made use of when any subject or item of business is before the body is that every item of business, under any category, is a *main motion*, or in the nature or status of main motion (p. 50), and main motions *yield* to motions of *higher* rank (such as these three classes). Master pages 10 and 11, and glance often at page 52.

What can an assembly do to an order of business? Since, as stated in the preceding paragraph, a subject or item of business under any category of business has the status of a main motion, and all *main motions* (p. 52) yield to (are superseded by) subsidiary, privileged and incidental motions, members have the right to propose appropriate subsidiary, privileged or incidental motions while a main motion is pending. Hence:

(1) When the minutes are about to be read, a member can move to dispense with the reading, or to postpone or table the reading — and this because the minutes are in the nature of a *main* motion.

(2) On reports of officers, boards and committees (standing or special), a member can move to postpone or table the report (or move any other subsidiary motion), and this because such reports are in the nature of main motions.

(3) When special orders are before the body, such questions are main motions; hence they yield to the subsidiary, privileged and incidental motions.

(4) Subjects or questions taken up under unfinished business are also main motions; hence they yield to the subsidiary, privileged and incidental motions.

(5) Questions or propositions proposed under new business are also main motions; hence they can be amended, postponed, tabled, etc., if a majority vote will favor such action. A member proposes, but the body disposes.

In like manner, a member has the right to propose any subsidiary or privileged motion (or pertinent incidental motion) on such other types of proceedings as shown below; and it is up to the body then to decide the member's proposal one way or the other: (a) applications for membership or reinstatement; (b) any and all amendments to bylaws, for which previous notice was duly given; (c) motions to censure or commend an officer or member; (d) motions to assess or to fine members; (e) motions to impeach, suspend or expel; (f) to abolish or modify a term of office, or any individual's office or his term of office, etc.

Note: The mere giving of previous notice, such as to amend bylaws or to reconsider, rescind, etc., is not subject to the subsidiary, privileged or incidental motions.

Models of Order of Business

Well-regulated organizations, clubs, and societies have a program, plan, or order of business for the orderly and efficient transaction of their agenda. Six models of order of business are listed below.

Organization A

Taking of Password
Prayer
Roll Call of Officers
Pledge of Allegiance
Opening Ode
Reading of Minutes
Reports: Officers and Committees
Second Reading: Applications
Balloting for Members
Unfinished Business
New Business
Good of the Order

Organization B

Prayer
Roll Call
Reading of Minutes
Communications and Bills
Report: Board, Officers
Names proposed for Membership
Reports on Candidates
Balloting on Candidates
Obligation of Candidates

Organization D

Prayer
Roll Call of Officers
Pledge of Allegiance
Minutes of Club and Board
Communications; Correspondence
Reports: Officers, Boards
Unfinished Business
New Business
Good of the Association
Adjournment

Organization E

Invocation
Roll Call of Officers
Reading of Minutes
Executive Board Report
Communications, Bills
Report of Business Agent
Report: Standing Committees
Report: Special Committees
Report: Board of Trustees
Unfinished Business
New Business

Report: Delegates, Committees
Accidents, Sickness, or Death
Unfinished Business
New Business
Good of Union
Receipts and Expenses

Organization C

Invocation
Presentation of Colors
National Anthem
Address of Welcome
Response to Address
Credentials Committee Report
Adoption of Convention Rules
Memorial
Reports of Officers, Boards, and
    Committees
Nominations, Elections
Installation
Banquet

Good and Welfare
Reading of Financial Report

Organization F

Opening the Convention in Due
    Form
Calling Roll of Officers
Reports of Officers
Appointment of Committees
Reports of Committees
Unfinished Business
New Business
Elections
Installation of Officers
Close Convention in Due Form

Note: This national organization
also provides in its order of business
the following instructive declaration:
This order of business is suspendable
by $\frac{2}{3}$ vote any time.

III. MINUTES (S, D, A, M)

Purpose of minutes. Minutes are recorded and read for three main reasons: (1) to refresh the memory of the members who attended the last meeting; (2) to inform those who were absent; and (3) to compile a history of the organization's acts and accomplishments.

Other names. The term "minutes" is known by at least three other names: "record," "report," or "journal." All are synonymous terms. The most common is minutes. For *your* correct term see your bylaws.

Basic rules. Minutes are in the nature of a main motion (technically called "incidental main motion"); on a formal motion to accept or adopt them, they are secondable, debatable, amendable (correctable), and require a majority vote. They cannot be reconsidered; instead, the motion to amend them is used in place of reconsideration. That is, minutes can be corrected (or recorrected) whenever the error is noticed, even if it be months or years later. Simply rise and offer the needed correction.

Amending (correcting) adopted minutes. If a set of minutes has been voted as accepted either by silent consent or by formal vote, and it is afterward desired to correct or amend them, the rule is as follows: It requires only a majority vote to amend the minutes during the same session in which they were adopted, but a $\frac{2}{3}$ vote to amend or correct them in subsequent sessions. They may also be corrected by rising to a question of privilege.

Quorum during reading of the minutes. If the point of no quorum is *openly* raised, the minutes are *not* read; if it is not raised, a quorum is presumed present. The point of no quorum can be made at any time.

How minutes are transacted. Normally, minutes are acted on in three ways: (1) they are read and approved as read; (2) they are read and corrected, and approved as corrected; or (3) their reading is dispensed with; thus:

1. *Acceptance of the minutes*

(*a*) Acceptance of the minutes, as read, by silent consent.

CHAIR: "The secretary will please read the minutes of the last meeting." (After they are read:) "Are there any corrections to the minutes?" (No corrections being proposed, he says:) "There being no corrections, the minutes will stand approved as read."

This constitutes acceptance of the minutes by silent or general consent, since the reading is purely a routine matter. This form of acceptance of the minutes is transacted on the initiative of the Chair. This is the quickest and most efficient way to adopt minutes if no corrections are proposed; it saves time. But the members have the right to move to accept the minutes, thus:

(*b*) Acceptance of the minutes by vote of the body.

CHAIR (after minutes are read): "Are there any corrections?"

MEMBER: "Mr. Chairman, I move to accept the minutes as read."

CHAIR: "It has been moved and seconded that the minutes be accepted as read." (Pauses for possible corrections, and then the vote:) "Those in favor of the motion will say aye; those opposed will say no; the ayes have it, and the minutes are accepted as read."

2. *Correcting and accepting the minutes*

CHAIR: "The secretary will read the minutes of the last meeting." (Reading completed.) "Are there any corrections?"

MEMBER A: "Mr. Chairman, my name was omitted from the Ball Committee."

CHAIR: "The secretary will make the necessary correction. Are there any further corrections?"

MEMBER B: "Mr. Chairman, the net receipts from our card party were $39.45, not $41.45 as recorded."

CHAIR: "The secretary will make the necessary correction. Are there further corrections?" (He keeps using this form.)

MEMBER C: "The last meeting adjourned at 10:15, not 10:45."

CHAIR: "The secretary will make the necessary correction. Are there further corrections? There being no further corrections, the minutes will stand approved as corrected." This constitutes adoption of corrected minutes by silent consent.

Note: Avoid asking, "Are there any errors, omissions, or additions?" The word "corrections" covers all these words. The secretary may, but is not required to, rise to read the minutes. But he must read them distinctly and audibly for all members in the room to hear. A majority vote adopts the minutes if put to a formal vote.

3. *Differing opinions on accuracy of the minutes.* If there are differing opinions as to the accuracy of an entry in the minutes, and its correctness cannot be established by proof or facts, a vote can be taken to determine the entry in dispute; the opinion receiving the largest vote establishes the correct entry. All officers and members present (including the secretary) are entitled to vote on the question, even if any were absent at the last meeting. If such opinion is afterward found to be erroneous, it can be corrected at *any* meeting.

4. *Dispensing with the reading of the minutes.* To "dispense with" the reading is to omit the reading of the minutes, thus:

CHAIR: "The secretary will read the min—" (interrupted).

MEMBER: "Mr. Chairman, I move that we dispense with the reading of the minutes of the last meeting." (This motion is secondable and amendable but is undebatable, and requires a majority vote.)

CHAIR: "Those in favor of dispensing with the reading of the minutes will say aye; those opposed will say no; the ayes have it, and the reading is dispensed with," or as the case may be.

The motion to dispense with the reading of the minutes is proposed when some urgent business is to be first attended to, or when the secretary has not yet arrived, etc. The reading can also be postponed or laid on the table, but the more appropriate form is to dispense with the reading. Omitted minutes can be read anytime later during the same session when called for, and when no other business is then pending before the house; if not read, they are read at the next meeting, unless again dispensed with at such or any further meeting.

Minutes of boards, committees and conventions. Board and committee minutes are not read to the body except by rule, or by vote of the body, or by custom. Convention minutes are read on each succeeding convention day, and those of the last day of the convention may be ordered approved by a committee or board, etc. Minutes of a previous convention are not read at the next convention, except by rule or custom. Minutes in conventions, or bodies having two or more sittings the same day, are not read that day unless it is the *final* day of the session or unless the body orders otherwise. But if the body holds a sitting next day, then such minutes are read at that time.

Demands to record one's vote. Demands by a member to record his vote in the minutes is allowable if no one objects. If there is objection, a majority vote is necessary to authorize it.

Slander recorded by secretary. A secretary can be sued for slander for recording in the minutes such words as "liar," "thief," etc., uttered by members in the heat of debate. Defamatory or scandalous charges or derogatory remarks uttered in the course of *debate* should not be recorded, but formal charges during impeachment proceedings *are* recorded.

Guardianship and disposition of minutes. In the absence of express authority the secretary should never exhibit the minutes to a nonmember. The organization has the right to inspect at reasonable hours, or order to be inspected, all such records, minutes, papers, etc. Official books, papers, records and organization property belong to the organization, not to the officer or member charged with their keeping, and it is the duty of such member or outgoing officer to surrender the same to his successor promptly and peaceably.

Essentials of minutes. The secretary is not required to include in the minutes all that takes place at meetings. Generally speaking, only decisions should be embodied. A record is made of what is done, not what is said. Lengthy or detailed minutes are not necessary. The following constitute the most essential points for inclusion (others are not excluded):

1. Kind of meeting (as regular, special, etc.).
2. Name of the organization.
3. Date and place of meeting; also presence of quorum.

4. Names of substitute officers.

5. Action taken on minutes of last meeting.

6. Main motions and resolutions, whether adopted or lost, but not those withdrawn, and any and all other motions (such as postpone, table, refer, etc.) that were adopted.

7. Name of proposer of a motion (seconder's name if required).

8. Reports of boards, officers and committees.

9. All required previous notices, such as notice to rescind, to reconsider, to amend the bylaws at the next meeting, all proper points of order and appeals, and all votes taken by hand or rising, ballot, roll call (or by mail, or proxy).

10. Any other action or proceeding worthy of record.

11. Hour of meeting and adjournment.

12. Socials or other events of the meeting occurring before, during or after the session, including names of guest speakers therein may be included for the record.

Models of minutes

Model 1. At a regular meeting of C Club, held in B Hall, on Tuesday, October (date and year), at 8:10 P.M., a quorum being present, the minutes of the last meeting were read and approved. The treasurer reported $500 in D Bank as of this meeting, with all bills paid to date. The following committee reports were submitted: Executive, Program, Music, House, Annual Ball, and Legislative. Under unfinished business, the motion to buy a new clubhouse postponed from the last meeting was considered and, after considerable debate, was defeated. Under new business, on motion of E duly seconded, it was voted to organize a bowling team. On motion of F duly seconded, it was voted to appoint a committee to revise the bylaws, and the Chair appointed G, H, I, J and K to the committee. The meeting adjourned at 10:05 P.M.

Respectfully submitted,
(signed) A. BROWN, Secretary

Model 2. A special meeting of N Club was held in O Hall, on Tuesday, April (date and year), at 8:05 P.M., and was called to order by Vice President P in the absence of President Q, a quorum being present. The secretary read the call of the special meeting as follows: "A special meeting of the N Club will be held in O Hall, on Tuesday, April (date), at 8:00 P.M. The object of the meeting will be to consider the advisability of buying a new clubhouse."

On motion of U, duly seconded, it was voted to limit debate on the question to three minutes a member, and no one to speak a second time except by unanimous consent. The following members spoke in favor of buying a new clubhouse: V, W, X, Y and Z; and the following spoke against: A, B, C, D, E, F, G, H and I. On motion of J, it was voted to order the previous question. The motion to buy a new clubhouse was then put to a vote and on a rising vote the result was 87 in favor and 91 against. Member K, who voted with prevailing side [the negative here] then moved reconsideration of the vote. Reconsideration was then duly seconded, put to vote and was defeated. Then L rose and moved to have the vote *again* reconsidered. The Chair ruled that the same question cannot be reconsidered more than once.

On motion of N, duly seconded, the meeting adjourned at 10:45 P.M.

Respectfully submitted,

(signed) A. BROWN, Secretary

Note to Secretary: (1) *Unseconded* motions are not recorded in the minutes; unseconded motions are not "lost" (defeated) motions; to be lost a motion must first be put to vote and be defeated. Theoretically, the body's refusal to second a motion implies forbiddance to record it. (2) *Withdrawn* motions are not recorded in the minutes. It may sometimes be damaging or unwise to record them in the minutes: hence their withdrawal. (3) A convenient form for recording members' motions is: "On motion of A, duly seconded by B, it was voted to do thus-and-so."

Previous notice. It is the duty of the secretary to record in the minutes all the essential previous notices duly given that have not been withdrawn, which the organization's bylaws prescribe or its parliamentary authority may authorize, such as a previous notice to amend the bylaws or to rescind some motion, or to reconsider it or reconsider and enter, etc.

Recording the vote. All votes on bylaws should be recorded (and the record should also say whether a quorum was present). All other votes should be recorded as "47 Yes, 51 No," or "87 voted in the affirmative, 65 in the negative."

Chapter 3
BASIC PROCEDURES: DEBATING, VOTING
I. DEBATING

Fundamental rules of debate. To enable the members to share the floor equally in the discussion of questions before the body and to prevent its being monopolized by anyone, parliamentary law has devised the following fundamental rules governing members' rights to discuss questions.

Note: Your bylaws or special or convention rules may create exceptions. Know them.

1. Every member is automatically entitled to speak *once* on a debatable motion before the body unless the body, by a $\frac{2}{3}$ vote, has ordered the discussion closed. After discussion has been voted closed, no one can debate a motion—except by unanimous consent.

2. A member is also automatically entitled to speak a *second* time on the same question the same day, unless other members who have not yet spoken on the question actually *rise* to claim the floor to speak. If no one rises, he may then speak a second time.

3. No one may automatically speak a *third* or further time if anyone in the assembly objects. To object, one need simply say: "Mr. Chairman, I object to anyone speaking more than twice on the same question." (This is the rule you can invoke to enable you to prevent members from monopolizing the floor.) But if no one objects, he may speak as many times as the body cares to permit him.

4. The *time limit* for each speech is ten minutes under common parliamentary law. But in some organizations the limit is five minutes, and in others seven, etc.; in such cases the said limit prevails. At the end

of the time limit, if no one objects, the speaker may continue; but if anyone objects, he cannot continue unless granted permission by a $\frac{2}{3}$ vote, because by thus extending debate, fewer members will be able to debate.

5. The ten-minute rule (or five or seven) applies to all questions whatsoever, such as main motions, resolutions, reports, etc.

Note: Although reports of officers, boards, etc., are usually permitted to occupy unlimited time, at the end of the first time period any member may rise, interrupt the report and ask: "Mr. Chairman, how much more time will the report occupy?" Following this, a motion can be made, when need be, that only so much more time shall be used, and no more.

Who may debate a motion. A proposer can in any desired case, vote against his own motion, but he may not speak against it. A seconder can do both. But the fact that a member has spoken against his own motion does not invalidate either his motion or any action taken on it by the body.

Members who were absent or who failed to vote when present can vote on and also debate any question when they are present.

One who spoke on a question can also speak on amendments to that question, as well as on any other proceeding which involves or affects that question, such as reconsideration, rescission, or any subsidiary, privileged or incidental motion (pp. 47, 48); reason: the question is in a different stage.

Abide by the final result. Defend or oppose motions and questions with all your skill and eloquence, but always abide by the final result — thus preserving harmony and the unity of the members and safeguarding the organization's dignity and integrity. Show the same spirit and good sportsmanship at meetings and conventions as in sports and political elections.

Forms of debate. A smart debater uses recognized parliamentary forms and effective parliamentary phraseology when discussing a motion before the house. For the best results, he should begin and conclude his remarks on a question by using the following forms:

To speak in favor of a motion, he begins: 'Mr. Chairman, I rise [or, I wish] to speak in favor of the motion," and gives his reasons. Or, "Mr. Chairman, I am in favor of the motion." He concludes: "I therefore hope that the motion will prevail." Or, "I therefore hope and trust that the motion will be adopted." Or, "I therefore hope and sincerely trust that the motion will be carried." Or, "I therefore urge the members to vote *yes.*" (Use these forms interchangeably.)

Model debate in favor of a motion. "Mr. Chairman, I rise [or, I wish] to speak in favor of the motion," and immediately follow this up with a statement of your reasons; for example: "In the first place, there is enough money in our treasury; secondly, we need these articles at this time; thirdly, the price at which we can now buy them is reasonable," etc. Now conclude emphatically: "Therefore, I hope and trust that the motion will prevail."

To speak in opposition to a motion, he begins: "Madam President, I rise [or wish] to speak against the motion," and gives his reasons. Or "Madam President, I am opposed to the motion." He concludes: "I therefore hope that the motion will not prevail." Or, "I hope and trust that the motion will not be adopted." Or, "I earnestly hope and sincerely trust that the motion will not be carried." Or, "I therefore urge the members to vote *no*."

Model debate against a motion. "Mr. Chairman, I rise to speak against the motion. I think the price at which these articles can be bought is still high. The best materials are not yet available. Besides, the sum we have in our treasury does not permit further expenditure at this time. Therefore, I earnestly hope and trust that the motion will not prevail."

How the Chair opens the meeting. An effective way of getting the members or delegates to respond quickly to the Chair's command to come to order is this preliminary warning:

CHAIR (strikes *once* vigorously with gavel): "The Chair is about to call the meeting [or, convention] to order. The officers will take their respective stations, and all members [or, delegates] will please be seated."

He then calls it to order, using one of these forms: (1) "The meeting will now come to order." Or, (2) "The meeting will be in order." Or, (3) "The meeting is now called to order."

If the assemblage is a convention, conference, annual meeting or committee or class meeting, substitute these words in place of the word *meeting;* thus: "The annual meeting will now come to order," "The class will be in order," "The conference will please come to order," etc. The word "please" is not required.

How to obtain the floor. Before a member can, properly speaking, be permitted either to propose motions, or to debate, he must observe the following three rules: (1) He must rise. (2) He must address the presiding officer by his proper title: men are addressed "Mr." and women, married or single, "Madam"; thus: "Mr. President!" "Madam President!" etc. (3) He must be recognized, that is, he must wait until the Chair recognizes him by name, or by nodding to him, or by other mode of recognition.

When the Chair appears not to know or remember a member's name the member should instantly aid the Chair by giving his name, whereupon the Chair repeats it, and the member has thus duly obtained the floor. In any event, to expedite business the Chair may always use the following convenient form: "The Chair recognizes the member [lady, gentleman, delegate, etc.] in the third row" or "in the front of the room" or other appropriate designation.

Note: Never address a presiding officer as "chairwoman." The women frown on it. Say "Madam Chairman" instead. Authority: National Association of Parliamentarians; American Institute of Parliamentarians. "Toast-mistress" is correctly applicable to women. Authority: International Toast-mistress Clubs. The title "postmistress" is proper for a woman presiding officer in a convention of postmasters, and "Moderatrix" is appropriate in town meetings.

Rule for recognizing members and assigning the floor. Under basic parliamentary law, when two or more persons rise to claim the floor at about the same time, the member who, in the Chair's sound judgment, first *rose* and *addressed* the Chair is entitled to recognition. The proposer of the motion, however, is always entitled to the floor first, provided he rises and asks for the floor immediately. For the finer points of this problem, see pp. 43–45.

Speaker's right to demand order. Although the assembly cannot be compelled to listen to a speaker, it is the duty of the Chair to compel it to observe order. When the members are disorderly or noisy, or the Chair disregards observance of order, or when the speaker himself is unable to hold the interest of the assembly, he is nevertheless entitled to due courtesy and he can demand order; thus: "Mr. Chairman, I respectfully demand order!" Or, "I demand quiet!" The Chair then enforces order. This can be repeated at intervals when need be.

How to Manipulate Motions for Passage or Defeat

The following tactics or proceedings can be used at meetings and conventions by proponents or opponents to help *adopt* or *defeat* a motion, resolution or question.

Note: Vote and function at meetings and conventions. Do not be idle or sleep on your rights; when you do, you forfeit them at adjournment, or sooner.

To Help Defeat a Motion

1. Do not second it. Remain silent.
2. Speak against it while it is before the body.
3. Vote against it.
4. Move to postpone it indefinitely to "kill" it.
5. Amend it adversely to encumber it or complicate it.
6. Move to refer it to a committee to delay it.
7. Move to postpone it to the next meeting to delay it.
8. Move the previous question to shut off debate on its good points.
9. Move to table it.
10. Move to recess to go after more votes.
11. If their motion wins, move to reconsider it.
12. If their successful motion remains unexecuted by a later meeting, then move to rescind it.
13. Move to adjourn, to prevent action on their motion at this meeting.
14. Only *votes* win. Get your voters to the meeting. Require them to stay to the end, and to vote as you or another key leader will vote.

To Help Pass a Motion

1. Second it immediately. Say: "I second it."
2. Speak in favor of it while it is still before the body.
3. Vote for it.
4. Vote against postponing it to rescue it.
5. Amend it sensibly to perfect or improve it.
6. Vote against referring it, to achieve action now.
7. Vote down all postponements that delay it.
8. Defeat the previous question so you can continue the debate.
9. Vote against tabling it.
10. Defeat recess so they may not go seeking more votes.
11. Vote against their motion to reconsider your motion.
12. Execute motions promptly so that they may not be subject to rescission at any later meeting.
13. Vote down all motions to adjourn, so as to achieve adoption of your motion now.
14. It is *votes* that win elections and other proceedings at meetings and conventions. Have your supporters there to help you with their votes.

Filibuster. Filibuster, or talking a question to death, is a parliamentary proceeding practiced in the Senate of the United States. Under Senate rules, senators are allowed unlimited debate on a bill, unless a $\frac{2}{3}$ vote is mustered to end the debate on it. If a $\frac{2}{3}$ vote is not mustered, senators may then continue to debate a pending objectionable bill for as long as they wish — for days and weeks, as has been the case at times — thus causing stoppage of all other public business in the Senate and ultimately forcing the proponents of the objectionable bill to withdraw it in order to save the Senate's public image.

But since debate in all other bodies than the U.S. Senate is limited, such as to ten minutes a member — or seven or five minutes — in assemblies such as fraternal orders, labor organizations, veterans associations, women's clubs, PTA's, etc.; or from 20 minutes to one hour in other assemblies, such as the U.S. House of Representatives, state senates, houses of representatives or general assemblies, and city councils or boards of aldermen, etc.; a filibuster cannot occur in these organizations and it need be of no concern to you.

Note: Originally, debate in the U. S. House of Representatives was unlimited, as in the Senate; but in 1820 the House adopted the one-hour limit when the brilliant and erratic John Randolph of Virginia consumed so much time in debate that the rule was adopted to prevent his holding the floor indefinitely.

What Motions to Use for the Greatest Efficiency

To conduct business with the greatest possible efficiency, and, therefore, to best advantage, make use of the following steps and proceedings.

1. First of all, before proposing a main motion give it some thought in order to make it as complete and comprehensive as practicable, so that it will require as few amendments as possible to perfect it, thus eliminating extra parliamentary proceedings and conserving the assembly's time; thus:

Don't say simply, "I move that we buy a desk." Say, preferably: "I move that we buy a new desk from Wilson and Company, at a cost not to exceed [so many] dollars, and that the House chairman be instructed to buy it in time for our next meeting." Be specific and comprehensive.

2. If a proposed motion is incomplete and imperfect, or is loose and ungrammatical, improve on it if you can by moving to amend the motion.

3. If it is complicated, to save time, move to refer it to a committee.

4. If it is worthless, useless, injurious or ill-advised, move to postpone it indefinitely.

5. If the attendance is slim, it is wise to move to postpone it to the next meeting.

6. If the question is of great importance — such as revision of the bylaws, or consideration of the sale of the clubhouse — in order to bring it before as many members as possible move to postpone it to the next meeting, and make it a special order for a particular hour.

7. If it is desired to transact some very urgent business ahead of a pending piece of business, move to suspend the rules ($\frac{2}{3}$); or, move to lay the pending business on the table.

8. When that urgent business has been attended to, move to *take* that piece of business from the table.

9. If the hour is late, or the question has been sufficiently discussed and speakers are repetitive, to expedite business move the previous question to terminate the debate.

10. On the other hand, if it is apparent that many members are eager to discuss a question, to hear as many of them as possible, move to limit debate to one or two minutes a member.

11. If the question is contentious and the debate heated, to prevent disorder or disruption, move to adjourn; or, in mild form, to "cool off," move to take a recess.

12. If the question is of an inflammatory nature, such as politically, racially, religiously, or otherwise discriminatory, instantly move to lay it on the table; or, move to postpone it indefinitely; or, object to its consideration.

13. If you think the meeting erred in adopting or defeating some question, then while the meeting is still in session move to reconsider the action taken.

14. On the other hand, if the meeting has adjourned, provided the action taken has not been carried out or executed between that meeting and the next, give previous notice to rescind that action at the next meeting.

15. If some urgent or worthwhile business has been passed in a quorum-less meeting (one in which it was *openly* disclosed that a quorum was not present), or some beneficial action was taken by officer or committee in good faith but without previous authority from the body, then at the next meeting move to ratify the action taken.

16. If a meeting took outrageous action or transacted some unconscionable business injurious to the best interests of the organization, to rectify this malfeasance — provided the motion is proposed before that meeting has adjourned — move "to reconsider the action taken and have it entered in the minutes to be reconsidered at the next meeting."

This is the technical form for saying: "Mr. Chairman, I move to reconsider the question and have reconsideration acted on [voted on] at the next meeting [in organization having regular meetings as often as quarterly]."

17. If a situation appears hopeless, with neither side yielding to or heeding reason (whether from sheer obstinacy or in good faith), or the obstacles to a final and befitting decision loom insurmountable, or the mission and duty of the assembly are destined to fail, or are seemingly unaccomplishable or unrealizable, in a last attempt to save the situation, lead the assembly to prayer and try business again.

18. To prevent hopeless deadlocks, vote to appoint a co-equal committee from each faction, then a chairman acceptable to *both* factions, and bind the assembly in advance by a motion to accept their majority report as decisive and final by arbitration.

Who should propose the above steps? The question might be asked: Who is supposed to suggest or propose the steps enumerated above for the efficient transaction of the assembly's business? There is but one answer—*you!* It is *your* organization and *your* duty to be vigilant at meetings and conventions and to be consistently aware of what transpires therein and to take the initiative in proposing the proper steps or proceedings. Do not sleep on your rights. When you do, you forfeit them.

Personalities in Debate

It is a principle of parliamentary law that a member of an assembly shall confine himself to the question before the house and shall avoid personalities. Resort to personalities often leads to the excitement of personal feeling and disturbs harmony and courtesy. Therefore, strictly speaking, the mention of a member's *name* in the course of debate is unparliamentary. This is especially true, and is strictly enforced, in legislative bodies. Members can be referred to in some other way, as "the maker of the motion," "the delegate [or, brother] who just spoke" or "who just took his seat," or "the preceding speaker," "the member who offered the amendment," etc. Appropriate adjectives when fittingly and deservingly applied may be used as "the learned member," "the distinguished brother," etc.

Members have the right to propose and discuss motions, and when they exercise their rights they must not be denounced. The measure or motion can be denounced or attacked, but never the person. Members are entitled to express their opinion on questions without incurring the enmity of their fellow-members.

Profanity in debate. Profane words and disorderly language or gestures at meetings are prohibited. Public assembly decorum requires propriety of speech and conduct; therefore, when profane or disorderly language is used, whether in anger or for emphasis, the Chair should instantly strike the gavel, interrupt the speaker and warn: "The member will refrain from unparliamentary language," or "from improper or unbecoming language." A second warning may be given, if a repetition of the offence occurs, before a member is denied further use of the floor.

Rule of censure in the U.S. House of Representatives. Rule XIV, 5, of the U. S. House of Representatives provides: "If a member is called, to order for [disorderly] words spoken in debate, they shall be taken down in writing at the Clerk's desk and shall be read aloud to the House." Such a member is subject to censure.

Rule of censure in the British Parliament. Under "Conduct of Members" the rule in the House of Commons declares: "The Speaker orders Members whose conduct is grossly disorderly to withdraw immediately from the House during the remainder of the day's sitting." (The English rule is abler, and less personal.)

Public apology. Members should be eager to apologize to the assembly for disorderly conduct or abusive language. It is noble to proffer a public apology. Simply say: "Mr. Chairman, I regret any improper remarks uttered in the heat of debate," or "I regret any unbecoming conduct on my part, and I apologize to the body" or "to the member," as the case may be.

Temper in debate. Speakers fall into two general classes: those who debate a question in temperate and tactful language, and those who resort to intemperate or tactless language: thus:

Intemperate Language. "I rise to kill this motion. The motion is revolting, nauseating. It would be asinine to pass it. Let's murder it. I have my own opinion why it was introduced. And only those who support it will be blamed. And they must be held responsible if this passes. Therefore, throw this motion out the window!"

Temperate Language. "I rise to speak against the motion. Its adoption will endanger the standing of our organization. I have no fault to find with those who proposed it; it is their privilege. Personally, however, I can never endorse or encourage such action. If the motion has any merit at all, its many disadvantages far outweigh any points in its favor. Its overwhelming defeat will be a blessing. I trust that the motion will not be adopted."

Violent temper and language, or insulting and insidious references and remarks should be avoided; they are unparliamentary and often cost votes. Tact and diplomacy can win votes.

Examples of tactful forms of debate:

1. "Mr. Chairman, I hesitate to rise to speak in favor of the motion when such able and experienced [or, distinguished] members as those who preceded me in debate have spoken against it; but let me point out why I am in favor of the motion," etc. Flatter your opponents (if you wish), then give abler arguments.

2. "Mr. President, much as I dislike to, I feel compelled to take the floor at this time to oppose the motion before the body proposed by my good friend and eloquent colleague who just spoke," etc. Assail the motion, never the member.

3. "Mr. Moderator, the sincerity with which previous speakers spoke in support of the motion commands my respect and admiration, and if I were not truly and sincerely convinced that the motion they supported will have detrimental results, I would not rise now to oppose it; and I'll tell you why," etc. Differ with fellow-members, but remain friends.

II. VOTING

Forms of voting. The three most common forms of voting are: (1) voice vote, often referred to as a viva voce (oral) vote, (2) hand vote, and (3) rising vote. Other methods of voting are: (4) by roll call, members answering yes or no when their name is called, (5) by secret ballot, (6) by mail, provided the bylaws so specify, (8) by proxy, provided the bylaws authorize it, or (9) by any other method desired.

When a roll call or secret ballot may be taken. Basically it requires a majority vote or general consent to order a vote on a question to be taken either by ballot or by roll call, because it is time consuming. But by special rule in some organizations fewer members can ask for a roll call or secret ballot. Check your bylaws.

Note: "Ballot" means "secret ballot," so the "secret" is superfluous, but "secret ballot" is a popular term. The Congress uses it.

Which method used. Motions requiring a simple majority vote are voted on by voice vote (it is the easiest). If the vote is doubted or the Chair himself is in doubt, it is then verified by show of hands, or finally by a rising vote when need be.

All motions requiring a $\frac{2}{3}$ vote (or three-fourths, etc.) are normally put to vote by a hand or standing vote. But if the Chair feels that such motion is not controversial, he can take it by voice vote in the first place; but when announcing the result he should (for the record) indicate *that* motion's required $\frac{2}{3}$ vote; thus: "There is a $\frac{2}{3}$ vote in favor of the motion, and the motion is carried." Any member can challenge the result, whereupon a vote by hand, etc., is taken.

Special use of some methods. If voting by telephone, mail or referendum is not authorized in the bylaws, these methods may nevertheless be resorted to as "feelers" of organization sentiment on a question or proposition. Majority vote is needed to authorize it.

When voting by mail is useful. When the scattered membership of an organization warrants voting by mail, it is ordinarily used for the following purpose: (1) election of officers; (2) amendments to bylaws; and (3) proposals of policy or principle. Other proceedings may be included.

An appropriate provision to effect the above can be incorporated in the bylaws as follows: "ARTICLE X. VOTING BY MAIL. Voting by mail is hereby authorized and the Board is hereby empowered to prescribe appropriate procedure therefor. The following matters shall be embraced: (1) election of officers, (2) amendments to bylaws, and (3) matters of policy or principle," or such other questions as may be authorized for inclusion.

Voting by proxy. "Proxy," short for "procuracy," from the Latin *procuro* (to attend to, to care for) is a form of voting, the voting being done not by the person himself who is entitled to vote, but by another person designated by him to vote in his place and stead. Hence, "voting by proxy" means voting done by a substitute person. The person so designated is known as the "proxy."

Voting by proxy is not permitted and is not valid in ordinary assemblies (fraternal orders, labor organizations, women's clubs, veterans associations, etc.) unless the organization's charter, articles of association, certificate of incorporation, or its bylaws expressly authorize it. And if these laws do *not* prohibit voting by proxy, the body can pass a law permitting proxy voting for any purpose desired. But unless a bylaw or rule expressly allows it, proxy is illegal.

Voting rights of alternates and proxies. (1) In the absence of his delegate in any meeting or convention of a club, society, organization or association, including conventions of political bodies, the *alternate* has all the privileges of voting, debate and participation in the proceedings to which the delegate is entitled.

But (2) in the absence of his principal from the annual meeting of a business corporation, the *proxy* has the right to *vote* in all instances, but he has not the right to debate or otherwise participate in the proceedings unless he is a stockholder in that same corporation.

And (3) where a *proxy* votes in the absence of his principal, or the *alternate* in the absence of his delegate, the vote in either case can be cancelled on the appearance of the principal or of the delegate prior to the announcement of the result, and the vote of the principal or of the delegate is then registered instead if the principal or delegate so desires.

How the Chair Takes the Vote

Form used by the Chair. Every presiding officer and vice president should master the correct form, or language, for putting motions to vote. Everyday experience shows that failure to put questions to vote properly and to announce the result decisively confuse both the issue and the assembly.

When the Chair puts a question to a vote, he begins with either "As many as are . . ." or "Those . . ." For example, "As many as are in favor of the motion," or "Those in favor of the motion," or mingled, thus: "As many as are . . ." (for the affirmative) and "Those . . ." (for the negative). Use no others — avoid others.

The form "as many as are" is the most authoritative form. It is the official Congressional form prescribed for use in the U. S. House of Representatives (Sec. 940). The next most acceptable form is "Those in favor," and "Those opposed." These forms are used interchangeably in the manual. The forms "all in favor," and "all opposed" are inelegant.

Duty of the Chair when putting motions to vote. Chairmen are in no small degree responsible for frequently confusing both the issue and the assembly when putting a question to vote. It is the duty of the Chair (1) to repeat the member's question accurately, just before the vote is taken; then (2) to put it to vote clearly and audibly; and (3) to announce, or declare, the result correctly and distinctly (note well the three stages), thus: ((There being no further discussion, the Chair will put the motion to vote." (1) "The question is on the motion that we buy a new radio." (2) Putting it to vote: "Those in favor of the motion will say aye; those opposed will say no." (3) Announcing the result: "The ayes have it, and the motion is carried," or "The noes have it, and the motion is lost."

1. *Voice vote.* "Those in favor of the motion will say *aye* [pronounced "I"]. Those opposed will say *no*." Then say: "The *ayes* have it, and the motion is carried"; or, "The *noes* have it, and the motion is lost." Repeat word for word — every word.

2. *Hand vote.* "Those in favor of the motion will raise their right hands." (Count the hands and say "Down," thus:) "Thirty. Down. Those opposed will raise their right hands. Seven. Down." Then say: "The affirmative has it, and the motion is carried"; or, "The negative has it, and the motion is lost."

3. *Rising vote.* "Those in favor of the motion will rise." Count the persons and say "Be seated," not "Down," thus: "Fifteen. Be seated. Those opposed will rise. Six. Be seated." Then add: "The affirmative has it, and the motion is carried"; or, "The negative has it, and the motion is lost." Avoid saying "stand up" and "sit down"; they are ungracious phrases. *Rising vote of thanks.* "Those in favor will rise; [start applauding, then say:] be seated." The negative is never put unless seriously asked for; hence do not say "Those opposed will rise."

4. *Roll call vote.* "Those in favor will answer yes; those opposed will answer no. The secretary [clerk] will call the roll."

5. *Secret ballot.* "Those in favor will vote yes; those opposed will vote no."

Note: The negative vote is never put first. The affirmative vote must always be put first, followed by the negative.

Vocabulary of voting. The words "ayes" and "noes" are used only on voice vote; in all other cases "affirmative" is used in place of "ayes" and "negative" in place of "noes." He should say, "The ayes have it," or "The noes have it," or "The affirmative [or, negative] has it."

The Chair should never say only "It is a vote"; this does not show which side won, especially if a stenographic, stenotyped or disc or tape record is being made, as in conventions.

"Carried" and "adopted" are synonymous terms: use them interchangeably; but never say "The motion carries," or "The motion carried." Instead, use the passive voice and say, "The motion is carried," or "The motion was carried"; and, too, do not say, "The ayes have it and the motion adopts"; say, "The motion is adopted," or "The motion was adopted," and never "The motion adopted."

Always say "down" to hands, but "be seated" to persons.

Affirmative and negative are singular terms, not plural. Hence say, "The affirmative [or negative] *has* it," not "*have* it."

What is "prevailing side"? Prevailing side is the winning side — it can be either side, affirmative or negative (ayes or noes), depending upon which side wins. In the case of tie votes the negative is always the prevailing side on all motions except appeals.

On $\frac{2}{3}$ or unanimous votes, if a $\frac{2}{3}$ vote or a unanimous vote is not attained, the negative is then the winning side always. In other words, if the affirmative side does not win, then the negative side necessarily wins. Once a motion is put to vote, there is always a prevailing side, and there is always a result to be announced, even if no one votes.

One negative destroys unanimous vote. If a unanimous vote is required, or even a request for general consent, a single negative vote destroys unanimity.

Full announcement of vote. Always announce the vote in full. Say: "The ayes have it" (this shows how the vote resulted), then add: "and the motion is adopted" (this tells what happened to the motion); or 'The noes have it, and the motion is lost."

Announcement of a tie vote. A tie vote is announced thus: CHAIR: "There being a tie vote, the motion is lost." (A motion is *lost* when a tie vote results because it takes a majority vote to adopt a motion. A tie vote is less than majority.)

When no one votes. If no one votes on a question, no predicament is involved, since the Chair can declare the result as (1) "The ayes have it," which indicates *he* voted with *that* side; or (2) "The noes have it," for a like reason; or (3) "There being a tie vote, the motion is lost." The vote can be doubted, of course, at any stage. Once a motion is put, there is a result.

The two-thirds vote announcement. The announcement of a $\frac{2}{3}$ vote is made thus. "There being two-thirds in favor of the motion, the affirmative has it and the motion is carried." Or, "There not being two-thirds in favor of the motion, the negative has it and the motion is lost."

How to compute a $\frac{2}{3}$ vote. To determine instantly (without the aid of pencil and paper) whether or not you have a $\frac{2}{3}$ vote on motions that require it, apply this simple formula: *double* the number of votes cast for the *negative* side; if the negative votes exceed (are more than) the number of votes cast for the affirmative side, you do not have a $\frac{2}{3}$ vote; thus you do *not* have a $\frac{2}{3}$ vote in a 9 to 5 vote, or 27 to 15 vote, or 75 to 40, or 158 to 90, or 603 to 310, etc. But if the negative vote cast either *equals* or is *less than* the affirmative vote cast, you have a $\frac{2}{3}$ vote; thus you have a $\frac{2}{3}$ vote in a 10 to 5 vote, or 18 to 9, or 30 to 15, or 88 to 44, or 180 to 90, or 1,200 to 600; and also in a 12 to 5 vote, or 19 to 8, or 51 to 25, or 94 to 45, or 305 to 150, etc.

Computing a majority vote and a $\frac{2}{3}$ vote. *Majority vote* means more than half of the votes actually cast, ignoring blanks, as in votes of 19/18, 41/27, 87/86, 196/194, etc. A *tie vote* is not a majority; it is less, as in 8/8; 19/19, etc.

Two-thirds vote means that for every negative vote you must have at least two affirmative votes, as in 10/4; 33/15; 50/25; 91/45.

On a *three-fourths vote* you need three *yeses* to every *no* vote.

A Majority Vote of:		A $\frac{2}{3}$ Vote of:	
1 vote is...............	1	1 vote is...............	1
2 votes is..............	2	2 votes is..............	2
3 votes is also..........	2	3 votes is..............	2
4 votes is..............	3	4 votes is..............	3
5 votes is also..........	3	5 votes is..............	4
6 votes is..............	4	6 votes is also..........	4
7 votes is also..........	4	7 votes is..............	5
8 votes is..............	5	8 votes is..............	6
9 votes is also..........	5	9 votes is also..........	6
10 votes is..............	6	10 votes is..............	7
11 votes is also..........	6	11 votes is..............	8
12 votes is..............	7	12 votes is..............	8
13 votes is also..........	7	13 votes is..............	9
14 votes is..............	8	14 votes is..............	10
15 votes is also..........	8	15 votes is also..........	10
16 votes is..............	9	16 votes is..............	11
17 votes is also..........	9	17 votes is..............	12
18 votes is..............	10	18 votes is also..........	12
19 votes is also..........	10	19 votes is..............	13
20 votes is..............	11	20 votes is..............	14
21 votes is also..........	11	21 votes is also..........	14
33 votes is..............	17	22 votes is..............	15
34 votes is..............	18	26 votes is..............	18
40 votes is..............	21	27 votes is..............	18
42 votes is..............	22	30 votes is..............	20
50 votes is..............	26	31 votes is..............	21
52 votes is..............	27	45 votes is..............	30
61 votes is..............	31	46 votes is..............	31
62 votes is..............	32	51 votes is..............	34
73 votes is..............	37	52 votes is..............	35
80 votes is..............	41	61 votes is..............	41
85 votes is..............	43	70 votes is..............	47
90 votes is..............	46	72 votes is..............	48
92 votes is..............	47	82 votes is..............	55
94 votes is..............	48	85 votes is..............	57
96 votes is..............	49	90 votes is..............	60
98 votes is..............	50	98 votes is..............	66
99 votes is also..........	50	99 votes is also..........	66
100 votes is..............	51	100 votes is..............	67

When members doubt the vote. When a member wishes to doubt or to challenge the Chair's announcement of the vote on a motion, he must immediately call out (without having to rise) "I doubt the vote," or "I challenge the vote," and the vote is taken again, thus:

CHAIR: "The ayes have it, and the motion is carried."

MEMBER X: "I doubt the vote." (No second is needed.)

CHAIR: "The vote has been doubted." He then takes the vote once more, this time either by show of hands or standing vote, for a surer verification, instead of by voice vote again, thus: "Those in favor of the motion will raise their right hand; fifteen hands. Hands down please. Those opposed will raise their right hand; thirteen. Hands down. The affirmative has it, and the motion is carried."

The Member's Role in Voting

Right to abstain. It is the duty of every member to vote on every question before the house because he should be willing to participate in the responsibility of the decision. But no one can be compelled to vote. If a member abstains from voting, he helps the stronger side (the side that prevails).

Members may doubt either side of the vote. A member has the right to doubt either side of the vote, affirmative or negative, if he thinks the Chair's announcement is incorrect, thus:

CHAIR: "Those in favor of the motion will rise; twenty-nine. Be seated."

MEMBER Y: "Mr. Chairman, I challenge that vote."

CHAIR: "The vote for the *affirmative* has been challenged. Those in favor of the motion will rise and stand until counted again." (He counts 27.) "The corrected count is now twenty-seven. Please be seated. Those opposed will rise; thirty-one. Be seated."

MEMBER Z: "I challenge the negative vote."

CHAIR: "The vote for the negative side is doubted. Those in favor of the motion will rise and stand until again counted." (He counts 33 this time.) "There are thirty-three in the negative. Please be seated. The negative has it, and the motion is lost."

The Chair's rights. The presiding officer can *vote* on any and every motion members can vote on (unless the bylaws specify that he shall not vote); but he cannot *propose, second* or *debate* motions if anyone objects. If the Chair participates in debate with the members and no one raises a point of order to prevent him from doing so while in the chair, then the assembly wants him to do so.

When a member may change his vote. A member has the right to change his vote from one side of the question to the other (on motions taken by voice, hand or standing vote) before or as the Chair announces the result. After the vote has been announced, it is too late to change a vote except by unanimous consent, provided the member rises at once after the announcement of the vote and *before* any other matter or business whatsoever is taken up. The Chair, however, must never put a question to vote or to announce the result with such rapidity as not to afford a member reasonable *momentary* opportunity to rise to change his vote, either because he voted under a mistake in the first instance, or because he changed his mind, or to change his vote so as to qualify to move reconsideration. These are fundamental rights and he can exercise them at will, if he acts immediately.

Changing or recording a vote on a roll call. On roll call votes, members who wish to change their vote (or who "passed" or were not previously recorded) must wait until the last name is called, and then *promptly* rise to change their vote or to be recorded. It is too late to change or to record one's vote after the call has been completed and the voting process has been declared closed, regardless of *when* the result is computed or verified and announced after that.

Changing or recording a vote on a ballot. On secret ballot voting, the right to change one's vote ceases when the voter deposits or parts with his ballot (as when he hands it to a teller or casts it in the container, ballot box, computer, etc.). The right to change one's vote, or to be recorded when not previously recorded also ceases when balloting time has expired, or the presiding officer has duly declared the balloting closed—regardless of when, after such closure, the ballots are counted or computed or the result thereon is verified and announced. It is not in order to change one's ballot (or the vote on that question) if *any* matter or thing (business or social) has intervened after such closure.

All voting must be done and all changes of votes must be made, while the assembly is engaged in the *process* of voting. When that process ends, voting and changes in the voting automatically end.

A member may vote on a recount. On a recount or retake of a vote, a member who previously refrained from voting or who was absent can now vote on the question. This includes every proceeding.

A member may vote for himself. A member has the right to vote for himself for any office. He may, if he wishes, refrain from voting for himself when he is sure he will be elected, or he may cast a blank ballot when he is the sole candidate and the unanimous choice; but he should never cast his vote for his opponent, as this reflects inconsistency and insincerity.

A member may not vote for direct personal interest. A member cannot vote on a question in which he has a direct personal or financial interest, such as on motions relating to his suspension or expulsion; or awarding him a trophy, decoration, money or other gift; or buying from him property he owns, such as purchasing his home (if it is in his name) for a clubhouse, or a parcel of land or an automobile which he owns and offers for sale, etc. But he is not prevented from voting on questions where others are included with him, such as casting a ballot in elections where he is also a candidate, or voting for a catered supper for which he will partake out of the funds of the treasury, or (as in legislative bodies) voting for a salary or increase in salary, etc.

Secret ballot reconsidered or rescinded. A vote taken by secret ballot can be reconsidered or be rescinded under the same rules as for other motions. All a member need say is, "I voted with the prevailing side." When reconsidering or rescinding votes taken by secret ballot, the vote on such reconsideration or rescission should also be taken by secret ballot.

Chapter 4
THE PRESIDING OFFICER'S ROLE IN MEETINGS

Chair chosen for skill. According to Robert, "The Chair is supposed to be an expert parliamentarian and able to inform members as to correct parliamentary procedure in ordinary cases" (*Parliamentary Law*, p. 172); and "The presiding officer of a large assembly should never be chosen except for his ability to preside" (*Rules of Order*, p. 241); and "There is nothing to justify the unfortunate habit some chairmen have of constantly speaking on questions before the assembly" (Ibid., p. 240).

Chair's duty to stand. Unless disabled, the Chair is supposed to stand under the following circumstances: (1) When opening the meeting; (2) when formally welcoming or greeting speakers, officials or guests, or when introducing them; (3) when actually putting motions to vote; (4) when he formally addresses the assembly; (5) when answering points of order and parliamentary inquiries, and on appeals from his decisions (and on questions of information asked of him); (6) when he can better control, or be heard by the assembly; (7) when declaring the meeting adjourned; and in general as good sense may suggest or require at any time.

Except as just explained, the Chair may sit or not as he chooses. He need not stand (1) during the reading of the minutes; (2) when recognizing members and their seconds, and when stating motions; or (3) during debate on motions. But he may stand all through the meeting, if he so chooses.

Need not leave the chair during appeal. The Chair is never required to surrender the gavel on an appeal from his decision (unless the bylaws say so) because, since such decision is of his own making, it is logical and proper to hear his reasons or explanation for so ruling (in self-defense, as it were) and asking him to leave the chair would be like asking any other member whose motion is before the house to refrain from discussing his motion or to leave the room or his seat while his motion is being considered.

Note: No more than two persons, speaker and Chair, may stand at any time except when yielding the floor to another for a question or for more than one question.

The gavel. The gavel is a symbol of the presiding officer's authority and right to act officially in his capacity. The gavel should be used sparingly, and at all times so as to command respect. A light tap after a vote merely implies (needlessly) completion of that vote.

Proper use of the gavel. 1. To attract attention and call a meeting to order. In most organizations, two raps raise and one rap seats the assembly; in others, two raps raise and three raps seat it.

2. To maintain order and restore it when breached in the course of the proceedings. (Rap the gavel once, but vigorously.)

3. To be handed over to successors in office or to officiating officers at ceremonials, etc. (Always extend the holding end.)

4. To be laid aside at all other times.

Improper use of the gavel. 1. Using it to lean on. 2. Juggling or toying with it, or using it to challenge or threaten. 3. Using it to emphasize remarks. 4. Pounding it to drown out a member's remarks or shut him off. Instead, give one vigorous rap at a time at intervals.

When president temporarily vacates chair. If the president vacates the chair temporarily, the first vice president takes the chair; and in his absence or refusal, the next one in order takes it. If there is no vice president, the president can designate a chairman pro tem, who presides only up to adjournment. If the designated appointee is not acceptable to the body, the body can proceed to elect a chairman pro tem in his place, and such action overthrows the president's action. In either case, when the president returns to the meeting room he automatically resumes presiding, preferably as soon as the pending matter, if any, has been voted on or is otherwise disposed of.

When presiding officer is not a member. If the presiding officer is not a regular member of the body, but he is added to the body either by superior law or by vote of the body itself, his rights therein are as follows: (1) if he is made a member (note the word "member") without mention of any restrictions, then he is vested with all and the same rights as any constituent or regular member; (2) if he is made its presiding officer (note the words "presiding officer") without mention of the word "member" or of any grant of specific rights to go with it, then he acts only as presiding officer and has no other rights of membership; (3) if he is not a constituent member of the body, but by superior law he is made its presiding officer with the right to vote *only* in case of a tie, then he may vote either to break or to make a tie vote. This is the case under the Constitution of the United States, which says: "The vice president of the United States shall be president of the Senate, but shall have no vote, unless they be equally divided" (Art. 1, sec. 3).

Note: In determining the rights of a nonmember who is annexed as presiding officer, or any other officer, by superior law or by vote of the body, look for the words "presiding officer" or "member" and note if any rights have been taken away from him as member, or any rights have been added to him as presiding officer.

Chair's Role in Debate

How to control meetings. If the assembly is slow to respond to the call to order or becomes unruly in the course of the meeting, the Chair strikes firmly *once* with the gavel and then commands: "The Chair is waiting for the members to come to order," or, "Will the members [or, delegates] in the back of the hall [front, right, left, etc.] take their seats immediately?" Or, "The Chair will state that business cannot commence [or, continue] unless there is quiet."

It is the duty of the Chair to preserve order (reasonable order, or reasonable quiet or attentiveness), and he can designate others to assist him, such as the sergeant-at-arms or monitor.

How to control individual members. In the first place, the Chair should never shout to or command the members or the delegates to "Sit down!" or, "Sit down, you are out of order!" This is bad assembly or public manners.

Instead, the Chair advises, speaking in the third person: "The member [delegate] will be seated!" "The member [delegate] is obstructing the business of the meeting, and he will please be seated at once," etc.

In the second place, the Chair should never ignore a member or delegate who rises to claim the floor. It is his duty to attempt to attend to each claim and then be able to control it or cope with it: thus, for example:

CHAIR: "The Chair can recognize but one member [or, delegate] at a time; the Chair *now* recognizes Mr. A; all others will please be seated." Or, "The Chair will not overlook anyone; the members are requested to cooperate and be patient until their turn comes."

In other words, a sagacious chairman in tense moments assures these members that their right to the floor will not be denied to them at the proper time, thus propitiating or pacifying and controlling them, and preserving orderly procedure.

Members departing from the question. If, after he is duly recognized and has obtained the floor, a member does not speak on the pending question, or departs from speaking germanely to it, the Chair (on his own initiative, or on point of order from the floor) admonishes the speaker. He raps the gavel and commands:

CHAIR: "The Chair will respectfully ask the member to confine his debate to the pending question"; or, when need be, "The Chair will not grant the floor to the member further unless he confines his discussion to the pending motion," or similar words.

Note: In public assemblies like Congress, parliaments, city councils, state legislatures, etc., speakers are often permitted to debate questions ungermanely and irrelevantly, on the theory that thus possible schemes could be unveiled unwittingly, or a dormant plot disclosed which is injurious or inimical to the public good, and a presiding officer in such bodies usually (but not always) awaits a point of order from the floor before admonishing a speaker to confine himself to the question before the body.

Chair usually refrains from debating. According to Cushing, "The presiding officer [of the main body] does not usually engage in the debate, and votes only when the assembly is equally divided" (Sec. 5); and "It is a general rule ... that the presiding officer shall not participate in the debate. ... He is only allowed to state matters of fact within his knowledge; to inform the assembly on points of order or the course of proceeding when called upon for that purpose, or when he finds it necessary to do so, and on appeals from his decision, on questions of order" (Sec. 202).

When the Chair does debate. When presiding, the presiding officers of the main body may not propose motions or second them or debate them if anyone objects, unless they surrender the chair. But committee chairmen can do all these things without surrendering the chair.

The Chair, while presiding in the main assembly, has, strictly speaking, no right to propose or second or discuss motions, and thus take sides on questions. If the Chair feels that his active participation in a proceeding is necessary, he should surrender the gavel to the vice chairman and then debate the question.

This is based on the principle that the chairman cannot be expected to be a fair and impartial presiding officer after he has spoken on and shown partisanship in a question. When he takes the floor in the main body and speaks on a motion, he cannot properly resume presiding until the question on which he spoke has been disposed of and is no longer pending before the body.

This, however, does not apply to committee chairmen or to chairmen of a small board. They can propose and debate any motion, and they do not surrender the chair.

On the other hand, in the exercise of sound leadership and initiative, the presiding officer is within his rights to shed light on a motion, to inform the members of the status or effect of a question, or to enlighten the assembly on facts within his knowledge to spur the assembly to action; and if such liberty is not abused by him the practice is not only tolerated but frequently welcomed.

But the Chair's comments and remarks commending or condemning speeches or opinions of members expressed in debate are unwise and unparliamentary. Judicious and efficient presiding officers avoid it; they are expected to be outwardly impartial and nonpartisan.

Where the Chair abuses his powers, objection can be made to the Chair himself; thus: "Mr. Chairman, I object to the Chair's speaking [or, frequent speaking] on motions before the house. As I understand the rule, the presiding officer of the main body must surrender the chair before he can participate in the discussion with members; it stands to reason that the Chair, as such, has no more right to take sides and discuss motions than an umpire would have a right to be a player on one of the ball teams." Members are as jealous of their rights, as the Chair is of his prerogatives.

When objection is raised against his participation in partisan discussion, the Chair instantly ceases his discussion or surrenders the chair and then continues. When the Chair surrenders the gavel to debate a question, he is recognized, as a mark of courtesy, to speak ahead of other members.

Note: The fact that the Chair has debated a question while presiding does not void that question or make invalid the action taken on it by the body. And, too, if he proposes or seconds a motion and the body adopts it, the vote thereon is valid. Nevertheless, it is unfair and prejudicial to good order for presiding officers in the main body to take sides in debate, or to propose or second motions while in the chair, if anyone objects. If no one objects, the Chair is not culpable or censurable, and he may participate actively in the proceedings, while presiding, as frequently as the body cares to permit him. A point of order duly raised by any member, can put an end to it.

How the Chair can influence business. It would be a pity if the talents and leadership of capable and conscientious presiding officers could not be made use of at meetings and conventions. Therefore, while presiding officers are forbidden, while in the chair, to debate motions before the house or to otherwise engage in direct partisan participation in the proceedings unless they first surrender the chair, nothing prevents them from having their pet programs or policies transacted indirectly—through others—if it is so desired.

Thus, presiding officers with progressive programs and abundant initiative who aspire to achieve a successful administration or who have ambition for higher office in the organization or broader service in the community, state or nation, can covertly designate other members of the body to "carry the ball" for them — to propose their will at meetings in the form of a motion, to direct it through any obstructive intervening proceedings, and to bring it to successful accomplishment.

Accordingly, one competent member, for instance, can be assigned the duty to propose the Chairman's motions; another (or several others) to second them; then one or more members (planted in different parts of the hall or meeting room) who are good debaters, can rise in turn and speak for the motion; still others, skilled in rebuttal, can rise and attempt to counteract or refute damaging arguments or points advanced by the opposition; or, when the proposal unexpectedly takes an unfavorable twist in the course of the proceedings and a change of strategy appears advisable, presiding officers, when necessary or prudent, can confer on the spot, quickly and unobtrusively, with one of their leaders at the rostrum or platform, or hand him or send to him a note with written instructions about what to do next; or, in brief, they can in any number of ways maneuver or promote a favorite formula, policy or proceeding without direct participation in the pending proceedings.

Chair remains outwardly strictly neutral. In the event of and during such a proceeding, the Chair's duty, or attitude, toward the pending matter should be clearly and solemnly borne in mind; he must appear and remain strictly impartial, should assign the floor equally and alternately between those favoring and those opposing the question, and should otherwise preside with absolute and unquestioned fairness, justice and dispassion.

If he feels he cannot conduct the proceeding impartially or the efforts of his leaders do not prove adequate to "swing" the proceeding to certain victory, he can then surrender the chair, take the floor like any member and attempt in debate to exert his direct influence or his leadership and personal magnetism or popularity.

Recognizing Members and Assigning the Floor

The general rule. Except in assemblies whose special rules or bylaws provide a different method by which a presiding officer recognizes members, the general rule, under parliamentary law, is that when two or more persons rise to claim the floor about the same time, the one who first *rises* and *addresses* the Chair is entitled to recognition over the others. An appeal lies from the decision of the Chair when he misassigns the floor.

Exceptions to the general rule. (1) The member who introduced the motion before the house is entitled to recognition over others, provided he rises to claim the floor promptly—that is, before another member, already recognized, has commenced speaking. (2) A member who has already spoken on a motion cannot be recognized to speak a second time if others who have not yet spoken on that question rise to speak; but if no one rises he is entitled to recognition. (3) The member who has introduced the motion before the house is entitled to close the discussion on that question provided he has not (a) already spoken twice on it, or his allotted number of times, or (b) that the discussion has not been closed. (4) Claimants to the floor should be recognized in alternate turn between those favoring and those opposing a question, provided the Chair knows or is informed on which side each intends to speak. (5) The member who introduced a subject before the body is entitled to speak last on it, provided he has not already exhausted his allotted turns at debate. (6) As between members who are necessarily identified or concerned with a motion or proceeding, and those not so identified or involved, the former are given preference in the assignment of the floor, provided they *rise* promptly to claim the floor; thus:

(*a*) A member who gave notice to amend a bylaw is given the floor ahead of others at the next meeting to call up the proposed amendment, or to debate it.

(*b*) A member who moved to postpone a motion to the next meeting is assigned the floor to speak first under unfinished business.

(*c*) One who moved to reconsider a motion, or to rescind it, or to expunge it, etc., is likewise recognized before others.

(*d*) One who moved to table a motion is recognized first to move to take it from the table.

(*e*) On committee reports, the committee chairman (and in his absence some other member of the committee) is recognized ahead of others when a committee report is before the body.

If a member who has the kind of prior rights enumerated in the above proceedings is absent, or is unwilling to exercise them when present, any member can exercise them.

Motions which may interrupt

A. The following motions can arbitrarily interrupt a speaker:
    1. A point of order
    2. A question of privilege
    3. A point of no quorum (doubting a quorum)
    4. A call for the orders of the day
B. The following motions cannot interrupt a *speaker* without his consent, but may interrupt the *occupant* of the floor:
    1. An appeal from the decision of the Chair
    2. A parliamentary inquiry
    3. A question of information
    4. Giving previous notice of reconsideration or of rescission
    5. An objection to the consideration of a question
    6. A motion to divide a compound question

If the interruptions raised under classification (A), above, are not legitimate or appropriate, they cannot interrupt the speaker, and the Chair instantly returns the floor to the speaker interrupted. If the interruptions enumerated under (B), above, are not deemed urgent at the time they are raised, the Chair so informs the interrupting member and returns the floor to its previous occupant.

Appeal from ruling of the Chair. A member who is aggrieved by a ruling of the Chair on any of the foregoing proceedings may appeal from the decision. But if members fail to exercise their rights, they must not complain; they have forfeited them.

Distinction between speaker and occupant of the floor. If a member has been recognized and assigned the floor but has not commenced speaking, he is known as occupant or holder of the floor; he is said to be in possession, or the possessor of the floor. But after he has commenced speaking, he is called speaker; that is, he alone does the speaking. A few words uttered in addition to "Mr. Chairman" constitute speaking within the meaning of the word "speaker."

Distinction between "out of order" and "not in order." It is the Chair's duty to recognize and properly deal with motions which are out of order or which are not in order at a given time. A motion or proceeding which cannot be entertained at all is ruled as being *out of order* when proposed; and a motion or proceeding which cannot be entertained at the time it is proposed but can be entertained at some time is, properly speaking, ruled as being *not in order*.

Thus, a motion to endorse John Jones for mayor is out of order if the bylaws prohibit political endorsements; and discussion of the motion to lay on the table is out of order, because the motion is not debatable.

On the other hand, a main motion which is proposed while another main motion is already pending is not in order at the time, but would be in order when no other motion is pending; and a motion to postpone is not in order while the privileged motion to adjourn is pending because to adjourn outranks to postpone, but would be in order when no motion of higher rank is pending.

The Chair's Role in Voting

Motions concerning the presiding officer. When the Chair is a nominee, alone or with others, or he is to be voted a gift or compliment, he need not (although he may) surrender the chair. If, out of sense of delicacy, he prefers to surrender the chair, he merely asks the vice president to put the question to a vote. If he himself puts it to a vote, the action taken is not invalid or illegal; indelicacy does not constitute illegality.

The Chair's right to vote. Presiding officers never surrender the chair in order to *vote*, and they can vote on any question whatsoever that members can vote on, unless the bylaws specify otherwise.

The Chair has the right to vote on questions just like any other member, if he is a voting member of the assembly. He wisely refrains from voting, however, when his vote cannot alter the result (as, for instance, when the vote is 77 for and 55 against) thus avoiding show of feeling or partisanship. He can vote to *break* a tie (if he so wishes), as when the result is 35 for and 35 against, by voting with the affirmative side, thus breaking the tie vote and adopting the motion; or he can vote to create a tie, as when the vote is 35 for and 34 against, by voting with the negative, thus creating a tie vote and defeating the motion. The Chair can thus change the result either way if he so desires.

In other words, the Chair, if he is going to vote at all, should vote on that side of the question which can change or affect the result; but if he is satisfied to let the result stand as is, he need not vote. He can vote with the members, however, when the vote is taken by secret ballot, because no one knows how he votes.

When the vote is taken by roll call, the Chair's name is called last so that he will not influence the vote of others. He *can* then (after examining the result) vote on the question or not, as he may choose. But he is never entitled to cast two votes. Thus, if he has already voted on a question or on an election and a tie results, he may not cast a second vote to break the tie unless the bylaws give him *two* votes (as some bylaws do), or unless by unanimous consent of the members present, upon a question, or by unanimous consent of the nominees or candidates involved in the vote in an election to office.

Note: If the Chair's name is called first, or it is called in its alphabetical order instead of last on roll call votes, this does not invalidate either his vote or the result on a question. But the practice can be stopped when a point of order is duly raised at the time.

Form used by the Chair to vote. When the Chair votes either to break a tie or to create one, he says: "On this question, thirty-five having voted in the affirmative and thirty-four in the negative, the Chair votes with the negative; therefore, there being a tie vote the negative has it, and the motion is lost." (Note that to break a tie he votes with the affirmative; to create a tie he votes with the negative.)

Chapter 5
CLASS AND RANK OF MOTIONS

Seven classes of motions. There are seven classes, or types, of motions in parliamentary law. No matter what motion or proceeding is proposed at meetings or conventions, it is possible to know (and it is well to know, as part of our education in parliamentary procedure) in which of these classes a motion belongs. They are as follows:

Note: Repeat them aloud. You can fix them in mind in four minutes. Notice the distinction between class 4 and 6.

Their rules. The symbols S, D, A, M, $\frac{2}{3}$, and R alongside each motion reveal their rules and give you on-the-spot information; thus: S means the motion requires a Second; D, it is Debatable; A means that it is Amendable; M, it requires a Majority vote to adopt it; and $\frac{2}{3}$, a Two-thirds vote is necessary; R means that the motion can be Reconsidered.

You must know a motion's negative rules as well as its positive ones, otherwise you will only half know its rules. If it shows an S, say: "It requires a second"; if no S, say: "It does not require a second," and similarly if it shows a D, an A, an M, $\frac{2}{3}$, or an R. A motion with none of these symbols is unsecondable, undebatable, unamendable, unvotable, and unreconsiderable, and should be learned as such.

Rank of motions. It is necessary to memorize the rank of three classifications of motions: main motions and resolutions, subsidiary motions, and privileged motions. These are the most frequently used kinds of motions. Memorization of the motions classified as main, subsidiary, and privileged, and mastery of their ranks, will give you at once a 50 percent skeleton knowledge of basic parliamentary law and practice.

The main motion is outranked by all the subsidiary motions, and each subsidiary motion is outranked by all the privileged motions. And within each classification there is rank: certain subsidiary motions outrank certain other subsidiary motions, and certain privileged motions outrank certain other privileged motions. For instance, the motion "to lay on the table" (subsidiary motion number 1) outranks the motion "to refer to a committee" (subsidiary motion number 5).

The main motion, the most important of all motions, is the lowest of all in rank. The least important (that is, the least relevant to the transaction of the main motion) is the highest in rank. A motion of *higher* rank is always in order when a motion of *lower* rank is pending, and a motion of *lower* rank is out of order if proposed while a motion of *higher* rank is before the assembly — just like bids in an auction sale.

Think of motions as occurring in sets. Only one *main motion* may be pending at a given time; but adhering to each main motion may be several less important (thus higher-ranking) motions. These higher-ranking motions also have rank among themselves so that the Chair and members will know in what order they should be taken up.

Key to Abbreviations

S — it must be seconded   M — it requires majority vote
D — it is debatable $\frac{2}{3}$ — needs two-thirds vote
A — it is amendable   R — it can be reconsidered

Privileged Motions

Privileged motions have no direct relationship to pending business, but relate to the integrity of the organization, or the safety, health, and welfare of the members, or observance of orderly procedure. Coexisting motions (p. 110) are a special kind of main motion rising out of the privileged motion of question of privilege.

1. Fix a day to which to adjourn (S, A, M, R)...... page 119
2. Adjourn (S, M).................................... 113
3. Recess (S, A, M)................................... 112
4. Raise a question of privilege (no symbols).......... 106
5. Call for the orders of the day (no symbols)......... 104

Subsidiary Motions

Subsidiary motions are helping, aiding or assisting motions, invented to aid, assist or help in disposing of a pending main motion.

1. Lay on the table (S, M)....................... page 98
2. Previous question (S, $\frac{2}{3}$, R)....................... 92
3. Limit or extend debate (S, A, $\frac{2}{3}$, R)................ 90
4. Postpone to a definite time (S, D, A, M, R)......... 88
5. Refer to a committee (S, D, A, M, R).............. 82
6. Amend the main motion (S, D, A, M, R)........... 68
7. Postpone indefinitely (S, D, M, R)................ 66

Main (or Principal) Motions

Main motions or resolutions (S, D, A, M, R)...... page 50

Main motions and resolutions are proposals which introduce a principal subject or proposition before the house. Any motion introduced when no other main motion is pending before the body, is itself a main motion.

Only one main motion can be pending before the body at a time. For the only exception to this rule, see "Coexisting Motions," page 110.

The following four classes of motions do not have absolute ranks, either between classifications or within classifications. They are used where applicable and may or may not yield to the subsidiary, privileged, and incidental motions. See the drill on transacting the rank of motions on page 11.

Incidental Motions

The class name of these twenty motions happens to be "incidental motions." The order in which they are listed has no meaning. There is nothing either to memorize or to be alarmed about just because there are so many of them listed. All you need to know about them is (a) that all of them are undebatable except two, namely appeal from a decision of the Chair, and consideration by paragraph (or *seriatim*); note that they are the only two with the symbol D; and (b) that they have no order of rank among themselves and you therefore use each one when needed.

Restoratory Motions

Restoratory motions are such as restore the status quo of a question; that is, they bring a question back to its original status — as it was prior to the last vote on it. Basically these motions are quasi-main motions, or in the nature of main motions. But restoratory is a more precise term.

Incidental Main Motions

Incidental main motions are either former main motions or they are quasi-parliamentary forms.

And any other action or motion pertaining to some previous act or decision of the body which is still in force, or any parliamentary action or proceeding which proposes some course of action on business already disposed of or about to be proposed.

Coexisting Motions

A privileged main motion (S, D, A, M, R)   page 110

A coexisting motion is an original main motion which emanates from (that is, which is proposed and entertained as a result of) a member's having risen to a "question of privilege" while another main motion is actually pending before the body. If another main question is not pending, then it is not a coexisting main question; it is instead a main motion.

A coexisting motion is the *only* exception to the rule that only one main motion can be pending before the body at a time.

How to Transact Motions by Rank

Transacting motions according to their rank as shown in the scale on pp. 46–49 is as simple as transacting bids in an auction sale — higher motions, like higher bids, being always in order; and lower motions, like lower bids, being always out of order.

To illustrate their operation, assume the following main motion pending before the body (and assume all motions are duly seconded):

MAIN MOTION: "To build a new clubhouse."

MEMBER A: "Mr. Chairman, I move to *table* the main motion." (To table is a subsidiary motion of higher rank than a main motion, and the Chair entertains it; he has to know its *rank;* thus:)

CHAIR: "It is moved and seconded to lay the motion on the table."

MEMBER B: "Mr. Chairman, I move to *refer* the main motion to the House Committee, with instructions to report back at the next meeting."

CHAIR: "The motion to refer [note the language used] is not in order now; it is of lower rank than the pending motion to table."

MEMBER C: "Mr. Chairman, I move to *amend* the main motion by adding at the end thereof the words 'at a cost not to exceed $250,000.'"

CHAIR: "The amendment is not in order at present; it is of lower rank than the pending subsidiary motion to table."

MEMBER D: "Mr. Chairman, I move to *postpone* the main motion."

CHAIR: "The motion to postpone is not in order at the present time; it is of lower rank than the pending motion to table."

MEMBER E: "Mr. Chairman, I move we *recess* for five minutes." (The privileged motion to recess is in order; it outranks to table.)

CHAIR: "It is moved and seconded to recess for five minutes."

MEMBER F: "Mr. Chairman, I move we *adjourn*." (The privileged motion to adjourn outranks to recess and to table. The Chair says:)

CHAIR: "It is moved and seconded to adjourn."

MEMBER G: "Mr. Chairman, I move that we buy a new desk."

CHAIR: "The *main* motion just proposed is presently not in order, as only one *main* motion at a time may be considered."

MEMBER H: "Mr. Chairman, how many motions are now properly pending?"

CHAIR: "Four: to *adjourn*, *recess*, *table* and the *main* motion to build a new clubhouse." (Only one *main motion* is pending; the other three are mere parliamentary *forms*, which outrank it.)

Taking the vote on many pending motions. When more than one motion is pending, as above, the *highest* motion in rank is voted on first, then each *next highest*, for example:

CHAIR: "The first vote is on the motion to adjourn. Those in favor will say aye; those opposed will say no; the *noes* have it. Next, the motion to recess. Those in favor will say aye; those opposed will say no; the *noes* have it. Now, the motion to lay on the table. Those in favor will say aye; those opposed will say no; the *ayes* have it, and the main motion to build a new clubhouse has been *tabled*." (Then he asks:) "Is there further new business?"

Other sets are similarly transacted. Master pages 10 and 11.

Note: Presiding officers are expected to know the *rank* of the motions shown on pp. 46–49, otherwise they have no business presiding.

Chapter 6
MAIN MOTIONS AND RESOLUTIONS

I. INTRODUCTION

Definition of main motions and resolutions. Main motions and resolutions are proposals which introduce a principal subject or proposition before the house; hence, they are called main or principal motions. "Main" and "principal" motions are synonymous terms, and the rules that apply to them are the symbols S, D, A, M, R. All through the book the symbol S means a motion is Secondable; D, it is Debatable; A, it is Amendable; M means Majority vote; R, it can be Reconsidered.

Examples of main motions: "To build a hospital," "to buy a new desk," "to donate fifty dollars to the United Fund," and similar subjects, topics, or questions of substance — they are conceived by the members, and are also known as **original main motions**.

Important Note: The following proposals are also main, or principal, motions, and when they are pending before the body they are subject to the same rules (S, D, A, M, R) as all main motions. (1) recommendations, (2) motions on town articles, (3) orders, (4) resolves, (5) propositions, (6) measures, (7) a bill, (8) petition or request, (9) questions of policy, (10) motions or resolutions on taking the assembly's sense, attitude or stand on questions, or on putting the assembly on record for or against any proposition or question. Since they are main motions, you can debate them, or table them, etc. In other words, all main motions and resolutions are subject to all the subsidiary and privileged motions (p. 47) and to such incidental motions as properly apply to them (p. 48).

Motions which are not main. A motion which does not introduce a main, or principal (substantive), question or topic, is not a main motion; it is some other class of motion, such as privileged, subsidiary, etc. (See pages 47–49).

Examples of motions which are not main: "To adjourn," "to lay on the table," "to postpone," "to refer to a committee," etc. These are motions, too, but they are not main, or principal, motions within the meaning of the words *main* and *principal*, for they do not introduce a proposal, topic or motion of substance; they are procedural forms invented by the rules of parliamentary law.

Distinction between main motion and resolution. Strictly speaking, a resolution can have a preamble and is normally put in writing, whereas a main motion does not have a preamble and unless lengthy is not put in writing. A resolution is a more formal expression of a proposal which often suggests questions of sentiment or feeling, such as expressions of joy, sorrow, approval, disapproval or other attitude or state of mind, whereas a main motion primarily suggests concrete business proposals. In other words, if a proposal concerns or borders on opinion, policy, principle or feeling, it is better parliamentary form to express the state of mind through a resolution rather than a motion; thus:

MEMBER: "Mr. Chairman, I move the adoption of the following resolution: *Resolved*, That this organization go on record in favor of prohibiting immigration during the next three years."

On the other hand, if a proposal relates to sheer business matter, the motion and not the resolution serves the purpose more appropriately, thus:

MEMBER: "Madam President, I move we buy a new desk."

However, they can be proposed either way and both ways are correct. The proposer himself decides in what form the question will be offered, whether as a motion or resolution.

Who can propose motions and resolutions. Only *voting* members may propose motions and resolutions in the main body, and only committee members in committees.

Questions should be well conceived. A main motion or resolution should be well thought out before it is proposed, and should be made as complete and comprehensive as practicable so as to require as few amendments as possible to perfect.

What motions may be put in writing. There are at least six kinds of motions which, because they can be lengthy or complex, must be put in writing if the Chair so directs. They are as follows: (1) Main motions and resolutions.   (2) Amendments of any kind.   (3) Instructions to committees.   (4) Points of order.   (5) Appeals.   (6) Questions of privilege.

II. THE MAIN MOTION (S, D, A, M, R)

Rules of a main motion. The same rules apply to both resolutions and Main motions.

These rules comprise the basic or most essential rules of a main motion; hence, if you are asked: "What do you know about main motions?" or "What are the basic rules of a main motion?" you would say: "A main motion is secondable, debatable, amendable, requires a majority vote and can be reconsidered (S, D, A, M, R); it possesses the lowest rank of all motions, and can be proposed when no other business is pending before the body; while it is pending, other motions of higher rank, such as to amend it, postpone it, lay it on the table, etc., can be proposed and are entertained ahead of it."

Note: In other words, a main motion is like the foundation of a house upon which you can apply many floors. Now, with eyes off the page, give the basic rules of main motions and resolutions as stated just above.

Since only one main motion at a time can be considered, when a second main motion is proposed while one is already pending, the Chair says: "The motion just proposed is not in order at the present time because there is another main motion now before the body; after the pending motion has been disposed of you may propose your motion."

Motions must first be proposed, then seconded, and then stated by the Chair before they can be debated or amended.

No one may propose two or more motions at once if anyone objects.

Form used for main motions. When proposing a motion, a member first rises when the floor is free, addresses the Chair, waits until he is recognized and then begins with the phrase "I move," never "I *make* a motion." Never say "I move *you*." It is indelicate. You do not move the Chairman. Leave out "you." Say, instead: "I *move* that we . . ."

He proceeds to state his motion in full, thus:

MEMBER: "Mr. Chairman, I move that we donate fifty dollars," etc.

VOICE: "I second the motion."

CHAIR: "It has been moved and seconded to donate fifty dollars. Is there any discussion on the motion?" (After discussion, if any, he further prompts the assembly:) "Is there any further discussion?" (There

---

KEY QUIZ

Q. Must main motions be seconded? *A.* Yes.
Q. Can they be debated? *A.* Yes.
Q. Can they be amended? *A.* Yes.
Q. What vote adopts them? *A.* Majority.
Q. Why majority? *A.* Because the majority rules.
Q. Can they be reconsidered? *A.* Yes.
Q. What is their rank? *A.* Lowest of all motions (pp. 10, 11).
Q. Can more than one *main* motion be before the body at the same time? *A.* No. (Notice it says *main.*)
Q. Can other motions not main be proposed or applied upon a main motion? *A.* Yes.
Q. Give examples. *A.* Adjourn, postpone, amend, etc. (pp. 10, 11).

being no response, he continues:) "There being no further discussion, the Chair will proceed to put the motion to a vote." (This preparatory language alerts the assembly for the vote to come; he then repeats the pending motion if necessary, thus:) "The question is on the motion that we donate fifty dollars. Those in favor of the motion will say aye. Those opposed will say no." (And he announces the result distinctly, thus:) "The *ayes* have it, and the motion is carried," or "The *noes* have it, and the motion is lost," depending upon which side unquestionably prevailed.

The phrase "I so move." When a member starts a proceeding by discussing a motion or an amendment which he intends to propose in due form before he sits down, and he afterward avoids proposing it in its required form because he either cannot properly phrase it or he cannot extract a concise proposal out of all that mass of words in his discussion of it, or because he intentionally avoids it as a shortcut process, being content to let the Chair do it for him, the term "I so move," or "I therefore *so* move' is acceptable, and the Chair phrases it for him if possible. If the Chair cannot or will not, the proposal is repeated, or is put in writing.

Note: If your motion is defeated, and you have not the votes to reconsider it, you can reintroduce it at any future new session. The body can, however, defeat the same motion as often as it chooses. By the same token you can reintroduce it from session to session as often as you choose.

Seconding motions. Main motions must be seconded on the principle that at least two persons in the assembly (mover and seconder) must be interested in the same subject matter to warrant taking up the assembly's time in its consideration. Seconding is approving a motion. A member cannot second his own motion.

If an unseconded motion is adopted, its adoption is valid; a second is implied and cannot be questioned afterward; the time to question the absence of a second is while the motion is still before the body.

More than one second. A motion can be seconded by more than one person, as is often the case. On certain motions some organizations require seven seconders, others thirty seconders; and still others, one-fifth of the members, etc.

Chair enforces the rule. Until a motion has been seconded it is not open to debate. Hence, if a member rises to discuss a motion before it has been seconded, the Chair may interrupt (if he wishes to enforce the rule) and say: "Under the rules, a motion which has not been seconded is not open to debate; will you please [or, the member will please] be seated until the Chair asks for a second," and the Chair asks only once, "Is the motion seconded?" If no second is voiced then, the Chair describes the situation thus: "There being no second, the motion cannot be entertained." But if it is seconded a bit late and *before* any other matter or thing intervenes, it can be entertained.

The phrase "Do I *hear* the motion seconded?" is not good form and should be avoided; it involves one's sense of hearing. The Chair must not plead with the members "Will someone *please* second the motion?" The phrase "Is the motion seconded?" is a pure and impersonal form of asking for a second; use that form and no others. (Legislative bodies in general omit seconding certain motions, such as appeals, and others.)

It is not necessary to rise or to be recognized in order to second a motion in small assemblies, although it may be done. Simply call out: "I second the motion," or "I second the resolution," or simply "I second it," or rise and second it, if required by rule, and rise also in large assemblies, conventions, etc.

Seconding sensible or routine motions is a good way for beginners and shy members to start active participation in proceedings and gradually acquire confidence and proficiency. (See "Motions which do not require a second," p. 173.)

Note: Before proposing motions — amendments, postponement, reconsideration, or any others — it is well to arrange in advance for someone to *second* your motion.

Stating the motion. After a motion is seconded, it is the duty of the Chair (if the motion is in order at the time), to state it; that is, he must officially take notice of and repeat the motion (or have the clerk or secretary read it) so all may hear it. It is inexcusable for the Chair not to state a motion; stating it is a vital and extremely important stage of orderly procedure.

Inaudible or complicated motions. If the Chair cannot hear or understand the motion, he says: "Will the member please repeat his motion." Or: "Will you repeat your motion?" Or: "The member will please repeat his motion." If it is lengthy, loose or complicated, he has the right to require that the motion be put in writing. He says: "Will the member please put the motion in writing?" Or: "The member will put his motion in writing." Of course, the secretary or clerk usually assists the Chair by taking down the motion when proposed, or the Chair himself may do so for his own guidance.

If the proposer is asked to put his motion in writing, the Chair is not duty bound to stop all other business and to await that motion. It is the duty of the proposer to have a lengthy or complicated motion ready and in acceptable form before he offers it, so that progress in business may not be obstructed. But where the delay would be but momentary, the courtesy is usually extended (if no one objects to the delay).

Improving a member's motion. The Chair may, if he wishes, improve the phrasing of a member's ungrammatical or incoherent motion or resolution, but he must not change its sense or meaning. If he attempts an improvement, after stating it in its improved form he should immediately ask the original proposer: "Is that the sense of your motion?" Or, "Did the Chair state the motion correctly?" If there is doubt, the motion is put in writing.

How the Chair entertains motions. When entertaining a member's motion, the Chair should always begin with the word "It" (except in some legislative bodies) and follow it with the phrase "has been moved and seconded," which describes the act of proposing and seconding a motion; thus: "It has been [or, It is] moved and seconded to appropriate the sum of $500 for . . ." "It has been [or, It is] moved and seconded to adjourn." "It has been [or, It is] moved and seconded to amend the main motion." etc.

The form "It has been [or, it is] moved and seconded" is the most direct, efficient and impersonal form. On the other hand, phrases like "Mr. Jones moves" injects personalities, (except in legislatures); and "a motion is made" is incomplete and unparliamentary. Therefore, use the phrase: "It has been moved and seconded." Adhering to the correct form insures greater accuracy and orderly procedure. (Presiding officers in legislatures mention proposers' names for the *record*, on the grounds of public policy: they act on public questions.)

When motions become debatable. A motion is not open to debate until it has been stated (repeated) to the body by the Chair; and the Chair, in the interest of orderly procedure, should *not* permit any member (including the proposer) to discuss or amend it before he has stated it. Therefore, if anyone attempts to discuss or amend it out of turn, the Chair may intervene; he says: "The member will please wait until the Chair first states the motion." Or, when a member rises out of turn the Chair may ask: "For what purpose does the member rise; the Chair has not yet stated the question?" This anticipates irregular procedure and prevents waste of time.

Strictly speaking, in other words, no member may discuss a motion before it has been seconded and stated by the Chair.

But convenience often allows the proposer of a motion the following liberties in ordinary assemblies — if no one objects; thus:

(a) He may *discuss* his motion first by way of preface, and then propose it; or (b) he may *propose* it first and (while on his feet) discuss it then even before it is seconded and stated by the Chair, and this because no one cares to object.

But if anyone objects (and it is not usual to object unless the privilege is abused), he must propose his motion first, then wait, or sit down, until it is seconded and the Chair repeats the motion (states it to the body) before he may, according to the strict rule, discuss his motion; thus:

MEMBER A: "Mr. Chairman, before proposing an important motion, I should like to preface it with these fine points in its favor: in the first place, our treasury is very . . ." (interrupted).

MEMBER B: "Mr. Chairman, with all due respect to the member, in the interest of orderly procedure I object to a motion being debated before it is *proposed* and *seconded*."

CHAIR (addressing Member A): "Will the member please propose his motion first?" Or, "Since, under the rules, a motion is not open to debate until after it has been proposed, seconded and stated by the Chair, the member will propose his motion first." The member then proposes it, and it is entertained in due course.

Note: If a member is allowed to speak for five minutes, or seven, or ten minutes on his motion and he then does *not* get a *second* to it, that much time will have been wasted in futile debate. Hence, a question must first be *seconded* before it may be *debated*.

The proposer of a motion is always, logically, recognized to speak on his motion ahead of others, provided he rises at once to claim the floor (that is, before another, if another has already been recognized, has commenced *speaking*).

It is the duty of the Chair, after repeating a member's motion, to look to the proposer to be the first to speak on it, so he may to enlighten the assembly thereon; if that member does not rise to speak on it, or to claim the floor, the Chair then recognizes another member. The proposer can, however, rise to discuss his motion afterward, if discussion has not been voted closed.

Prompting the assembly. A main motion becomes debatable as explained above, only after it has been stated by the Chair. It is then that members can and should take the floor to discuss it. It is both useless and absurd to rise to discuss a motion after it has been disposed of; it is then too late. If the members are slow to respond to the requirement of a proceeding, then, to speed up business the Chair methodically prompts them. He says: "Is there any further debate on the motion?", and eventually he puts it to a vote.

Other correct forms of prompting the assembly to action are: "Are you ready for the question?" "Is there any discussion on the motion?" "Are there any remarks?" "Is there debate?"

All the above forms mean and convey the same thing; namely: "If anyone wishes to discuss the motion, *now* is the time to do it." The most practical form is: "Is there any discussion [or, debate] on the motion?" But the most accomplished form is: "Are you ready for the question?" However, since members often shout "Question! Question!" when this form is used (which is discourteous), this form is avoided in this book in favor of the more practical form: "Is there any debate on the motion?" This form is preferable.

Note: Members who wish to discuss or amend a motion must ask for the floor promptly after the Chair states it; if they do not, they must not complain if the Chair puts it to vote. There is nothing else he can do when they delay or they do not seek the floor. Members who sleep on their rights forfeit them.

Right to vote and debate one's own motion. A member can vote for *or* against his motion; and he can speak *in favor* of it. But he may not *speak against it;* and if he attempts to do so, a point of order (or the chairman) can stop him. If he is not stopped, the fact that he spoke against it does not at all void his motion or any action taken on it. To speak *against* one's own motion is a mere inconsistency; it is not illegal.

Since members can *vote against* their own motion, and thus vote it down, they can propose any motion of theirs and then intentionally defeat it (whatever their reason may be). They can thus prevent a mischievous and opportunistic minority or opposition from introducing that particular question later at that same session.

Who owns the motion. A proposed motion belongs to its mover and he can modify it or withdraw it at will, provided the Chair has not *fully* stated the motion to the body. After it has been completely stated, it belongs to the assembly, and is then modifiable or withdrawable with its consent. See Withdrawal.

Chair prepares assembly for the vote. If no one rises to claim the floor to discuss a debatable motion, the Chair prepares the assembly for the vote. He says: "There being no debate [or, further debate], the Chair will put the motion to vote," and if no one then asks for the floor, he proceeds:

CHAIR: "Those in favor of the motion will say aye. Those opposed will say no. The ayes [or noes] have it and the motion is carried [or, lost]," as the case may be.

A motion which has been defeated, or one substantially similar, cannot be offered again at the same session, but it can be introduced again at any future session.

Distinction between motion and question. Strictly speaking, a motion is correctly referred to as a "question" *after* the Chair has stated it to the body; before it is fully stated, it is properly known as "motion." But in practice they are synonymous terms and are used interchangeably, thus: "Mr. Chairman, what is the *motion* [or, question] now before the house?" Or, "The *question* now before the body is on the *motion* to buy a new desk."

Life of the main motion. When a main motion is adopted, it assumes one of three forms of life: (1) temporary, (2) limited, or (3) continuous, depending on the motion and the assembly's intent; thus: (1) Motions obviously intended to be carried out *promptly*, assume temporary life, such as "to paint the meeting room green," "to buy one hundred shares of U. S. Steel," etc. When such motions are executed their life expires. When they are left unexecuted, the body can, at any meeting, amend them or rescind (repeal) them, and thus *end* their life. If an adopted main motion is never carried out and is never rescinded, its life never expires; it stays on record as a live motion, awaiting execution.

(2) Motions which are given *restricted* duration assume limited life, such as "to hire an extra typist for *four* weeks," or "to conduct a drive for new members at half the initiation fee during the next *six* months," etc. The life of such limited motions ends when their *duration* expires, unless, prior to such expiration, the body votes to shorten their duration, or to extend it, or to amend it, or rescind it.

(3) Motions which, when passed, have *recurring* effect and application assume continuous life, such as "to mail *birthday* cards to our members," "to give *annually* fifty dollars to X Fund," etc. Such self-executing motions assume continuous life, until changed or rescinded.

Ambiguous motions. Oftentimes, motions passed by the body are found after adjournment to be ambiguous, or interpretable in two senses. This is especially true when these motions are connected with or applied to matters or events which take place regularly, or recurringly.

For instance, the meaning of the three motions below (given here in the exact wordage passed by assemblies) was challenged. Some members thought that the motion, in each case, applied only *once;* others thought it applied *repeatedly* until rescinded; namely:

(1) "Members must add one dollar to their *annual* dues for our Home Fund."

(2) "Any member being the first endorser of a new candidate will receive a free ticket to our Ladies Night" (an *annual* affair).

(3) "At installation time the incoming president shall be presented with a parliamentary law book" (installations are *biennial*).

No one asked at the meeting if the motion was to apply only just this *once,* or at each event's *recurrence.*

Intention must govern. Legally and parliamentarily, where the act (motion) of the body is not apparent or manifest, the *intention* must govern. Hence, ask what the proposer's intention was; and what the presiding officer's and other members' *understanding* of it was at the time the motion was passed; and whether the language used in debating the motion was guardedly in the singular or plural; or was it carelessly mixed, now singular, now plural.

Where it is impossible to ascertain the body's actual intent on an ambiguous motion, then if that motion is connected with or is applied to established functions or events that take place regularly or recurringly, then the motion recurs with the recurrence of the event with which it is connected, until rescinded; but in the meantime, the assembly in any meeting can (by majority vote) apply its own interpretation, until it is modified or rescinded.

Caution: Since motions passed by the body remain in force until modified, executed, or rescinded, if previously passed motions which remain unexecuted have become obsolete, useless or are no longer desirable, move to *rescind* them (under new business) regardless of *when* they were passed. If you leave them standing, the authority to carry them out is still there, and they can be clandestinely carried out and may involve or perpetuate fraud upon innocent third parties, for which the organization could be held legally liable.

Out-of-order and null and void motions. Motions which conflict with the society's bylaws or rules are out of order when proposed, and if adopted, are null and void, and of no force or effect, even if they are adopted by a unanimous vote. Thus, if the bylaws provide that "candidates for public office shall not be endorsed at meetings," a motion "to endorse X for governor" would be out of order. If it is provided that the "bylaws can be amended by a ⅔ vote, provided thirty-day notice shall have been given," an amendment to the bylaws adopted prior to the expiration of thirty days is null and void, even if adopted by unanimous vote. The same is true of conflict with the laws of the land — local, state or national — as well as with the constitution, bylaws, rules or mandates of a higher body or authority within the organization itself.

Absurd, frivolous and dilatory motions. Motions without sense or merit and those clearly obstructive to the progress of business are out of order and unentertainable, the Chair saying: "The motion just proposed is out of order on the grounds that it is an absurd [frivolous or dilatory] motion." Thus, a motion "to empower the president to stop the rain," "to postpone a question a million years," or "to require new members to know every word in the dictionary prior to their admission," and similar meritless, exaggerated or facetious proposals are absurd and frivolous motions.

Dilatory motions are those which mischievously or unreasonably obstruct or delay business. Thus, if one or more members constantly rise to points of order, or move to adjourn, or doubt the quorum repeatedly with the *evident* intent to delay or obstruct business, the Chair firmly rules the motions out of order, because it is his duty to protect both the assembly and the pending proceeding from unnecessary annoyance or interference.

Note: This, however, cannot prevent members from proposing the motion "to adjourn" at any early part of the meeting or at reasonable *intervals* thereafter (the Chair cannot compel members to remain at the meeting against their will). If it is not deemed wise to adjourn, the members will vote it down.

III. THE RESOLUTION (S, D, A, M, R)

Basic rules of a resolution. Resolutions (like main motions) require a second, they are debatable, amendable, need a majority vote, and can be reconsidered (in symbol form, S, D, A, M, R).

How to propose a simple resolution. When proposing a simple resolution (without a preamble), always begin with the form "I move . . ." and follow it with the phrase "that we adopt the following resolution"; then, add the word "Resolved"; thus:

"Mr. Chairman, I move that we adopt the following resolution: *Resolved*, That this convention express its profound appreciation to the Mayor and city council for the free use of the city auditorium." Or, "Mr. [or, Comrade] Commander, I move that we adopt the following resolution: *Resolved*, That it is the sense of this convention that the United States shall maintain an adequate standing army."

Other forms of proposing a resolution are: "I move to adopt [or, I move the adoption of] the following resolution: *Resolved*," etc.

Example of a simple resolution:

MEMBER: "Mr. Chairman, I move (that) we adopt [or, I move the adoption of] the following resolution: *Resolved*, That the United Nations adopt an international anthem." (Seconded.)

CHAIR: "It has been moved and seconded to adopt the following resolution: *Resolved*, That the United Nations adopt an international anthem. Is there any debate on the resolution?" and the resolution is ultimately put to vote and the result announced. [Observe the comma after *Resolved*, and the capital first letter of the first word that follows it. *Resolved* is italicized in print.]

How to propose a resolution with preamble. Resolutions with preamble (or introduction, which can consist of one or more than one "whereas") are proposed and entertained in much the same way as a simple resolution, except that the "whereas" comes between the form "I move . . ." and the word "*Resolved*," thus (observe the form and punctuation marks):

Example of a resolution with preamble:

MEMBER: "Mr. Chairman, I move that we adopt [or, I move the adoption of] the following resolution:

"Whereas, Our radio is useless; and

"Whereas, We need a new one this year; and

"Whereas, There is a special sale on radios this week; be it [or, be it therefore]

"*Resolved*, That the treasurer be authorized to buy a new radio at a cost not to exceed" etc., stating the resolution in full.

CHAIR: "It has been moved and seconded that we [or, to] adopt the following resolution:

"Whereas, Our radio is useless; and

"Whereas, We need a new one this year; and

"Whereas, There is a special sale on radios this week; be it *Resolved*, That . . . [etc.]. Is there any debate on the resolution?" (After discussion, if any, it is put to vote).

With the above as a model, you can compose any kind of resolution with a preamble, just as you can offer or compose any kind of a simple resolution without a preamble, as previously shown.

Four Model Types of Resolutions

These models cover all conceivable types of resolutions. There are four types of resolutions: (1) those not having any preamble at all;

(2) those with a preamble of only one "whereas"; (3) those with a preamble of two or more "whereases"; (4) those having only one or more than one "resolved" part (resolution part), thus:

(1) *Without a preamble:*
"Mr. Chairman, I move the adoption of the following resolution: *Resolved,* That we express our deep appreciation to the Mayor and city council for the free use of the city auditorium."

(2) *With a preamble of one whereas:*
"Mr. Chairman, I move that we adopt the following resolution:
"Whereas, The Mayor and city council granted us the free use of the city auditorium during this convention; be it
"*Resolved,* That we express our deep appreciation."

(3) *With more than one whereas:*
"Mr. Chairman, I move the adoption of this resolution:
"Whereas, The Mayor and city council provided this convention with the free use of the city auditorium; and
"Whereas, On Tuesday they tendered a complimentary luncheon; and
"Whereas, His Honor the Mayor presented our national president with the key to the City; be it therefore
Resolved, That this convention go on record expressing to the Mayor and the city council our profound gratitude."

(4) *With more than one Resolved:*
"Mr. Chairman, I move the following resolution:
"Whereas, the mayor and the city council did [thus and so]; and
"Whereas, They also extended [thus-and-so]; and
"Whereas, On Tuesday [thus and so took place]; be it
"*Resolved,* That we express our appreciation; and be it further
"*Resolved,* That a copy of this resolution be forthwith transmitted to His Honor the Mayor and each member of the city council."

There is no limit to the number of "whereases" or of "resolved" parts that can be included in a resolution. It is up to the proposer to decide the form it will take. The assembly can amend any part of the resolution, including the preamble, just as it can amend any part of a main motion. The preamble is amended last when it becomes necessary to amend it, and thus include the changes, if any, made upon the resolution itself.

Forms for recording assembly's sense. Use the following standard forms when you wish to have the sense or attitude of the assembly recorded on a question:

1. "Mr. Chairman, I move that we go on record [or, that this convention, body or organization, go on record] as being in favor of [or, as being opposed to] such-and-such question."

2. "Madam President, I move that it be the sense of this meeting [or, of this body, assembly, convention, or organization] that we deplore discrimination against our fellow-men on account of race, color, or religion."

3. "Mr. Chairman, I move that we petition the Mayor [or, the Governor, the Congress, etc.] to do thus-and-so."

The above forms can also be in the form of resolutions; thus: "*Resolved,* That we go on record," or "*Resolved,* That we petition," or "*Resolved,* That it is the sense," etc. (Note the capital T's).

Other forms of proposing resolutions. In addition to the above strictly formal or technical forms of proposing resolutions, the following forms, with or without preamble, are equally authoritative. (Use in separate paragraph form or combined form; thus:)

(1) "Mr. President, I move the adoption of the following resolution: *Resolved,* That it is the sense of this body [or, That this body, assembly, convention or meeting, etc.] that we go on record as follows: *First* [or 1, or A], That we detest war; *Second* [or 2, or B], That all munition plants or factories be immediately converted to commercial purposes; *Third* [etc.], That future production or manufacture of war equipment be and is hereby prohibited; and *Fourth,* That the General Assembly of the United Nations be petitioned to authorize the creation of such supervisory commission within each nation throughout the world, as shall be deemed adequate to enforce the objects hereof; *Fifth* [if necessary], or *Sixth* [if necessary] . . ." etc.

(2) "Madam President, Be it *Resolved* as follows: *First,* So-and-so; *Second,* So-and-so," etc. "I move its adoption."

The quickest and surest way to learn the correct and accomplished form of composing resolutions is to *write* out one or two of them (copy any of the choices shown, or compose your own).

How the Chair entertains simple resolutions. The Chair entertains resolutions (those without a preamble) as follows: He begins, as in the case of motions, with the word "It" and the customary phrase "has been moved and seconded," and adds the member's proposal, thus:

CHAIR: "It has been moved and seconded to adopt the following resolution: *Resolved,* That we go on record . . ." etc. And he prompts: "Is there any debate on the resolution?"

How a resolution is put to vote

CHAIR: "Those in favor (of the adoption) of the resolution, will say aye. Those opposed will say no. The ayes [or, noes] have it, and the resolution is adopted [or, lost]."

Explanation of terms. "I move" means I propose, I offer, I submit. "Motion" means proposal. "To adopt" means to pass, to approve. "Adoption" means passage or approval. "Resolution" means motion, proposal, decision, etc. "Whereas" means since, in view of the fact that, inasmuch as, because, etc. "Resolved" means decided, determined—that is, "let it be decided," or "let it be here determined." The word "preamble" means introduction, preface, prologue, etc.

Note: Do not use the ungrammatical and corrupt form, "I move *for* the adoption of the motion." Leave out the word "for"; say simply, "I move *the* adoption of," etc.

Correct form and punctuation for resolutions. Observe carefully the written form of a resolution, and note particularly the punctuation marks. Note the colon (:) after the phrase "I move to adopt the following resolution:" Each "Whereas," as shown above, begins with a capital "W" and a separate paragraph, and a comma follows it. The first letter of the first word after each "Whereas" begins with a capital letter. A semicolon (;) ends the statement of each whereas; and there are *no* punctuation marks after each "and" or "be it" or "be it therefore." The word *Resolved* is *italicized* when it appears in print, and when not printed it is underscored; it is always followed by a comma, as shown above, and the first word that follows it begins with a capital letter.

The words "be it" or "be it therefore" are not absolutely necessary, as the word *resolved* itself is sufficient; thus:

"Mr. Chairman, I move the adoption of the following resolution:

"Whereas, The war is over; and

"Whereas, World peace must endure;

"*Resolved*, That we go on record favoring total disarmament."

Resolutions as published in newspapers. When published in newspapers, to speed up the copy and to conserve space, resolutions are not always given their full and correct form in separate paragraph arrangement. Capitals and punctuation marks are also frequently omitted.

Chapter 7
THE SUBSIDIARY MOTIONS

There is a class of motions in parliamentary procedure known as *subsidiary motions*. This is the technical name for them.

In its parliamentary sense, the word "subsidiary" means helping, aiding, or assisting; that is, these motions were invented to assist, aid or help dispose of (act on) a main motion—as when a motion is amended, or postponed, or laid on the table, etc. Therefore, the subsidiary motions can be entertained as such only while a main motion is pending and they are then acted on ahead of it.

The subsidiary motions are the most frequently used motions in parliamentary procedure. In the course of the proceedings, motions are debated, amended, postponed, referred to committees, tabled, etc. Hence, unless you know the rules pertaining to each motion you cannot make proper use of them and, therefore, you cannot apply or promote efficiency in the transaction of the assembly's business.

Rules and rank. There are only seven subsidiary motions in the whole body of parliamentary law. If you know the rules and rank of these motions, you can operate or manipulate them to affect the business before the assembly in any way desired. They are as follows:

1. Lay on the table (S, M).................... page 98
2. Previous question (S, $\frac{2}{3}$, R).................... 92
3. Limit or extend debate (S, A, $\frac{2}{3}$, R)............. 90
4. Postpone to a definite time (S, D, A, M, R)..... 88
5. Refer to a committee (S, D, A, M, R)......... 82
6. Amend the main motion (S, D, A, M, R)........ 68
7. Postpone indefinitely (S, D, M, R)............. 66

Their key symbols: S means that the motion is Secondable; D, it is Debatable; A, it is Amendable; M means Majority; $\frac{2}{3}$, two-thirds vote; and R means it can be Reconsidered.

How to memorize their name and rank. A convenient way of remembering the name and respective rank, or order, of the above subsidiary motions is by their first letter; namely: L, P; L, P; R, A, P.

Each motion, as listed, beginning with number one, is of higher rank than every motion listed below it; and conversely, each motion, commencing with the bottom one, is of lower rank than every motion listed above it.

This means that a motion of higher rank can always be entertained while a motion of lower rank is pending before the body but a motion of lower rank cannot be entertained if a motion of higher rank is before the body — just like bids in an auction sale.

No one may propose two or more motions at once (as for example: "I move reconsideration and I also move that it be tabled"), unless no one objects to this being done.

Some collective rules.

1. There are only seven subsidiary motions.

2. All of them require a second (observe the S sign in the parentheses of each motion).

3. All of them can be reconsidered (note the R), except the top one — to lay on the table. (Reread this.)

4. All of them require a majority vote (observe the M), except two of them — the previous question and to limit or extend debate.

5. The top three motions are undebatable (no D indicated), but the bottom four are debatable (note the D).

6. The top two motions and the bottom one are not amendable (no A symbol shown), but the other four motions are amendable (note the A sign in them).

7. Each subsidiary motion, beginning with the top one is of higher rank than the motions listed below it; thus, motion number four outranks motions five, six and seven, but is of lower rank than, or is outranked by, motions three, two and one. This means that a motion of higher rank is in order and can be entertained if a motion of lower rank is pending; but a motion of lower rank cannot be entertained if a motion of higher rank is pending before the body.

8. None of them can be tabled, postponed or referred apart from their motion. The previous question cannot be ordered on the motion to table, but it can apply on all the rest. To limit debate applies to all of them except to table and the previous question.

Why subsidiary motions were invented.

The subsidiary motions were invented to promote efficiency in the transaction of business; that is, to help accomplish the business of a meeting in the quickest and wisest possible manner.

In other words, some subsidiary motions were deliberately invented to be used in delaying consideration of a question when the assembly is not ready to take final action on a matter; other subsidiary motions were intentionally designed to accelerate final action.

For instance, if attendance at a meeting is slim, an important question then pending before the body is wisely postponed to the next meeting when more members can be expected to be present. If it needs further study and investigation, it can be referred to a committee. If some urgent business has to be acted on ahead of it, the pending question can be laid on the table. If the hour is late and further discussion is inadvisable, the previous question (terminates debate), or the motion to limit debate (reduces debate) can be proposed, thus speeding up action. If it needs changing or improvement, it can be amended. If it is a useless or unprofitable motion, it can be postponed indefinitely (which is an indirect or polite way of killing it outright).

It is up to the members to take the initiative to propose and maneuver these motions as best befits business efficiency. (When in doubt what motion to make, ask the Chair to guide you. It is his duty to do so; he is presumed to know procedure.)

Subsidiary motions outrank the main motions. Since the subsidiary motions were invented to promote wise and efficient action and to aid or assist in disposing of a main motion, to serve that purpose the subsidiary motions were necessarily given precedence over, or were assigned higher rank than, the main motion. They are entertained while a main motion is pending before the assembly, as when an amendment to the main motion is acted on ahead of it, and then the main motion as amended (or not) is acted on next.

Consequently, if a main motion (such as to buy a desk) is before the body, it is in order to propose an amendment to it, or to postpone it, or to lay it on the table, etc., but it is not in order to propose another *main* motion, such as, to sell the clubhouse, because only one main motion at a time can be considered.

Subsidiary motions also have rank among themselves. Besides having higher rank than the main motion, the subsidiary motions also have rank among themselves. This means that when any one of the subsidiary motions is pending with the main motion, every subsidiary motion listed *above* it can be proposed because it outranks it (just like the higher bids in an auction sale), but no motion listed *below* it can be entertained, because it is of lower rank.

Whenever a motion is proposed while a motion of *higher* rank is immediately pending, the Chair uses this language: "The motion just proposed is not in order at the present time because it is of lower rank than the immediately pending motion [naming it]."

Numerous subsidiary motions can be pending. In other words, since subsidiary motions outrank the main motion and also outrank each other, any number of subsidiary motions can be pending at the same time with a main motion, provided they have been proposed in the order of their rank.

Thus, it is possible to have pending at the same time a main motion and several subsidiary motions with it, as shown in the following sets.

The motions in these sets are numbered according to the order in which they were made. They will be acted upon in the opposite order, beginning with the subsidiary motion of highest rank; the main motion is voted on last.

Set 1	Set 2
4. Lay on the table	4. Lay on the table
3. Refer to a committee	3. Postpone to next meeting
2. Postpone indefinitely	2. Amendment to main motion
1. MAIN MOTION	1. MAIN MOTION

In each set there are four motions pending before the body; all are in order, because only one *main* motion is pending in each set; the other three motions in each case are subsidiary motions which have been proposed in the order of their rank. In each set, the main motion is *proposed* first, then the motion just above it, and the one just above that, and finally the top motion.

Highest ranking motion always voted on first. When two or more motions are before the body, as in these two sets, the motion having the *highest* rank is always put to vote first (motion 4), and if any motions remain pending after each vote, the motion having the next highest rank is then put to vote, then the next, and so on successively down the line until the set is disposed of as follows.

Illustration of the vote. For instance, set number 1 would be transacted in this manner:

CHAIR: "Those in favor of laying the question [meaning always the entire pending set] on the table will say aye; those opposed will say no. The noes have it, and the motion to lay on the table is lost." (Since the motion to table is defeated, the other three motions under it are still pending before the body, and the Chair continues:) "The question now is on the motion to refer to a committee." (If it is put to vote and lost, the Chair continues:) "The question now before the body is on the motion to postpone indefinitely." (If it is put to vote and lost:) "The question now is on the *motion*, which is . . ." The main motion is then put to vote and is adopted or lost. The vote on the second set is taken in the same manner. Indeed, all *seven* subsidiary motions (plus their respective amendments) can be pending before the body at the same time if they are proposed in their proper order.

The logic of rank of the subsidiary motions. When the seven subsidiary motions were being invented and their inventors sought to determine what rank to assign to each one, it was decided to base their rank on the speed and wisdom with which each motion can accomplish business.

In other words, the nearer to completion a subsidiary motion brings the business before the house, the *higher* its rank. Thus, (1) the motion to "lay on the table" was assigned highest rank among the seven subsidiary motions because its adoption sets a main question aside only *temporarily* (since a tabled question can be taken from the table at any time during the same session, which may be but five minutes later or even less, or after the urgent business to which it gave way is disposed of.) Theoretically, therefore, the motion to lay on the table does not hold up business long. (2) The motion called "previous question" (which terminates debate), and (3) to "limit debate" (which reduces the time for debate) were assigned second and third rank respectively and given position in that order, next to the motion to table, because by ending or cutting down further debate on a pending question they expedite accomplishment of business. (4) The motion to "postpone to a definite time" (that is, to a later time within the same session or to the next session) was given fourth rank because when the time to which it was postponed is reached, the question is automatically taken up for consideration, thus assuring accomplishment of business. (5) The motion to "refer to a committee" was assigned fifth rank because a committee requires time to organize and may not report for a session or two and, logically, has lower rank than the above four motions which accelerate business. (6) The motion to "amend the main motion" was given sixth rank and assigned position *near* the main motion because it belongs *close* to the motion it is amending; and it was assigned higher rank than the motion to "postpone indefinitely" because the act of amending a main motion is a more profitable or useful proceeding than the motion to "postpone indefinitely" (to kill) a question. (7) The motion to "postpone indefinitely" was assigned lowest rank among the seven subsidiary motions because its adoption kills outright a main motion which cannot be introduced again at the same session or it might never be introduced again.

Outranked by the privileged motions. While the subsidiary motions outrank the main motion, they are themselves outranked by the *privileged* motions and by such of the *incidental* motions as logically pertain to them (pp. 47, 48).

Each subsidiary motion will now be separately considered beginning with the motion to postpone indefinitely — the lowest in rank.

7. POSTPONE INDEFINITELY (S, D, M, R)

This is not a motion to *postpone* at all. Its name is misleading. It is purely a technical term for "killing" the motion before the body, and if it is adopted it actually ends the life of the main motion for that session. It is proposed when it is desired to "kill" the pending main motion outright.

When a member says: "I move to postpone a motion *indefinitely*," it is the same as if he said: "I move that we suppress [or, kill] the pending main motion." And if the motion to postpone indefinitely is carried, the main motion is then no longer before the body; it is suppressed, or eliminated; but if indefinite postponement is defeated, the pending main motion remains unaffected; it is *still* before the body and is put to vote in due course.

Basic rules. The motion to postpone indefinitely is secondable and debatable, but is unamendable; it requires a majority vote; it is a subsidiary motion with lowest rank, and can be reconsidered. It outranks only the main motion; hence, it can only be proposed when only a main motion is before the body. When it is adopted, it automatically removes the main motion from before the house and prevents it from being reintroduced at the same session; it can, however, be introduced again at any future *new* session. In other words, a motion that has been indefinitely postponed does not automatically come up for action at the next or any future meeting; it has to be reintroduced.

How proposed and entertained. Assume the following main motion pending before the body: "To buy a new radio."

MEMBER: "Mr. Chairman, I move that we postpone the motion to buy a radio indefinitely." (It is seconded.)

KEY QUIZ

Q. Must this motion be seconded? *A.* Yes.
Q. Is it debatable? *A.* Yes.
Q. Is it amendable? *A.* No.
Q. What vote adopts it? *A.* Majority.
Q. What class of motion is it, and what is its rank? *A.* It is a subsidiary motion of lowest rank.
Q. Can it be reconsidered? *A.* Yes, if *adopted*.

CHAIR: "It has been moved and seconded that we postpone *indefinitely* the pending motion 'to buy a new radio.' " (And since the actual consequence of this motion is not always understood by the average member, the Chair can explain:) "The Chair would like to state that if the motion to postpone indefinitely is adopted, it will automatically kill or eliminate the main motion from before the body. Is there any discussion on the motion to postpone?" (No response; he continues:) "There being no discussion, the Chair will put the motion to postpone indefinitely to a vote. Those in favor of the motion to postpone indefinitely will say aye; those opposed will say no. The ayes have it, and the motion to postpone indefinitely is carried." (Thus the adoption of indefinite postponement automatically ends the life of the main motion and nothing is then before the body.)

When indefinite postponement can be reconsidered. An affirmative vote on the motion to postpone indefinitely can be reconsidered; in other words, if the motion to postpone indefinitely is carried, it can be reconsidered; but if the negative side prevails, it cannot be reconsidered. The only way a main motion that has been postponed indefinitely can come before the body at the *same* session is to reconsider the motion to postpone indefinitely which suppressed the main motion. If this is *not* done, that main motion stays killed for that session.

Points to remember about indefinite postponement. To postpone indefinitely is a tricky motion. It can be manipulated so as to gain advantage in the proceedings. Therefore, the following significant points should be remembered:

(1) It is an indirect or polite motion by which a main motion may be killed outright.

(2) It is a test motion, and as such it gives its proponents an opportunity to ascertain their strength (how many votes they have or can rely on) to vote down the main motion if put to a direct vote. This helps you to "size up" situations.

(3) Since it opens the main motion to debate, those who previously spoke their allotted number of times on the main motion can now speak on the main motion again.

(4) It opens to debate the merits of the main motion at the same time with itself; that is, when it is proposed, members may discuss or touch on both the main motion as well as this motion, or either of them. (It is an exception to the rule which requires that discussion must be confined to the immediately pending question.)

Illustration of its dual discussion

MEMBER: "Mr. Chairman, I am in favor of the *main* motion to buy a new radio [he is discussing the main motion], and I am opposed to the motion to postpone it indefinitely [he is now discussing indefinite postponement]. Radios can be bought at very low price all this week [he is discussing the main motion]. I therefore hope that the motion to postpone it indefinitely [he is discussing it] will not prevail, and when the vote is taken on the main motion [he is discussing *it*], it will be overwhelmingly adopted."

If an amendment to the main motion and the motion to postpone indefinitely are pending at the same time with a main motion, thus (read them from bottom upward):

> 3. Amendment to main motion
> 2. Postpone indefinitely
> 1. MAIN MOTION

the *amendment* is voted on first, then *postponement*, then, if indefinite postponement is defeated, the *main motion* as amended, thus:

CHAIR: "The ayes have it and the amendment is carried. The question now is on the motion to postpone the main motion indefinitely. (He then puts postponement to vote. If it is defeated, the main motion as amended is then put to vote, the Chair continuing:) "The question now is on the main motion *as amended*, which is . . ." (stating it, and the vote is taken and announced).

But if postponement *prevails*, the main motion as amended is not put to vote because adoption of postponement removes it from before the meeting, and nothing would be pending to postpone.

Note: Since the *adoption* of indefinite postponement kills outright a pending main motion, as previously stated, to avoid or to minimize heated arguments on a controversial question, move to postpone it indefinitely. If this is carried, the controversial question is suppressed and is no longer before the body. Similarly, apply indefinite postponement (in preference to "to table") on useless, unwise, unjust, or unwarranted proceedings or main proposals — such as to impeach, suspend, expel, raise the dues, assess the members or fine a member, sell the clubhouse, buy a new desk, increase or decrease a salary, a vote of confidence, etc. But if such proceedings are just, wise and merited, then vote *against* indefinite postponement and thus be enabled to vote directly upon the merits of any such proceeding or any main motion.

6. AMEND THE MAIN MOTION (S, D, A, M, R)

Amendments to main motions never require anyone's consent to be proposed; they automatically outrank their motions.

Why amendments were invented. Amendments were invented to afford all members of the assembly an opportunity to contribute their talent and skill to the improvement of incomplete or imperfect motions. In other words, since a single mind is not always capable of conceiving every phase of a question or proposition, through amendments an assembly is enabled to achieve business with fuller wisdom.

Many motions, when first proposed, are not made complete enough in their most essential particulars. For example, the following is not a complete motion: "Mr. Chairman, I move that we buy a radio." The proposition is not sufficiently complete or comprehensive. It does not specify price, size, make, color, whether new or used, or when and where to buy it.

When the main motion is so vague, it may be necessary to act on many amendments, and this is a slow-moving and time-consuming process. On the other hand, fewer amendments would be required if the motion when first proposed were as follows: "Mr. Chairman, I move that we buy a radio from Roosevelt and Co., about the size of the old one in our banquet hall, at a cost not to exceed fifty dollars, and that the chairman of the House Committee be authorized to purchase it in time for our next meeting."

Basic rules. Amendments are secondable, debatable, amendable, and require a majority vote. They can be reconsidered. They belong in the subsidiary class of motions and have sixth rank; that is, amendments to main motions can be proposed only when nothing of higher rank than the motion to postpone indefinitely is pending.

KEY QUIZ

Q. Do amendments require a second? *A.* Yes.
Q. Are amendments debatable? *A.* Yes.
Q. Are they amendable? *A.* Yes.
Q. What vote do amendments to main motions require? *A.* Majority;
but to bylaws, usually 2/3.
Q. What class of motions are amendments? *A.* Subsidiary.
Q. What is their rank? *A.* Sixth.
Q. Can they be reconsidered? *A.* Yes.
Q. When an amendment has been acted on, is it necessary to vote afterward on the motion? *A.* Yes, regardless of what happens to that amendment.

Vote on main motion as amended. The fact that an *amendment* is voted on does not mean that the *main motion* has also thereby been voted on. The main motion must also be put to vote.

When indefinite postponement is pending. If an amendment to the main motion is adopted while the motion to postpone indefinitely is pending, the motion as amended is not put to vote until after indefinite postponement is voted on and is lost.

If only one amendment is pending with a main motion, after the amendment is put to vote and adopted, the words contained in that amendment are then automatically absorbed by and incorporated in the pending (and as yet *unvoted* on) main motion, and the main motion, as thus amended, must then be put to vote. The mere adoption of the amendments does not constitute completed action upon the *main* motion.

Note: Despite this rule, when, in the assembly's mind and understanding, the action taken on an *amendment* is unknowledgeably deemed final and conclusive also upon the *motion* itself, the adoption or defeat of the amendment implies the adoption or defeat of the motion and is charitably allowed so to stand unless someone raises a point of order at the time or before the meeting adjourns. Remember: no matter how the vote results on an amendment, you must still put the main motion *also* to a vote, or there can be trouble and confusion later.

How an amendment is entertained. The language in transacting an amendment is as follows:

CHAIR: "The ayes have it and the amendment to add to the main motion the words 'before our next meeting' is carried. The question now is on the main motion as amended, which is: that we buy a new radio before our next meeting. Is there any discussion on the motion *as amended?* There being none, the Chair will put it to vote. Those in favor of the *main* motion as amended will say aye." (Response.) "Those opposed, will say no." (Response.) "The ayes have it and the main motion is carried, and we will buy a new radio before our next meeting," or "The noes have it and the motion as amended is lost."

If the **amendment** above is defeated, the Chair says: "The noes have it, and the amendment is lost; the question now is on the main motion to buy a new radio," which he puts to a vote and declares it as "The ayes have it," or "The noes have it," as the case may be. (Practice on this paragraph, and the one above for quick mastery.)

In other words, when you vote on the amendment to a motion you are voting only on the words of that amendment; you are not voting on the words of the main motion.

Chair's role in transacting amendments. It is the duty of the presiding officer to take, first, a separate vote on the *amendment* to a motion, and then, if the amendment is adopted, a separate vote on the motion *as amended*, or if the amendment is lost, on the motion itself as originally proposed. Otherwise he mispractices parliamentary law and he exasperates progressive and knowledgeable members (who resent it, even if in quiet desperation they endure it out of a sense of delicacy, or out of deference to the office).

After an amendment has been proposed and seconded, the Chair should always repeat the member's amendment by prefacing it with the phrase: "It has been moved and seconded to amend the main motion . . ." and then specify in the proposal the method by which the amendment can best be made, as "by adding the words . . .".

If members fail to propose amendments by recognized parliamentary form (as is often the case), it is the duty of the Chair (who is supposed to know the correct forms and procedure) to state them correctly. Thus if a member says "I would like to move an amendment so that the price won't go over fifty dollars," the Chair should state it: "It has been moved and seconded to amend the motion by adding the words 'at a cost not to exceed fifty dollars.'"

Amendments can be reconsidered. Amendments, like main motions, can be reconsidered (whether adopted or lost). An amendment can therefore be moved to be reconsidered the moment it has been voted on, if so desired. If it is desired to reconsider an amendment after it has been passed with its motion, the motion to reconsider must also include reconsideration of its motion; thus: "Mr. Chairman, I move to reconsider the main motion and its amendment(s)." If this is adopted, the said amendment and the motion are in the same position they were in before the vote was taken thereon. Both the primary and secondary amendments can be reconsidered.

Members can amend their own motion. A member has the right to amend his own motion, just as he may amend another's motion, whenever he feels his motion can be improved or made more acceptable.

Informal acceptance of amendments to motions. If an amendment is proposed upon a pending motion and the maker of the pending motion calls out "I accept the amendment," if no one objects to it such informal acceptance of the amendment is then deemed adopted by general consent; and the Chair then puts the main motion to a vote as thus amended; but if anyone objects to this informal practice, the amendment must then have a second and is put to vote separately.

Rule of "germaneness" of amendments. Amendments to a motion must be germane to it, otherwise the amendment is not entertained.

In its parliamentary sense, "germane" means related or pertinent.

In other words, the subject matter of an amendment must relate to the subject matter of the motion to be amended.

If the amendment does not relate to the text of the motion, or it introduces a different subject from that contained in the motion, then it is not a legitimate amendment; it is, instead, another main motion proposed in the guise of an amendment, and it is not entertained.

Illustration of germane amendments. If the motion before the body is, say, "to buy a new desk," any amendment is germane to it which, for instance, relates to its price, make, color, who will order it, etc.

Illustration of ungermane amendments. Assume the same motion before the body: "to buy a new desk." Are the following proposals, offered in the form of amendment, germane: "and to donate fifty dollars to X Fund"; "paint the meeting room"; "buy the adjoining lot for club parking," etc.? Obviously these are **ungermane** amendments and are not in order as amendments (but they can be proposed as main motions afterward).

How ungermane amendments are disposed of. When an amendment is deemed not germane, the Chair, on his own initiative or on a point of order from the floor, rules it out of order; thus:

CHAIR: "The amendment just proposed is not germane to the motion, and it cannot be entertained as an amendment to it."

Whenever the Chair entertains ungermane amendments to a motion, or declines to entertain germane amendments, discerning members can rise to a point of order to correct the error.

If the Chair rules incorrectly on a point of order, the member can appeal from the Chair's decision. (See Appeal.)

If, while an ungermane amendment is before the body, no one challenges the amendment, it is too late to raise a point of order or to challenge the amendment after it has been put to a vote, and the vote thereon is legal. (Mere procedural mispractice does not constitute illegality of action.)

Unparliamentary and confusing proposals. It is not only unparliamentary but also confusing and misleading to propose or to entertain amendments to motions in loose, inefficient or improper language. Thus:

(1) It is incorrect to say: "I'd like an amendment to the motion 'to buy a new radio' so that it won't cost over fifty dollars." It should be stated in its proper parliamentary language; namely: "I move to amend the motion by adding the words 'at a cost not to exceed fifty dollars.' " Use this form.

(2) It is incorrect to say: "I want the motion 'to buy a new gavel' amended so that a mahogany one will be bought." It should be phrased in its proper parliamentary form: "I move to amend the motion by inserting the word 'mahogany' before the word 'gavel.' "

(3) It is incorrect to say: "I want an amendment to the motion so that the state senator will not be invited." It should be correctly phrased, thus: "I move to amend the motion by striking out the words 'state senator.'"

(4) It is incorrect to offer to amend the motion "to buy a new desk from Allen's Stores" by loosely saying: "I'd like to see Allen's Stores eliminated and the desk bought from Jordan's." Instead, the proposed amendment should be offered thus: "I move to amend the motion by striking out the words 'Allen's Stores' and inserting the word 'Jordan's.' "

(5) It is incorrect to say: "I have a different motion than the pending one, 'to donate from our treasury one thousand dollars for scholarships this year' and it is this: 'to give a dance, proceeds of which shall go toward scholarship awards,' and would like this carried in place of it." Instead, it should be stated correctly, thus: "I move to substitute for the pending

main motion the following: 'that we hold a dance, proceeds of which shall go for scholarships.' " Use this form and you avoid confusion.

Active or passive forms. Amendments and motions can be proposed either in the active or passive voice, thus: "I move *to amend* the motion," or "I move that the motion *be amended*"; "I move ,that *we buy* a new desk," or "that a new desk *be bought*," etc.

Amending motions previously adopted. When an amendment is proposed not to a pending motion but to a motion or question that was previously adopted and which is still in effect, such amendment is not the *subsidiary* to amend (p. 68), but is a *main* motion (technically called an *incidental main* motion); and since it is a main motion, it is subject to all the subsidiary and privileged actions, and to apt incidental motions; pp. 47, 48. Hence such a motion to amend something previously adopted may be voted postponed, referred, tabled, etc.

For instance, say the assembly, two meetings ago, voted to buy a new desk and no price was set; or at the last meeting it voted to donate $50 to X charity; or earlier at this meeting it was voted to have the meeting room painted brown. If these motions have not yet been carried out, they are still in effect. But since they already *have* been adopted (passed), they are not now actually pending before the meeting. Since they are still effective and executable, and while they still so remain, then at any meeting they can be amended by the incidental main motion to amend by setting the price to be paid for the desk, or to amend the $50 donation to $75 or $25, or to amend, changing color from brown to green.

It requires a $\frac{2}{3}$ vote to amend motions adopted in past sessions, unless previous notice is given, but only a majority vote to amend motions previously adopted at the present session.

Debating the amendment. Debate on an amendment to a motion must be restricted to the amendment, except where it is necessary to mention its motion for comparison or clarification for better grasp of the object of the amendment.

Absurd amendments. No amendment is in order which strikes out the parliamentary forms "Resolved," or the words "I move," or "I propose that . . . ," etc. And no amendment is in order which converts one parliamentary form or identity into another, such as to amend by striking out the words "to table" and inserting in their place the words "to postpone," or to change "refer" to "table," or to change to "postpone indefinitely" to "definitely," etc.

Debatability of amendments. An amendment is debatable if the motion which it seeks to amend is debatable; thus, amendments to main motions are debatable because main motions are debatable; but amendments to the motion to limit debate, for instance, are not debatable because to limit debate is not debatable — and similarly with other motions.

Note: Wherever the symbol D, meaning Debatable, is shown with listed motions, as on page 62, and with it, is shown the symbol A, meaning Amendable, then when these motions are amended, their amendments are debatable until debate is voted ended. *Query:* How many of the seven subsidiary motions (p. 62) are *both* debatable *and* amendable? Name them.

Hostile amendments. Hostile amendments to a motion are in order, provided they are germane to the overall purpose or objective of that motion.

There is nothing strange or puzzling about "hostile" amendments. A hostile amendment is merely a *contrary* amendment — just as contrary debate on a motion is hostile debate. There is nothing improper in proposing a hostile amendment upon a pending proceeding, just as there is nothing improper about expressing a contrary view on a pending proceeding. Therefore, if, for instance, the motion before the body is "to have a catered lobster supper after our installation," it is in order to amend it (contrarily) changing "lobster" to "chicken a la king," or "steak," or "Boston baked beans and brown bread," etc. Such amendments are technically known as hostile amendments, but they are in order because they are germane to the overall subject matter of the pending question, which is food.

If, for instance, the pending motion is "to give the outgoing president a briefcase," it can be amended to "suitcase," or "desk set." Such amendments oppose (are hostile to) "briefcase," but they are in order because they are germane to the overall idea of that motion, which is a gift.

If the pending motion is "to censure" or "condemn," it can be adversely amended, changing it to "to commend" or "to praise." Such changes or amendments are in order because they are germane to the frame of mind or one's attitude on a matter.

More than two pending amendments prohibited. Not more than two amendments can be pending before the body at the *same* time. Experience has shown that the human mind can best comprehend and entertain no more than two amendments at once.

For instance, it is intelligible or understandable to say "I move an amendment to the main motion," or "I move an amendment to the amendment of the main motion," but to say "I move an amendment to the amendment of the amendment to the amendment of the main motion" is absurd and confuses the assembly. Therefore, having more than two formal amendments before the body at one time is prohibited.

No limit to additional amendments. There is no limit, however, to the number of additional or successive amendments that can be *proposed* to a motion; that is, as soon as one amendment is adopted or defeated, another one can be proposed if need be.

Thus, if two amendments are pending, after the second one is out of the way, another one can then be proposed in its place, provided it is germane or related; or if only one amendment is pending, after it has been disposed of, another amendment can be proposed to the motion; and when no further amendments are proposed, the motion, as amended or not, is then put to vote in due course.

Note: The subsidiary motion to *amend* applies only to main motions and to no others. All other motions that are amendable are amendable by their very nature. Look on page 62. How many subsidiary motions are amendable by their very nature? That is, which ones there have the symbol A?

Primary and Secondary Amendments

Amendments are known by definite and specific names. The amendment *first* proposed can be referred to in the course of the proceedings as a "primary" amendment, or amendment to the main motion, or amendment of the first degree (or order), or first amendment. If one amendment is already pending before the body and another one is then proposed, the *second* amendment can be referred to in the course of the proceedings as a "secondary" amendment, or amendment to the amendment, or amendment of the second degree (or order), or second amendment.

The terms "primary" and "secondary" are the most literate and best descriptive parliamentary terms; but "first" and "second" are practical and popular terms.

There is no such parliamentary term as *third* or "tertiary" amendment, or *fourth* or "quartiary" amendment, etc.

Whenever numerous amendments are spontaneously suggested or simultaneously called out by the members, such suggestions or calls are treated not as formal amendments or proposals, but as suggestions for filling blanks. (See Filling Blanks.)

Amendments to motions die or survive with their motion (to which they are applied). When adopted as amendments, their further life is contingent upon their *motion* being adopted, too. If their motion is defeated, they go down in defeat with it.

Secondary amendments outrank primary amendments. When *two* amendments are pending with a motion, the secondary amendment is considered and put to vote first, because it is of higher rank than the primary amendment and the motion. If a secondary amendment is carried, it is automatically absorbed by and incorporated in the *primary* amendment.

The fact that the secondary amendment is carried does not mean that the primary amendment is also thereby carried, and/or that the motion itself is also thereby carried. The primary amendment as thus amended must then be put to vote. If the primary amendment as amended is carried, it is then automatically incorporated into the motion, and the motion as thus amended must then be put to vote.

How to transact two pending amendments. To illustrate the procedure for transacting a secondary amendment, a primary amendment and a main motion, assume the following set of motions before the body: (1) *main motion:* "to buy a new radio"; (2) *primary amendment:* to add to the main motion the words "from Smith and Company"; and (3) *secondary amendment:* to add to the primary amendment the words "before our next meeting."

On paper or on the blackboard the set below would look like this (Read from bottom upward):

      2nd Amendment.   Add: "Before our next meeting."
      1st Amendment.   Add: "From Smith and Company."
      MAIN MOTION: "To buy a new radio."

CHAIR: "The question before the body is on the secondary amendment, which is: to add to the primary amendment the words 'before our next meeting.' Is there any debate?" (After debate:) "Those in favor of the secondary amendment will say aye; those opposed will say no. The ayes have it, and the secondary amendment is carried." (Take special note of the language used.) "The question now is on the primary amendment as amended, which is: to add to the *main* motion the words 'from Smith and Company before our next meeting.' Is there any discussion? There being none, the Chair will put it to a vote. Those in favor will say aye; those opposed will say no. The ayes have it, and the primary amendment is carried. The question now is on the main motion as amended; namely: 'to *buy* a radio from Smith and Company before our next meeting.' Is there any debate on the question?" He then puts it to a vote and it is voted to buy or not to buy a radio.

Observe that a secondary amendment is progressively voted on three times, the primary *twice*, and the main motion only *once*, unless the vote is doubted.

Note: Properly practiced, the *secondary* amendment, if one is pending, is voted on first; the *primary* (as amended or not) is voted on next; and finally the *motion* is voted on, as amended or not. Why *three* steps, or three different votes, instead of only *one* for all three? Because all members may not want to adopt all three proposals; some may not like the secondary or the primary amendment. Hence each amendment is supposed to be voted on *separately* in its own capacity, so as not to confuse the members or frustrate their vote under conflicting voting. But where there is apparent approval of all three pending proceedings, the Chair may (and he often does) put all three of them to a *single* vote, for convenience, if no one objects to it; but if anyone objects to such mass voting, the Chair then takes the vote separately.

Function of primary and secondary amendments. All amendments to a motion must be germane to the overall purpose of that motion.

It should be noted, however, that primary and secondary amendments vary in one important respect; namely, although both amendments (primary and secondary) have to be germane to the overall purpose of the pending question or motion, the notable function of the primary amendment is to concern, or be germane to, the motion, whereas the function of the *secondary* amendment is to be germane to both the primary amendment and the main motion.

In other words, if, while a primary amendment is pending, a secondary amendment is proposed which directly relates to (or connects itself with) the motion and ignores the primary amendment (which is the immediately pending question), then this secondary amendment is not a legitimate secondary amendment; it is, instead, another primary amendment offered (innocently or designedly) in the guise of a secondary amendment (conceivably to get action ahead of the pending primary amendment).

For instance, if the *main* motion is "to buy a new desk for fifty dollars," and the *primary* amendment is "from Smith and Co.," a proposed secondary amendment "to insert the word 'mahogany' before the word 'desk,'" is out of order, because the proposed amendment "mahogany" properly belongs in the main motion (when reached), where the word "desk" is, and not in the primary amendment where the firm "Smith and Co.," is — because it is not Smith who is to be mahogany, but the desk.

But if the secondary amendment is, say, "to strike out the words Smith and Co., and insert Baker and Co.," it would be germane to the primary amendment since it relates to business firms, which is the subject matter of the primary amendment.

Whenever a primary and secondary amendment are pending with their motion, the secondary amendment is voted on first because it outranks the primary amendment, then the primary amendment is voted on (as amended or not), then the main motion (as amended or not).

Note: Under enlightened parliamentary practice, as in the Congress, state legislatures, city councils, etc., secondary and primary amendments are judged and transacted strictly as stated just above. But in some less informed bodies they are not practiced strictly according to parliamentary form. Nevertheless, if no one (Chair or member) challenges a mispractice when it is being done, it is too late to do so after the vote thereon has been taken. Hence, if an ungenuine secondary amendment is acted on ahead of a legitimate primary amendment, or if the Chair puts the amendment(s) and the main motion to a vote *collectively*, instead of each one *separately*, and no one objects, it is too late to question the mispractice after the vote has been taken on it; reason: the body's approving vote cures such mispractice.

Primary amendment bypassed if supplanted by secondary. Where the adoption of a secondary amendment supplants the entire substance of the primary amendment, the vote is then directly on the main motion (instead of on the primary amendment as amended); that is, the primary amendment in such case is bypassed, because it has no substance left in it worth voting on. Thus if the words "Baker and Co." (contained in the secondary amendment previously shown) replace the words "Smith and Co." of the primary amendment, since only the word "from" remains in the primary amendment, the vote then is on the main motion as *thus* amended, ignoring the word "from" in the primary amendment.

Words retained in main motion when taken from the primary amendment by secondary. When the secondary amendment strikes out from the primary amendment word(s) which the primary amendment aims to strike out from the main motion, the effect is to *retain* those words *in* the *main* motion. For example:

If the main motion is, say "to direct the treasurer to buy a new desk, a flag, gavel, radio and a Persian rug," and the primary amendment is "to strike out the words 'radio' and 'Persian rug' " from the main motion (so as thus *not* to buy a radio and a Persian rug), if a secondary amendment is then adopted striking out from the primary amendment the word "radio" (thus *not* wanting the radio *not* to be bought — note the double negative form), the word "radio" (thus exempted or freed by the secondary amendment from the primary amendment) is then automatically retained in the main motion (which proposed to buy a *radio* with the other articles) and is voted on with the main motion when reached. If the motion is then defeated, the treasurer buys nothing; but if it is adopted, he buys all the articles (including the radio) except the Persian rug (which the primary amendment struck out, or eliminated, from the main motion which proposed to buy it).

Five methods of amending motions. There are five (and only five) ways of amending a main motion (and the same is true of any other motion which is amendable).

In other words, no matter how (in what words or form) an amendment is proposed, it has to fall in one of these five correct ways of phrasing the amendment; namely:

(1) By adding words to the end of the motion; or,
(2) By inserting words within it; or,
(3) By striking out words from it; or,
(4) By striking out words and inserting others in their place; or
(5) By substituting another main motion.

Note: It is *words, words, words* you must always specify (correctly and parliamentarily speaking). You either amend a motion by adding needed *words* to it, or inserting needed *words*, or striking out certain objectionable *words*, etc., as also explained in next section.

(1) By *adding words* is meant to add to the pending motion any words it may need to render it more complete. Thus, if the main motion is simply "to buy a new radio" without specifying price, make or when to buy it, this motion may need amendments to make it more acceptable before being put to a vote. Hence, members can, for instance, move to amend the main motion by adding the words "before the next meeting."

(2) By *inserting words* is meant to insert in the pending motion any word or words it may need to render it more definite or more complete Thus, if the motion is "to buy a new TV," a member can move "to amend the motion by inserting the word 'MacArthur' before the word 'TV.' "

Note: You *add* words to a motion when they logically belong *after* the period or end of the motion; you *insert* words when they properly belong somewhere *before* the period or end of the motion.

(3) By *striking out words* is meant to strike out any word or words from the motion which are in any way objectionable, redundant or undesirable. For instance, if the main motion is "to buy a brand-new typewriter," the word "brand" is unnecessary or undesirable from a scholarly standard. Hence, a member may, for instance, move to amend the main motion by striking out the word "brand."

(4) By *striking out words* and *inserting other words* in their place is meant to strike out from the pending motion any word or words which are considered undesirable, and to insert more acceptable words in their place. Thus, if the pending main motion is "to buy a new radio from Jones and Co.," and it is considered more advantageous or more desirable to do business with a firm other than Jones and Co., a member can move to "amend the motion by striking out the words 'Jones and Co.' and inserting in their place the words 'Brown and Co.' "

(5) By *substituting another main motion* for the pending main motion is meant to replace the question by another related whole (or substantially whole) question. Thus, if the pending main question proposed for adoption is "to go fishing in Maine this weekend," and it occurs to a member that it would be more desirable for the members to go duck shooting on Cape Cod, he can move to "substitute duck hunting on Cape Cod."

Distinction between inserting and adding. Words by insertion are words logically insertable anywhere before the end of the motion. Words added after the end of the motion are accurately called words by addition. Words of insertion should specify the exact place of insertion, such as to insert the word "mahogany" before the word "table"; to insert the word "green" before the word "rug."

Meaning of "substitute." It is incorrect to use the term "substitute" when amending a motion only partially, as when merely striking out the word "green" and inserting in its place the word "blue," or replacing the words "by bus" by the words "by airplane." The correct form is to move "to strike out the word 'green' and insert' blue,' " "to strike out the words 'by bus' and insert 'by airplane.' "

Correctly used, the term "substitute" applies when it is desired to substitute a whole or substantially whole related motion or proposition (such as a whole article of the bylaws, or a whole or entire section, or paragraph, or an entire new set of revised bylaws, etc.) for the existing motion, proposition, or question.

"Substitute" is also correctly used when unconnected or unconsecutive words in a motion are to be amended. Thus if the pending motion is "to buy a good used desk, a dictionary, two flag stands, a gavel and two folding chairs," and if it is desired to amend the motion so that a new desk will be bought instead of a used one, and also to buy four chairs instead of two, it is in order to include such unconnected words or parts of a motion under the motion to "substitute," instead of offering separate amendments for the purpose; thus, the motion to amend unconsecutive words correctly stated would be: "Mr. Chairman, I move to substitute for the pending motion the following: that we buy a *new* desk, a dictionary, two flag stands, a gavel and *four* folding chairs."

How five methods proposed and entertained. When proposing amendments to a motion, it is the duty of the members to use the correct form or language of the method by which the amendment is to be made.

The correct procedure in proposing, entertaining and disposing of the five ways of amending a motion is as follows (repeat aloud):

(1) *By adding words to the main motion.*

MEMBER: "Mr. Chairman, I move to amend the main motion 'to buy a new radio' by adding at the end thereof the words 'at a cost not to exceed fifty dollars.'" (Seconded.)

CHAIR: "It has been moved and seconded to amend the motion by adding the words 'at a cost not to exceed fifty dollars.' Is there any debate on the amendment?" (After debate, if any, it is put to vote, thus:) "Those in favor of the amendment will say aye; those opposed will say no. The ayes have it, and the amendment is carried." (He then states the main motion as amended, thus:) "The question now is on the main motion as amended, which is, that we buy a new radio at a cost not to exceed fifty dollars. Is there any debate on the motion? There being none, the Chair will put it to a vote. Those in favor of the main motion as amended will say aye. Those opposed will say no. The ayes have it, and the motion is carried, and we will buy a new radio at a cost not to exceed fifty dollars." The amendment is always voted on first, then the main motion as amended, or "as is" if the amendment is defeated.

(2) *By inserting words.*

MEMBER: "Madam Chairman, I move to amend the main motion 'to buy a new desk' by inserting the word 'oak' before the word 'desk.'" (Seconded. The logical place of insertion should be specified.)

CHAIR: "It has been moved and seconded to amend the motion by inserting the word 'oak' before the word 'desk.' Is there any discussion on the amendment? Those in favor of the amendment will say aye; those opposed will say no. The ayes have it, and the amendment is carried." (The Chair then states the main motion as amended.) "The question now is on the main motion as amended, which is, that we buy a new oak desk. Is there any debate? There being none, the Chair will put it to vote. Those in favor of the motion will say aye; those opposed will say no. The ayes have it and the motion is carried." The amendment is always voted on first, then the main motion.

(3) *By striking out words.*

MEMBER: "Mr. President, I move to amend the main motion 'to buy a new desk for the secretary and twenty-four folding chairs' by striking out the words 'and twenty-four folding chairs.' " (Seconded.)

CHAIR: "It has been moved and seconded to amend the main motion by striking out the words 'and twenty-four folding chairs.' Is there any discussion on the proposed amendment?" (After which the amendment is disposed of, thus:) "The ayes have it, and the amendment is carried." (He now states the main motion as amended; he says:) "The question now is on the main motion as amended, which is, that we buy a new desk for the secretary," which is then put to vote.

(4) *By striking out words and inserting other words.*

MEMBER: "Madam President, I move to amend the pending 'to buy a new flag from Smith's' by striking out the word 'Smith's' and inserting in place thereof the word 'Stone's.' " (Seconded.)

CHAIR: "It has been moved and seconded to amend the main motion by striking out the word 'Smith's' and inserting the word 'Stone's.' Is there any debate on the proposed amendment?" (No response.) "Those in favor of the amendment will say aye; those opposed will say no. The ayes have it, and the amendment is adopted." (The Chair then states the motion as amended.) "The question now is on the main motion as amended; namely, that we buy a new flag from Stone's. Is there any discussion?" (After which the Chair puts it to vote and the vote is announced accordingly. The amendment is voted on first, then the main motion as amended, or as is, if the amendment does not prevail.)

The same procedure as shown above governs when two amendments are pending before the body; the secondary amendment is always voted on first (because it supersedes or outranks the primary amendment), then the primary as amended, or as is, if the secondary amendment is defeated, and then the main motion as amended or not.

(5) *By substituting another related motion* to the pending motion, as shown in next section.

The Substitute Motion (S, D, A, M, R)

Definition of a substitute motion. A "substitute," properly speaking, is a proposal which germanely seeks to replace an entire (or substantially an entire, or unconsecutive parts of) a motion, or an article, paragraph, section, or rule, and whose *ultimate* objective is the same as that of its motion, or question. In other words, a substitute motion is another motion or proposition whose goal or end is the same as that of the main motion but whose method or means of achieving that end is different. The motion is also known as a "substitute amendment" or just "substitute."

Procedure for substitute motion. The procedure for disposing of a substitute motion is slightly different from that of the other four methods of amending; namely: whereas on a regular or ordinary amendment, the amendment is always considered and discussed ahead of the motion, and the main motion is acted on afterward, in the case of a substitute motion the substitute is merely stated by the Chair when proposed, and it is then automatically left unacted on until the pending main motion is first attended to by its being opened to debate and amendment only, not to a final vote; and after the main motion has been perfected as desired, the substitute motion is *then* also automatically open to debate and amendment, so that it, too, can be perfected before a choice between the two is finally made by the body. When the vote is taken, however, the substitute motion is always voted on first (because it is an amendment), after which the main motion is put to vote as substituted, or as is, if the substitute is defeated, just as on any regular amendment.

How to transact a substitute. To illustrate the procedure of a substitute motion, assume the following main motion pending:

MAIN MOTION: "To have a catered supper after our installation of officers" (which is now, say, being debated pro and con. Observe and employ the language used here:)

MEMBER: "Mr. Chairman, I move to *substitute* for the pending main motion the following: that the Ladies Auxiliary be requested to furnish a home-cooked supper after our installation." (Seconded.)

CHAIR: "It has been moved and seconded to substitute for the pending main motion the following motion: to request the Ladies Auxiliary to furnish a home-cooked supper after the installation. Under the rules [he can explain, the better to guide the assembly], before the substitute motion can be acted on, the pending main motion must first be attended to, by being open to debate and amendment, after which the substitute will be similarly considered and the vote then taken. Is there any discussion or any amendments to the *main* motion first?"

MEMBER: "Mr. Chairman, I move to amend the *main* motion by adding the words 'provided the cost of said catered supper is not more than four dollars a person.'" (Seconded.)

CHAIR: "It has been moved and seconded to amend the *main* motion by adding the words 'provided the cost for the catered supper does not exceed four dollars a person.' Is there any discussion on this amendment?" (After discussion, if any, the amendment is put and the vote announced:) "The ayes have it, and the *amendment* is carried. The question now is on the *main* motion as amended, which is 'to have a catered supper after our installation provided the cost thereof does not exceed four dollars a member.' Is there any discussion, or any further amendments to the *main* motion before we take up the proposed substitute motion?" (No response. He describes:) "There being no further discussion or amendments to the main motion, the *substitute* motion is now open to debate and amendment. Is there any discussion or any amendments to the substitute?"

MEMBER: "Mr. Chairman, may I move an amendment now to the *main* motion?"

CHAIR: "Not at this moment, because the substitute is now being considered; but after the substitute has been debated or perfected by amendments, if any, then the pending main motion would again be automatically open to further debate and amendment before the vote is taken on the question."

MEMBER: "Mr. Chairman, I move to amend the *substitute* motion by striking out the word 'after' and inserting in its place the word 'before.'" (Seconded.)

CHAIR: "It has been moved and seconded to amend the *substitute* motion by striking out the word 'after' and inserting in its place the word 'before.' Is there any discussion on the proposed amendment? There being none, those in favor of striking out the word 'after' and inserting in its place the word 'before' will say aye; those opposed will say no. The ayes have it and the amendment is carried. The question now is on the substitute motion *as amended*, which is, 'to request the Ladies Auxiliary to provide a home-cooked supper *before* our installation.' Are there any further amendments or any discussion on the substitute motion?" (No response. The Chair says:) "There being none, before the Chair puts the substitute motion to vote, are there any further amendments proposed to the original *main* motion? If there are any, now is the time to propose them." (No response.) "There being no further amendments to the original *main* motion, are there any further amendments to the *substitute* motion before the vote is taken?" (No response.) "There being none, the Chair will put the question to a vote. The substitute motion [he can elucidate] will, under the rules, be put to vote first, because a substitute is essentially an amendment. Those in favor of the substitute motion will say aye; those opposed will say no. The ayes have it, and the substitute motion is carried." (He then puts the substitute motion to vote once more, this time as the *main* motion *as substituted*, thus:) "The question now is on the main motion as substituted" (repeating the same substitute motion, which is again put to vote as, and in the place of, the original *main* motion).

A substitute is a primary amendment. When a main motion and a substitute motion are pending, only one amendment to each motion in turn can be offered and acted on, because the substitute motion is in the nature of and has the status of a primary amendment. Hence, only a single amendment at a time to either one can be considered. After its adoption, the substitute motion (which then becomes the main motion as amended, or as substituted) may be amended further, if desired, by adding only new matter to it unless it is first reconsidered so as to allow any other amendment desired upon it.

A "substitute" is known by two other names: "substitute motion" and "substitute amendment."

Further rules of a substitute. Further rules of a substitute are as follows:

Substitute motions must be germane, or must relate to, the same subject matter or purpose as the motion or proceeding which it seeks to amend. A substitute is secondable, debatable and amendable; and it requires only a majority vote for its adoption. It can be reconsidered, just like any other amendment to a motion.

It outranks the motion to postpone indefinitely and the main motion; therefore, it may not be proposed when a motion of higher rank than indefinite postponement is pending.

If the substitute is voted laid on the table or referred to a committee or postponed, both the substitute and the main motion go together to the table, or committee, or to the next meeting by postponement.

When a substitute and its motion are pending, the previous question (shutting off debate) can be proposed separately on each one when reached, or it can be proposed combinedly on the two, if so desired, like any other pending main motion and its amendment.

Examples of legitimate substitute motions. Substitute motions can, like amendments, be hostile, provided they are germane, as in the instances shown below.

(1) *Main motion:* "To donate five hundred dollars to the Red Cross."
Genuine substitute: "To give a dance, proceeds of which shall go to the Red Cross." The *goal* is the same: to help the Red Cross. (Note that the substitute is hostile, but is germane to the overall purpose.)

(2) *Main motion:* "That we charter an airplane to Washington, D. C., this weekend."
Legitimate substitute: "To hire a bus and all go to the beach over this weekend." The *end* is the same: fun, relaxation, etc. (It, too, is hostile, but is related, germane.)

(3) *Main motion:* "To present the retiring president with airplane luggage for her fine administration this past year."
Appropriate substitute: "To give the retiring president a beautiful loving cup, appropriately inscribed, in recognition of her extraordinary leadership in her term of office." The *goal* is the same: to show appreciation by a different means.

(4) *Main Motion:* "To organize in each state weekly meetings and conferences of eminent leaders of Catholics, Protestants and Jews, for the promotion of tolerance and understanding."
Proper substitute: "To urge all public and private elementary schools to recite a 'Pledge of National Unity' at weekly assemblies, as one of the most effective means of minimizing and eventually eradicating racial and religious bigotry from early youth." The *object* is the same: to suppress bias and prejudice.

(5) *Main motion:* "To go on record in favor of prohibiting the manufacture of all war armaments and equipment throughout the world."
Appropriate substitute: "To go on record favoring immediate conversion to commercial use of all plants in the world capable of producing war materiel, nuclear weapons, missiles, etc." The *goal* is the same: to attempt to prevent wars; it is hostile, but an equivalent (germane) proposal in place of the other.

5. REFER TO A COMMITTEE (S, D, A, M, R)

The terms "to commit" or "to refer" mean the same thing — to refer a question to a committee. To recommit means to refer a motion back to the same committee. Recommit is more euphonious than rerefer.

Basic rules. The moment it is voted to refer a pending question to a committee, the question is instantly and automatically removed from before the body, and nothing is then pending; but if the motion to refer is defeated, the question is still before the body and it is voted on in due course.

The motion to refer is secondable, debatable and amendable, and requires a majority vote for adoption. It is a subsidiary motion of fifth highest rank and can be reconsidered.

How proposed and entertained

MEMBER: "Mr. President, I move that we refer the pending motion to sell the clubhouse to a committee of three to be appointed by the Chair with instructions to report back at the next meeting."

CHAIR: "It has been moved and seconded to refer the pending question to a committee of three," etc. "Is there any discussion on the motion?"

KEY QUIZ

Q. Is the motion to refer secondable? *A.* Yes.
Q. Is it debatable? *A.* Yes.
Q. Is it amendable? *A.* Yes.
Q. What vote adopts it? *A.* Majority.
Q. What class of motion is it? *A.* Subsidiary.
Q. What is its rank? *A.* Fifth highest.
Q. Can it be reconsidered? *A.* Yes.

(If none, he continues:) "There being no discussion, the Chair will put the motion to vote. Those in favor of referring the question to such committee will say aye; those opposed will say no. The ayes have it, and the question is referred to a committee of three. The Chair appoints the following committee: A, B, and C."

No new business until the committee named. After it has been voted to refer a matter to a committee, or the Chair is authorized to appoint a committee, no new question can be entertained until the committee has been *named*, thus completing the action, or carrying out the mandate just authorized by the body. If a committee is not appointed before adjournment of the meeting at which it was authorized, it is invalid if challenged.

Chair can name committee later. If the Chair is unprepared to name the committee the moment it is voted into being, or he cannot appoint it prior to adjournment of that meeting, he should *so* inform the body; thus:

CHAIR: "The Chair will not [or, is not prepared to] appoint the committee at this moment, but will do so either before the meeting is adjourned [or, after adjournment]." If no objection is then raised, the Chair chooses his committee accordingly.

If objection is made by a member's simply rising and saying: "I object to the committee being appointed later," or "after the meeting," the Chair proceeds to appoint the committee then, unless he is differently authorized by a majority vote. If a committee is appointed after adjournment without the prior consent or approval of the body, the motion to ratify the Chair's appointment of such a committee can be proposed at the next meeting and if adopted by a majority vote the appointment is validated. If not challenged when such committees are announced late, they are automatically valid.

When Chair's committee appointments are unwise. If the Chair appoints an unrepresentative or incompetent committee, move to reconsider the motion by striking out the words "to be appointed by the Chair," and inserting the words "to be nominated from the floor."

To discharge a committee. After it has been voted to refer a matter to a committee, the assembly cannot consider a question involving substantially the same matter. Committees can be discharged when they fail to perform their duties or neglect to make reports, or when it is desired to take a matter out of their charge. The proper motion to use is to "discharge the committee from further consideration and action" on the question. Such motion requires a $\frac{2}{3}$ vote unless prior notice is given. Another way of accomplishing the same result, provided it is proposed during the same meeting at which appointment of the committee was authorized, is to move reconsideration of the motion by which the committee was chosen; such motion requires only a majority vote. If the committee has actually taken up consideration of the question, or has reported in part, a $\frac{2}{3}$ vote is required "to discharge it," or "to relieve it of further consideration of its assignment."

Committees can report in part or in entirety under "Reports of Committees." They may be reprimanded or censured for failure or neglect to perform by majority vote.

Note: Where the bylaws say "*All* committees shall be appointed by the president," this merely means that the Chair is the one who can *name* the members who will serve thereon; it does *not* mean that the body cannot *create* additional committees for any desired purpose. Hence, on motion of a member (under new business, and by majority vote), the body can add new committees, but it is the Chair who then designates the members who will serve on any committee the body so establishes.

If the body is dissatisfied with the type of appointments a president has been making, either (a) amend the bylaws repealing the above provision *in toto*, or (b) amend it to suit.

Methods of choosing committees. There are numerous methods of choosing committees. The most common are:

(1) Committees *appointed* exclusively by the Chair.
(2) Committees *nominated* by the Chair but elected by the body.
(3) Committees *nominated* and *elected* exclusively by the body.

All three methods are authorizable by a majority vote.

When method number 1 is used the Chair alone has the exclusive power to name the committee. If method number 2 is decided on, the Chair names the members who will comprise the committee but his choices are made final only by vote of the assembly. If method number 3 is authorized, the assembly both nominates (from the floor) and elects the committee members.

In other words, the power to choose the committee in each case belongs to: with method 1, the Chair exclusively; with method 2, the Chair and assembly jointly; and with method 3, the assembly exclusively.

Why have different methods of choosing committees. Parliamentary law established these three methods of selecting committees in order to insure impartiality, efficiency and progress in the business of the organization.

For instance, if the Chair has been appointing wholly partisan or biased members to committees (thus destroying the principle of impartiality), or he has been nominating incompetent and unfit members (thus impairing efficiency) or lacks initiative and sound leadership, such as failing to inquire into the capabilities of members for committee appointment (thus obstructing progress), then instead of using method number 1, the members can authorize that the Chair nominate, but not appoint (method 2), or they can directly authorize nomination and election by the assembly (method 3).

Note: Absorb this paragraph; you can then restrain an unfair, incompetent, unprogressive or dictatorial chairman.

The vote and effect of each method

1. *Appointment by the Chair.* If method number 1 is authorized, the

Chair's choices are final (unless the motion authorizing him to appoint is reconsidered before adjournment of the meeting); thus:

MEMBER: "Mr. Chairman, I move that the Chair be authorized to appoint a committee of three." If this method is adopted, the Chair names his three choices and the act is final.

2. *Nominations by the Chair.* If method number 2 is authorized, the Chair merely nominates his choices but they must be put to vote for approval, and if approved or endorsed by the assembly they then become final; thus:

MEMBER: "Mr. Chairman, I move that the pending motion to buy a new clubhouse be referred to a committee of three to be nominated by the Chair." If this method is authorized, the Chair nominates three choices and then he puts those choices to a vote. If they are approved they become final and compose the committee; thus:

CHAIR: "It has been moved and seconded to refer the pending motion to a committee of three, to be nominated by the Chair." (After debate, if any, he puts the motion to vote:) "Those in favor of reference will say aye; those opposed will say no. The ayes have it, and the motion is carried." Now he names his three choices: "The Chair nominates Mr. A, Mrs. B, and Miss C." Then he puts these choices to vote, because the body must elect or approve them: "Those in favor of A, B, and C constituting the committee will say aye; those opposed will say no. The ayes have it, and A, B, and C have been elected, and they will comprise the committee." This ends it.

Method number 2 is amendable because under its authority the body shares the responsibility jointly with the Chair; hence any member can move to amend the Chair's nominations by striking out A's name or B's, etc., and if this amendment is carried it is the Chair who supplies another choice, because under this method the Chair does the nominating of names; thus:

CHAIR: "The Chair nominates Mr. A, Mrs. B, and Miss C."

MEMBER: "Mr. Chairman, I move to amend the nomination by striking out Miss C's name and inserting Miss D's name."

CHAIR: "The amendment just proposed is out of order because the member's right extends only to amending by striking *out* a name, but does not extend to *nominating* other names; under the motion previously adopted, the Chair alone can nominate other names in place of any names that may be struck out by the body."

MEMBER: "I beg the Chair's pardon, I forgot the rule."

CHAIR (continuing): "It is moved and seconded to amend the Chair's nominations by striking out the name C. Those in favor of striking out Miss C's name will say aye; those opposed will say no. The ayes have it, and Miss C's name is struck out. The Chair now nominates Miss X in place of Miss C. Those in favor of the Chair's nomination as amended, namely, Mr. A, Mrs. B and Miss X, will say aye; those opposed will say no. The ayes have it, and these three members will comprise the committee.

3. *Nominations from the floor.* If method number 3 is authorized, namely, nominations and elections by the assembly, nominations come from the floor; and when no further nominations are proposed, the Chair puts each name in the order in which it was nominated and the *first* three

receiving a majority vote are declared elected and they constitute the committee; the remaining names, if any, are ignored and are not put to vote — just as when there are only two nominees: if the first one is elected, the second nominee is not voted on; thus:

MEMBER: "Mr. Chairman, I move that we refer the pending motion 'to buy a new clubhouse' to a committee of three to be nominated from the floor." (Seconded.)

CHAIR: "It has been moved and seconded to refer the pending motion [etc.]. Those in favor of such reference will say aye; those opposed will say no. The ayes have it, and the motion to refer is carried." (Now he must entertain nominations, hence he says:) "Nominations are now in order. Three are to be elected." (Nominations normally need no second, except where expressly required.)

MEMBER: "I nominate Mr. M."

CHAIR: "Mr. M has been nominated. Are there further nominations?" (Keep using this phrase after each nomination, if no one rises to nominate further.)

MEMBER B: "I nominate Mrs. N."

CHAIR: "Mrs. N is nominated. Are there further nominations?"

MEMBER C: "I nominate Miss O." (Chair replies as above.)

MEMBER D: "I nominate Mrs. P." (Chair replies as above.)

MEMBER E: "I nominate Mr. Q." (Chair replies as above.)

CHAIR (after nominations have been duly closed): "There are five nominees for three places. Each name will be voted on in the order nominated, and the *first three* who receive a majority vote will be declared elected, and will comprise the committee. The first name is M. Those in favor of Mr. M will say aye; those opposed will say no. The ayes have it, and Mr. M is elected. Next, Mrs. N. Those in favor [etc.]; those opposed [etc.]. The ayes have it, and Mrs. N is elected. Next Miss O. Those in favor [etc.], those opposed [etc.]. The ayes have it and Miss O is elected. All three places have been filled, and further elections automatically come to an end. Hence, M, N and O will comprise the committee.

MEMBER D: "Mr. Chairman, I rise to a point of order."

CHAIR: "The member will state his point of order."

MEMBER D: "My point of order is that the names of Mrs. P and Mr. Q have not been put to vote, and they should be voted on just like the previous three members." (Now note carefully:)

CHAIR: "The point of order is not well taken. Under the rules, when the necessary places on a committee have been voted filled, further voting on any remaining names automatically ceases because there are no places to fill; besides, the combined majority of those who voted to elect the successful candidates M, N, and O is, logically, not expected to undo its action by electing additional names and thus invalidating the election. The majority having voted to elect M, N, and O, it would be a waste of time to take a vote on P's and Q's name.

Note: In all cases of oral vote-taking, as in the above instance, members who wish to vote for nominees whose name *follows* that of earlier nominees ought to know their right to vote "No" on every prior name they do not want to see elected when put to vote, in the hope that these earlier nominees may be defeated and the later nominees may survive long enough to be voted on to fill a place. It would be prejudicial and indelicate for the Chair, in such instances, to advise members to vote against any prior name so that a subsequent name might survive.

In the event none of the nominees are elected, or fewer than the required number have been elected, further nominations are automatically in order and the same procedure continues.

Completeness of the motion to refer. The motion to refer should be made as complete as necessary; thus: "Mr. Chairman, I move that the pending motion be referred to a committee of . . . [specify number] members, to be chosen by . . . [specify method], with instructions to report back at . . . [specify time]"; instead of merely "to refer to a committee." The motion to refer should designate the number of members (usually odd numbers, to avoid tie votes), the manner in which they shall be chosen, and instructions when to report back. You thus impel action and compel results.)

"Ad hoc" committee. Another expression for special committee is the Latin term, *ad hoc* committee. *Ad* means "for," and *hoc* means "this"; this is, for this purpose or special case.

Other methods of choosing committees: (1) As designated in the by-laws. (2) By choosing only the chairman and empowering him to add other members. (3) By a nominating ballot, the members receiving the highest vote constituting the committee. (4) By roll call. (5) Any other method designated by the assembly. A majority vote is required in all cases.

Referring to a committee with full power. Sometimes, a committee is chosen "with power"; thus: "I move that this be referred to a committee of three *with full power*," that is, with power to do all that is necessary and proper to carry out an assignment (a duty or function). When the words "with power" or "with full power" are inserted in the motion to refer, the committee is clothed with power to carry out a mission with plenary authority. But the assembly can amend from time to time the authority given, because the committee is an agent of the assembly.

Distinction between "refer" and "appoint." If no motion is pending before the body and it is desired to designate a committee, the proper motion to use is "to appoint a committee," or "to authorize the Chair" or "that the Chair be authorized to appoint a committee." Such motion is a main motion. But if a main motion is pending before the body and it is desired to transfer it to a committee, the motion "to appoint a committee" should not be used; the correct motion is "to refer to a committee." Such a motion is the subsidiary motion. When members erroneously propose the form "to appoint a committee," when "to refer" should be used, the Chair treats it as a motion to refer. The motion to refer is a subsidiary motion, while the motion to appoint is a main motion (technically called incidental main motion).

Meaning of words "appoint," "elect," "choose," etc. The terms appoint, elect, choose, select, designate and other similar words are often used as synonymous terms. However, "appoint" normally means selection of a committee by the Chair; "elect" signifies election by the body; "choose," "select," and "designate" are used interchangeably, as in the form: "How shall the committee be chosen [or selected, or designated]?

Besides its specific meaning, "appoint" may also be used as a synonym for "choose," "select" and "designate," as in "How shall the committee be appointed?"

Note: One who holds membership in a committee is not a holder of office. A committee is not an office.

4. POSTPONE TO A DEFINITE TIME (S, D, A, M, R)

This is the genuine and most popular motion to postpone — usually to the next meeting. Business so postponed is automatically taken up under *unfinished* business at the time designated. It is called a motion to postpone to a definite time (or to "postpone definitely") which can be to postpone to the next meeting, or to a later time of the *same* meeting when so specified.

Note: Do not confuse this motion either with the motion to postpone indefinitely, or to lay on the table. The rules differ for each.

Basic rules. The motion to postpone to the next meeting is secondable, debatable and amendable, and requires a majority vote for adoption. It is a subsidiary motion of fourth highest rank, and can be reconsidered.

How proposed and entertained

MEMBER: "Mr. Chairman, I move that we postpone the pending motion 'to buy a new piano' to the next meeting." (Seconded.)

Note: Avoid saying "to lay it on the table until next meeting"; say "to *postpone* to the next meeting."

CHAIR. "It has been moved and seconded to postpone the question to our next meeting. Is there any debate on the motion?" (After debate, if any, it is put to vote, and the result announced; thus:) "Those in favor of postponement will say aye; those opposed will say no. The ayes have it, and the motion is postponed to the next meeting." (In this case, no motion is now pending before the body, because it was voted postponed to a definite time; but if the motion to postpone is defeated, the main motion would still be before the body and, after further debate, if any, would be put to vote.

A motion which has been postponed to the next meeting automatically comes up for consideration under unfinished business; thus:

CHAIR: "The next business in order is unfinished business." (He turns to the secretary:) "Is there any unfinished business?"

KEY QUIZ

Q. Must this motion be seconded? *A.* Yes.
Q. Is it debatable? *A.* Yes.
Q. Is it amendable? *A.* Yes.
Q. What vote adopts it? *A.* Majority.
Q. What class of motion is it, and what is its rank? *A.* It is a subsidiary motion having fourth highest rank.
Q. Can it be reconsidered? *A.* Yes.
Q. Is this motion the same as to postpone indefinitely? *A.* No. This motion defers or puts off business; the other kills it outright.

SECRETARY: "Yes. The motion to buy a new piano for the reception hall was postponed from the last meeting to this meeting."

CHAIR (informing the members): "Under unfinished business there was postponed to this meeting, from the last, a motion to buy a new piano. The question before the body is automatically on that motion. Is there discussion?" (After discussion it is put to vote, and the vote is duly announced.)

Synonymous terms. The motions "to postpone to a definite time," "to postpone to a certain time," and "to postpone to a time certain" are synonymous expressions.

What is "certain" or "definite" time? The element of "certainty" or "definiteness" contemplated in this motion means "not beyond the next regular meeting." That is, to retain its rank as fourth highest motion among the subsidiary motions, the motion to postpone must not put off or defer consideration of a question beyond the next regular meeting.

Hence, it must specify a time that falls (1) within the same session, (2) at the next regular session, or (3) at another time or meeting held between the present session and the next regular session, as in meetings from day to day in conventions and annual meetings, or in adjourned meetings, and as in town meetings from week to week.

Questions previously postponed can, by majority vote, be again postponed from session to session when taken up, and thus be kept alive as long as desired. But once this continuity is broken, the postponed question is dead; but that question can be reproposed at any subsequent meeting in the same or any other form desired.

A postponed question can be taken up prior to the time specified if no one objects, or if the rules are suspended for the purpose (a $\frac{2}{3}$ vote is required).

Postponement beyond the next regular meeting. A motion to postpone a question until after the next regular meeting (such as two or three meetings from now) or until after a certain event which will not occur until after the next regular meeting, is not the genuine definite motion to postpone definitely or to postpone to a certain time within the meaning of the definition conveyed above; in such a case it loses both its identity as a motion of definite postponement and its rank as fourth highest among the subsidiary motions; and as a result, it automatically falls into the class, and assumes the rank of, the motion to postpone *indefinitely* and is treated as a motion to postpone indefinitely, which has lowest rank among the subsidiary motions, and therefore, it can only be entertained when only a main motion is before the body, because indefinite postponement outranks only a main motion.

Note: Motions postponed beyond the next regular meeting do not come up for consideration automatically under any heading of business whatsoever (strictly speaking); but if they are taken up and no one objects, the vote thereon is valid.

If a postponed motion is not taken up when its time is reached, it dies with adjournment.

To postpone is out of order when the purpose is absurd. Thus, if a pending motion is to attend a July 4th event, a motion to postpone attending the July 4th event until after July 4 is absurd; but it is in order to "postpone it indefinitely," and thus attempt to suppress the motion to attend it at all.

Various forms of the motion to postpone. A motion can be postponed (1) to a later time or after a certain event to occur later at the same meeting, (2) to the next meeting, or (3) to a meeting between the present one and the next regular meeting. In all such cases and in all other cases of forms of postponement (except "special" postponement which will be discussed next), postponement requires only a majority vote for adoption. In each case, the postponed proceeding cannot be taken up if other business happens to be before the house when taken up. It must wait until pending business is out of the way.

Special postponement. When the assembly desires to postpone a question to another hour so that it shall have the right to interrupt a pending piece of business when that hour arrives, then the proper motion to use is "to postpone the question to the desired time and make it a special order." "Order" means "business," hence the word "business" may be used in place of it for that hour. In such case, however, the motion to postpone specially requires a $\frac{2}{3}$ vote, because it automatically interrupts the business that may be pending before the body when taken up. (Amendments to this motion, however, require only a majority vote.)

The form of postponing a special piece of business, or of proposing a special order, must specify or contain the words: "and be made a special order for . . . [specify hour]"; thus:

"Mr. Chairman, I move that we postpone the pending motion 'to build a new clubhouse' until the next meeting and make it a *special* order for nine o'clock." Or, "Mr. Chairman, I move that the pending question to 'buy a new clubhouse' be postponed to our next regular meeting and be made a special order for nine o'clock." Merely postponing a question to a certain hour does not make it a special order unless it is so *specified*.

Special postponement can also carry a pending motion to a time beyond the next regular meeting, provided a $\frac{2}{3}$ vote is obtained; and the question so postponed can then be automatically considered when that time or hour arrives.

When the specially postponed question is before the body, it can be further postponed from meeting to meeting for as long as desired, and thus be kept alive.

More than one special postponement. When two or more special postponements have been ordered, the one first *proposed* is taken up when its set time is reached, even though another special postponement has been made *afterward* for an earlier time that conflicts with the former, unless otherwise agreed to. Thus, if at 8:15 motion X is voted specially postponed to 9:30, and later, at 8:30, a motion Z is specially postponed to 9:15, if the 9:15 postponed question is not finished by 9:30 it can be interrupted by motion X (which was given *postponement* before Z; and after motion X is disposed of, motion Z is then automatically resumed.

3. LIMIT OR EXTEND DEBATE (S, A, $\frac{2}{3}$, R)

This is the technical term of the motion to decrease (limit) or to increase (extend) debate on motions before the body; that is, since parliamentary rule allows members ten minutes' debate on a debatable motion (or in some organizations five or seven minutes, etc.), when you wish to reduce the time for further discussion such as to two or three minutes a member, the proper motion to use is "to limit debate"; and when you wish to allow more than ten minutes debate, propose the motion "to extend debate," such as to fifteen or twenty minutes.

In other words, the designation "to limit or extend debate" is in reality two motions: "to limit" is one, "to extend" the other. Propose limitation whenever time is of the essence, or when many members desire to speak on a pending question.

Basic rules. The adoption of the motion to limit debate does not kill the main motion before the body; it merely lessens the length of time it can be discussed by each member. To limit debate requires a second; it is not debatable but it is amendable; it requires a $\frac{2}{3}$ vote for adoption; it is a subsidiary motion of third highest rank, and can be reconsidered.

It is not debatable because to allow debate on it would be inconsistent with its nature which seeks to shorten debate (just like the "previous question" which is also undebatable, because its object is to terminate debate). It is amendable because while some members may desire only three minutes' debate, others may wish less than three minutes, and still others more than three. It requires a $\frac{2}{3}$ vote because its adoption deprives members of their inherent right to discuss a debatable motion before the body to the full ten minutes.

When it is voted to limit debate to perhaps two or three minutes a member, all interrupting debatable motions are debatable to the same shortened limit.

How proposed and entertained

MEMBER: "Madam Chairman, I move that we limit debate on the main motion 'to paint the room green' to two minutes a member. (Seconded.)

CHAIR. "It has been moved and seconded to limit debate on the motion before the body to two minutes a member. [Pause.] Those in favor of limiting debate — it requires a two-thirds vote — will rise. Twenty. Be seated. Those opposed will rise. Four. Be seated. There being two-thirds in favor of the motion, the affirmative has it, and debate is now limited to two minutes." (Instead of a standing vote, a hand vote may be taken first.)

Variations of motion to limit or extend debate. There is no limit to the kinds of motions that can be used for limiting, extending, or controlling debate on a question before the body. Here are a few variations on the motion:

(1) When you wish to limit the number of speakers, say: "Madam

---

KEY QUIZ

Q. Is this motion secondable? *A.* Yes.
Q. Is it debatable? *A.* No.
Q. Is it amendable? *A.* Yes.
Q. What vote does it require. *A.* Two-thirds.
Q. What class of motion is it? *A.* Subsidiary.
Q. What is its rank? *A.* Third highest.
Q. Can it be reconsidered? *A.* Yes.

President, I move that further debate be limited to not more than two speakers," or three, or four.

(2) When you wish to specify the number of speakers for each side, say: "Mr. Commander, I move that further debate be limited to two speakers on each side of the question," or three, or four.

(3) When you wish to specify particular speakers, say: "Mr. Moderator, I move that debate be limited to two speakers on each side, with Mr. A and Mrs. B for the affirmative, and Mrs. X and Mr. Y for the negative."

(4) When you wish to increase debate to more than is allowed by the fundamental rule, say: "Madam Speaker, I move that debate be extended to fifteen minutes a member," or 20 minutes, or 25, etc.

(5) If it is desired to fix the hour for finally terminating all discussion and the vote taken at that time, simply say: "Comrade Commander, I move that all discussion on the motion close half an hour from now," or whatever time is desired.

Chair may propose limiting debate. In all these and similar cases of debate regulation and control, a $\frac{2}{3}$ vote is required. Besides such formal motions, the Chair on his own initiative can suggest or attempt to apply these rules when necessary to expedite business, provided no one objects (silent consent).

Can apply to more than one motion. The motion to limit or extend debate can apply to one or more than one motion before the body, provided they are embraced in consecutive order and the immediately pending motion is included.

Can always be reconsidered. The motion to limit or extend debate can be reconsidered at any stage of its proceeding, even if a motion under it has been voted on (unlike the previous-question rule).

Previous question in order. After it has been voted to limit debate, it is in order to move the previous question (which, if carried, stops debate altogether). This is so because the previous question (ending debate) accomplishes business faster than the motion to limit debate (which allows some debate and thus prolongs business).

Amendments to motion to limit debate. Although the motion to limit debate requires a $\frac{2}{3}$ vote, amendments to it (changing the time for debate or number of speakers, etc.) require only a majority vote, because the power to deny to the members the right to limit debate on a motion is embodied not in the amendments, but in the motion to limit.

2. PREVIOUS QUESTION (S, $\frac{2}{3}$, R)

This is a *motion*. Its name is misleading, and hence it is frequently misunderstood and misapplied. "Previous question" is the technical term for proposing to terminate further discussion and amendments on a question before the body. Note that it includes two elements: (1) to shut off debate, and (2) to shut off amendments. Alert leaders move the previous question when time is of the essence, or the hour is late, or there has been enough debate, or the pending motion is obnoxious or of a personal or delicate nature.

Basic rules. The motion known as "previous question" (ending debate and further amendments) must be seconded. It is undebatable and unamendable, and requires a $\frac{2}{3}$ vote for adoption. It is a subsidiary motion and has second highest rank. It can be reconsidered.

It requires a $\frac{2}{3}$ vote because its adoption deprives members of their inherent right to discuss a motion as long as the ten minutes which the fundamental rule allows (or whatever limit the organization's rules allow). It is undebatable because to allow debate would be inconsistent with its purpose of ending discussion. It is unamendable for a parallel reason. It yields to motions of higher rank (p. 47). It cannot be tabled by itself.

The adoption of the previous question does not kill the main motion before the body. All it does is prevent further debate and amendments on it. Hence, after adoption of the previous question, the main motion which is still pending is put to vote.

May not interrupt a speaker. Members must duly obtain the floor to propose it, under correct practice.

Effect of the previous question. The term "previous question" means to end discussion and amendments on pending motions. In other words, when a member says: "Mr. Chairman, I move the previous question," it is the same as if he said: "I move that further discussion and amendments on the motion before the house be prohibited." Either form of the motion may be used; but the correct form is to "move the previous question," instead of "I move that discussion and amendments cease."

If the previous question (closing debate) is adopted, then further discussion and amendments cease.

The motion, however, must be seconded, then put to vote, and must be carried by a $\frac{2}{3}$ vote before discussion and amendments can legally cease (except where general or silent consent is granted).

In other words, the mere shouting "Question, question!" or "I call for the question," or, without rising, "I move the previous question," does not end discussion and amendments. The assembly alone can decide that, by vote or by general (silent) consent.

Note: Notwithstanding this rule, if *no* member objects when the Chair entertains the previous question wrongfully, the vote on it is valid and cannot be challenged afterward; members must not sleep on their rights; they must protect them at the time they are violated—as when a member, without obtaining the floor, shouts "Question, question!" and the Chair, instead of putting the previous question to a vote, arbitrarily stops further debate, and wrongfully deprives members of their right to continue the discussion. In other words, it is not sound to regard one member's shout of "Question,

---

KEY QUIZ

Q. Does this motion require a second?   *A.* Yes.
Q. Is it debatable?   *A.* No.
Q. Is it amendable?   *A.* No.
Q. What vote adopts it?   *A.* Two-thirds.
Q. What class of motion is it?   *A.* Subsidiary.
Q. What is its rank?   *A.* Second highest.
Q. Can it be reconsidered?   *A.* Yes.
Q. Can it interrupt a speaker?   *A.* No.
Q. Can a member propose it on his own pending motion?   *A.* Yes.
Q. Why would he want to do that?   *A.* To prevent hostile debate or unfavorable amendments on his motion by opponents.

---

question?'' as a mandate to close the discussion. If the previous question is not carried, discussion continues.

How proposed and entertained. To illustrate its procedure, assume the following motion before the body: "To buy a new desk."

MEMBER A: "Mr. Chairman, it occurs to me that the motion has been sufficiently discussed and the hour is late. I therefore move the previous question." (In other words, "I move that further debate and amendments cease." A brief explanation why the previous question is proposed is allowable. Seconded.)

CHAIR: "It has been moved and seconded to adopt [or, to order] the previous question." (It is undebatable and unamendable, and requires a $\frac{2}{3}$ vote; hence, it is put to vote thus:) "Those in favor of adopting the previous question will raise their right hand. [Counts.] Forty-one. Down. Those opposed will raise their right hand. Eleven. Down. There being two-thirds in favor of the motion, the affirmative has it and the motion is carried; and the members will please remember that the motion before the house, to buy a new desk, is now undebatable and unamendable." (He then puts the main motion to vote:) "Those in favor of buying a new desk will say aye; those opposed will say no. The ayes have it, and a new desk will be bought," or "The noes have it," as the case may be.

When a member violates the previous question. If a member rises to discuss the main motion, to buy a new desk, after the previous question (which renders it undebatable) has been adopted, the Chair should say to him:

CHAIR: "The Chair would like to remind [or, inform] the member that the adoption of the previous question has put an end to further debate and therefore the motion is not debatable."

If a member rises and proposes an amendment to the motion after the adoption of the previous question (which renders it unamendable), the Chair says:

CHAIR: "The amendment is out of order because the assembly adopted the previous question which puts an end to amendments."

Since most members are unfamiliar with the rules and effect of the previous question, it is well for the Chair (who is expected to know procedure and the operation of motions) to explain the effect of the previous question after it has been proposed and just before it is put to vote, thus:

MEMBER: "Mr. Chairman, I move the previous question."

CHAIR: "It has been moved and seconded to adopt the previous question." (Here is the best place to explain it to the members, the Chair saying:) "The Chair would like to point out, for the information of all the members, that the adoption of the previous question will terminate further discussion or amendments on the motion before the body." (Then he puts it to vote:) "Those in favor of ordering the previous question," etc.

Note: There is no way to prevent moving the previous question on motions it outranks. If its proposer cannot be prevailed upon not to propose it, or he will not withdraw it, your most effective action is to vote against it, and thus attempt to defeat it, which should be easy to achieve because you need only one-third of the votes cast plus only one more vote to defeat it — whereas they need at least a $\frac{2}{3}$ vote to pass it.

Two elements of previous question. The previous question combines two elements, namely: to end debate and to end amendments. Hence, when the previous question is moved, the object is to terminate both discussion and amendments. But when it is desired to end debate only and not amendments, or amendments only and not debate, the motion is specifically proposed in that form or language. The same rules, however, apply to either statement as to the previous question itself, and a $\frac{2}{3}$ vote is required.

Motions after the previous question. Motions which arise after the previous question is ordered and while it is still in force automatically become undebatable, and are therefore decided without debate — such as reconsideration, appeal and others.

Previous question may be moved on part or all of a set. If the previous question is proposed when other motions are pending with the main motion, such as (read from bottom upward):

> 3. To refer it to a committee of three
> 2. To amend the main motion
> 1. MAIN MOTION (to buy a new radio)

all of which are in order, because there is only one main motion, the others being subsidiary motions which outrank it, the previous question can be moved on all three, or on only two of them, or only one of them, as the proposer may choose.

If the previous question when proposed does not specify to the contrary, only the immediately pending motion (the motion last stated) is affected, which in this set is the motion to refer to a committee. If it specifies more than one, then more than one are affected. But when it is proposed on more than one motion, the motions (like the links in a chain) so included must follow in consecutive order, beginning with the immediately pending motion.

Thus, in the above set, the previous question can apply to the motion to *refer* alone, or to *refer* and *to amend* (they follow in consecutive order), or all three, to *refer*, *amend* and the *main motion* itself, since all three follow in successive order.

In other words, the previous question cannot apply to the motion to refer and the main motion, and thus leave out or skip over the amendment; nor can it apply to the main motion and leave out or skip over the other two. When more than one motion is covered under the previous question they must follow each other in consecutive succession. When the previous question is proposed in differing applications, the proposal which covers the largest number of motions outranks proposals for a lesser number.

Forms of its proposal. If it is desired to stop debate and amendments on the immediately pending motion only, the form of the proposal is simply "I move the previous question." If it is desired to include all pending motions, the proposal is "I move the previous question on all pending motions." If it is desired to apply it to specific motions, then it should be so specified, as "I move the previous question on the motion to refer and the amendments to the main motion." In all cases, a $\frac{2}{3}$ vote is required.

When a member may move the previous question on his own motion. A member may not move the previous question with his own other motion, except by general consent. Instead, he should propose his *first* motion, and debate it or not; then be seated. If after that no one rises to claim the floor to debate that motion or for any other purpose, then that member may, when the floor is free, move the previous question preventing further debate on his own pending motion.

Premature previous question. When the previous question (shutting off debate and amendments) is mischievous, malicious or untimely and premature, simply vote it down. If it is defeated, it can be reproposed a bit later.

Previous question can be reconsidered. The previous question can be reconsidered when either the affirmative or negative side prevails. But it cannot be reconsidered after a motion it covered has actually been voted on. In other words, if the previous question has just been voted on, the vote on it can be reconsidered; but if, after it has been voted on, some motion under it (not over it) which is then pending has been voted on, it is too late to reconsider the previous question. Hence, if the motion to refer is voted on and defeated, it is too late to move reconsideration of previous question because execution of a vote on a motion under it stops reconsideration of the vote on the previous question, since it has been executed in part. But the motion to refer can be reconsidered.

If the previous question is reconsidered, it is not submitted for adoption again; the pending question becomes automatically free of its effect because a ⅔ vote for reordering the previous question is presumed logically unattainable after a mere majority voted to reconsider it; it would be a waste of time.

After the previous question has been adopted, the pending question is under the power of the previous question, and therefore no motion of lower rank than the previous question can be proposed. But motions of *higher rank* than the previous question (such as to lay on the table, to recess or adjourn) can be proposed. Thus if the previous question has been adopted it is not in order to move to refer the main motion to a committee, the Chair saying: "The motion just proposed is out of order because it is of lower rank than the effect of the previous question just adopted."

Power of the previous question over motion to limit debate. The previous question can be entertained after it is voted to limit debate, but the motion to limit debate cannot be entertained after the *previous question* has been adopted and while it is still in force, because the superior motion of the two is the previous question, whose adoption ends debate altogether and thus expedites business, whereas to limit debate prolongs it. Hence, if debate has been voted limited to, for instance, two minutes a member, adopting the previous question afterward stops the debate on the motion altogether.

Where both the previous question and the motion to limit debate are pending and the previous question is voted adopted, the motion to limit debate is then ignored and is not put to vote, because it would be inconsistent to vote to *limit* the debate on a motion after the body voted to *stop* the debate on it.

Previous question and tablement or postponement. If a main motion on which the previous question was ordered imposed (thus rendering the main motion undebatable and unamendable) is laid on the table or is postponed to a definite time within the same session and if that main motion is then taken up for further consideration during that session it remains undebatable and unamendable until it has been voted on, because it is still under the imposed effect or power of the previous question. But if it is taken up at the next new session (by its being "untabled," or under unfinished business), the said motion is free of the imposition of that previous question and automatically becomes debatable and amendable — because it is then in a new and different stage of proceeding, and consequently is subject anew to all the subsidiary motions, and the privileged and incidental motions (pp. 47–48).

In other words, motions which regulate debate or impose limitation on debate (such as previous question or to limit debate) do not extend to any next new, called meeting.

Previous question and referral or indefinite postponement. However, if a main motion on which the previous question was imposed is voted postponed indefinitely or is voted referred to a committee, that main motion is automatically free of that previous question regardless of when the main motion is taken up again or when the committee reports on it (even if it reports during the same meeting or session). *Reason:* the moment the body refers a motion to a committee, it transfers its immediate and direct control of that motion to an intervening *other* body (the committee), and when it postpones it indefinitely, the body suppresses or puts that motion out of its direct control over it.

When the force of previous question ends. The power of the previous question to continue to prevent debate or amendments on motions ends automatically when the body has voted on the motion or motions on which it was imposed. For instance:

1. *One motion pending.* When the previous question is moved and only one motion is pending before the body, the previous question loses its power to stop debate and amendments the moment that main motion has been voted on (and is adopted or defeated). Hence, if reconsideration of that main motion is afterward proposed, its reconsideration is then debatable and the main motion to be reconsidered is also debatable, because the main motion is in a new stage of proceeding, and, as such, it is subject anew to the subsidiary, privileged and apt incidental motions.

2. *More than one motion pending, previous question not specific.* When more than one motion is pending and the previous question does not specify which motion or motions it applies to, only the motion most recently stated is affected. The moment that motion is voted on (and is adopted or defeated) the remaining motions become debatable and amendable.

3. *Previous question moved on more than one motion.* When the previous question is imposed on more than one pending motion, its force to end debate and amendments does not end until every motion it specified has been voted upon. Supposing (a) a main motion, an amendment to this main motion, and a motion to refer are all pending; and (b) the previous question is moved on the referral and the amendment but not on the main motion itself; and (c) the motion to refer is voted upon; after which (d) reconsideration of the referral is proposed; then both the motion to reconsider and the referral are undebatable and unamendable, because the pre-

vious question's power to stop debate and amendments does not cease until the amendment is also voted upon (see *b*). The pending main motion, in this case, is not affected by that previous question, but it can be ordered on it when the main motion is reached.

1. LAY ON THE TABLE (S, M)

The original intent of the motion to lay on the table ("to table") was to lay a pending question aside only temporarily, in order to give way to some more urgent piece of business, immediately after which the tabled question would be "taken from the table" for its further consideration by the body.

But modern artifice has added a different phase to it which transforms this motion into a motion which can kill a question if members are unaware of their rights to move to take it from the table (if they *want* to take it from the table) during either the same session or the next new session (in organizations having regular meetings as often as quarterly).

Note: Since a tabled question can be thus taken from the table (1) during the current session, or (2) during the next called session, as specified, obviously the act of tabling a question keeps that question *alive;* it is killed only after failure to take it from the table within its due time.

Basic rules. The motion to lay on the table (or to table) must be seconded; it is undebatable and unamendable and requires a majority vote. It is a subsidiary motion of the highest rank and cannot be reconsidered. If it is adopted, it automatically removes the main question from before the body together with any and all other motions that may be pending at the time (such as amendments, or to refer, or postpone, etc.), in which case nothing remains before the house, and the Chair takes up the next business. But if the motion to lay on the table is defeated, the question is still before the body and is put to vote in due course.

No subsidiary motion can be tabled by itself; the main motion to which a subsidiary motion adheres is tabled with it.

How proposed and entertained

MEMBER: "Mr. Chairman, I move that we lay on the table the pending motion to buy a new desk"; or "I move that the motion be laid on the table." Propose it in that simple form. (Seconded.)

CHAIR. "It has been moved and seconded to lay the motion on the table." (It is undebatable and unamendable; the Chair continues:) "Those in favor of laying the motion on the table will say aye." (Response.) "Those opposed will say no." (Response.) The ayes being in

---

KEY QUIZ

Q. Does the motion to table need a second? *A.* Yes.
Q. Is it debatable? *A.* No.
Q. Is it amendable? *A.* No.
Q. What vote does it require? *A.* Majority.
Q. What class of motion is it? *A.* Subsidiary.
Q. What is its rank? *A.* Highest.
Q. Can it be reconsidered? *A.* No.

the preponderance, he announces: "The ayes have it, and the pending motion is laid on the table."

Nothing now remains before the body, because the motion has been voted tabled. "Table" means the secretary: his file, records, or custody.

Taking a motion from the table. A motion that has been laid on the table can be "taken from the table" (this is the technical phrase) at either (1) the *same* session, or (2) the *next new* session, provided no other business is before the body when it is proposed.

In other words, a tabled motion remains alive in the secretary's file during the life of this and the next session only, and if not taken from the table by the end of the next session, it no longer lies on the table; it is said to be dead. After the next session the original question may be reintroduced if so desired.

A tabled motion does not come up automatically under any heading whatsoever at the next meeting. It can only come before the body through adoption of the motion to "take it from the table."

It is not the duty of the Chair or the secretary to move to take it from the table. Any member can do so, however, including the member who originally moved to table it, who is given preference to make the motion if others rise at the same time with him.

Cannot be reconsidered. The motion to lay on the table cannot be reconsidered because it can be made again after a few minutes, or after the motion has been discussed further or some other business has intervened since its defeat. The motion to lay on the table is the only subsidiary motion that cannot be reconsidered; all the other subsidiary motions can be reconsidered (see the symbol R shown with the subsidiary motions). It is outranked, however, by the privileged motions such as to adjourn, recess, etc. (p. 47), and the incidental motions (p. 48).

Note: Questions or motions previously tabled can, when they come up for action before the body, be again laid on the table from session to session thereafter and thus be kept alive for as long as desired (such as, for instance, an application for membership pending further investigation, or an amendment to the bylaws raising the dues, etc.) Once this continuity is broken, the tabled motion dies; but it can be reintroduced at any next new session.

When tabled motions may be taken from the table. A main motion (such as to buy a new desk) which has been tabled can be "taken from the table" under two stipulations: (1) during the same session, or at the next new session in organizations having regular meetings at least quarterly; or (2) it can be taken from the table only during the same session in organizations, clubs or societies which do not hold meetings this often.

Note: Notwithstanding the above rule (namely, that a tabled motion can be taken from the table at the next session only in organizations meeting regularly at least quarterly), if the organization customarily meets regularly less frequently than quarterly, such as semiannually, and it regards such meetings as fixed and established meetings, and it practices the motion to table and to take from the table at such meetings, then such usage or practice has the force of law in the organization and overthrows the general rule of parliamentary law to the contrary.

Difference between to postpone and to table. Normally, a *postponed* question is taken up under unfinished business at the next session, unless otherwise ordered, whereas a *tabled* question can be taken up during the same session if desired. Hence, at first glance, a *tabled* question has notable earlier advantage over a *postponed* question; it can receive earlier consideration.

Members often confuse the motion "to postpone to the next meeting" with the motion "to lay on the table." They say: "I move to lay the motion on the table until the next meeting," thus combining into one single proposal two motions which are antagonistic and which are governed by different rules.

When the motion to table is proposed in that uncanonical form, the parliamentary sense of such proposal is not to table it (which permits it to be taken from the table even during the same session), but to postpone it (which means the next new session).

Therefore, when the proposal is made in that combined form it should be treated not as the motion to lay on the table (which has top rank among subsidiary motions and is undebatable), but to postpone (which has fourth rank among the subsidiary motions and is debatable).

Accordingly, when the motion "to lay on the table" is modified in any way, as by combining with it the words "until the next meeting," or "until the committee chairman arrives," or "until after the election," etc., such combined proposals constitute postponement, not tabling, and they reduce the motion to lay on the table to the rank of definite postponement.

Interference with a tabled question. The assembly may not discuss or consider a question previously tabled unless it first takes that question from the table, and thus bring it before the body again for further action.

Hence, if the following motion is tabled, "to give a dance, half the proceeds of which shall go for scholarships and half toward our Home Fund," it is out of order to entertain a main motion afterward "to invest all the proceeds of the dance in stocks for the next two years" or to propose any other disposition of the proceeds. Such motion interferes with the tabled question, and cannot be entertained.

Instead, the proper course to pursue is first to move to take the question from the table and this done, move then to amend the original question or substitute the new proposal in its place; or, vote down the question and then propose the new one.

Tabling a question after discussing it. An effective way of opposing a pending question (besides speaking against it, for example) is to move to table it, because it takes only a majority vote to table it; or, you can first speak against the question (pointing out its faults and disadvantages), and then move to table it just before you sit down, thus: "I therefore move to lay the motion on the table." You have the right to debate a question and then move to table it.

Note: Where it is not wise to have a question tabled, simply vote it down — vote against it. It is perfectly proper parliamentary (and legislative) practice to speak against an undesirable question, and while on your feet, then move to lay it on the table — just as it is proper and common practice to speak against a pending motion and then move to amend it, and thus attempt to improve or perfect it; or, instead, move to refer it, or postpone it after discussing it.

Motion to table can supplant suspension of the rules. Since the motion to lay on the table requires only a majority vote, whenever you wish to act on some question out of its proper place in the order of business, and ahead of other business, if you cannot command a $\frac{2}{3}$ vote "to suspend the rules," you (and your supporters, taking turns preferably) can move to lay on the table each piece of business when taken up, and eventually you will reach the desired motion, thus supplanting "suspension of the rules."

It is not in order to lay on the table mass action, or mass proceedings, such as to suspend all reports, or the entire agenda, except by unanimous consent.

Tabling a reconsideration. The restoratory motion to reconsider yields to the motion to lay on the table. Therefore, the reconsideration of a main question previously passed by the body (such as "to sell the clubhouse") may be tabled; but such tablement automatically takes with it to the table the question to be reconsidered (the clubhouse question here).

Accordingly, when the reconsideration of a previously decided main question is voted tabled, the question lies on the table, and it therefore cannot be executed until after the time has expired for taking that question from the table, since the body can, up to that time, take the question (the clubhouse question here) from the table and reverse or modify its previous decision on it. But if the question is not taken from the table before adjournment of the next session (in organizations holding at least quarterly meetings) or is not taken from the table before adjournment of the session at which it was passed (in organizations which do not hold at least quarterly meetings), the question is then automatically free of both the reconsideration and its tablement and it can be carried out. In other words, the body's previous affirmative decision (in this case, "to sell the clubhouse") automatically then becomes effective (and the clubhouse can now be sold).

Note: Shrewd leaders and assemblies at times purposely move to reconsider a passed motion (such as to sell the clubhouse), and then vote to table it, thus keeping it lying on the table, and hence still alive, in hopes of getting a better bargain in the interim, or in case it may be to their advantage to reverse the decision later.

Tabling an appeal from the Chair's ruling. Appeals from the decision or rulings of the Chair can be tabled without taking to the table the question from which the appeal is taken, except where the appeal is taken from the Chair's ruling on the germaneness of amendments to main motions in general.

Hence, if the Chair rules that an amendment to a question is (or is not) germane and an appeal is taken therefrom, if the appeal is then voted laid on the table the question goes to the table with it.

In other instances, an appeal can be tabled separately and apart from the question out of which it arises, as shown below.

Motions which may or may not be tabled. A glance at the structure of parliamentary law discloses that some motions or proceedings can be tabled, while others may not; thus, in general:

Tablable Proceedings	Untablable Proceedings
All main motions (original or those in the nature of incidental main ones)	All subsidiary motions
	All privileged motions
Reconsider, rescind, ratify (but not reconsider and enter, because it is in the nature of a notice, which cannot be tabled)	Quorum requirement
	Parliamentary inquiry
	Appeals (except if they concern germaneness of amendments to main motions)
A coexisting motion	Close nominations or polls
A point of order	Reopen nominations or polls
Suspension of the rules	Division of the assembly, or doubting the vote
Appeals from Chair's ruling (except on germaneness of amendments to motions)	Objection to reading from paper, manuscript or book (which is the same as objecting to anyone debating a question)
Motions to take the vote by ballot, roll call, referendum, or by mail (but not voice vote or hand or standing vote)	Withdraw a motion or second
	Requests of any kind
	Filling blanks
Division of a question	Nominations (proposing them)
Objection to consideration of original main questions	Take from the table
	Reconsider and enter
Consideration by paragraph, section, or article	Notices of *any* kind (such as notice to reconsider, rescind, amend the bylaws or standing rules, or any other required previous notice, necessary announcement, or reminders).
The above proceedings can be tabled *alone* and *apart from* whatever motion is concerned under them at the time they are made.	

Note: When it is not desired to table any question (motion, appeal, reconsideration or any of the proceedings listed above), all you have to do is vote against tabling it. If you do not vote against it, it means you *want* it tabled.

Chapter 8

THE PRIVILEGED MOTIONS

Rules and rank. There is a class of motions in the framework of parliamentary law technically known as "privileged motions." There are only five such motions. If you know their rules (S, D, A, M, R) you can help promote efficient parliamentary practice at meetings and conventions, or gain some advantage therein. Here are the five privileged motions:

1.	Fix a day to which to adjourn (S, A, M, R)	119
2.	Adjourn (S, M)	113
3.	Recess (S, A, M)	112
4.	Raise a question of privilege (no symbols)	106
5.	Call for the orders of the day (no symbols)	104

Explanation of symbols. S means the motion requires a second, D (wherever seen) means it is debatable, A means the motion can be amended, M means it needs a majority vote, and R, it can be reconsidered. Motions without symbols, such as motions 4 and 5, are, when raised, unsecondable, undebatable, unamendable, unvotable and unreconsiderable — as, for instance, when you say "I rise to a question of privilege." Your right to rise to a question of privilege does not necessitate a second, debate, amendment, or a vote by the body to determine whether or not you can rise to a question of privilege. Note that none of the privileged motions are debatable, and only the motion to fix a time to which to adjourn may be reconsidered.

Rank of privileged motions. The privileged motions are listed in the order of their established rank; namely: each outranks those below it and each is outranked by those above.

In other words, when any one of the privileged motions is immediately pending (number 3, to recess, for instance), motions 2 or 1 can be proposed and can be acted on ahead of it because they outrank it, but motions 4 or 5 cannot be raised because they are of lower rank than motion number 3. (Review page 11.)

Privileged motions may become main motions. (Aside to beginners: Bypass this paragraph for now.) The top three motions listed above as "privileged motions" often assume the role of a main motion, in which case they take its rank and are debatable, whereas as privileged motions they retain their high rank and are undebatable. (Observe their privileged status and symbols, p. 102.) In other words, these three motions are not always privileged. When are they privileged? (1) The highest ranking motion, to fix a time to which to adjourn, is privileged only when either another question is actually pending at the time, or when its purpose is to continue the present meeting as an adjourned meeting (a continued meeting) to another day. (2) The second highest motion, to adjourn, is always a privileged motion, and hence undebatable and unamendable in assemblies which hold regular scheduled meetings at least quarterly, such as daily, weekly, or monthly; but the motion to adjourn loses its privileged status and becomes a main motion when its purpose is not to adjourn instantly but to adjourn qualifiedly (as "in one hour from now," or "after we hear the next report," etc.); and it also loses its privileged status when it is proposed in unorganized assemblies that have no provision for reconvening (such as at a protest meeting). (3) The third highest privileged motion, to recess, is privileged (and hence undebatable) only when some other business is actually pending at the time it is proposed. When these three motions are performing in the role of a main motion they are subject to debate, amendment and the subsidiary motions.

Why privileged motions were invented. Privileged motions were invented to achieve the following three general aims: (1) observance of orderly procedure; (2) protection of the organization and the well-being of the members; and (3) perpetuation of the existence of the organization. In other words, privileged motions deal with, or concern, questions relating to the above three general aims.

Thus: When the Chair fails to take up the business in its scheduled or announced order, any member may "call for the orders of the day," and thus compel the Chair to follow the proper order of business; or: When meetings are prolonged far into the day or night, the motions "to recess" or "to adjourn" can be used to provide time for food or rest, thus protecting the well-being of the members — just as "question of privilege" can be used to protect the members from present or impending threat or danger; or: The motion "fixing a day to which to adjourn" (or the setting of another day to which to continue the present meeting), enables an assembly to hold future meetings under the same call, thus assuring fulfillment of the organization's needs.

Logic of rank of the privileged motions. When the privileged motions were being invented and their inventors (the British Parliament originally) sought to determine what rank to assign to each motion, it was resolved to base the logic of their respective rank on the degree of usefulness each motion can render to the cause of the organization and the pending proceedings.

Of the five privileged motions, "to fix a time to which to adjourn" (to hold an adjourned or continued meeting another day) was assigned highest rank because it enables an assembly to meet at will for the accomplishment of business, thus serving the highest possible service to the organization, namely: it perpetuates its existence and thus serves to sustain its objectives and purposes. The motion "to adjourn" was given second highest rank because its adoption ends the session and frees the members from the cares of business entirely, while the motion "to recess" was assigned lower rank next to the motion to adjourn because its adoption frees the members only temporarily. The "question of privilege" was given fourth highest rank because it is a means of protecting the well-being of the members of the assembly from danger or violation of personal rights. Lastly, a "call for the orders of the day" suggests correct business procedure and encourages respect for law and order.

No relation to the pending business. Actually, privileged motions have no direct relation to a pending piece of business; they are proposals to adjourn, or recess, or which introduce a wholly different question, one that is privileged in status, or which insures orderly pursuit of the agenda or a program.

Why they are called "privileged" motions. It will be observed that the privileged motions, when raised or proposed, have no direct bearing upon the *disposal* of a pending motion (if one is pending before the house); they concern, as explained above, purely matters or proposals which affect (1) orderly procedure at meetings, (2) the well-being of the members, and (3) the preservation of the organization; this distinguishes them from the subsidiary motions which directly affect a pending motion.

Because the privileged motions serve such a high purpose they were given the appellation "privileged" motions, and were accordingly assigned higher rank than the subsidiary motions (which directly concern the disposal of pending business).

Each privileged motion will now be considered separately in the order of its rank, beginning with the lowest in rank, call for the orders of the day.

5. CALL FOR THE ORDERS OF THE DAY

It is the duty of the Chair to carry out the program or order of business of the assembly in the customary, announced, or scheduled order; and if he neglects to do so (designedly or unintentionally), any member may rise and say: "Mr. Chairman, I call for the orders of the day." (No second is necessary nor is it subject to the subsidiary motions.)

Calling for the orders of the day is parliamentary language for saying to the Chair: "Mr. Chairman, business is not being taken up in its proper order, and I rise to call this to your attention, so that its correct order may be followed."

The same result can be achieved by simply rising to a point of order and calling the departure from the regular or specified order of business to the attention of the chairman. As a matter of fact this is a more effective (and a more readily understood) remedy. However, the formal motion in parliamentary law is to rise and "call for the orders of the day." This proceeding is also used as a reminder that the hour to which a piece of business was previously postponed has been reached.

Once the subject of an order of the day is before the body it is then treated like any other main motion.

Basic rules. This motion, to call for the order of the day, is undebatable and unamendable, and is not put to vote; it is a privileged motion of lowest rank and is unreconsiderable. Calling for the orders of the day is in order only if the Chair has ignored or departed from the scheduled order of business.

Synonymous terms. "Orders of the day" means "business of the day." The word "order" means a motion or piece of business previously scheduled or postponed. Hence, the phrase "special orders" simply means special motions or special business. "General orders" means general business, motions, subjects, or topics scheduled for action.

Special orders. The term special orders (or special business or motions) refers to a motion (or motions) set for or postponed to a particular time. Business so scheduled or postponed is taken up when the particular hour arrives, otherwise it forfeits its status for special consideration and hence is usually actable under unfinished business.

Form of the special order. "Mr. Chairman, I move that the motion before the body (to buy a new clubhouse) be postponed to the next meeting and be made a special order for 8:30 p.m." Such a motion requires a $\frac{2}{3}$ vote because it can interrupt a motion, if any, that may be pending when that hour is reached at the next meeting.

While the motion to postpone a question to the next meeting and make it a special order for a particular hour requires a $\frac{2}{3}$ vote for adoption, amendments to the motion (changing, for instance, the hour from 9:15 to 9:30) require only a majority vote, because the force or power of con-

---

KEY QUIZ

Q. Does it require a second to call for the orders of the day? *A.* No (just like a point of order).
 Q. Is it debatable? *A.* No.
 Q. Is it amendable? *A.* No.
 Q. Can it be reconsidered? *A.* No.
 Q. Is it put to vote? *A.* No.
 Q. What class of motion is it? *A.* Privileged.
 Q. What is its rank? *A.* Lowest in the privileged class.

sideration is contained in the act of *postponement* and not in the selection of the *time*.

The motion to postpone specially is subject to the same rules in all respects but one as the regular motion to postpone; namely: it is seconable, debatable, amendable, can be reconsidered and is a subsidiary motion of fourth highest rank; but it requires a $\frac{2}{3}$ vote.

When two or more special orders have been voted, the one which was first proposed is taken up when its time is reached, even though another special order had afterward been set for an earlier time that conflicts with the former, unless otherwise agreed to.

General orders. General orders, as practiced in permanent organiza- tions, means business or motions postponed to the next meeting; and such postponed matters automatically come up under unfinished business un- less otherwise specified. In other words, if a motion at the present meeting is voted postponed to the next meeting (without specifying it as a special order and a special hour for its consideration), such a postponed motion can be referred to in technical language as a "general order." Special orders are acted on ahead of general orders.

4. RAISE A QUESTION OF PRIVILEGE

Grave injustices and countless wrongs have been and are constantly being done both to business and to members because of misuse of this proceeding. The motion to "raise a question of privilege" is one of the least understood and most abused and misapplied motions in parliamen- tary law. It must be stressed that this important privileged motion must be understood and properly applied by both members and presiding officers. Therefore, study the discussion on the following pages with extra care.

Definition and scope of question of privilege. In enlightened parlia- mentary practice a question of privilege implies that the member raising it will reveal some matter which concerns the rights and privileges of the members collectively or individually. Question of privilege relates in a broad interpretation to the following subjects: the members' Safety, Health, or Integrity, or protection of their Property (catchword: S-H-I-P). When a member rises to a question of privilege or personal privilege and is asked to state it, he is expected to reveal or point out something con- cerning these four subjects; namely, the subjects S-H-I-P.

Therefore, raising legitimate questions of privilege does not relate to business matters already pending before the body.

Basic rules. Rising to a question of privilege (like rising to a point of order) does not require a second; it is not debatable or amendable, and it is not put to vote.

There are two types of questions of privilege: general and personal (or special). A general question of privilege concerns the assembly collec- tively; and a question of personal (or special) privilege concerns one or more members individually. The decision of the Chair on whether a question is privileged is appealable.

A proper question of privilege has fourth rank among the privileged motions, and as such it is superseded by the privileged motions for adjournment and recess; but it outranks or supersedes a call for the orders of the day and all the subsidiary motions, and, of course, all main motions.

How proposed. The form of the motion is: "Mr. Chairman, I rise to a question of privilege," which means that the mover wishes to make known or to disclose to the body some matter detrimental to the organization's safety, health, integrity or property. Or he can say: "Mr. Chairman, I rise to a question of personal [or, special] privilege," which implies that he wishes to reveal some matter or subject detrimental to himself or some other member.

Examples of questions of personal privilege. (1) A member who cannot hear a report has the right under the formal rules of parliamentary procedure to rise to a question of personal (or special) privilege and can interrupt the reading of the report (which is the pending business at the moment) long enough to have it read louder or have the Chair call the reporting member to the front of the room or rostrum so that the report can be heard.

(2) Similarly, he can rise to a question of personal (or special) privilege to call to the attention of the Chair that the room is uncomfortably hot or cold, and he can thus interrupt the pending piece of business, if one is pending, long enough to have steps taken to correct the situation.

(3) Or he can rise to a question of personal (or special) privilege to call to the attention of the Chair that there is unnecessary conversation or other disturbance around him which the Chair (whose duty it is to preserve order and maintain reasonable quiet) has allowed to go unnoticed and which is an invasion of the member's fundamental right to enjoy reasonable comfort and quiet during the meeting.

(4) Or, when a member sees that automobiles in the assembly's parking area are being damaged by hoodlums, he can rise to a question of privi-

---

KEY QUIZ

Q. What is a legitimate question of privilege? *A.* One which affects the organization or assembly or any member(s) thereof with respect to their safety, health, integrity or the security of their property, and many similar protective measures or proceedings, such as concerning their honor, reputation, peace of mind, dignity, or their conduct or status therein.

Q. Can a question of privilege interrupt a speaker or a pending motion? *A.* Yes, if it is legitimate (S-H-I-P).

Q. If it is not legitimate, then what happens? *A.* The Chair says: "The subject raised does not constitute a proper question of privilege and cannot interrupt the speaker."

Q. What is the correct form for proposing a question of privilege? *A.* "Mr. Chairman, I rise to a question of privilege."

Q. What does the Chair do then? *A.* He says: "The member will state his question of privilege."

Q. Who decides or rules whether a question of privilege is or is not a legitimate one? *A.* The Chair — subject to appeal.

Q. Does it require a second to rise to a question of privilege? *A.* No.

Q. What class of motion is it? *A.* A privileged motion.

Q. What is its rank? *A.* Fourth among them.

Q. Is a question of privilege always in order? *A.* No; motions to fix adjourned meetings, or to adjourn or recess, outrank it.

lege and interrupt a speaker or pending business, and move to have necessary steps taken at once to protect the members' property.

(5) Or he can rise to a question of personal privilege when his good name or reputation is attacked, as when shown a newspaper in which he is charged with being a spy, or he is accused of being a holdup man, etc. (which accusations could subject him to expulsion from the organization), or of other charges against his good name and reputation, and he can interrupt any pending business (except the privileged motions relating to adjournment and recess) to have steps taken to deny the accusations, and adopt some motion to cope with, meet or otherwise attend to or answer such charge or accusation.

Remember: questions of privilege cannot be raised haphazardly or capriciously. They must be proper, legitimate, or germane to the members' safety, health, integrity or the safety of their property at the meeting.

How ordinarily handled. Of course in an ordinary assembly simple matters are, in practice, generally attended to informally, as by a member's simply calling out, "I can't hear the report"; "I can't hear the member"; "I didn't hear the motion"; or "It's stuffy in this room"; or "Mr. Chairman, it's awfully cold here," etc.; and usually, without offering the formal motion, "I rise to a question of privilege," the windows are closed, or opened, or the inaudible member is asked to speak louder, or the members causing the disturbance complained of are asked to refrain from causing further disturbance. Disrespect for a member's fundamental rights entitles him to rise to a question of personal privilege, and it is the duty of the Chair to enforce these rights. Failure to enforce them is appealable.

Note: Enforce your rights when need be; do not sleep on your rights.

Examples of general privilege. These concern the assembly as a whole: A member can formally rise, under the strict rules of parliamentary procedure, to a question of privilege to (1) warn the assembly, for instance, of leaking gas in the service kitchen adjoining the meeting room; or of smoke, or fire, or a broken water pipe in the building, or of some other physical danger; or (2) to warn the assembly that individuals parked in a car near to the entrance to the hall threaten to harm the officers or members after the meeting; or that (3) the late edition of the local newspaper carried an article charging that the organization is subversive and its members disloyal citizens.

U. S. House of Representatives foremost authority. The foremost authority in the United States on what constitutes proper questions of privilege in parliamentary and legislative procedure is the U. S. House of Representatives. Rule IX of "Rules of the House" defines questions of privilege thus:

(1) "Questions of privilege shall be, first, those affecting the rights of the House collectively, its safety, dignity, and the integrity of its proceedings; second, the rights, reputation and conduct of members individually, in their representative capacity only; and shall have precedence of all other questions, except motions to adjourn." The rule further explains:

(2) "Questions of privilege also relate to its [the House's] organization, the conduct of officers and employees, admission to the floor of the House,

the conduct of representatives of the press, the accuracy of its Journal and of its documents and messages," etc.

For instance, a "menace to the personal safety of Members from an insecure ceiling in the Hall" (U. S. Representatives' Chamber) was held to involve a proper question of privilege; also "an assault on a Member within the Capitol"; and any definite and specific charge made in the newspapers against "the members in their *representative* capacities."

Therefore, on the authority of these extracts of the rule of the U. S. House of Representatives, and as further expounded by this author, the following also necessarily constitute proper questions of privilege in ordinary assemblies:

(1) To proceed to fill vacancies in the offices or personnel of an organization; (2) to punish members; to censure officers or members for being tyrannical, abusive or disorderly; to engage or dismiss employees; (3) to vote to admit nonmembers or special guests or a speaker into the meeting room; (4) to check disturbances by reporters or visitors; and (5) to insure the accuracy of the minutes (a member can rise to a question of privilege, for instance, when he wishes to correct the minutes at any time after their adoption), and the safety from damage or theft of its mail, and, generally, of the integrity or safety of the organization's documents, papers, files, books, or other property. Indignities to a member, his eligibility status, his good standing or his being erroneously recorded as absent or his vote erroneously recorded, and his right to be sworn in or be installed in office belatedly are also proper questions of privilege.

Abuses of question of privilege. A question of privilege is abused or misapplied: (1) When a member rises to a question of privilege to take the floor away (innocently or intentionally) from a speaker in order to debate a motion (as is often done); instead, he should wait until the member has finished and then take the floor. (2) When he rises to a question of privilege to make some explanation or correct a misstatement uttered in the course of debate; instead, he should wait until the member has finished and then rise to make the explanation or correction. (3) When it is used as a point of order, or as a question of information, or a parliamentary inquiry; instead, he should use the motions just mentioned.

When a question of privilege is misapplied or abused, or is improperly used in the place of another proceeding, the Chair tactfully applies the rule correctly; thus if a member rises to a question of privilege and when directed by the Chair to state it, he asks: "How much will the radio cost us?", the Chair tactfully informs the member: "The question just raised does not constitute a question of privilege; it is a question of information." The Chair could also say, "The question is not one of personal privilege," or "The subject raised by the question of privilege does not constitute a proper question of privilege," or "This is not a proper question of privilege."

Note: It is only when a question of privilege is raised while another motion is before the body, or it interrupts a speaker, that it becomes important to make sure that the question of privilege (or a motion arising under it) *is* a proper one. If no one has the floor and no other business is actually pending and a question of privilege is misapplied, the misapplication is simply ignored.

Misrulings by the Chair. If the Chair admits an improper question of privilege, or does not admit a proper one, members should raise a point of order to prevent parliamentary mispractice and misrulings by the Chair.

If no one takes notice of such mispractice or misrulings, it is too late to do so after the question has been disposed of.

When the Chair is in doubt about whether to admit a question of privilege, he should always give it the benefit of the doubt.

Whether a question of privilege is or is not a proper one is a matter of judgment and opinion; hence it is appealable.

Motion resulting from question of privilege. If, after raising a proper question of privilege (when *no* other business is pending), a motion is propounded to cope with the matter or condition disclosed by the question of privilege, such proposal is a main motion, and it is treated as a main motion in all respects (S, D, A, M, R).

But when a question of privilege is raised while other business or another motion *is* pending before the body and a motion arises from it to cope with the condition stated by the question of privilege, such motion is technically known as a *coexisting motion* (it coexists with another pending main motion), and is subject to the following rules.

Coexisting Motion (S, D, A, M, R)

A legitimate coexisting motion is simply a main motion and is subject to the same rules as a main motion (S, D, A, M, R).

Another essential rule to remember about a coexisting motion is that since it is proposed while another question is pending it automatically interrupts and suspends further consideration of the other pending question until the coexisting motion is first considered, acted on, or disposed of. This is simply an exception to the rule, and the only circumstance under which a pending main motion is allowed to remain pending while another main motion is taken up ahead of it.

How proposed and transacted. To illustrate the full practice and procedure of the unique "coexisting motion" emanating from a proper question of privilege, assume the following main motion pending before the body: "to donate five hundred dollars to Y charity" (being discussed pro and con at the moment). Member X has the floor.

Member X: "Mr. Chairman, I am in favor of donating five hundred dollars to this charity, because . . ." (interrupted by member A, who just arrived).

Member A: "Mr. Chairman, I rise to a question of privilege."

Chair: "The member will state the question of privilege."

Member A: "I have here a copy of the newspaper *Evening Dash*, in which it is charged that this organization is composed of anarchists and disloyal citizens." This is a proper question of privilege, since it concerns the *integrity* of the members collectively, so he properly interrupts member X's speech and is allowed to continue. He proceeds:) "Mr. Chairman, I am stunned by such an accusation against an outstanding patriotic organization such as ours. We all know that these charges are false and malicious. We must take immediate steps to deny them and to answer this accusation. I therefore move the adoption of the following resolution:

"*Resolved,* That the members of this organization have read with inde-scribable regret the false, malicious and unfounded charges made against them in the *Evening Dash* which are herewith categorically denied in their entirety, and for which we demand an immediate apology and re-traction; and be it further

"*Resolved,* That a copy of this resolution be immediately forwarded to the said newspaper." (Seconded.)

CHAIR: "It has been moved and seconded to adopt the resolution. Is there any discussion?"

MEMBER X (who was interrupted by Member Z): "Mr. Chairman, I rise to a point of order." (He is asked by the Chair to state it, and he says:) "My point of order is that this resolution cannot be entertained, because another main motion is pending; to donate five hundred dollars."

CHAIR: "The point of order is not well taken. The resolution is in the nature of a coexisting motion. It arises out of a proper question of privilege affecting the integrity of the membership, and on that account it supersedes the further consideration of the pending main motion; but as soon as the resolution is disposed of, the Chair will reassign the floor to you." (The Chair proceeds to dispose of the coexisting motion; thus:) "Is there further debate on the resolution?" (After which the vote thereon:) "Those in favor of the resolution will say aye; those opposed will say no; the ayes have it, and the resolution is carried. The Chair now recognizes Member X who had the floor at the time the question of privilege was disclosed."

Business then continues as though no interruption had occurred.

Note: Since, as previously stated, a coexisting motion arising out of a proper question of privilege is a main motion, and is subject to all the rules of a main motion (S, D, A, M, R), then while the said resolution was pending any member could apply on it any subsidiary, privileged or incidental motion (pp. 47–48).

Hence, when a "coexisting" motion emanates from a proper question of privilege while other business is pending, the coexisting motion auto-matically interrupts the pending business and is attended to first (as shown in the above drill), after which the pending motion (which was interrupted) is resumed at the point interrupted. But if no other business is pending at the time, the motion is acted on and is disposed of just like any other main motion.

Any member can propose the coexisting motion. If a member raises a proper question of privilege but does not propose suitable action to meet the situation raised, then any member may propose the necessary steps to be taken.

General privilege outranks special privilege. When a question of gen-eral privilege (involving the assembly as a whole) and one of personal or special privilege (involving individuals) come into conflict, the question of general privilege takes precedence over a question of personal (special) privilege.

In other words, a question of general privilege outranks a question of personal privilege because it affects more members. Only one question of privilege at a time can be before the body, except that a question of general may be proposed while a question of personal privilege is pending.

3. RECESS (S, A, M)

The motion to recess is normally used when it is desired to suspend business temporarily and when it is to be resumed within reasonable time thereafter, as when recessing for lunch, or to admit some person to address the assembly, or to await the counting of the ballots, etc. It is also used by strategists so as to permit them to go after more votes or to seek more support for some motion or project.

"Recess" and not "adjourn" is the appropriate motion to use between sittings of a convention or in any assembly desiring to have a short intermission. But if the motion to "adjourn" is used instead of the motion to "recess," it is still a *recess* when that is what is intended, even if adjournment is voted on.

Basic rules. The privileged motion to recess is secondable and amendable, but it is not debatable. It requires a majority vote. It cannot be reconsidered. To recess is equivalent to having an intermission in the proceedings of a session. If members move to adjourn when they mean to take a recess, as is often done in conventions, the Chair treats the motion as the motion to recess. Regardless of which of the two motions made is put and voted on, the action taken is deemed a recess.

As a privileged motion, to recess outranks two privileged motions — a question of privilege, and a call for the orders of the day; all the subsidiary motions (p. 47); and all main motions; but it is itself outranked by the privileged motions to adjourn and to fix a time to which to adjourn.

It is not necessary to have a quorum in order to recess for any purpose; hence it is in order to recess even to await a quorum.

How proposed and transacted

MEMBER: "Mr. Chairman, I move we take a fifteen-minute recess." (Seconded.)

CHAIR: "It is moved and seconded to recess for fifteen minutes; those in favor of recessing will say aye; those opposed will say no; the ayes have it, and the meeting is [or, stands] in recess."

After recess, the Chair again calls the meeting to order; thus:

CHAIR: "The meeting will come to order." (He then reminds the members:) "Just before recessing the following business [for example] was pending before the meeting: a main motion to hold a public installation, and an amendment to it to add the words 'in the Town Hall.'" (He takes the vote on the amendment first, then on the main motion no

---

KEY QUIZ

Q. Is the motion to recess secondable? *A.* Yes.
Q. Is it debatable? *A.* No, not as a *privileged* motion.
Q. Is it amendable? *A.* Yes; it is always amendable by nature.
Q. What vote adopts a recess? *A.* Majority vote.
Q. What class of motion is it, and what is its rank? *A.* It is a privileged motion and has third highest rank in that class.
Q. Can it be reconsidered? *A.* No, not as a privileged motion.
Q. What makes the motion to recess a privileged motion (and hence undebatable and unreconsiderable)? *A.* It is privileged only when other business is actually before the body when it is proposed.

matter what happens to the amendment; thus:) "Those in favor of the amendment will say aye; those opposed will say no; the ayes have it, and the amendment is carried. The question *now* is on the main motion as amended: to hold our public installation in the Town Hall" (which is then put to a vote).

Forms for proposing a recess. Any form for recessing, modified or not, is appropriate for taking a recess immediately, such as: "to recess for one hour [or, for lunch]"; "to recess pending the report of the nominating committee"; "to recess until the business manager arrives"; "to recess until we have a quorum," etc.

When the motion to recess is a main motion. It is a *privileged* motion when another motion or piece of business is actually before the body when it is proposed. It is a *main* motion when no other business is pending when it is proposed.

The motion to recess at a *future* time, or after a future event (such as after the next report, or after we vote on the pending motion, etc.) is not the motion to recess *immediately*, and hence is not a privileged motion. It is a *main* motion, and it is so treated; it is in order provided no other motion or business is pending at the time it is proposed.

Rules applying to recess as main motion. To recess is always amendable (as a privileged or as a main motion) so as to suit the object of a recess.

It is not debatable as a privileged motion, nor can it be reconsidered; but it is debatable as a main motion, and, as such, it can be reconsidered like any other main motion.

Changing the hour set for recess. If the body passes a motion to recess at some future time or after a certain event or stage in its proceedings, the body can (by majority vote during the same meeting) change or amend its previous motion in any way desired.

But if the body's agenda designates time for taking a recess, then a $\frac{2}{3}$ vote is necessary to modify or change the time designated in the agenda.

2. ADJOURN (S, M)

To "adjourn" is properly used when it is desired to end (under its present call) the meeting which is being held. Adjourn denotes separation and departure from that meeting or session, as in a convention, annual meeting or other whole meeting. The next meeting is held under a *new* call.

If more than one sitting is held in a whole session or meeting, the motion to recess is used rather than to adjourn.

Basic rules. The privileged motion to adjourn requires a second; it is undebatable and unamendable, and requires a majority vote. It cannot be reconsidered. It is a privileged motion of second highest rank. It can be proposed at *any* time after the usual opening ceremonies — even before the minutes are read. It cannot be entertained by the Chair when another member has the floor, nor can it interrupt a speaker without his consent for the purpose. It can be renewed (proposed again) provided that reasonable time has elapsed since its last defeat, or that some other business has intervened. It does not require a quorum. Remember: if your organization has definite and regular meeting dates (as weekly, monthly, etc.), the motion to adjourn is never debatable or amendable, whether business is pending or not at the time it is proposed.

How proposed and entertained

MEMBER: "Mr. Chairman, I move we adjourn." (Seconded.)
CHAIR: "It has been moved and seconded to adjourn." (Pause.) "Those in favor will say aye; those opposed will say no." (Pause.) "The ayes have it, and the meeting is adjourned."

Consent of the body necessary. No adjournment is legal unless by vote of the body, or by its evident or general *consent* or approval. Therefore, arbitrary, spiteful or mischievous adjournment of a business meeting by the Chair is illegal; hence the body can continue the meeting without him and can legally transact business therein, provided a quorum remains, regardless of how many members may have walked out of the meeting with the presiding officer.

When it loses privileged rank. The motion to adjourn if qualified in any way loses its rank as a privileged motion. For instance, "to adjourn ten minutes from now" is not the privileged motion which adjourns forthwith; it is adjournment in the future, in which case the motion is debatable and amendable because it loses its privileged rank and becomes a main motion. "To adjourn till tomorrow" is likewise qualified, hence debatable, amendable, tablable, postponable, etc.

The motion to adjourn also loses its rank as a privileged motion and automatically becomes a main motion when an unorganized assembly is holding its first meeting (as in a protest meeting), or when it is holding the last meeting of its existence. In such cases it becomes a main motion and is both debatable and amendable, because when a group convenes for the first time, it is logical to permit discussion in order to determine when to meet again if necessary; similarly, when an assembly is about to go out of existence and is holding its last meeting, the motion to adjourn, when proposed, is a main motion and is both debatable and amendable, thus enabling the assembly to consider extending its life.

KEY QUIZ

Q. Is the privileged motion to adjourn secondable? *A.* Yes.
Q. Is it debatable or amendable? *A.* No.
Q. What vote adopts or can authorize adjournment? *A.* Majority.
Q. What class of motion is it and what is its rank? *A.* It is a privileged motion having second highest rank, and, as such, it outranks all the privileged motions except "fix a day to which to adjourn"; and it also supersedes all the subsidiary motions, as well as all the main motions.
Q. Can the Chair refuse motions to adjourn and keep the members at the meeting against their will? *A.* No. The members cannot be compelled by the Chair to remain in the meeting against their will, nor may he refuse to entertain the motion to adjourn *between* or *during* categories of business or at reasonable intervals after its last defeat, from the reading of the minutes to the end of the agenda. (Reread and absorb this question.)
Q. At what point of the agenda may members adjourn? *A.* At any point they care to after the usual *opening* ceremonies — even before the reading of the minutes (which usually commences the *business* part), or at any point desired thereafter (U. S. House, Rule 1).

What business can be transacted after adjournment voted. Voting to adjourn is one thing and declaring the meeting adjourned is another — there being two distinct steps to the proceeding; thus:

CHAIR: "The ayes have it; the motion to adjourn is carried."

At this stage it has only been *voted* to adjourn; the Chair has not *announced* adjournment and members should not leave their seats. Legally, a meeting is not considered terminated or adjourned until the Chair makes the formal declaration, "The meeting is [or, "stands"] adjourned," or some similar declaration which it is his duty to make.

Therefore, between the time the vote to adjourn is taken and its declaration, the following business can intervene:

1. The motion to "fix a day (time) to which to adjourn," because it is of higher rank than the motion to "adjourn."

2. Motions giving notice to reconsider, or to reconsider at the next meeting (technically known as "reconsider and enter") some motion or act passed at this meeting; or to rescind; or any other previous notice *required* under parliamentary law or the bylaws (such as to assess the members, to give notice of intention to appropriate or expend money above a *prescribed* sum).

3. Motion (or previous notice) to amend or revise the bylaws.

4. Announcements, such as appointment of committees, if any, that were previously authorized; reminders about a bowling date, the annual formal dance, officers' rehearsal, committee meetings, and other necessary and vital announcements.

After these necessary matters (if any) are attended to, the Chair then *announces* adjournment; he says:

CHAIR: "There being no further business to come before the meeting [he pauses], the meeting *is* adjourned."

After adjourning the meeting, it may not then be called back to order to take up omitted business except by unanimous consent, and provided no one left the meeting room (strictly speaking).

Effect of adjournment on unfinished business. Presiding officers and members are often baffled as to the effect an adjournment has upon a question actually pending before the body at adjournment. The rules stated below govern, unless the body has otherwise ordered or the bylaws provide to the contrary; namely:

(1) In assemblies having regular sessions as frequently as quarterly (as weekly, monthly, etc.) — as in fraternal orders, labor organizations, women's clubs or veterans' associations, the pending question automatically goes over to the next session and is taken up first under its own category.

For instance: If the interrupted question at the time of adjournment was on a committee report, that question is taken up at the next session under committee reports of its own class — as under reports of boards, or standing or special committees, as the case may be. If it was pending under unfinished business, it is taken up under unfinished business, etc.

Note: If the interrupted question was pending under new business, the adjournment automatically makes it unfinished business for the next session.

(2) In bodies which do not have regular meetings, but which hold occasional meetings at their pleasure, or as the need arises, as in patriotic

gatherings, mass meetings or protest meetings, a pending question of business expires upon adjournment; but it can be introduced anew at any future meeting as new matter.

(3) In conventions and annual meetings or town meetings, any question (motion, article, etc.) which is left unfinished automatically *expires* upon final adjournment.

Note: These bodies have inherent power, while in session, to put off by majority vote to the next annual convention or meeting the further consideration of any proposition from its present agenda, or any article from the town warrant, and thus keep it alive for more advantageous future consideration than the current session can give it — as by referring a proposition to a committee or commission for study and report at the next annual session; or by directing the town selectmen to include it in the next town warrant, unless the bylaws or existing laws prohibit it.

(4) In an executive board or a standing committee, elected or appointed, if the term thereof expires *in toto* for all its members simultaneously, or it expires only for a portion of them (as one-third, etc.), and a wholly new board or a re-formed board succeeds it, unfinished business of the former board can thereafter be introduced before the new board as new matter.

(5) In any body (parent, or board or committee) which holds more than one sitting a day during its whole meeting or session, if the body uses the term "adjourn" (instead of "recess") for intermission between sittings, or the body votes an adjourned meeting to another day under its current call, the interrupted pending business is resumed at the next sitting, or adjourned meeting, at the point it was interrupted, and business continues as if there had been no adjournment.

(6) And, generally, *when* an adjournment dissolves the assembly, all unfinished business therein is dissolved.

How meetings are adjourned. Meetings are normally adjourned in three ways: on motion of a member (when no one has the floor), when duly seconded and voted on or agreed to by general consent; on the initiative of the Chair, but with the assembly's consent; or according to established form or ritualistic custom.

Illustration of the three ways of adjourning:

(1) *On motion of a member.* "Mr. Chairman, I move we adjourn."

CHAIR: "It is moved *and* seconded to adjourn; those in favor will say aye; those opposed will say no; the ayes have it, and the meeting is adjourned" (stating to when if need be).

(2) *Upon the Chair's initiative.* "It appears we have completed all our business." (He then wisely asks:) "Before adjourning, is there anything to come before this meeting?" (He pauses, just in case, and if there is no response he says slowly:) "There being no further business . . . the meeting is adjourned."

Note: Enlightened presiding officers never adjourn the meeting willfully, arbitrarily or hastily — as this can lead to disorder, disunity and litigation. In all instances, the assembly must *want* the adjournment.

(3) *According to form or custom.* Follow the usual or customary form or ritualistic practice. (See your ritual book.)

Agenda need not be completed. It is never obligatory to finish the agenda before adjourning. The members have the right to adjourn by majority vote at any business stage or under any category of business. The body can adjourn even though business is before it.

Chair should entertain motion at intervals. It is because of its precedence that it is in order when other business is pending; and it is also in order if made between categories of business or during them at any time, as well as at reasonable intervals during the course of the proceedings from the reading of the minutes to the end of the meeting, and, therefore, the Chair should entertain it at such intervals. If the body does *not* wish to adjourn, it can defeat it.

When adjournment is not in order. The motion cannot be made and put to vote when another member has the floor; if this is done and anyone objects, the vote is void.

The motion to adjourn is not in order while the body is engaged in voting, or during a division or verification of a vote; nor can it be made after a roll call has begun, or after it has been voted to take a vote by ballot.

To adjourn is not in order when it is *obvious* that it is offered for purposes of delay or obstruction, in which case it may be ruled dilatory — subject to appeal, however.

It is not in order if made when new members or unsworn officers-elect await the taking of the oath.

It is out of order if made after it has been voted to go into committee of the whole, nor is it in order in such committee.

When bylaws prohibit adjournment except at certain hour. A bylaw which directs members to remain in session up to a certain hour is merely a directory or advisory bylaw, especially when it does not attach any penalty for its violation. Hence, if a bylaw reads: "All members shall stay in session until 10:30," or "shall not adjourn before 10:30," such bylaw is voidable and may be ignored, because members cannot be compelled to remain in session by mere *direction*. Business done after that hour is not invalid, provided it is valid in all other respects. (But see the next rule.)

When bylaws prohibit transaction of business after certain hour. Where a bylaw declares: "Business transacted after eleven o'clock shall be *void*," business transacted after that hour is then automatically null and void by force of that compelling and binding bylaw. But if the bylaw reads: "No business shall be transacted after 11 o'clock," such bylaw is purely declaratory or merely advisory, having no binding force, especially when it prescribes no penalty for its violation. Hence, business transacted after that hour is not void if it is valid in all other respects.

When holding a meeting is impossible. If, at meeting time, it is impossible or unsafe to begin or continue the meeting due to emergency (fire, blackout, surrender of the meeting room, etc.), and the body adjourns without transacting business or a necessary piece of business (as election of officers) such unfinished business may not be conducted or completed by mail unless existing bylaw authorizes voting by mail. Instead, another meeting, with due notice to the members, should be held as soon as practicable thereafter, if it is not in the best interests of the assembly to wait until the next regular meeting at which to hold the election. But when, in an organization with scattered membership which meets but once a year or so, *all* the candidates or nominees of an unc-om pleted or unheld election *agree* to conduct the election by mail, and no one else registers objection, then an anomalous election or proceeding which is never challenged is valid.

Adjournment "sine die." The term "sine die" (Lat.) literally means "without day." It denotes a *final* adjournment of the body — its dissolution. Following are several ways in which it is interpreted:

(1) In legislative bodies (as in state legislatures or in a city council, board of aldermen, etc.), in which term of office is limited to a two- or four-year term, etc., when that term expires it automatically *ends* or dissolves the life of that body by operation of statutory law, or by a charter or bylaw provision, and the newly elected body then replaces it. Hence the *final* adjournment of that body properly constitutes an adjournment sine die, since it has no days left for itself in which to meet again; it has been replaced by another body.

(2) In lodges, chapters, locals, posts, or units of fraternal orders, labor organizations, veterans' associations or women's clubs, etc., in which membership is continuous and successive, or which have bylaws which provide regularly scheduled future meetings, an adjournment of the meeting in these bodies is never an adjournment sine die; instead, it is a *simple* adjournment or mere suspension of the body's deliberations, which the body automatically resumes on another day or at the next regular meeting.

(3) In a convention of delegates (annual, biennial, etc.), if the organization's bylaws have *no* provision authorizing the convention to call itself back into session between adjournment of the current session and the next scheduled new convention session (under a *new* call), then the final adjournment of the current session dissolves the life of this convention or annual meeting, and hence such final adjournment properly constitutes an adjournment sine die. All unfinished business of this session falls to the ground upon adjournment. The next convention then starts business anew, elects new officers, appoints new committees and it can adopt new rules.

(4) In a convention, however, whose bylaws expressly authorize the body of delegates either, for instance, (*a*) "to serve as delegates until the next convention" (as some bylaws do), thus continuing the body's life, or (*b*) "to reconvene itself in special session when necessary between conventions," then the adjournment of the assembly in such bodies is a simple adjournment (not a sine die adjournment), and means only the ending of its sittings in the current convention session, since the body of delegates has authority to meet again. When they do meet again under their same call or in a special meeting, as stated above, then they meet as a body already organized, with the same officers and convention rules; and they remain so organized until the day the new convention of delegates has been called to order, at which moment Parliamentary Time automatically dissolves the old body, or adjourns it sine die.

Distinction between "adjourn" and "fix a day to which to adjourn." It is the motion to "adjourn" that *closes* the meeting, and not the motion to "fix a day to which to adjourn." The latter motion merely designates another sitting to which to *continue* the present meeting's business so that it can be attended to before the next called meeting. If the body has no need to hold additional sittings, there would be no need to move to "fix a day to which to adjourn."

1. FIX A DAY TO WHICH TO ADJOURN (S, A, M, R)

To fix a *day* to which to adjourn, and to fix a *time* to which to adjourn are synonymous terms, but the former is more authoritative; U. S. House Rules and Manual, 784.

This is not the motion to adjourn. It is, instead, the technical form for the motion to designate another *day* to which to continue a sitting of the present whole meeting.

For example, assume that an assembly has not time enough to transact all of its desired business, scheduled under its call for this meeting or session, and that it wishes to extend its life and thus have additional sittings or meetings under it, so as not to have to wait until the next regular session to complete the desired business, which may be two weeks away, or as much as a year (as in annual town meetings and conventions). In such a case, a motion can be made at the current meeting designating an additional sitting (technically called "adjourned meeting") for the continuation of its business. If this motion prevails, the body has "fixed an adjourned meeting" for the purpose, and reconvenes on that day. In such case, the adjourned meeting is part of the same, original session.

In parliamentary law, there is no such motion as "I move to designate . . . [another day] to which to continue the current session"; the correct motion for that purpose is "I move that *when* we adjourn we adjourn to meet on . . ." (specify day), and this is the motion used in enlightened parliamentary practice. But either form will do, because they are synonymous.

Basic rules. The privileged motion "to fix a day [time] to which to adjourn" requires a second and is amendable, but is not debatable. It requires a majority vote for adoption. It is a privileged motion of the highest rank, and can be reconsidered.

It can be proposed even when the motion to adjourn is pending, because it outranks it; and it can be proposed even after it has been voted to adjourn, provided the meeting has not been actually declared adjourned by the Chair.

How proposed. While the motion itself is called a motion to fix a day (or time) to which to adjourn, the actual language or form of this motion, when proposed, is as follows:

KEY QUIZ

Q. Is the motion "to fix a day to which to adjourn" secondable? *A.* Yes.
Q. Is it debatable? *A.* No; not as a privileged motion.
Q. Is it amendable? *A.* Yes.
Q. What vote adopts it? *A.* Majority.
Q. What class of motion is it and what is its rank? *A.* It is a privileged motion having highest rank.
Q. Can it be reconsidered? *A.* Yes.
Q. Does *this* motion adjourn (*end*) the sitting? *A.* No.

MEMBER: "Mr. Chairman, I move that when we adjourn, we adjourn to meet . . ." (specify time, such as "a week from tonight").

Its adoption thus designates the date for continuing the present meeting's business, and both of these meetings constitute one and the same session — as if there were no cessation of business at all.

What times cannot be specified. The motion is out of order if it fixes a time that falls beyond the next regular meeting; it is in order only when it fixes a time which falls between the present meeting and the next known or stated meeting.

It is not in order to fix a time to which to adjourn for the same day or the next day of the current meeting. (Recess is the proper proceeding.)

What business can be considered in adjourned meetings, regular or special. In any adjourned meeting of either a regular or special meeting, any business which would have been proper to consider at that meeting may be considered and acted on at the adjourned meeting. In other words, nothing can be considered at an adjourned meeting unless it could have been considered and acted on at the original meeting.

Adjourned meetings resume business under the same officers and the same rules, limitations and rights as the original meeting.

Does not mean adjournment of present meeting. If the motion to "fix an adjourned [continued] meeting" is carried, the meeting is not adjourned, because this motion does not adjourn a meeting; it merely designates another day on which to meet again.

When it becomes a main motion. "To fix a time to which to adjourn" is a privileged motion (with the rank of highest of its class), *if* proposed when other business is actually pending before the body. If proposed when no other business is before the body, it loses its status of privileged motion and automatically becomes a main motion, technically known as an incidental main motion, and is subject to the same rules as any other main motion.

Legal without notice to members. Legally, members are bound to take notice of such adjournments and to be present at the time and place thereof without renewed notice to them. Hence, it is not required that additional notices be mailed by the secretary to announce this adjourned meeting. However, it is good policy to do so. But if it is neglected or omitted it does not render the business of the adjourned meeting illegal or null and void, provided a quorum is present.

Chapter 9
INCIDENTAL MOTIONS

There is a class of motions in parliamentary procedure known as "incidental motions," so called because they are incidental to, or arise out of, a motion on which they have a bearing — as, for example, when a point of order is raised pertaining to a pending motion, or when information about it is asked for. They are as follows:

Note: *Starred motions in the following list may be raised (whenever applicable) upon any question or motion whatsoever, regardless of rank.

Incidental motions have no rank or order of precedence among themselves. They are in order when they logically pertain to any motion before the body. They are each individually decided as each one is raised. Each one will be treated separately below beginning with the motion known as a "point of order."

POINT OF ORDER

A question of order, or point of order, is raised when there is a violation of the rules of order, or of the bylaws, or the laws of the land, or the mandates or rules of a higher or superior body; or, generally, any violation occurring in the course of the proceedings, as when a member is not speaking on the motion before the body. A *proper* point of order can interrupt a speaker. It is raised to insure orderly procedure.

Members often call this motion "a point of clarification."

Note: A point of order should first be raised before there can be any appeal from any improper decision of the Chair.

How proposed and entertained. Assume before the body the following motion:

MAIN MOTION: "To endorse Mr. A for mayor."

CHAIR: "Is there any discussion?"

MEMBER: "Mr. Chairman, I rise to a point of order." (He pauses until the Chair asks him to state it.)

CHAIR: "The member will state his point of order."

MEMBER: "It seems to me the main motion before the body is out of order because it violates our bylaws. As I remember it, under Article X of the bylaws, endorsements of candidates for political office are prohibited." (Sits.)

CHAIR: "The Chair is looking it up." (He then reads from the bylaws:) "Section 1 of Article X reads as follows: 'This organization shall be nonpartisan in politics and shall not endorse candidates for public office.' This provision is clear and unmistakable; it prohibits endorsements of candidates for political office. Therefore, the point of order is well taken; the Chair was in error in entertaining the main motion; and the motion to endorse Mr. A is out of order.''

Note: Since this is the *law* under Article X, the Chair's decision is not appealable. No appeals can be taken from matters of *law*, or from *facts, truths* or *rules*. Instead, if a bylaw or rule is objectionable, *amend* it canonically.

Basic rules. A point of order needs no second, and, strictly speaking, is not debatable or amendable; and it is not put to vote, because the Chair usually decides it. But if the Chair is in doubt, he may consult the parliamentarian or some other member of experience for advice, or submit it to the body for a decision.

When submitting it to the assembly, he says: "The Chair is in doubt whether the motion just proposed is in order. The Chair would like to submit it to the body for decision." (After debate, or exchange of views on it, he puts it to vote:) "Those who are of opinion that it *is* in order will say aye. Those who are of *contrary* opinion will say no. The ayes [or, noes] have it, and the motion is [or, is not] in order.''

If the Chair rules that the point of order is well taken, the violation comes to an immediate end; but if the Chair decides that the point of order is not well taken, the proceeding continues. An appeal may be made in either case.

A member can appeal from the Chair's decision, but no appeal is possible from the decision of the body itself, unless an appeal to a higher body is authorized by a bylaw or existing rule.

The vote on the appeal can be reconsidered.

When a point of order is raised, the speaker interrupted is supposed to resume his seat but does not lose his right to the floor by such interruption if the point of order is ruled not well taken or is not sustained.

It is an incidental motion, and can be raised against any proceeding or motion deemed in violation of the pending proceeding or of the rules of procedure, bylaws, etc.

A point of order must be raised at the time of the violation or breach. If any other business has intervened, it is too late to propound a point of order.

Failure to raise the point of order that an amendment to a motion violates parliamentary law does not render such amendment or motion inoperative or invalid after adoption. But, whether a point of order is raised or not, all motions or action in violation of the bylaws are null and void automatically.

A *proper* point of order automatically interrupts a speaker.

KEY QUIZ

Q. Does a point of order require a second? *A.* No.
Q. Is it debatable? *A.* No, except by the Chairman.
Q. Is it amendable? *A.* No.
Q. Is it voted on? *A.* No.
Q. Who decides the point of order? *A.* The Chair.
Q. Is it a motion, and if so, what is its class? *A.* It is an incidental motion.
Q. Can it interrupt a speaker? *A.* Yes, if it is a proper one.

Note: Answers to parliamentary inquiries or to information are not decisions, hence not appealable. But it is clever first to raise a question of information to ascertain the Chair's viewpoint, then make a point of order from which you can subsequently appeal if the Chair's decision is adverse to you.

Abuse of point of order. Points of order are often proposed intentionally to confuse or to take the floor away from one who is speaking. This is unparliamentary, and the Chair should always be on his guard to protect members equally in this respect. A member who wishes to discuss a motion or to correct a misstatement should wait until the speaker has finished and the floor is free, and then rise to take the floor for the purpose.

Frivolous or dilatory points of order. Frivolous or dilatory points of order can be laid on the table without taking to the table the question out of which they arise. Usually (but not always), the Chair awaits a further point of order from the floor before directly acting on a frivolous or dilatory point of order; but if it is not so raised, he may do so, for it is his duty to enforce the body's rules.

Debatability of a point of order. Points of order are not debatable (except by the Chair and the member who propounds it, who may explain their reasons). No others may debate it unless recognized by the Chair because he needs information, or unless the Chair submits it to the body for fuller discussion.

May be withdrawn. A point of order may be withdrawn before decision on it; but when so withdrawn, another member may immediately raise it, so as to get a decision on it.

Further point of order. A point of order having been made and overruled on a particular phase of a question, a further point of order on a different phase of that question is in order.

Chair's role when points of order are raised. Here is what the Chair must do when a point of order is raised:

When a member rises to a point of order, the Chair says: "The member will please state his point of order." Then he listens to what the member has to say. If he cannot hear or understand his point of order, he says: "Will you [or, will the member] repeat the point of order?"

After hearing it, the Chair must judge (he must not dodge it), as follows: Did the member raise a sound or *proper* point of order? Is he right?

If he is, the Chair says: "The point of order is well taken," and he orders the violation to stop immediately.

On the other hand, if the member did not point out any violation — in other words, if the member is wrong — the Chair says: "The point of order is not well taken," and the interrupted business continues.

Point of order, it must be remembered, was created by the founders of parliamentary law to prevent violation of the rules and misuse of proceedings. Therefore, when genuine or proper points of order are raised by members in an effort to call attention to some breach or violation in the course of the proceedings, presiding officers are expected to take notice of them and to rule without delay or evasion that "the point of order is well taken," or that "it is not well taken."

If a presiding officer is unfamiliar with the requirements of this simple proceeding, it is his duty to study it, as given herein, so that confusion and injustice can be minimized or avoided.

The Chair may require a point of order to be presented in writing when needed for clarity.

The greatest abuse on points of order in ordinary assemblies arises from a member's anxiety or design to take the floor away from one who possesses it legally. In such cases, the Chair should quickly say to the interrupting member: "The point of order is not a proper one; it is debate. Points of order may not be raised to seize the floor from other members" (or like words).

PARLIAMENTARY INQUIRY

This motion is correctly known as "question of parliamentary inquiry."

A parliamentary inquiry is properly used when a member rises to ask for information on parliamentary procedure, such as, "What vote does the motion require?" "Is an amendment to the motion now in order?" "Is the motion to recess [or adjourn] debatable?" It cannot interrupt a speaker without his consent. Replies by the Chair to such inquiries are not appealable.

Basic rules. Since the object of a parliamentary inquiry is to obtain information or guidance on procedure, and since it is the duty of the chairman to *know* procedure and be able to inform the members thereon, a parliamentary inquiry is directed to the Chair. It cannot interrupt a speaker, as can a legitimate point of order, except with his consent. If the member speaking will not be interrupted, the Chair should not entertain the inquiry until the speaker has concluded, as the speaker must not be unduly interrupted by the raising of such inquiries, which sometimes can be endless. It is an incidental motion, and can be proposed on motions pertinent to questions before the body regardless of their rank.

How proposed and entertained

MEMBER: "Mr. Chairman, I rise to a question of parliamentary inquiry." (Pause. The Chair should then say:)

CHAIR: "The member will state his question of parliamentary inquiry" (or simply "his inquiry").

MEMBER: "What vote does the motion to postpone require?"

CHAIR: "The motion to postpone requires a majority vote." (And this ends the matter.)

KEY QUIZ

Q. Does a parliamentary inquiry need a second? A. No.
Q. Is it debatable? A. No.
Q. Is it amendable? A. No.
Q. Is it voted on? A. No.
Q. Who decides it? A. The Chair.
Q. What class of motion is it? A. Incidental.
Q. May it interrupt a speaker? A. No, except with his consent. A speaker who does not want thus to be interrupted need only call out, "Mr. Chairman, I do not yield the floor."

INFORMATION

This motion, correctly known as "question of information," is used when it is desired to ask a question on the merits, or *contents*, of the motion itself, such as "How much will it cost?" "Who will buy it for us?" "Is it new or secondhand?" It cannot interrupt a speaker without his consent.

A speaker who will not be interrupted need only call out: "Mr. Chairman, I do not yield the floor."

How proposed and entertained

MAIN MOTION: "To buy a new desk."

MEMBER A: "Mr. Chairman, I rise for information" or "I rise to a question of information" (some members call it "point of clarification").

CHAIR: "The member will state his question of information."

MEMBER A: "How much will it cost?"

CHAIR (looking in the direction of the maker of the motion): "Can the maker of the motion enlighten the member?"

MAKER OF MOTION: "I don't believe it should cost over fifty dollars."

This ends the question; additional questions can be asked.

The Chair should not ask inquiring members: "Does that answer your question?" Or, "Are you satisfied with the answer?" etc. This is being overly "nice," and is superfluous; it delays business, and it usually provokes additional and often unnecessary inquiries. The Chair should, instead, proceed with business.

When speaker yields the floor.

Under enlightened parliamentary practice, all questions of information and replies made by the yielder of the floor and the yieldee are addressed through the Chair, as follows:

MEMBER F (who has the floor): "This is a good motion, and I will explain why. In the first pl —" (interrupted by Member G).

MEMBER G: "Mr. Chairman, I rise to a question of information."

CHAIR (knowing he must have F's consent to interrupt him, he looks at F and asks him): "Does the member yield?"

MEMBER F (sees who it is): "I yield for a question only."

MEMBER G: "Mr. Chairman, who can get the discount for us?"

MEMBER F: "Mr. Chairman, it so happens our treasurer is the vice president of that TV Company, and he can get us the discount."

MEMBER G: "Mr. Chairman, how much discount?"

MEMBER F: "Mr. Chairman, thirty percent. Mr. Chairman, I do not yield the floor further," and F then continues his debate since he still has the floor.

KEY QUIZ

Q. Is this motion secondable? *A.* No.
Q. Is it debatable? *A.* No.
Q. Is it amendable? *A.* No.
Q. Is it put to vote? *A.* No.
Q. What kind of motion is it? *A.* Incidental.
Q. Can it interrupt a speaker? *A.* Only with his consent.
Q. What does the speaker say? *A.* "I yield," or "I do not yield."
Q. Are answers to a question of information appealable? *A.* No.

Note: When you yield the floor you relinquish it for all purposes, strictly speaking, unless you restrict it, as in the above case. Hence, whoever receives the floor unrestrictedly can use up all of the yielder's remaining time for debate, or make any proper motion — such as an amendment to a pending motion, or a motion to adjourn. You can also shut off further inquiries or questions if you still have the floor, as shown in the above drill.

When speaker refuses to yield the floor.

MEMBER H (who has the floor): "Other organizations would love to have this applicant. Why then are we . . ." (interrupted).

MEMBER J: "Mr. Chairman, will the member yield?"

CHAIR: "Does the member yield?"

MEMBER H (seeing who it is): "No, Mr. Chairman, I cannot yield," or "I regret I cannot yield at the moment," or "I am about to conclude and he can then have the floor," or "I will yield in a moment as I do not wish to interrupt my train of thought right now," or "I yield for one question only and for no other purpose," etc.

Speaker can yield time to another. A member who has original control of the floor for debate may yield any portion of his allotted time to another member for purpose of debate; as, for instance:

MEMBER X: "Mr. Chairman, will the speaker yield?"

MEMBER K: "Mr. Chairman, I yield two minutes of my debate to Member X." (Make sure beforehand that the Chair is aware of this right. Such practice is common in legislatures, but in ordinary assemblies it is virtually unknown and is scarcely ever practiced; members are not familiar with it.)

Note: One who debates on someone else's time is not charged with having had his own rightful turn at debate. Hence he is still entitled to the floor in his own right, if debate is not closed.

Distinction between parliamentary inquiry and question of information. Parliamentary inquiry is properly used when guidance is desired on parliamentary procedure. Question of information is used when it is desired to inquire into the contents of a pending motion. The former is asked of the Chair, who is expected to know parliamentary law and to guide members thereon; the latter is asked, through the Chair, of the maker of the pending motion.

APPEAL FROM A DECISION OF THE CHAIR (S, D, M, R)

The right of members to appeal from a ruling or decision of the Chair protects the assembly against the arbitrary control of the meeting by its presiding officer.

Therefore, when a member is dissatisfied with the Chair's ruling on an essential question, he has the right to appeal to the body to decide the merit of the Chair's decision. A decision by the Chair has to be rendered first.

To appeal to the body means to ask the body to judge the matter in dispute.

When appeals are made. Appeals from the decision of the Chair most often arise out of the following circumstances in which the decision is a matter of opinion or deviation from proper procedure: (a) if the Chair misassigns the floor or incorrectly recognizes a member, such as if he gave the floor to B when A should have been recognized; (b) if the Chair rules on a motion as not within the scope of the organization's purposes; (c) when the Chair rules on germaneness of an amendment; (d) when he rules on points of order and questions of privilege; (e) when he rules on the interpretation of words, phrases, provision, etc.; (f) when the Chair misapplies the rules of a motion, as when he entertains a motion of lower rank over a pending motion of higher rank, or refuses to entertain a higher ranking motion over a pending lower ranking motion — as often happens when chairmen do not know the rank of motions.

Basic rules. The appeal must first be seconded before the Chair can entertain it. Appeals are debatable if the motion out of which they arise is debatable at the time. They are not amendable. They may not interrupt a speaker. Appeals require a majority vote to reverse the Chair's ruling, and the vote on an appeal can be reconsidered.

An appeal can be made from any decision of the Chair on essential questions; but it must be made immediately after the Chair renders his decision. It is too late to appeal if other business or motion whatever has intervened.

How proposed and entertained. Assume this motion before the body:

MAIN MOTION: "To buy a new desk for the secretary."

MEMBER: "Mr. Chairman, I move to amend the motion by adding at the end thereof the words 'and paint our meeting room green.'"

CHAIR: "The amendment just proposed is out of order because it is not germane to the subject matter of the main motion."

Note: Whether amendments to a motion are *germane* or not is a matter of judgment or opinion; hence appealable.

MEMBER: "I appeal from the Chair's ruling [or, decision]." (Seconded.)

CHAIR (note the Chair's direct and simple language): "It has been moved and seconded to appeal from the decision of the Chair." (Then he adds:) "The question before the body now is, 'Shall the *decision* of the Chair be sustained [or, upheld]?' Is there any debate?"

Here, now, under debate, the Chair is first entitled to debate it, if he wants to, in defense of his decision, giving his reasons for the ruling;

KEY QUIZ

Q. Must an appeal be seconded? *A.* Yes.

Q. Is it debatable? *A.* Yes.

Q. Is it amendable? *A.* No.

Q. What vote reverses the Chair's decision? *A.* A majority vote against it.

Q. On a tie vote is his decision reversed? *A.* No; it is sustained; a *tie* vote is not a *majority* against it.

Q. What is put to vote, the member's appeal or the Chair's decision? *A.* The Chair's decision.

Q. Can the Chair debate it? *A.* Yes, in order to give reasons.

Q. Must he leave the chair to debate it? *A.* No, unless he wants to, or unless the bylaws require it.

Q. Can the Chair vote on it? *A.* Yes, if he wants to.

Q. What class of motion is "appeal?" *A.* Incidental.

Q. Can the vote on an appeal be reconsidered? *A.* Yes.

then any member may discuss it (just once), giving his reasons pro or con; and when all debate has ended, the vote:

CHAIR (continuing): "There being no further debate, those in favor of *sustaining* the decision of the Chair will say aye; those opposed, will say no. The ayes have it, and the decision is sustained," or "The noes have it, and the decision is *not* sustained," as the case may be.

If the Chair's decision is upheld, the above proposed amendment is not entertained; but if the Chair's decision is not sustained, the amendment is then entertained (notwithstanding the fact that this amendment is clearly *not* germane; the *body* has the final say).

Other forms of putting Chair's decision to vote. The modern form, "Shall the decision of the Chair be sustained?" is not the only form of putting to vote the Chair's decision on an appeal. This old English form is still in good use: "Shall the decision of the Chair stand as the judgment of the assembly?" (Observe the word "decision" is used in both cases, not "appeal.")

Note: Experience has shown that in ordinary assemblies the two forms just stated are not instantly understood and members are confused. In such cases, use any one of the following forms instead: "Shall the Chair's decision be approved?" Or, "Shall the decision of the Chair be upheld?" Or, "Shall the decision of the Chair be accepted?" Or, "Is the Chair right?" Or, "Is the Chair's ruling correct?"

Voting on appeals. In all cases of appeals from the Chair's decision, the proceeding to be voted on is the Chair's decision, and not the member's appeal. Yet in many bodies the member's appeal is (erroneously but sometimes conveniently) put to vote.

When the *appeal* is put to vote, instead of the Chair's *decision*, a different vote decides the question; namely:

(1) If the question put to a vote is, "Shall the *decision* of the Chair be sustained (approved)?" it takes a majority vote in the *negative* to reverse the decision. Hence, if a *tie* vote results in such a case, the decision is sustained.

(2) But if the member's *appeal* is put to vote, instead of the Chair's decision (as is often the case), then a majority vote in the *affirmative* is necessary to approve the *appeal*. Hence, if a tie vote results, the appeal is disapproved (since a tie vote is not a majority vote in favor of it).

The Chair has the right to vote in either case.

Note: Appeals confuse members more than any other parliamentary proceeding — but not in legislative bodies. Hence, presiding officers in ordinary assemblies must make thoroughly clear and intelligible *what* the members are voting on in appeals from rulings.

Right of Chair and members to debate an appeal. The rules for debating an appeal from the Chair's decision *differ* both for the Chair and for the members from the rules for debating any other question; namely: the Chair, without surrendering the gavel, is entitled to debate an appeal from his decision (in self-defense, so to speak — in defense of his ruling) as many as *two* times (at the beginning, to give his reasons, and at the end, to answer arguments advanced by opponents). The members may discuss the appeal only *once*. On debatable questions other than appeals the Chair may not debate motions unless he first surrenders the chair (or if no one objects), and the members may speak thereon as many as *two* times.

Rank of the appeal. In point of rank, an appeal cannot be postponed indefinitely, amended or referred to a committee; but it can be postponed *definitely*, in which case it yields to the motions to limit debate, the previous question and to lay on the table, and also to privileged motions and to apt incidental motions (such as a point of order, or a motion to have the vote on it taken by ballot, etc.). See pp. 47–48.

When the body, despite the rule that an appeal cannot be referred, votes to refer the appeal to its board (or other authority) with intent to obtain a more enlightened opinion on the Chair's ruling, as bodies sometimes do, or when the appeal is postponed temporarily with intent to take it under advisement and report on it later, then the appeal and its question go to the board or to the postponement stage, as the case may be, and consideration thereof is not resumed until the board's opinion or the awaited report is again before the body. This is so because the body's *intent* overpowers the *form* of parliamentary practice.

If, however, the body votes to lay on the table a pending appeal, then only the *appeal* is tabled; the question out of which it arises does *not* go to the table with the appeal — unless the appeal is from a ruling of the Chair involving the germaneness of an amendment to a question, in which case *both* the appeal and the amendment are laid on the table with the question.

Accordingly, in all other respects *tabling* the appeal (in practice usually proposed by a member favorable to the Chair's ruling) has the parliamentary and legislative effect of upholding the Chair's ruling and rejecting the appeal, in which case the said appeal is ignored and the pending question is then disposed of in due course.

Note: For illustrations of appeals that are tablable separately from their question, see "*When an appeal is not debatable*" further on.

One appeal at a time. When a pending question has an appeal adhering to it, a second appeal is not entertained on the *same* question until the pending appeal on that question has first been disposed of. This can occur when, for example, successive amendments to the same question are erroneously ruled admissible or inadmissible, and aggrieved members appeal from the Chair's rulings on that pending same question or motion.

More than one appeal when arising out of proceedings of higher rank. The fact that only one appeal at a time can be considered does not mean that additional appeals may not be pending when they canonically arise out of successive *pending* proceedings that have higher rank than the immediately pending one.

For instance, if a main motion has an appeal pending with it when the motion to limit debate is made (which motion outranks the pending main motion and its appeal), if an amendment to the motion to limit debate is overruled by the Chair and the aggrieved member appeals, you then properly have *two* appeals pending (one with the *main* motion, and one with the motion to *limit* debate, in accordance with their canonical rank).

Moreover, if, while the above two motions and the two appeals are pending, the motion to "fix a day to which to adjourn" is proposed (which is of higher rank than both of the *pending* motions and their respective appeals), and an amendment to *it* is overruled by the Chair, should the aggrieved member appeal from the Chair's ruling you will then have *three* different appeals properly pending before the body, because each one is canonically pending with, or adheres to, its respective motion of *higher* rank. Each one is then decided in turn.

When appeal is not debatable. An appeal is not debatable (1) if taken after the body has voted to shut off further debate; (2) if the immediately pending question is itself undebatable; (3) when it relates to transgression of the rules of debate, as when a member violates the rules of debate by insisting on speaking more than the prescribed *length* of time, or he insists on speaking more than twice on the same question the same day; (4) if it relates to indecorum, as when a member is directed to sit down for uttering offensive words or for disorderly or obnoxious conduct, or for failure to confine himself to the pending question; (5) when it reflects derogatorily upon an act of the assembly, or arraigns or denounces the motives of members, or otherwise indulges in personalities or ignominies; (6) when it is obviously dilatory; (7) if made during a division of the assembly or during a roll call; (8) on replies to parliamentary inquiries, or questions of information; (9) on the same question on which an appeal has just been decided.

In other words, if an appeal arises under any one of the above proceedings it is undebatable, because its goals are good order, discipline and law and order; to allow debate would be incompatible with these goals.

Note: The above instances of appeal-taking are good illustrations of appeals which can be laid on the table *without* taking to the table the question out of which they arise. Hence, each such appeal *can* be tabled by itself; and if it is tabled by majority vote, or by general consent, only the appeal is banished.

When an appeal is debatable. Outside of the few instances enumerated under which an appeal is not debatable, all other appeals which normally arise out of main motions, resolutions, recommendations, town articles, and other main propositions in the course of parliamentary practice *are* debatable.

It is far more important for members to remember that in general *all* appeals from rulings of the Chair are debatable, than it is to remember the few specific instances under which an appeal is not debatable. Therefore, when in doubt, always regard the appeal as being debatable. And if it is not then desired to have debate on it, simply move the previous question (thus shutting off debate) or (better still and quicker) move to table the appeal (thus banishing it for good).

Note: Under enlightened parliamentary practice, no appeal from a ruling is entertained unless a point of order is first raised, so as to thus establish valid ground for taking up the appeal.

If an appeal arises after debate has been voted *limited* to, say, one or two minutes a member, the appeal is then debatable one or two minutes; and if the previous question is then ordered upon it, the appeal then becomes undebatable.

The Chair may vote on appeals, or he may vote to sustain his decision thereon; and it is within his discretion whether he will vacate the chair on an appeal, unless in either case a bylaw compels otherwise.

If a ruling or appeal becomes personal, factional or otherwise quarrelsome, to prevent disunity or disruption take the vote on the appeal by secret ballot, and thus save face all around; or, move to *table* the appeal, and thus banish it by majority vote.

An appeal may be withdrawn at any time before final action on it.

No appeals taken from laws, facts, or rules. Appeals from the Chair's rulings can be taken only on questions involving the exercise of his personal judgment or opinion and not on those involving the operation of existing laws, established facts, known truths, or existing rules.

Matters of opinion can be corrected on the spot by the assembly, whereas matters of law, or rules and bylaws, can be corrected or changed only through the organization's prescribed *amending* process.

Nor can appeals be taken from known facts, evident truths or established rules, because they are self-evident or uncontradictable (such as: 2 and 2 equal 4; the ball is round; the week has seven days; snow melts), nor from established rules of parliamentary law (such as: main motions are debatable; to adjourn requires a majority vote; the subsidiary motion to table supersedes the motion to postpone, etc.).

One way of remembering the general rule that no appeals can be taken from the Chair's rulings which arise out of known Facts, evident Truths, established Rules or operative Laws, but can be taken only from rulings which are based on his personal Judgment, Opinion or Discretion, is by the first letters thereof: F, T, R, L and J, O, D.

Examples of appeals that cannot be entertained

MEMBER B: "Mr. Chairman, what vote adopts adjournment?"
CHAIR: "Majority vote."
MEMBER B: "I appeal from your decision; it needs a $\frac{2}{3}$ vote."
CHAIR: "The appeal cannot be entertained; the rule says majority."
MEMBER C: "Madam Chairman, how many delegates can we elect?"
CHAIR: "Article nine states: 'nine delegates shall be elected.' "
MEMBER C: "Madam Chairman, I move that we elect eleven instead."
CHAIR: "The motion is out of order; it violates the bylaw."
MEMBER C: "Madam Chairman, I appeal from your ruling."
CHAIR: "The appeal is out of order; the bylaw is inviolable."
MEMBER D: "Madam Chairman, is the motion to postpone debatable?"
CHAIR: "Yes."
MEMBER D: "I appeal from your decision; it is not debatable."
CHAIR: "The appeal is out of order; the rule says it is."
MEMBER E: "Mr. Chairman, how many months has the year?"
CHAIR: "Twelve."
MEMBER E: "I appeal from your ruling; it has eleven months."
CHAIR (calmly, patiently): "The appeal is out of order. The calendar says twelve months."

In other words, if you were presiding in the above instances and such appeals were taken, should you waste the assembly's time or affront its intelligence by submitting such absurd appeals to the members to back up your rulings — that there are seven days in the week, or twelve months in the year, or the main motion can be debated, or any other law or rule, or any self-evident and incontestable facts?

Note: Robert applies the above doctrine thus: "The Chair should not entertain an appeal from a decision to which there can be no two rational opinions." Also, "The case is so plain that the Chair cannot entertain the appeal."

SUSPEND THE RULES (S, ⅔)

For all practical purposes in ordinary assemblies, the motion to suspend the rules is made when it is desired (*a*) to suspend temporarily the operation of some standing rule (not a bylaw, however) or an act of the assembly previously passed which is still in force; or (*b* to take up out of turn some particular business ahead of other items in the scheduled agenda or order of business.

Basic rules. Suspension of the rules requires a second; it is not debatable or amendable; it needs a ⅔ vote for adoption. It cannot be reconsidered.

It outranks all the subsidiary motions (p. 47) except to lay on the table; hence it can be tabled apart from, and *without* taking with it to the table, the question out of which it arises.

It yields, however, to apt incidental motions, and to all privileged motions except a call for the orders of the day (since such call sets up the orderly schedule of business, after which it is in order to move suspension of the rules, if so desired).

It also yields to special orders (but not to general orders).

Main motion or incidental motion. Suspension of the rules can be made either (1) when no other business is before the body (in which case it is a main motion — technically an incidental main motion — and it is so treated), or (2) while other business is actually pending, provided its proposal has to do with that pending business (in which case it is the genuine incidental motion to suspend).

How proposed and applied. (1) When a *standing rule* says, "A ten-minute recess shall follow the initiation," or "Refreshments shall not be served before eleven o'clock," by adopting suspension of the rule you eliminate the ten-minute recess that night, or the rule preventing service before eleven; or (2) when you wish to get to an item of business in the agenda (unfinished business for instance) ahead of other items that precede it, simply say: "Mr. Chairman, I move to suspend the rules and take up unfinished business"; and if this is adopted by a ⅔ vote, unfinished business is then taken up before the other items.

Note: If in illustration (2) you do not command a 2/3 vote to suspend the

---

KEY QUIZ

Q. Does this motion require a second? *A.* Yes.
Q. Is it debatable or amendable? *A.* No.
Q. What vote adopts suspension of the rules? *A.* Two-thirds.
Q. What class of motion is it? *A.* Incidental.
Q. Can it be reconsidered? *A.* No.
Q. Can you suspend the organization's bylaws? *A.* No.
Q. Can you suspend rights to give previous notices? *A.* No.

rules, but do control a majority vote, move to lay on the table (which needs only a majority vote) each intervening piece of business until your topic is reached. You and your adherents in such a move have that right; but by the same token opponents have the right to move to lay on the table your motion "to suspend the rules" and thus frustrate the proposed suspension, since the motion to suspend yields to the motion to table.

Unanimous consent for renewal. If suspension of the rules is defeated, it cannot be renewed for the same purpose at the same sitting except by unanimous consent.

Bylaws cannot be suspended. In general, essential rights of members secured to them in the bylaws may not be suspended, unless any suspension thereof is authorized therein.

If bylaws are illegally suspended. Bylaws cannot be suspended even by unanimous vote. But sometimes circumstances, expediency or strong assembly determination in behalf of a cause or proposition make violations necessary. In all such cases of violations, the action taken is illegal per se; but if no one objects at the time, or never challenges it at any time thereafter, a violation never challenged is never a violation.

CHOOSE THE METHOD OF VOTING (S, A, M, R)

The assembly can take the vote on a question by any method it desires, unless the bylaws prescribe or forbid a particular method.

Basic rules. A second (or more, if your bylaws specify) is required for the motion to vote by secret ballot or roll call. A motion proposing the method of voting is not debatable, but is amendable. It can be reconsidered.

How proposed and transacted

CHAIR: "Is there further debate on accepting X's resignation?"
MEMBER: "Mr. Chairman, I move that the vote on the resignation be

---

KEY QUIZ

Q. Which are the methods of voting that *never* require a *second? A.* Voice vote, show of hands, and rising vote.

Q. Is a second required on motions for secret ballot or roll call? *A.* Yes (unless agreed to by general consent; and in some cases more than one seconder is necessary, as the rules or bylaws may otherwise prescribe).

Q. Can the vote on a question be taken by absentee ballot, by mail or referendum, by proxy, telephone, etc? *A.* Yes, *if* authorized by the organization's bylaws; otherwise, no.

Q. What vote adopts voting by ballot or roll call (or the methods named in the preceding paragraph)? *A.* Basically, a majority vote (or by general consent).

Q. Are any of the above methods of voting debatable? *A.* No.

Q. Are any of them amendable? *A.* Yes (changing one form to another, as by changing a roll call vote to a secret ballot).

Q. Can you table a motion to vote by ballot or roll call? *A.* Yes.

Q. What class of motions are these motions? *A.* Incidental.

Q. Can a member who has to leave the meeting ask another member to cast his vote for him on an election, or other question? *A.* No, unless the bylaws expressly authorize such proxy voting.

taken by secret ballot" (or, "I move that when the vote on the resignation is taken it will be taken by *ballot*"). Seconded.

CHAIR: "It is moved and seconded . . ." (repeats the above motion, then puts it to vote to see if it is desired to take it by ballot; thus:) "Those in favor of a secret ballot will say aye; (response); those opposed will say no; the ayes have it, and the vote on the resignation will be taken by ballot."

CHAIR (continuing): "Is there further discussion on the resignation before it is put to a vote?" (After debate pro or con:) "There being no further debate, the Chair appoints M, N and O as tellers. The tellers will proceed to distribute the ballots, afterward collect and count them, and report back to the body through the Chair. Those in favor of the acceptance of the resignation will vote yes. Those opposed will vote no."

TELLER (reporting after the vote): "Mr. Chairman, the vote on the resignation is as follows: seventy-two votes were cast; thirty-seven affirmative votes were necessary. Fifty-nine votes were affirmative and thirteen were negative."

CHAIR: "There being fifty-nine votes for acceptance of the resignation and thirteen against, the resignation is accepted."

Rank of special voting methods. Motions to take the vote by ballot or roll call (which can be used in any and every organization, unless a bylaw therein expressly bars their use), and motions to take the vote by telephone, absentee voting, proxy, or by mail or referendum (if these processes are authorized by the organization's bylaws) yield to all the privileged motions.

They also yield to the motion to lay on the table. The above motions are subject to the motion to lay on the table because they waste time, they occasion expense, and they can also be obstructive.

Therefore, when any one of the above mentioned motions is voted *tabled*, it does *not* take to the table with it the question out of which it arises. Hence it can be tabled alone, and in such case the parliamentary effect is outright rejection of the voting method.

In other words, while, as stated above, you may have the right to offer the motion for a secret ballot, roll call, etc., other members have the right, in the interest of economy of time, expense, etc., to move to table your motion (by majority vote).

Note: The reason most organizations do not authorize voting by mail is because the process is both time-consuming and costly.

Voting by custom. A long-established usage or practice in the assembly's mode of voting has the force of law. Thus if voting has for years been conducted by mail, although the bylaws do not authorize voting by mail — or by proxy, or otherwise — such voting by mail and continuous custom has the force of law, and the proceedings are valid. And where members *mail* their ballot on a current election (as they have been doing uninterruptedly for years), their ballot is valid, and is counted as in previous elections. Hence, at the *current* election it is not in order to invalidate these ballots by mail, since the members who voted by mail would be wrongfully disfranchised, unless there was previous notice to the membership in the call for the meeting that "voting by mail will be objected to."

How many times a vote can be verified. A vote can be verified automatically if a member calls out "I doubt [or, I challenge the accuracy of] the vote," when the vote is taken by voice, by hand, or by rising.

To anticipate and discourage dilatory tactics on vote-taking, the Chair can say (in ordinary assemblies, not in legislative bodies), "Does any one doubt the accuracy of this count? If so let him count the hands." He does this for both negative and affirmative counts.

If the vote is not then questioned, or doubted, in either case, the Chair need not entertain another verification. But a member has then the right to move if he so chooses, to have the vote taken by ballot or by roll call (requires majority vote), so as to either conceal how members vote on a question or to put them on record. Hence the Chair cannot deny him the exercise of this right. But the body can table his motion or vote it down.

CLOSE NOMINATIONS (S, A, $\frac{2}{3}$)

Nominations can be closed in three ways: (1) on motion of a member; (2) on the initiative of the Chair (with silent or general consent); (3) as prescribed in the bylaws.

Basic rules. The motion to close nominations is secondable and amendable, but not debatable. It requires a $\frac{2}{3}$ vote if it is put to a formal vote (two-thirds because it deprives members of their right to continue to nominate further). It is an incidental motion, and it cannot be reconsidered.

How proposed and transacted. Nominations must not be closed hastily. Sufficient time must be afforded to others to nominate. Usually, when the Chair asks, "Are there any further nominations before closing them?" and no one nominates further, then the Chair may close them by general or silent consent, thus: "There being no further nominations [pause], nominations are closed"; or on motion of a member, thus:

MEMBER: "Mr. Chairman, I move that nominations close." (Seconded.)

CHAIR: "It is moved and seconded to close nominations; those in favor will raise their right hand; forty-seven, hands down; those opposed will raise their right hand; none; there being two-thirds in favor, the motion is carried and nominations are closed."

Before closing nominations or entertaining a motion to close them, it is good practice for the Chair to say, "If there are any further nominations, *now* is the time to make them; are there any further nominations?" If no one then rises to nominate, nominations are announced closed, or a motion to that effect is entertained.

KEY QUIZ

Q. Does the motion to close nominations require a second?   *A.* Yes.
Q. Is it debatable?   *A.* No.
Q. Is it amendable?   *A.* Yes.
Q. What vote adopts it?   *A.* Two-thirds.
Q. What class of motion is it?   *A.* Incidental.
Q. Can it be reconsidered?   *A.* No.

Does not elect. Adopting the motion to *close* nominations does not elect any nominee(s); the nominee(s) must still be voted on, regardless.

Binding only for same meeting. When it is voted to close nominations at a meeting, such closure binds only the assembly of *that* meeting. Hence, if the election is held at the next meeting, nominations are automatically open at such next meeting, unless the bylaws expressly provide that "Nominations shall not remain open at the next meeting," or similar words.

The fact that the bylaws say that nominations shall not be made at the next meeting does not mean you cannot *vote* for anyone not previously nominated. It is only when your bylaws say that "Anyone not *previously* nominated shall not be voted on, and such vote shall be void," that you may not vote for anyone not previously nominated, because your vote will be void.

REOPEN NOMINATIONS (S, A, M, R)

While the motion to *close* nominations requires a ⅔ vote, the motion to reopen nominations requires only a majority vote (since it restores to members their rights to nominate further). A negative vote on this motion can be reconsidered, but not an affirmative one. To reopen nominations requires a second and is amendable, but it is not debatable. Nominations cannot be reopened when collection of the ballot has commenced.

Both the motion to close nominations and to reopen nominations yield to privileged motions (p. 47). Except that they can be amended, no other subsidiary motion can apply to them.

CLOSE THE POLLS (S, A, ⅔)

When time nears for closing the polls, or when a ballot vote is being taken on a question in assembly, the Chair should remind the members, or urge them somewhat as follows: "As previously voted, the polls will close in five minutes; if anyone has not yet voted he should do so promptly"; or "Have all voted who wish to do so?" In due course he says, "All having voted, the polls are now closed, and the tellers will proceed to collect the ballots"; or a motion to close the polls is made by a member.

If the place where the votes are cast is outside the meeting room itself (as in conventions), all members who are inside the polling place before the time fixed for closing the polls, or before the doors thereof are locked, are entitled to vote.

If the time for closing the polls has been fixed in the order of business, program, or agenda, and if it is desired to extend the time to, for instance, ten minutes more, this can be done by a ⅔ vote of the assembly.

In general, the rules that apply to closing nominations also apply to closing the polls, except as otherwise specified above.

REOPEN THE POLLS (S, A, M, R)

Members entering the meeting room after the polls have been voted closed, or voting has been closed, are not entitled to vote unless a motion is made to reopen the polls, or to open further voting.

Such a motion requires a second and is not debatable, but it is amendable. It requires a majority vote. A negative vote on it can be reconsidered, but not an affirmative one.

It is too late to reopen the polls if the ballots have been collected or have been removed from the ballot box.

DIVISION OF A QUESTION (S, A, **M**)

This motion is often known as a motion "to divide a question."

It is just as proper for a member to propose or set forth two or more subjects in one motion (instead of a separate motion for *each* subject) as it is for a person to set out to do two or more errands in one trip (rather than make a separate trip for each one).

In parliamentary practice, if a member's motion is deemed complicated, lengthy, or controversial, any member may move to divide the question, that is, to separate the parts of such question so that each part may be voted on individually to avoid confusion.

If a member's motion (however lengthy or complicated) presents no problem to the body, and the body can readily comprehend it and can dispose of it, there is no need to divide the question.

Note: Where parts of a question are deemed undesirable, contentious or unwise, instead of moving to *divide* the question, move to *amend* it by striking out the objectionable parts.

Basic rules. The motion to divide a question primarily applies to main motions, amendments to them and to instructions to committees. All three cases can be lengthy and complicated, and the function of a division of question is to eliminate perplexity, confusion and conflict in the vote.

It is undebatable, but can be amended. It requires a second and a majority vote. It is an incidental motion. A question can be divided only if its contents are capable of logical and intelligible separation into independent parts. In other words, a member may demand a division of the question provided it includes propositions so distinct that if one is taken away, a substantive proposition still remains in the question.

If a motion or question is not composed of independent propositions capable of logical separation, the motion to divide is out of order.

The motion to divide outranks only the subsidiary motion to postpone indefinitely; it yields to the other subsidiary motions, to the privileged motions and to apt incidental motions; pp. 47, 48.

It is not debatable, but this does not prevent a brief word about why it is proposed (as in Member B's brief remark in the following drill).

It can be proposed at any time before the question is voted on.

If it is mischievously proposed, it can be laid on the table apart from the pending question (it yields to tablement).

It is not in order after a roll call vote has been ordered or a secret ballot has commenced.

How proposed and transacted

MEMBER A: "Mr. Chairman, I move that the treasurer be authorized to purchase a new flag, to order new lodge stationery and to have the meeting room painted green." (Seconded.)

Note: Although these three matters are individually unrelated, they jointly relate to the organization's *needs*; hence they are in order as one motion.

CHAIR: "It has been moved and seconded to authorize the treasurer to . . . [repeating the above motion]. Is there any discussion?"

MEMBER B: "Mr. Chairman, while I appreciate the fact that we can conserve time by including in one motion *three* different subjects, I fear that some members may favor one subject but not the other; therefore, to avoid unnecessary confusion and conflict in the vote, I move to divide the question, so we can vote first on buying the flag, then on the stationery, and lastly on painting the room."

If this motion is not seconded, it is not entertained. If it is seconded, it is transacted as shown below.

CHAIR: "It is moved and seconded to divide the question, so that each subject may be transacted separately. Those in favor of the division of the question will say aye; those opposed will say no; the ayes have it, and the question will now be divided." (He then puts each proposition to a separate vote; thus:) *"First,* those in favor of a new flag will say aye; those opposed will say no; the ayes have it. *Next,* those in favor of new stationery will say aye; those opposed will say no; the ayes have it. *Now,* those in favor of painting the meeting room green will say aye; those opposed will say no; the noes have it. The treasurer is authorized to buy a new flag and have stationery printed." (And this ends it.)

Distinction between dividing a question and dividing the assembly. To divide a question is to separate the parts of a complicated question so that each part may be voted on separately (as illustrated above), whereas the technical term "to divide the assembly" merely means "I doubt [or, I challenge] the vote just taken," in which case the Chair puts that motion to vote again for further verification.

DIVISION OF THE ASSEMBLY (OR, DOUBTING THE VOTE)

The technical phrase "to divide the assembly" merely means "I doubt the vote," or "I question the vote." The object of doubting the vote (calling for a division of the assembly) is to verify the accuracy of the vote.

The following phrases therefore are synonymous; all mean the same thing. They are the less pure forms for "I move to divide the assembly"; namely: "I doubt the vote," "I challenge the vote," "I demand [or, I call for] a division," or the simple outcry "Division!"

Hence, when a member says to the Chairman, "I move to divide the assembly" (as purists sometimes do), all he means is "I doubt the vote, take it over again!" and the Chair puts it to vote again.

How proposed and entertained. "I doubt the vote" will be used here in place of other terms.

CHAIR: "The ayes have it" or "The noes have it."

MEMBER: "I doubt the vote!"

CHAIR: "The vote is doubted." (He then puts it to vote again by a surer method than by voice; thus:) "Those in favor of the motion will raise their right hand." (Counts 15 aloud, so members can check the count with him, and says:) "Fifteen. Hands down, please. Those opposed will raise their right hand." (Counts aloud 13.) "Thirteen. Hands down." (He then adds:) "The affirmative has it."

If this vote is further doubted, as when a member says "I further doubt the vote," the motion is put to a standing vote.

If a member votes with his left hand instead of the right, the vote is valid in all cases. If both hands are raised, count them as one.

Where the vote is close, or the Chair is in doubt, he says: "The Chair is in doubt" (instead of "I doubt the vote"). It is the members who say, "I doubt the vote" (or I challenge, or question it).

Doubting either side. Where either the affirmative or negative count of the vote is wrong, call out: "I doubt the vote for the affirmative [or, negative] count," so that *that* side may be individually voted on again, thus:

CHAIR: "There are twenty votes in the affirmative."

ALERT MEMBER (who checked the vote for himself): "I doubt the affirmative vote!" (No second is needed.)

CHAIR: "The affirmative count of the vote is doubted." (He then takes it by a standing vote; thus:) "Those in favor of the motion will rise and stand until counted." (He counts the vote aloud and says:) "Twenty-one; the correct affirmative vote is twenty-one." (He continues:) "Those opposed will rise and stand until counted. Nineteen. The affirmative has it, and the motion is carried."

Doubting the negative vote is conducted in a parallel manner.

Sagacious leaders and shrewd members always count the vote for themselves, so they can challenge any error in the count.

How far members can go. Voting by voice, show of hands and standing vote are automatic processes of *open* voting. They are intended to enable all members to see how the other members vote on a motion. Theoretically, such open voting processes are tests of loyalty, courage and constancy.

Accordingly, a member has automatically the right (1) to doubt a voice vote (since he cannot identify the voices), and (2) to doubt also a hand vote (because a hand vote is often shifty and uncertain, and it does not readily identify the hands). He is not entitled, however, to doubt a verified standing vote (because a standing vote can be accurate and it readily discloses the identity of the voters).

Hence, a member can go as far as to doubt a *voice* vote and a *hand* vote; and the Chair should always honor a member's two such doubts, no matter how one-sided the vote may be.

A member, however, may always propose a secret ballot or a roll call in *any* instance, but these two motions have to be seconded and they

---

KEY QUIZ

Q. Who can doubt the vote on a motion? *A.* Any member.
Q. When can it be doubted? *A.* As soon as the Chair declares it.
Q. Does it require a second to "doubt the vote?" *A.* No.
Q. Is "doubting the vote" debatable or amendable? *A.* No.
Q. Can it be reconsidered? *A.* No; say "I *further* doubt it" instead.
Q. Can the call "I doubt the vote" be tabled? *A.* No.
Q. Can either side, affirmative or negative, be doubted if the declaration or the count of the vote is wrong? *A.* Yes.

require a majority vote for adoption (or such greater vote as the organization's bylaws or rules expressly provide); or they may be authorized by general consent (silent approval), in any case.

Must be doubted immediately. The doubting of a vote must be voiced immediately after the Chair announces the result, or when the vote is deemed finished (if the Chair fails to announce the result, as is often the case).

Use of secret ballot. When the members do not want to expose their vote to open view, they can always take the vote by secret ballot instead.

A vote taken by secret ballot can be reconsidered, in which case the vote on the reconsideration is also taken by secret ballot.

Use of roll call. A member has the right (by majority vote, unless the organization's laws otherwise provide) to have the vote on a question taken by roll call, and thus put the members on record.

Voting recorded in minutes. All votes taken by any method other than by voice should always be recorded in the minutes.

Note to Chairmen: Humans are not automatons. You must allow them a few seconds to rise normally to claim the floor, or to change their vote. Hence, if your announcement has been hasty or inconsiderate, the vote is void, and members may still change their vote. A substantive right may not be overthrown by a mere technical requirement. It is too late to change one's vote if more than a few seconds have elapsed or any matter whatever has intervened in any case.

Obstructive calls for division. When repeated calls doubting the vote are needlessly or mischievously made, the Chair, in the interest of orderly procedure, rules these calls dilatory or obstructive, the Chair saying: "The vote is clear and unmistakable and has already been verified twice; it is unnecessary to put it to vote again, as this retards business," or similar statement. Or he may re-put it to vote for a final time; or he may, in small assemblies, ask the objector to count the vote himself, or with him.

Doubting in order to change one's vote. A member has the right to doubt the vote so as to vote with the prevailing side on the "retake," and thus qualify to move reconsideration (at the strategic time). Members can change their vote from "yes" to "no," or the reverse. They must do so either (*a*) before the Chair announces the vote, or (*b*) as he is about to announce it, or (*c*) even if he has *just* announced it, or (*d*) if the vote was taken hurriedly.

Illustrations of doubting in order to change one's vote on (1) voice vote, (2) hand vote, (3) roll call vote.

(1) CHAIR: "The ayes [or the noes] have it" (interrupted by A).

MEMBER A: "I doubt the vote!" (No second is needed.)

CHAIR: "The vote has been doubted." He then puts it to vote by show of hands, and A then intentionally votes with the prevailing side (thus qualifying to duly move reconsideration).

(2) CHAIR: "There were twenty-seven hands in the affirmative and nine hands in the negative" (interrupted by B).

MEMBER B: "Mr. Chairman, I wish to change my vote; I voted with the negative [the 9]; I wish now to vote with the affirmative [the 27]."

(3) CHAIR: "On this roll call ninety-six voted in the affirmative and ninety-nine in the negative."

MEMBER C: "Mr. President, I desire to change my roll call vote; I previously voted in the affirmative [the 96]; I wish to be recorded as voting with the negative [the 99]."

CHAIR: "Mr. C having changed his vote, the verified roll call vote is ninety-five in the affirmative and one hundred in the negative. Therefore the negative has it, and the motion is lost."

OBJECT TO THE CONSIDERATION OF A QUESTION ($\frac{2}{3}$, R)

Objection to the consideration of a question is used when an original main motion is of a delicate or personal nature, or is contentious or inflammatory (such as sectarian, political, racial, etc.), or is irrelevant, unprofitable, or otherwise objectionable or discriminatory. The motion can be avoided altogether by instantly objecting to the consideration of the question.

Basic rules. This motion needs no second and is not debatable or amendable. It is in order provided it is made before there has been any discussion or amendment to the objectionable question. It is an incidental motion requiring a $\frac{2}{3}$ vote to be adopted. It is in order even if another member has the floor. It yields to the motion to lay on the table, but not to the other subsidiary motions (p. 47). It also yields to all the privileged motions (p. 47) and to apt incidental motions (p. 48).

An objection to the consideration of a question can properly be raised only against original main motions and resolutions, and not against parliamentary forms, such as, the subsidiary and privileged motions (p. 47), incidental motions, the restoratory motions (p. 48), or any motions in the nature of incidental main motions.

If no notice is taken that an original main motion is in fact objectionable, the vote taken thereon is valid. It is too late then to challenge or question the vote on the ground that the question was inflammatory or personal. But the vote on it can be reconsidered or be rescinded under due process of parliamentary law. Or, if it is too late to object to the consideration of a pending contentious question, move to lay the question on the table.

How proposed and transacted

MEMBER A: "Mr. Commander [or, Comrade Commander], I move that our first meeting in November be open only to those of our members who served in wars overseas." (Seconded.)

CHAIR: "It has been moved and seconded . . ." (repeats A's motion).

MEMBER B (instantly sensing the discrimination): "Mr. Commander, I object to the consideration of the question on the ground that it is discriminatory." (No second is necessary.)

CHAIR: "Objection to the consideration of the question has been made. As this motion is neither debatable nor amendable, the Chair will put it to a vote; a $\frac{2}{3}$ vote is necessary to sustain the objection." (He continues:) "The question before the body is, 'Shall the *objection* be sustained?' Those in favor of sustaining the objection will raise their right hand. Forty-eight; hands down. Those opposed will raise their right hand.

One; hand down. There being two-thirds in favor of the objection, the affirmative has it and the motion will not be considered."

Note to Chairmen: Experience in the practice of the above proceeding in ordinary assemblies has shown that unless the Chair puts the proceeding to vote in this form: "Shall the *objection* be sustained" (as shown in the above drill), instead of "Shall the question be considered," presiding officers as well as assemblies will be confused. Hence, put the *objection* to vote (since the objection is the immediately pending question). If the objection is sustained by a ⅔ vote in the affirmative, the motion objected to will not be considered. On the other hand, a ⅔ vote must be *opposed* to the form, "Shall the *question* be considered," in order to sustain the objection. If you think the latter form is more effective and understandable, use that form (both are authoritative).

Motions which cannot be objected to. As stated, an objection to the consideration of a question can be applied only upon original main motions.

The following proceedings are not *now* original main motions (they *were* original when they originally were proposed for adoption). These proceedings cannot be objected to because they are not *now* original main motions (they run into hundreds); namely: none of the seven subsidiary motions, five privileged motions, twenty incidental motions, any incidental main motion, or the six "restoratory" motions (see pp. 47–49); and none of your organization's bylaws or amendments to them. You cannot object to the consideration of mandates, petitions, requests or communications that come from a superior body of the organization, but you *can* object to those of a subordinate body in the organization or those that come from sources outside the organization (requests for donations, purchase of tickets, etc.); and you cannot object to the consideration of committee reports that relate to subjects previously referred by the assembly to its committees, but you can object to any committee's own report, recommendation, motion or resolution.

The fact that you may not object outright to the consideration of the various types of motions mentioned in the preceding paragraph does not mean that you cannot move to table or postpone them instead, under due process of parliamentary practice while they are pending before the assembly.

Thus, although you cannot object to the consideration of a proposed bylaw amendment (because bylaws, once adopted, become incidental main motions), you can move to table any proposed bylaw amendment.

Note: Now and then a member or a delegate in convention boldly asserts: "I can object to any motion, I don't care what the bylaws or our parliamentary authority [Robert, or Demeter, etc.] says." This is like saying, "I don't care what the traffic sign says, I can object to any one-way street." Such assertions are false, misleading and in violation of the rules of orderly procedure and of established law and order.

READ FROM PAPER, MANUSCRIPT, OR BOOK (S, M, R)

To read from any paper or book in the course of debate means reading a prepared speech, or from paper, book, manuscript, newspaper or other document, in order to aid one's debate on motions.

In other words, a member may read his speech in debate, or he may read (from any source) any material pertinent to his remarks on a question before the body, unless objection is made to the reading. It is not usual to object, if the privilege is not abused.

But if objection is made, seconded and adopted by majority vote, he may not continue the reading; thus:

MEMBER A (continuing reading from a book): "As Shakespeare has so nobly said, 'To be or not to be . . .' " (interrupted by B).

MEMBER B: "Mr. Chairman, I regret that I must object to the member continuing to read from the book." (Seconded.)

CHAIR: "Objection has been made to reading from a book. The question now before the body is, 'Shall the *objection* be sustained?' Those in favor of sustaining the objection will say aye; those opposed will say no. The noes have it and the objection is not sustained; the member may continue to read," or, "The ayes have it and the member may not continue reading, but he may use the balance of his time to debate orally."

Objecting to reading from paper or book requires a second and a majority vote. It is not debatable or amendable. A negative vote on it may be reconsidered. It yields to privileged motions. If an objection to reading from a paper is sustained, the member has the right to continue to debate orally up to the limit of his debating time. Referring to one's notes does not constitute reading.

The reading of written or printed reports of officers or committees from paper, yearbook, etc., is not subject to such objection.

WITHDRAW A MOTION

To withdraw a motion is to recall it, or to take it back, in order to prevent further action on it. If a motion is withdrawn, all other proceedings pending with it are automatically withdrawn with it.

No *withdrawn* motion, or a second, or a previous notice is recorded in the minutes.

Motions are at times withdrawn so as not to put the organization on record on unwise, untimely, unnecessary or unprofitable questions.

Basic rules. The motion to withdraw is an incidental motion. It requires no second; it is not debatable or amendable; and it is not put to vote.

It is too late to withdraw a motion after it has been voted on, except by unanimous consent.

A withdrawn motion is regarded as having never been made; hence it can be reproposed later at the same session or at any future session.

How proposed and transacted. A motion can be withdrawn as follows:

(1) Before it has been stated in full by the Chair. In such case no one's consent is needed, not even the seconder's; thus:

MEMBER A: "Mr. Chairman, I move we buy a new desk." (Seconded.)

CHAIR: "It is moved and seconded to buy a new . . ." (interrupted).

MEMBER A: "Mr. Chairman, I withdraw my motion."

CHAIR: "The motion having been withdrawn, it is not before the body."

(2) After the Chair states it in full, provided no one objects. The

KEY QUIZ

Q. Who can withdraw a motion? *A.* Its proposer.
Q. Does it need a second? *A.* No.
Q. Is it debatable or amendable? *A.* No.
Q. Is it voted on? *A.* No (but see drill below).
Q. What class of motion is a withdrawal? *A.* Incidental.
Q. When can a motion be withdrawn? *A.* Before it is voted on.
Q. Are withdrawn motions recorded in the minutes? *A.* No.
Q. If a motion is withdrawn, can another member move it? *A.* Yes.
Q. Can you withdraw your challenge of a quorum? *A.* No.

seconder can object, but so can any other member. A seconder has no superior rights; thus:

CHAIR: "It has been moved and seconded to buy a new desk. Is there any debate?" (Observe the motion has been fully stated.)

MEMBER A: "Mr. Chairman, I withdraw my motion."

CHAIR: "As this motion is now in the assembly's possession, is there any objection to its withdrawal?" (If silence follows he continues:) "There being no objection, the motion is withdrawn."

(3) If there is objection to the withdrawal, the objection can be overcome. Simply rise and say, "I move we grant withdrawal"; thus:

MEMBER B: "Mr. Chairman, I object to the withdrawal."

CHAIR: "There being objection, the motion cannot be withdrawn."

MEMBER C (or any other member): "Mr. Chairman, I move that we grant withdrawal of the motion." (This has to be seconded.)

CHAIR: "It is moved and seconded to grant withdrawal of the motion." (It is undebatable and unamendable, hence the vote:) "Those in favor of granting withdrawal will say aye; those opposed will say no. The ayes have it, and the motion is withdrawn," or, "The noes have it, and the motion is not withdrawn." A negative vote can be reconsidered.

(4) If a member withdraws his motion, another member may renew it; thus:

MEMBER A: "Mr. Chairman, I withdraw my motion to buy a new desk."

MEMBER B: "Mr. Chairman, I move that we buy a new desk."

When previous notice can be withdrawn. A previous notice which is required to be given under the organization's laws or its parliamentary authority (such as previous notice to amend a bylaw, or to rescind or reconsider or assess the members) can automatically be withdrawn at the *same* meeting without the need of a vote to authorize its withdrawal. Reason: if such previous notice is withdrawn, any other member may give the same notice; thus:

1. MEMBER C: "Mr. Chairman, I withdraw the previous *notice* I gave just now [or, earlier at this meeting] to amend the bylaws increasing the annual dues from ten dollars to fifteen dollars." (Such withdrawal is automatic.)

MEMBER D: "Mr. Chairman, *I* give previous notice to amend the bylaws increasing the annual dues from ten dollars to fifteen dollars."

2. MEMBER E: "Mr. Chairman, I withdraw my previous notice to rescind [or, to reconsider, etc.]."

MEMBER F: "Mr. Chairman, *I* give previous notice to rescind."

When previous notice cannot be withdrawn. A previous notice cannot be withdrawn when it is too late for other members to propose it advantageously; that is, it cannot be withdrawn *after* the meeting at which the previous notice was given has adjourned. Hence it cannot be withdrawn at a subsequent new call for a meeting except by unanimous consent. The following two examples illustrate previous notice that cannot be withdrawn.

1. CHAIR (at the *next* regular meeting): "The next business is action of the proposed amendment to the bylaws to increase the annual dues from ten dollars to fifteen dollars, for which previous notice was duly given."

MEMBER D: "Mr. Chairman, *I* gave the previous notice at the last meeting to amend the bylaws increasing the dues. I now withdraw my previous notice."

CHAIR: "As this is not the *same* meeting at which the previous notice was given, it requires a unanimous vote to permit withdrawal of the previous notice. Is there any objection to the withdrawal?"

MEMBER G: "I object to its withdrawal."

CHAIR: "There being objection, the previous notice given cannot be withdrawn. Is there any debate now on the bylaw amendment?"

2. MEMBER J: "Mr. Chairman, at the *last* regular meeting I gave previous notice to rescind . . . [specifies motion]. I now withdraw my previous notice thereon."

CHAIR: "It requires a unanimous vote to permit such withdrawal at this meeting. Is there any objection to its withdrawal?" (If even one member objects, withdrawal is not granted, and action is then taken on the motion for which previous notice was given; if no one objects, the withdrawal is effectual and no action is taken on the motion.)

Note: In conventions and annual meetings with more than one sitting, a previous notice to rescind or to reconsider, etc., is not withdrawable at a sitting other than in the one in which the previous notice was given, except by unanimous consent, since it is then too late for other members to renew or offer that same previous notice and thus be enabled to reap presently the benefit of the parliamentary advantages of a legal previous notice.

WITHDRAW A SECOND

Withdrawing a second is similar to withdrawing a motion, namely: (1) the seconder can withdraw his second at will *before* the motion has been stated by the Chair; (2) it is automatically withdrawn when the *motion* itself has been withdrawn; and (3) a second can be withdrawn if the proposer of the motion varies (at any time) or *modifies* his motion in any way, as when he first proposes to "buy fifteen chairs," and then modifies it to "buy thirty-five chairs"; thus:

MEMBER A: "Mr. Chairman, I move that we buy fifteen folding chairs."

MEMBER B: "I second the motion."

CHAIR: "It has been moved and seconded that . . ." (repeating the above motion).

MEMBER A again: "Mr. Chairman, I meant to say thirty-five chairs."

MEMBER B again: "Mr. Chairman, in that case I withdraw my second."

CHAIR: "The seconder having withdrawn his second, is there a second to the modified motion to buy thirty-five chairs?" (And it is entertained if seconded, and not entertained if not seconded.)

The seconder can also withdraw his second after the Chair has stated the question and before it is voted on, if the body permits it either by silent consent, or by majority vote if put to a formal vote.

CONSIDERATION BY PARAGRAPH OR *SERIATIM* (S, D, A, **M, R**)

When a proposition, motion or resolution has many parts (paragraphs, sections, or clauses), or many articles (as a set of bylaws which is up for revision or amendment), it is best and most prudent that *no* vote be taken on each separate part. Instead, a single vote covering *all* its parts should be taken after each of them has been duly considered, amended, and perfected. *Seriatim* (Lat.) literally means "serially," and when applied to several or more parts of a parliamentary proposal or question it means consideration paragraph by paragraph or part by part.

Hence, under the doctrine of consideration by paragraph, or *seriatim*, each part is discussed and may be amended and perfected to suit; then, without putting it to a vote for final adoption, the next part or paragraph is similarly open to discussion and amendment, but is not voted on for final adoption yet; and, in like manner, each additional part is perfected in turn until all the parts of a proposal have been considered.

When the entire proposition, question or proposal has been thus attended to, and no further amendments are proposed, the Chair, before putting the entire proposition to a vote, asks: "Is there any further discussion or amendment to this question before it is put to a vote?" He then puts it to a final vote.

It requires only a majority vote to adopt a motion or resolution, but a ⅔ vote to adopt a bylaw or a revision of the bylaws (unless differently authorized in the bylaws).

REQUEST OF ANY KIND

Requests for any unallowable purpose need unanimous consent. A single objection defeats consent, unless the organization's laws or the assembly's usual practices allow otherwise. The procedure:

MEMBER: "Mr. Chairman, I ask unanimous consent to have Mr. X, a nonmember, address the body." (No second is needed.)

CHAIR: "Is there objection to granting the request?" (No response.) "There being no objection, the request is granted"; or, "There being objection, the request is not granted."

Note: To prevent delays which can arise out of such requests, but yet to give ear to meritorious ones, sagacious and alert members can rise and say: "Mr. Chairman, reserving the right *to object*, for what purpose does he want the floor," or "What will Mr. X discuss?" He is thus qualified to object if the purpose is not meritorious.

FILLING BLANKS (**M, R**)

To "fill a blank" means to fill a blank space in a motion, as when a motion is made to "buy a new television set at a cost not to exceed ——— dollars" (the amount is left blank for suggestions from other members).

Basic rules. Suggestions or motions for filling blanks do not require a second, and they are undebatable and unamendable. A majority vote is necessary for their adoption. They are incidental motions. They can be reconsidered. They apply to any motion to which they are pertinent and which requires fulfilling.

After it is voted to fill a blank, no further votes are taken; when the blank has been filled, the process for filling automatically ends.

How proposed and entertained

MEMBER: "Mr. Chairman, I move that we buy a new television at a cost not to exceed (blank) dollars." (Seconded.)

CHAIR: "It has been moved and seconded to buy a new television at a cost not to exceed the sum of (blank) dollars." And he asks the members: "How shall the blank be filled?" or "What sum shall be inserted to fill the blank?" or similar phrase.

MEMBERS (calling out): "One hundred dollars," "Four hundred dollars," "Seventy-five dollars," "Fifty dollars," "One hundred and fifty dollars," etc.

CHAIR: "Are there further suggestions before proceeding to fill the blank? There being none, the Chair will proceed to put each sum to vote beginning with the *largest* sum. Those in favor of filling the blank with the sum of four hundred dollars will say aye; those opposed will say no. The noes have it, and the blank is not filled. The next largest sum is one hundred and fifty dollars; those in favor of this sum will say aye; those opposed will say no. The ayes have it, and the sum of one hundred and fifty dollars is adopted and the blank is filled with that sum. The question now before the body is on the original motion as amended [or, as filled in] to 'buy a new television set at a cost not to exceed one hundred and fifty dollars.' Is there any discussion?" (And the motion is then put to vote.)

Allows more than two amendments at once. Filling blanks is in reality an informal method of amending a question plurally (with more than two pending proposed choices) at once, whereas the formal method of amending a motion does not allow more than two pending amendments before the body at one time. This informal method, that of filling a blank, allows *any* number of suggestions, fillers or amendments at one time, as when it is proposed to elect an unspecified number of directors, and members informally call out five, seven, nine, or three, etc.; or when it is proposed to buy more chairs for the banquet hall, and some suggest 35 chairs, others suggest 40, or 60, or 25, etc.

How to determine order of voting

(1) If the blank is to be filled with a sum of money and various sums are proposed, such as $60, $75, $50, and $40, the largest sum is voted on first; and if that is lost, each succeeding largest sum in turn is voted on successively until a choice is finally made by a majority vote.

Note: Voting on the largest number first applies only to filling blanks — not to formal amendments.

(2) If the blank is to be filled with a date, time, or distance, the most remote date, most distant time, or longest distance is put to vote first;

and if that is defeated, the next greatest is put to vote, and so on in turn by majority vote.

(3) If the blank is to be filled with names, as for committees, delegates, etc., the names are voted on in the order in which they were made, and each name is then put to vote successively until a choice is made or the desired number is elected.

Exception to the rule. The largest sum of money is not necessarily put to vote first. In some circumstances the smallest sum should be put to vote first. If the sum of money is to come out of the organization's own funds, which is nearly always the case, the largest sum, as just shown, is put to vote first; but if it is to come out of the funds of another organization or source, then the smallest sum is voted on first. Thus, if it is moved that "The assembly sell the old rug in the banquet room" and various sums are suggested, as $300, $15, $60, or $80, the smallest sum is put to vote first, because if the largest sum, namely $300, is put to vote first and adopted, and no buyer found for it at that price, all the action would be in vain and another motion would have to be made in a *future* meeting to authorize a more acceptable sum at which to sell it (which delays accomplishment of business).

In other words, if you are to *buy* goods, wares or merchandise you vote on the largest sum first; but if you are to *sell*, you vote on the smallest sum first.

Original motion still pending. After it is voted to fill a blank, the main motion is then put to vote as amended, that is, as filled in, because the fact that a *blank* has been voted filled or adopted does not mean that the main motion is thereby also adopted. This is just as in the case of any main motion which is put to vote as amended after an amendment upon it is adopted.

Blank can be filled later. Motions or suggestions to fill a blank can be proposed either while a main motion is actually pending or after its disposal. For instance, it can first be voted to buy a new television without specifying the price, and afterward entertain suggestions to determine the price.

QUORUM

A quorum in an assembly is the minimum number of members required by rule or bylaw to be present before business can be legally transacted in the organization.

The point of "no quorum" can be raised only against *business*, usually commencing with the reading of the minutes. Prayer is not business requiring a quorum, nor the national anthem or other ceremonial proceedings of any kind. A quorum is not necessary for officers to take the oath or for initiation of new members, unless bylaws specify otherwise.

A quorumless meeting may commence business and continue if no one openly challenges or questions the presence of a quorum; it is presumed to be present until someone openly doubts it. A point of no quorum may be raised at any time during a meeting.

Note: More than 70 percent of the public's business in state legislatures and the U. S. Congress is transacted in the absence of a quorum; usually no one challenges it, except where important or partisan questions are involved.

Basic rules. Any member, including the Chair, can doubt a quorum. The doubt must not be capricious or obstructive; it must be fairly apparent that a quorum is not present. The presence or absence of a quorum is determined by the number of members actually present, not by the number voting on a question; all present do not always vote. Once raised, the point of no quorum cannot be withdrawn or ignored, even by unanimous consent; and it may not be laid on the table.

Note: Unless a special rule so specifies, it is not necessary that any particular officer(s) shall be present before a meeting may commence, or before the quorum can be legal. If a quorum is present without them, you have a quorum; if the president and the vice president(s) are absent and you have a quorum, elect a chairman pro tem and then proceed to do business until they arrive.

When point of quorum can be raised. The point of no quorum can interrupt a speaker. A point of no quorum can be made at any time, but cannot be repeated after it is apparent that a quorum is present.

Note: Robert states that a member cannot be interrupted while speaking in order to make the point of no quorum.

A proceeding having been completed, and other business having intervened; it is too late to make the point that a quorum was not present; but if the point is raised immediately after such completion, and a quorum is not then present, the proceeding is invalidated.

Note: A speaker has had his turn at debate if he finishes his debate before the point of no quorum is raised: if he is interrupted by a point of no quorum he is deemed not to have spoken on the question.

Business in absence of a quorum. After it has been determined that a quorum is not present no principal or essential business can be transacted. If such business is transacted, it is deemed illegal, null and void, unless ratified or approved either later at the same meeting when there is a quorum, or at a subsequent meeting. The following procedural business can be legally transacted in a quorumless meeting: (1) Fix an adjourned (continued) meeting. (2) Adjourn. (3) Recess. (4) Take any measures to procure a quorum.

KEY QUIZ

Q. How is a quorum questioned or doubted? *A.* By a member's rising and saying: "Mr. Chairman, I doubt the presence of a quorum."
Q. Does this require a second? *A.* No.
Q. What does the chair do then? *A.* He says: "The presence of a quorum is doubted. All members will please rise to be counted."
Q. If there is then no quorum, what happens? *A.* The Chair says: "There being no quorum, business cannot continue [or commence]."
Q. And if a quorum is present? *A.* The Chair says: "A quorum being present, business will continue [or commence]."
Q. Is the motion debatable or amendable? *A.* No.
Q. Is it put to vote? *A.* No: the count decides the doubt.
Q. Is the quorum subject to the motion to lay on the table? *A.* No.
Q. Can the "doubt" of a quorum be withdrawn? *A.* No.
Q. Is this proceeding (the *quorum*) a motion? *A.* Yes; it is an incidental motion.

To get a quorum. Thus, when a quorum is lacking, the assembly can (1) fix another day at which to reconvene, so as not to have to wait until the next regular meeting before it can act on some urgent business. (2) The assembly can simply adjourn, and return at its next regular meeting. (3) The assembly can recess and await the arrival of other members. (4) It can entertain and adopt any motion intended to procure a quorum, such as to try to reach members by telephone or designate someone to call the members in from another room, etc. A majority vote is required to adopt any of these steps if it is put to a formal vote.

Note: If your meetings lack quorums frequently, insert at once in your bylaws: "When a quorum is not convened, the next called meeting shall be a valid meeting notwithstanding lack of a quorum, and the call shall so inform the members."

Business valid unless challenged. A quorum is always presumed to be present once a meeting has commenced, unless it is publicly challenged. Therefore, business that has been transacted in the unascertained absence of a quorum is legal unless challenged before other business has intervened. If challenged before other business has been taken up, the business acted on is automatically null and void. (Be alert; do not sleep on your rights.)

Quorum challenged. On the other hand, when quorum has been openly challenged and it is determined that a quorum is not present, all business automatically stops and the meeting remains quorumless until again a quorum is established.

A claim that there was no quorum in a previous meeting may not be entertained at a subsequent meeting unless the fact is recorded in the minutes. (But see the following note.)

Note: If a bylaw specifies that a quorum must be present before certain action may be taken, as, for instance, increase in salaries or adoption of a bylaw, and if such action is taken with a quorum present, alert members should make certain (and, of course, the secretary as well) that the minutes will record the fact that "a quorum was present." Otherwise the validity of the action taken can legally be subject to challenge later on.

Ratify quorumless action at next meeting. If a quorumless meeting finds it necessary to transact some urgent business, and then adjourns, someone at the next meeting should rise and explain the circumstances which warranted taking such action in the absence of a quorum, and then move "to ratify the action taken at the previous meeting." If it is not ratified, the action taken is void.

In like manner, if a legally convened meeting lacks a quorum and election of officers is scheduled or a vacancy in office is scheduled to be filled, the body may, by majority vote, postpone the election to the next meeting, or it may proceed to conduct the election or fill the vacancy (since previous notice thereof had been given), and then at the next meeting move to ratify the action. If ratification does not prevail, the action taken at the quorumless meeting is invalid and a new election is held.

If delegates to a convention are elected in a quorumless meeting to attend a convention which will occur before the next regular meeting, the said election is regarded as valid *ex necessitate*, if it is valid in all other respects (their eligibility to serve as delegates, etc.).

Basic rule for quorum requirement. If the bylaws of an organization do not prescribe a quorum, and no quorum has been accepted or established by long usage and practice, the quorum is as follows:

(1) In meetings of organizations which do not prescribe a quorum, a majority of the entire membership constitutes a quorum. If this is too large, adopt a smaller number in your bylaws.

(2) In committees, elected or appointed, including executive committees or boards, a quorum consists of a majority of those composing it. If it is too large or too small, change it.

(3) In conventions the quorum at any time consists of a majority of the total number actually *registered* as duly accredited delegates or representatives, counting also those, if any, who registered, but have left the convention, or are absent when a count is taken.

(4) In mass meetings, religious bodies, philanthropic, patriotic and other voluntary organizations with no prescribed quorum, no quorum governs; that is, the number of members present at any time constitutes the quorum — unless by vote the meeting establishes a quorum for its future sittings.

Reduction or increase in quorum. When, because of war, disaster, or other grave or enduring emergency, it is impracticable to secure a quorum, the size of the quorum should be forthwith reduced for the duration and then increased with its cessation (if need be in either case), provided previous notice of such action is given.

Note: Insert the authorization suggested above in your bylaws now — before an emergency arises.

What constitutes majority of the full membership. Members dead, disqualified, refusing to qualify or who have not yet been sworn or have resigned or been suspended or expelled are *not* counted as *members* of the body, and hence they are not computed in determining its majority quorum requirement.

Thus if a body's prescribed *full* membership is 18, say, and one member died, one resigned, one is unsworn and one was impeached, the full competent membership therein having dropped to 14 members, *eight* of the 14 members then comprise the body's majority quorum (until the vacancies have been duly filled, in which case the "majority quorum" is computed accordingly).

Note: In other words, a *majority* of the membership means "a majority of those chosen, sworn and living whose membership has not been terminated by resignation or by other action of the body" (U. S. House of Representatives, *Rules and Manual*, §53).

No best rule for a quorum. There is no best rule for a quorum. Each organization is the best judge thereof. It can fix its quorum at a specific number, as 3 members, or 9, or 21, etc.; or at 10%, 15%, etc.

Note: In the British House of Commons the quorum is 40 members out of its present full membership of 630. In the House of Lords it is only three members out of a total membership, currently, of 1022 members. In the U. S. Congress a "majority of each House constitutes a quorum." In some fraternal orders, some of whose lodges have over a thousand members, and in veterans' associations, some of whose posts also have thousands of members, their quorum is but nine, or seven or six members.

Origin of the word quorum. The term "quorum" (Latin for "of whom") was one of the words used in the diploma (commission or certificate, originally written in Latin) appointing justices of the peace in England. The language in the commission, or diploma, solemnly reminded the appointee that his presence at meetings was necessary for the transaction of the king's business. The wording in the commission read somewhat as follows: "We have hereby assigned you, and others as well, *quorum* [of whom] . . . *unum esse volumus* [it is our wish that you be one] . . ." to help make all action legal. Since then, the word quorum has by transference been taken to signify the minimum number of persons necessary to be present at meetings to constitute a legal sitting for the transaction of business.

Chapter 10
THE RESTORATORY MOTIONS

There are six motions in parliamentary procedure for which no suitable or satisfactory descriptive name or classification has hitherto been found. Hence, they could not be referred to as belonging to an exclusive and specific class of their own, like the subsidiary, privileged, and incidental classes of motions. These six motions are:

In other handbooks on parliamentary law, these motions are variously referred to as "unclassified," "miscellaneous," "certain other," or "specific" motions, etc. Since these designations are mere descriptions and not a name or classification, this manual confidently adopts the term "restoratory motions" as a fitting and appropriate designation.

Explanation for the term "restoratory." (1) When a main motion is voted from the table, the main motion is automatically restored before the body for further action; hence the designation of the motion to take from the table as a restoratory motion. (2) The three motions (all commencing with R) to *reconsider* a motion previously adopted, or to *rescind* it, or to *ratify* some act already executed automatically restore, or open, the merits of the main motion to further debate.

Each restoratory motion is considered and explained separately in this chapter, beginning with the motion to reconsider.

Note: The term "restoratory" is a new parliamentary term devised by this manual. In the interest of the uniform practice, permission to use the term "restoratory" is hereby granted without restriction.

RECONSIDER (S, D, M)

The motion to reconsider is normally used when it is desired to prevent hasty decisions, or to prevent undesirable motions, previously adopted by the body, from being carried out until they can be reconsidered. By the same token, it is also used when it is desired to undo (reconsider) adverse decisions on meritorious motions.

In other words, when you feel that the body's action on a motion was unwise, and you would like to have that question brought back before the body in hope of reversing or modifying the decision on it, then vote for reconsideration. But if you feel the action taken was wise and it should not be interfered with, then vote against reconsideration.

Basic rules. The motion to reconsider requires a second. It is debatable but not amendable and it requires a majority vote. It may not itself be reconsidered, and reconsideration may not be moved more than once on the same motion. A motion to reconsider may be made only by a member who voted with the prevailing side of the motion in question, though it may be seconded by any member. Reconsideration of more than one question at a time (mass reconsideration) is prohibited, except by unanimous consent.

Note: A tie vote, being less than a majority, defeats reconsideration.

How proposed and transacted. Correct forms for the reconsideration of either side, affirmative or negative, follow:

1. Assume the motion "to sell the clubhouse" was adopted.

MEMBER: "Mr. President, I move to reconsider the vote on the motion to sell the clubhouse, adopted earlier tonight." (Seconded.)
CHAIR: "Did you vote on the prevailing side?"
MEMBER: "Yes."
CHAIR: "It is moved and seconded to reconsider the vote on the motion to sell the clubhouse. Is there any debate on the motion to reconsider?"

KEY QUIZ

Mastery of this key quiz will enable you to acquire not only full basic knowledge of reconsideration, but also answers to questions often asked by members at meetings and conventions.

Q. Does the motion to reconsider require a second? *A.* Yes.
Q. Is the reconsideration of main motions debatable? *A.* Yes.
Q. Is it amendable? *A.* No.
Q. Who is eligible to move reconsideration and who can second it? *A.* Only one who actually voted on the prevailing side can move it; but anyone can second it, regardless of how, or whether, he voted.
Q. May the same question be reconsidered more than once? *A.* No.
Q. Are there any exceptions to the two above rules? *A.* Yes. The rules that "only one who voted with the prevailing side can move reconsideration" and that "the same question cannot be reconsidered more than once" are binding only in organizations whose bylaws so prescribe, or whose parliamentary authority so specifies (as do Robert, Demeter, and some others). Look this up in your parliamentary authority.
Q. What vote adopts reconsideration? *A.* Majority vote (unless the bylaws specify a different vote), even though the motion desired reconsidered may require a $\frac{2}{3}$ affirmative vote.
Q. When can you move reconsideration? *A.* Either immediately after the vote, or later during the meeting when you have enough votes. (See p. 158.)
Q. Is reconsideration in order at special meetings? *A.* Yes.
Q. Is a quorum necessary to a reconsideration? *A.* Yes.
Q. Can the vote on reconsideration be itself reconsidered? *A.* No.

(After debate, the vote:) "Those in favor of reconsideration will say aye; those opposed will say no. The ayes have it; the motion to reconsider is carried. The question now is on the original main motion to sell the clubhouse. Is there any debate on the main motion?" (After debate, the vote:) "Those in favor of the motion to sell the clubhouse will say aye; those opposed will say no. The noes have it; the clubhouse will *not* be sold," or, "The ayes have it and the clubhouse *will* be sold," as the case may be.

Note: When reconsideration of a question prevails, then that question always has to be voted on again, as shown above, otherwise the question remains unacted on, like a shoe lace which becomes loose and has to be retied.

2. Assume now the motion "to buy a new desk" was defeated.

MEMBER A: "Mr. President, I move to reconsider the motion to buy a new desk which was just defeated." (Seconded.)

CHAIR: "It is moved and seconded to reconsider the vote on the motion to buy a new desk, previously defeated. Is there discussion?"

MEMBER B: "Mr. President, did A vote with the prevailing side?"

CHAIR (to A): "The Chair neglected to ask you if you voted on the prevailing side [the negative side in this case]."

MEMBER A: "No; I voted on the affirmative side."

CHAIR: "In that case, reconsideration cannot be entertained."

MEMBER C: "Mr. Chairman, *I* move reconsideration; *I* voted on the prevailing side." (Seconded.)

CHAIR: "It is moved and seconded to reconsider the vote on the motion to buy a new desk. Is there any debate?" (After which, the vote:) "Those in favor of reconsideration will say aye; those opposed will say no. The noes have it and reconsideration is defeated"; or, "The ayes have it, reconsideration prevails, and the question *now* before the body is on the original main motion to buy a new desk." (The motion is now open for debate and must be voted on again.)

Exhortation: Rehearse and master the above two drills. Take turns at presiding in group or class study.

Origin of the motion to reconsider. The motion to reconsider is a distinctively American motion (it was first made the subject of a rule in the U. S. House of Representatives in 1802).

This motion was unknown to the early British Parliament. When Parliament (the British Congress) passed an act, that act then stood as the judgment of the body until another law or supplementary act was afterward passed explaining or amending the previous act — a slow-moving and time-consuming process in the estimation of American lawmakers.

Consequently, the American love for celerity invented the motion to reconsider, and cleverly made it a mere procedural or restoratory motion. As a result, the motion to reconsider now makes possible immediate reconsideration of a question, even on the same day.

What reconsideration accomplishes. The adoption of the motion to reconsider automatically restores, brings back or makes pending again before the body, the question that was to be reconsidered; and the body must then vote on the reconsidered question again. (A lone exception to this rule is the reconsideration of the previous question.)

The mere making of the motion to reconsider has the effect of automatically preventing anything being done to the question to be reconsidered until the motion to reconsider has been acted on. That motion cannot be carried out in the meantime.

Rank of motion to reconsider. The rank of the motion to reconsider varies. It takes the rank of the motion to be reconsidered. Thus if it is moved to reconsider a main motion, it takes the rank of the main motion, and in such case it can be acted on when no other business is before the assembly.

If it is moved to reconsider a motion other than main, such as to refer or postpone, it then takes the rank of such motion and is in order unless a motion of higher rank is pending at the time. Thus if a main motion to buy a new desk is pending, and the motion to refer it to a committee was previously voted on and defeated, before a motion of higher rank than the motion to refer is proposed (such as to lay on the table, or adjourn, etc.), reconsideration of that motion to refer is in order; but if a higher ranking motion is proposed ahead of it, such as to lay on the table, reconsideration of the motion to refer would not be in order at that moment, but would be in order if the motion to table is defeated, and no other motion of higher rank is proposed before reconsideration of the motion to refer is moved.

The motion to reconsider yields to motions to limit or end debate on it, and to the privileged and apt incidental motions. It is also outranked by the motion to reconsider and enter, and the motion to table.

When tabled or postponed definitely. When the reconsideration of a main motion is voted laid on the table or is postponed definitely, the question wished reconsidered as well as any motions adhering to it are tabled or postponed with it.

When tabled reconsideration expires. Suppose the motion "to authorize the sale of the clubhouse" (or any main question whatsoever) is adopted by the body, and reconsideration of it is proposed and is voted tabled or postponed to the next regular meeting; then, if the reconsideration is not taken from the table or is not taken up under unfinished business before adjournment of such next meeting, the reconsideration then automatically expires upon adjournment, with the result that the previously adopted motion ("to authorize the sale of the clubhouse") goes into effect and may be carried out.

Cannot be referred, amended, or postponed indefinitely. It cannot be referred to a committee because it was the assembly and not the committee which decided the original question and only the assembly can reconsider its own action. It cannot be amended because amendments properly adhere to the question to be reconsidered, and not to its reconsideration. It cannot be postponed indefinitely because the object of reconsideration is to restore a question before the body, whereas the object of indefinite postponement is to kill or suppress the question.

Who may not move reconsideration. Reconsideration in the main body (and this includes conventions and annual meetings) can be moved only by one who voted on the prevailing side of the motion wished reconsidered. Hence, it cannot be moved by one (*a*) who voted on the losing side, or (*b*) who was absent, or (*c*) who abstained from voting when he was present.

When reconsideration is proposed, the Chair should ask its proposer, "Did you vote on the prevailing side?" If the reply is "No," the Chair says, "The reconsideration is not in order."

If the proposer replies, "Yes, I voted on the prevailing side," but his veracity is challenged by a member (as is sometimes the case), he is given the benefit of the doubt in every case except where the record on a roll call vote shows otherwise.

Note: The rule in the U. S. House of Representatives supports this view. The rule says that except where a recorded roll call vote shows otherwise, "any Member, irrespective of whether he voted with the majority or not, may make the motion to reconsider." (U. S. House Rules & Manual, Rule XVIII, §813.) "Majority" is construed to mean the prevailing side in a tie vote, or in a $\frac{2}{3}$ or unanimous vote.

If an ineligible member moves reconsideration. If an ineligible member moves reconsideration and no one notices the fact or raises a point of order, the adoption of the reconsideration by the body implies and supplies a second and cures the ineligibility; the vote taken on it cannot be challenged afterward.

Vote with prevailing side in order to move reconsideration. If the organization's rules or parliamentary authority specify that reconsideration may be made only by one who voted on the prevailing side, if the minority feels that the body's decision on a question was hasty, unwise or detrimental to the best interests of the organization, or it was passed in a meeting with slim attendance, one or two alert members of the minority should purposely vote with the opposition (the majority side), and thus qualify to move reconsideration of the objectionable question at a more strategic time later at the meeting when votes have been switched, or some of the opposition departed, etc.

Who may second reconsideration. Only one seconder is necessary for reconsideration (unless bylaws otherwise specify), and any member at all can second it, regardless of how he voted or if he voted at all on the motion sought to be reconsidered (unless bylaws specify, as some do, that seconder(s) must also have voted on the prevailing side). Check your bylaws.

If a seconder withdraws his second, another member can second it.

When debatable. Reconsideration is debatable only if the motion sought to be reconsidered is debatable, otherwise it is not debatable. When debatable, the previous question and the motion to limit debate can apply upon it.

Must proposer of reconsideration give reasons? No one is obliged to give reasons for a reconsideration (or for any other debatable question); but unless he does so, it is unlikely that his motion will prevail.

How reconsideration is debated. It is often asked, "How is a reconsideration debated?"

It is debated pro or con just like any other motion.

If you want a previously decided question reconsidered, speak in favor of its reconsideration; if you do not want it reconsidered, speak against it; thus:

MEMBER A: "Mr. Chairman, I am in *favor* of the reconsideration of the motion to buy a new desk which was adopted earlier tonight. The desk is good enough as it is; we do not need a new one." (Gives further reasons.) "I therefore hope that reconsideration will prevail, and the motion to buy a new desk will then be defeated."

CHAIR: "Is there any further debate on the reconsideration?"

MEMBER B: "Mr. Chairman, I am opposed to reconsidering the motion to buy a new desk. The desk is ready to fall apart." (Gives further reasons.) "I trust that reconsideration will not prevail, so we can buy a new desk."

When the right to debate is exhausted. To reconsider automatically opens to debate the question under reconsideration, but no one may debate the reconsidered question who on that day has exhausted his right to debate that question further (as when he has spoken his permitted two times).

Second reconsideration in order if motion amended. If the affirmative side wins on a first reconsideration of the question (for instance, "to have new dues cards printed"), and the question is then materially changed (as by amending it, adding to it the words "and also new lodge stationery"), since this amended question is not the same one as before, it can be reconsidered if so desired, because it is a new question.

On a bylaw amendment. An adopted bylaw amendment may not be reconsidered, since a bylaw takes effect immediately upon its adoption unless it is expressly otherwise agreed at the time, or by unanimous consent. But a defeated bylaw amendment may be reconsidered by a majority vote, even though the amendment itself requires a $\frac{2}{3}$ vote for adoption.

If a bylaw provision states that "bylaw amendments shall not go into effect until after adjournment," the proviso "until after adjournment" does not constitute a reconsidering stage, unless it is expressly otherwise agreed at the time, or by unanimous consent, or unless the bylaws so provide.

Under previous question. When the previous question has been ordered imposed on all motions of a series (thus cutting off debate on *all* of them), the reconsideration of any one of those motions does not open that motion to debate. Voting on the entire series must be completed, at which time the previous question itself automatically becomes exhausted.

Under the rules of parliamentary law, the reconsideration of a question automatically opens to debate the merits of that question. If, however, the previous question (shutting off debate) is ordered on the reconsideration, debate on the question wished reconsidered also automatically ends, until either the reconsideration has been put to a vote and is defeated, or the question itself has been voted on.

Shortcut to reconsideration. If the assembly is unable or unwilling to act on a reconsideration of a question in accord with the technical parliamentary language and form, then simply adopt the motion "to consider the question previously decided [naming it], as *not* having been acted on."

If this motion is proposed by one who had voted on the prevailing side, a majority vote would be required to adopt it; but if it is proposed by one who did not so vote, a unanimous vote would then be required (since such a one is ineligible to propose it).

Right to move reconsideration expires with adjournment. The right of members to move reconsideration of some act of the body expires upon adjournment of the meeting or session, unless (a) the organization's bylaws or existing rules expressly authorize reconsideration at the next meeting (as some bylaws do), or (b) a member gives notice that he will have that act or question reconsidered at the next meeting, or (c) moves to reconsider and enter it on the minutes.

Reconsideration can be acted on at an adjourned meeting or special meeting if it was moved, or notice thereof was given, at the previous meeting, or if notice thereof is contained in the call for the meeting.

When an adopted motion may be safely executed. No question can be reconsidered which has been carried out or parts of which have been carried out.

It is not safe to carry out an adopted main question before the meeting has adjourned, because the question can be reconsidered during it and the vote could be reversed (unless before the meeting adjourns, reconsideration of the adopted question is purposely proposed and is purposely defeated, in which case it is then safe to execute the adopted question before the meeting adjourns, if so desired, since, under the rules, the same question cannot be *reconsidered* a second time; but if the said question is left unexecuted up to *any* next meeting, it can be *rescinded*).

Premature execution of a question. If a member gives notice to reconsider at the next meeting a main question adopted at the present meeting, or the organization's bylaws specify that reconsideration of a question may be made at the next meeting, then that question may not be executed in the meantime, since (a) this would interfere with the assembly's right to reconsider that question at the next meeting, and (b) the assembly can reverse the previous body's decision on it and then defeat it — or amend it to suit.

Therefore, if anyone executes that question prematurely (prior to the next meeting), he does so at his own risk.

Hence, where it is voted "to authorize the treasurer to buy ten tickets at ten dollars each to Senator X's testimonial banquet," and member Y then gives notice to reconsider the question at the next meeting, if the treasurer pays for those tickets with organization funds before the next meeting, and the assembly at such meeting defeats the motion (or amends it to buy only *"two* tickets for the president and his wife to attend"), the organization is then responsible for the payment of only two tickets; the treasurer is personally responsible for the other tickets.

To make an adopted question executable immediately:

CHAIR (announcing the vote): "The *ayes* have it, and we will buy fifty tickets to Senator Y's testimonial banquet."

MEMBER B (of the *majority*, alertly): "Mr. Chairman, I move that we reconsider the question to buy fifty tickets. I made that motion, and I voted in favor of it." (Seconded by one of the majority.)

CHAIR: "It is moved and seconded to reconsider the adopted motion to buy the fifty tickets. Is there any debate on the reconsideration?"

After debate and also after the majority has successfully defeated all attempts by the minority to postpone the reconsideration, or to table it, or to recess or adjourn; and assuming no one of the minority is aware of his right to move to reconsider and enter, which, under the rules, may be proposed, because it outranks the simple form "to reconsider"; the reconsideration is then put to a vote — the minority side being expected to vote *for* reconsideration and the majority *against* reconsideration; thus:

CHAIR (continuing): "There being no further debate, those in favor of reconsidering the motion to buy fifty tickets will say aye; those opposed will say no. The *noes* have it; reconsideration is *defeated*."

MINORITY MEMBER A: "I doubt the vote."

CHAIR: "The vote has been doubted. Those in favor of reconsideration will stand; forty-three; be seated. Those opposed will stand; sixty-one; be seated. The negative has it, and the motion to buy the banquet tickets is not reconsidered."

MAJORITY MEMBER B: "Mr. Chairman, may the treasurer now execute a check for five hundred dollars and hand it to the Senator's banquet chairman, who has been waiting in the corridor in hope that the motion would pass?"

CHAIR: "Yes, because that motion cannot be reconsidered a second time; hence the motion has now been made executable at once, and the treasurer may now pay for the tickets."

May be better to reintroduce. When a useful proposition is defeated, and you do not command enough votes to have it reconsidered, instead of giving notice to reconsider that question at the next meeting, it is more practical to introduce it all over again at the next meeting under new business.

May be better to give notice to rescind. If a useless proposition or question has been adopted by a willful majority, even though the question has been intentionally proposed for reconsideration and its reconsideration is purposely rejected, give notice anyway, at the meeting, that you will *rescind* that question at the next meeting, so that if the question will not have been executed by such next meeting you will then need only a majority vote to rescind it since you gave previous notice.

Reconsideration by Special Groups

Can directors decide reconsideration? A reconsideration of a question decided in a committee or board, standing or special, may be proposed therein at any meeting whatsoever, regardless of time, by anyone who did not vote with the losing side (provided that question has not been carried out in the meantime). Hence, reconsideration can be proposed (a) by one who was absent, or (b) by one who failed to vote when he was present, or (c) by one who voted on the prevailing side.

In committee of the whole. Reconsideration is not in order in a committee of the whole. But an adopted motion "to go into a committee of the whole" can be reconsidered.

Reconsideration in bodies meeting daily. In assemblies that meet daily, as in legislatures and conventions lasting more than one day (and also in annual meetings), unless the body's rules specify to the contrary, reconsideration of a question can be made either on the same day the vote to be reconsidered was taken, or on the next business day.

Reconsideration at a convention. Individual delegates of a district or county to a convention (or annual meeting) can move reconsideration of any question when in their own district or county, but when they have been instructed to vote as a unit in the convention, then reconsideration of a question in the convention must be moved in accord with the express wishes of a *majority* of the district or county.

When acting in the absence of their delegates in a convention (or annual meeting), the alternates can exercise and enjoy the same rights and privileges as their delegates; and they are bound by the same instructions as the delegates.

Where a convention or other body has many resolutions or items to consider and vote on, and, in order to expedite business, it is agreed that, unless a member claims the floor to debate or amend a resolution or item when read, each such question "shall be considered as having been carried," or similar language, a reconsideration afterward of any such resolution or item can be made by any member who was *present* at the time.

RECONSIDER AND ENTER (S)

Definition. Another form for saying "Mr. Chairman, I move to reconsider this question [naming it] and have the reconsideration taken up at the *next* meeting," is the technical parliamentary term, "I move to reconsider the question and have it entered upon the minutes of this meeting."

Note: Whenever a mischievous, arrogant or unscrupulous temporary majority passes undesirable business at a meeting, and the minority does not command enough votes to swing reconsideration and reverse it, if one of the minority who alertly voted with the prevailing side moves to reconsider and enter the objectionable act and it is seconded, this motion then has the effect of automatically restraining execution of the objectionable business until the proposed reconsideration has been acted on at the next meeting, since an adopted question is not considered as having been finally passed if a motion to reconsider it is pending.

Basic rules. The motion to reconsider and enter must be proposed by one who voted on the prevailing side of the question wished reconsidered; any member can second it. The motion to reconsider and enter, or its equivalent, previous notice to reconsider at the next meeting, is undebatable, unamendable, and is not voted on. Nothing else can be done to it. It may not be tabled, postponed, or objected to, because such a motion is essentially a previous notice to the members. The mere proposal, or the making, of this motion, duly seconded, is all that is required to be done in order to stop execution of an objectionable question until its reconsideration is acted on at the next meeting.

If simple reconsideration has been moved. To reconsider and enter can be moved even after the simple motion to reconsider has been made, provided the pending reconsideration has not been put to a vote, since after one reconsideration has been voted on a question, a second reconsideration of the same question is not in order.

Cannot be acted on at same session. The question on which to reconsider and enter has been imposed cannot be acted on at the same session, but only on another day: the next meeting, whether such next meeting be an adjourned meeting, a special one, or regular meeting.

Notice given when business pending. Reconsideration of a main motion can be acted on only when no other business is before the body at the time; but notice of intent to move reconsideration can be given even though other business is pending at the time, in which case the Chair can say: "The Chair is in receipt of the notice," or, "The secretary will make note of the notice of reconsideration to be acted on when the pending business is disposed of, if the member wishes to pursue the reconsideration [or, to call up his reconsideration]."

To call it up at next meeting. Any member may call it up at the next meeting; no formal motion is necessary, since the reconsideration was proposed at the last meeting. A simple request "that the reconsideration previously made be now taken up," or, "Mr. Chairman, I now call up the motion to reconsider which was entered on the minutes," is sufficient.

The question can be called up, or taken up, when that question's own category has been reached, or business of the same class, unless the assembly otherwise authorizes, as by suspending the rules in order to have the reconsideration of that question acted on sooner, or later, in the order of business.

If reconsideration not called up. If the motion to reconsider and enter a question is not called up before adjournment of the next meeting, the objectionable act then goes into effect upon adjournment.

When dilatory. To reconsider and enter is out of order when its purpose is obviously dilatory. Thus if it is voted to spend $300 for convention hall decorations and it is then moved to reconsider and enter it (for final action at the next meeting), if the next meeting will not be held until *after* the convention is over, the motion is absurd and unentertainable.

Out of order at last meeting. To reconsider and enter (or its equivalent form, previous notice to reconsider at the next meeting) is out of order if moved at the last meeting of a session, as in a convention or annual meeting having a sine die adjournment or in an assembly having regular meetings less frequently than quarterly. But if it has been made at a previous sitting or meeting of the same session in such convention or assembly, it may then be called up for final action on the last sitting of the session.

How proposed and transacted

CHAIR (announcing the vote on the pending question): "The *ayes* have it, and we will purchase fifty tickets at ten dollars each to Senator Y's testimonial banquet."

MEMBER A (of the minority, alertly): "Mr. Chairman, I move to have this motion reconsidered at the next meeting." (Seconded.)

CHAIR: "Did you vote with the prevailing side on this question?"

MEMBER A: "Yes. I sensed that this unnecessary and costly proposition would pass, and so I intentionally voted with the prevailing side in order to qualify to move to reconsider and enter."

CHAIR: "It is duly moved and seconded to reconsider and enter the question to buy the fifty tickets. Under the rules, reconsideration and entry automatically carries this question over to the next meeting, where it will be considered on its merits at that time. Hence, this question is neither debatable nor amendable at this meeting."

Withdrawal of previous notice to reconsider and enter. A member who gives previous notice at a meeting to reconsider a question, or to reconsider it at the next meeting, can withdraw his notice at will during the *same* session. When a member withdraws his notice at the same meeting, any other qualified member can give the same notice.

But such previous notice may not be withdrawn at the *next* meeting at which the reconsideration is expected to be acted on, except by unanimous consent, because it is then too late for others to give the same notice to advantage. To illustrate:

(1) MEMBER A (at the same meeting): "Mr. Chairman, I withdraw the previous notice I gave earlier tonight to reconsider at the next meeting the adopted motion to sell our clubhouse."

CHAIR: "Mr. A withdraws his previous notice." (No second is needed and no one's consent is required to withdraw it at the same meeting.)

MEMBER B (now rises): "Mr. Chairman, since that previous notice was withdrawn, *I* now give the same previous notice; I voted on the prevailing side." (Giving previous notice to reconsider must be made by one who voted with the prevailing side, since such notice is equivalent to *moving* to reconsider.)

CHAIR: "The Chair is in receipt of the notice." (Then, at the next meeting:)

(2) MEMBER B: "Mr. Chairman, I wish to withdraw the previous notice I gave to reconsider at this meeting the motion to sell the clubhouse which was adopted at the last meeting."

CHAIR (knowledgeable one): "As this is the meeting at which the motion to reconsider is expected to be acted on, withdrawal of that notice now requires a unanimous vote [or, unanimous consent]." (He may then ask:) "Is there any objection to the withdrawal of the notice?"

If even one member objects, there can be no withdrawal, and reconsideration is then acted on and disposed of in due course. But if there is *no* objection, the previous notice is automatically withdrawn, and with it is also withdrawn the motion to reconsider (which has now been rendered unactable by the withdrawal of its cohering notice), and hence the previously adopted motion to sell the clubhouse can now be carried out as the body had previously decided.

Note to the minority: It is conceivable that a conniving majority may deliberately give such previous notice ahead of interested minority members, and then purposely withdraw it later at the meeting when minority members, who had qualified to give notice of reconsideration of a question, have left the meeting, in which case there would be no reconsideration to act on at the next meeting.

To outwit or thwart such stratagem, either (1) stay through the meeting, so you can give the same notice if it has been withdrawn, or (2) give the previous notice ahead of them, which only you can then withdraw, or (3) give the same previous notice after they give theirs (if you may have to leave the meeting), saying to the Chair: "Mr. Chairman, I give the same notice [naming it], because I may have to leave the meeting shortly, and I want to make certain that the motion for which this notice has been given will be acted on at the next meeting," or similar words.

In other words, a member can give the same previous notice another member gives, to thus assure action under the notice at the proper time — just as he can second the same motion another member also seconds or sign a petition that also others are signing or have signed, etc.

Some exemplary rules on reconsideration

(1) No question or proposition which has been executed, or of which parts thereof have been executed, can be reconsidered. It is then too late.

(2) An affirmative vote entailing a proceeding or step in the nature of a contract cannot be reconsidered if the other party to the contract has been duly notified of the vote.

If A's application for membership is voted accepted and he has been notified of the fact via the usual and customary channels, the said application for membership may not then be reconsidered (strictly speaking), because A's contract with the organization has been consummated — his offer to join having been accepted; but if A's application was *rejected* by the body, the vote on it *can* be reconsidered.

If B's resignation is accepted, and he has been duly notified, or he is present when it is accepted, the resignation has been consummated, and it may not be reconsidered, strictly speaking; but if, as sometimes happens, it *is* reconsidered, in order, for instance, to encourage continuation of his membership, and no one objects to such reconsideration at the time, the action taken is not invalid.

If C is elected to office or position, and he is present at the time, or he is absent and when notified of his election does not decline, such election then becomes a vested right of possession to the office and it cannot be reconsidered or rescinded.

(3) If a bylaw specifies as follows: "In the event of the president's resignation, removal or death, the vice president shall assume the duties of president" (or similar language), the vice president is under those conditions automatically, and constitutionally, vested with the office of president and serves the balance of the term. Hence he cannot be ousted or removed from such office except upon charges for misfeasance or misconduct in office, or as the bylaws may otherwise prescribe in such connection.

If, after the vice president has thus become president, the opposition in the organization has a *special* meeting duly called, the purpose of which is "to amend so as to repeal the bylaw under which the vice president assuméd the duties of president, and if the bylaw is *repealed* we will then elect someone else as president," then two things must be noted: in the first place, there is no *vacancy* to be filled by this meeting; and hence an election to choose another president would be null and void, because the vacancy originally caused by the resignation or death of the president has already been constitutionally filled by the vice president; and in the second place, should the meeting *repeal* that bylaw (which it may do, since due previous notice was given), the legal effect of such repeal is to involve or apply only to *future* vacancies; it does not affect the previously filled vacancy at all.

(4) If a bylaw (or rule) states: "When a vote is carried it shall be in order for any member to move a reconsideration thereof at the same session," this does not mean that a member may not also move reconsideration therein of the vote on a question that was not carried, since

the bylaw does not say that a *negative* vote may not be reconsidered; it merely stresses that a *carried* vote can be reconsidered.

(5) If a bylaw (or rule, as in a city council) provides that "A member wishing to move reconsideration shall file written notice of same with the secretary or clerk within . . . [specified days or hours] after adjournment of the session," such a provision then makes it unnecessary for a member to move to reconsider and enter the question because the filing with the secretary or clerk of the notice to reconsider constitutes "reconsideration and entry" (or sufficient previous notice).

(6) If the rules of the body (as in a city council) specify that "the same question shall not be subject to reconsideration more than once," and the council has already reconsidered a question *once*, if a member afterward files written notice with the clerk "to reconsider that same question at the next session," the notice so filed is void, since it violates the council's existing rules; hence the clerk ignores such filing as being unconstitutional, and the question which had been previously decided then takes its course of proceeding (as by being sent to the board of aldermen for its action upon it).

(7) If a question has been adopted by the assembly, and a motion is then made to reconsider it at the next meeting (that is, to reconsider and enter it), the reconsideration of that question is taken up when business of the same category is taken up at the next meeting. Hence, if a question desired reconsidered was originally under the category of new business, then it can be reconsidered when new business is reached; if the question was adopted under the category of unfinished business or under reports of committees, or otherwise, then reconsideration of that question at the next meeting can be taken up when its category is reached. A motion to suspend the rules may be made to take up the reconsideration of an adopted question at any time or under any other category desired. It requires a $\frac{2}{3}$ vote.

Uses of Reconsideration

To expedite accomplishment of the assembly's business and thus carry out its will, or to obstruct its business and thus frustrate its will, the following parliamentary tactics or maneuvers can be utilized by either the majority or minority, when need be:

To frustrate it: (1) Move to reconsider the question (but first qualify by voting on the prevailing side). (2) If you have not enough votes to prevail on reconsideration at the same meeting, move to reconsider and enter on the minutes, or to reconsider the question and have it acted on at the next meeting. Such a motion automatically prevents execution of that question prior to the next meeting, since under the rules of parliamentary law the mere making of the motion to reconsider and enter made by one who voted on the prevailing side and seconded is sufficient to suspend execution of the question, because a question is not considered passed if a motion or notice to reconsider it is pending.

To carry it out: (1) Vote down their reconsideration of the question which your own side has adopted. (2) to prevent the minority from proposing reconsideration or to reconsider and enter (that is, to reconsider the question and have it acted on at the next meeting); or in order to make that question executable immediately and not have to wait even until the meeting adjourns, one of the majority side can purposely move reconsideration of the question, and then have it intentionally voted down by the majority. After the majority side has thus defeated the reconsideration of the question, the minority side may not propose reconsideration of the same question thereafter, because under the rules the same question may not be proposed for reconsideration a second time, either at the same meeting or at any next meeting.

RESCIND (S, D, A, $\frac{2}{3}$, R)

To rescind means to repeal (cancel or abolish) some motion previously adopted by the assembly.

The motion to rescind is usually applied to votes taken on main motions and on votes on an appeal from the Chair's decision, on orders of the day previously acted on, and such of the subsidiary and privileged motions as have been transacted as main motions.

Basic rules. The motion to rescind requires a second. It is debatable and amendable. To pass, it requires a $\frac{2}{3}$ vote, unless previous notice to rescind was given, in which case only a majority vote is required. Any member may move rescission regardless of how or whether he voted on the motion in question. Rescission may be reconsidered only if the negative side prevailed. It is not in order at the same sitting if reconsideration has been moved and lost. The motion to rescind is in order at any later meeting, regardless of how much time has elapsed since the original motion was passed. To rescind yields to the subsidiary, privileged, and apt incidental motions (see pp. 47–48).

How proposed and transacted

MEMBER: "Mr. Chairman, I move that we rescind the motion adopted two meetings ago to buy a new flag, a gavel and a dictionary." (Seconded.)

CHAIR: "It has been moved and seconded to rescind the motion passed two meetings ago, which has not yet been executed; namely: to buy a new flag, a gavel and a dictionary. Is there any discussion on the motion to rescind?" (After debate, if any, it is put to vote; a $\frac{2}{3}$ vote is required, thus:) "Those in favor of rescinding the motion will raise their right hand. Twenty-six. Hands down. Those opposed will raise their right

---

KEY QUIZ

Q. Does the motion to rescind require a second? *A.* Yes.

Q. Is it debatable? *A.* Yes.

Q. Is it amendable? *A.* Yes.

Q. What vote adopts the motion to rescind? *A.* Two-thirds, if previous notice to rescind has not been given, but only a majority vote if previous notice has been given.

Q. Who can propose rescission? *A.* Any member, regardless of how or if he voted on the motion he seeks to rescind.

Q. When can it be acted on? *A.* When no other business is actually pending before the body; but giving mere *notice* of intention to rescind may be given if other business is pending, provided no one is speaking on the pending business at the time, or if a speaker yields for the purpose.

Q. What class of motion is it? *A.* Restoratory.

Q. Can it be reconsidered? *A.* Yes, if the negative side prevails.

hand. Seven. Hands down. There being two-thirds in favor of the motion, the affirmative has it and the motion has been rescinded." This action means that the motion to buy the articles mentioned has been repealed or abolished, and the authority to buy them has been cancelled.

Previous notice of intention to rescind is given as follows:

MEMBER: "Mr. Chairman, I give notice that at the next meeting I shall move to rescind the motion . . . [naming it]." Only a majority vote is necessary to adopt rescission at the next meeting.

To rescind is a restoratory motion, and when proposed it automatically opens the original motion to debate. It can be acted on when no other business is actually before the body at the time.

Notice to rescind. When notice to rescind a question has been duly given, the rescission can be acted on when the category of that question is reached, or under unfinished business or new business, unless it is otherwise agreed to by the body.

Withdrawal of notice to rescind. A previous notice to rescind can be withdrawn during the same meeting, because when it is withdrawn any member can give the same notice; but it cannot be withdrawn at the next meeting except by unanimous consent, because it is then too late for other members to propose it to advantage.

Giving notice to rescind (as distinguished from moving to rescind) cannot be tabled or postponed because notices are not subject to tablement or postponement.

Method of voting affects rescission. Any vote taken by ballot or roll call on a main motion can be rescinded.

If voting by mail is permitted by the bylaws, the vote taken by mail or referendum on a proposition cannot be rescinded by the body at any meeting; such vote by mail or referendum is rescissible only by another vote taken by the same method.

Elections cannot be rescinded. Votes on elections can be recounted but not rescinded.

Rescission in same meeting. The motion to rescind usually applies to acts or questions decided in past meetings (because the motion to reconsider applies more advantageously to motions acted on in a present meeting). But when it is too late, during the same meeting, to move reconsideration, or when no one is eligible or willing to move it, to rescind can then be proposed.

Note: Since to rescind applies only to main motions and those in the nature of main motions, then no subsidiary or privileged motion can be rescinded, because they are not main motions.

Rescinded motion may be renewed. A question which has been rescinded is regarded as though it had not previously been proposed at all. Hence that same question can be renewed (reproposed) in the same form as before, or in changed form, during the *same* meeting, or in any next meeting.

Cannot rescind executed motion. If a motion has been executed in its entirety, it is too late to rescind the motion because it has been executed, and nothing remains to rescind, or cancel. But if it has only been partially executed, the unexecuted part can be rescinded.

Difference between reconsider and rescind. (1) Rescission can be proposed by anyone, whereas reconsideration can be proposed only by one who actually voted with the prevailing side. (2) Rescind can be proposed at any meeting, whereas reconsideration can be proposed only during the same meeting the action was taken, unless notice has been given to reconsider that action at the next meeting. (3) Rescind requires a $\frac{2}{3}$ vote, except where previous notice has been given, whereas reconsideration requires only a majority vote. (4) Giving notice to rescind does not prevent the carrying out or execution of the motion previously decided, whereas giving notice to reconsider prevents the execution of the action previously taken. (5) Rescind cancels a motion outright, whereas reconsider restores that question before the body to be voted on again.

Some exemplary rules on rescission. (1) The vote on a proceeding or question cannot be rescinded if something was done to the question that is now too late to undo, or is illegal, or is absurd to attempt to undo. (2) A proceeding entailing a contractual phase cannot be rescinded if the other party to the contract has been duly notified thereof; hence, (a) if X's application for membership is voted accepted and he has been duly informed thereof, the vote on the application cannot be rescinded; (b) if Y's resignation from membership or office is accepted, and he was duly apprised thereof or he is present at the meeting and sees it accepted, the vote thereon cannot be rescinded; (c) if Z is elected to office and he was so notified or is present at the meeting and sees himself elected, and he does not decline the office, the vote thereon cannot be rescinded; or (d) if A is voted suspended or expelled from membership or office, and he has been duly informed thereof, the vote on the proceeding is not rescissible.

No rescission if reconsideration pending. Where a question already adopted can be reached for further action thereon by calling up the motion to reconsider (which was previously made), neither the vote on the original question nor on its proposed reconsideration can be rescinded, because reconsideration keeps that question alive until the time for reconsideration has elapsed.

EXPUNGE (S, D, A, $\frac{2}{3}$, R)

To expunge is to obliterate or cross out. It is a form of the motion to rescind which implies strong condemnation or disapproval of the motion to be expunged, and is subject to the same rules as the motion to rescind.

The difference between the two is that when a motion has been ordered rescinded, the contents of that motion, although now null and void, still remain recorded in the minutes as originally passed without any alteration, along with the fact that the motion was rescinded. But when a motion has been ordered expunged, the contents of the motion in the minutes book are crossed out; a line is drawn through the words of the motion, or the words can be encircled instead. In either case a notation is made in the margin of the minutes stating that "this motion was ordered expunged by vote of the body." It is dated and signed by the secretary. The words should still be readable, to check that no words other than those ordered expunged have been crossed out.

Basic rules. To expunge is a restoratory motion. It is secondable, debatable and amendable. It requires a $\frac{2}{3}$ vote for adoption, unless previous notice to expunge was given in a previous meeting or in the call for the meeting, in which case only a majority vote is required. A negative vote on it can be reconsidered.

RATIFY (S, D, A, **M**, **R**)

To ratify means to approve, confirm, validate, make legal, etc. The object of the motion to ratify is to approve or legalize an act. No unconstitutional or illegal act or motion can be ratified.

Basic rules. The motion to ratify requires a second, and is debatable and amendable. It requires a majority vote for adoption. It is a restoratory motion and when proposed it opens to debate the merits of the motion to be ratified. It can be proposed when no other business is before the body. Anyone can propose or second the motion to ratify. A negative vote on it can be reconsidered.

Only such acts can be ratified as fall or come within the scope of the business or objectives of the organization.

When ratification is used. The motion to ratify is often used if a meeting in which a quorum was not present acted on some urgent business, and ratification is proposed at the next meeting to make that act valid.

To ratify is also used to approve acts of officers, boards or negotiating committees, or to approve contract agreements between the organization and another party which require the body's approval before they can be carried out.

How proposed and entertained

MEMBER: "Mr. Chairman, I move that we ratify the action of the treasurer in giving fifty dollars to X charity for our organization when the solicitor called at his office." (Seconded.)

CHAIR: "It has been moved and seconded to ratify the action of the treasurer. Is there any discussion?" (After discussion, if any, it is put to vote.) "Those in favor of ratification will say aye; those opposed will say no. The ayes have it, and the action is ratified." (The unauthorized act of the treasurer is now approved by the body. It is legalized as if authorized in the first place. If its ratification does not prevail, the fifty dollars comes out of the treasurer's own pocket since he acted without authority.)

KEY QUIZ

Q. Does the motion to ratify require a second? *A.* Yes.
Q. Is it debatable? *A.* Yes.
Q. Is it amendable? *A.* Yes.
Q. Who can propose or second it? *A.* Anyone.
Q. What vote adopts it? *A.* Majority.
Q. What class of motion is it? *A.* Restoratory.
Q. If adopted, what happens to the act in question? *A.* It is thereby approved.
Q. Can it be reconsidered? *A.* A negative vote can be.

TAKE FROM THE TABLE (S, M)

The motion to take from the table (that is, to take from the table a question previously tabled) is used when it is desired to bring that question back before the body for further consideration. If a question was not previously tabled, the motion to take it from the table is out of order.

Basic rules. The motion to take from the table (like the motion to lay on the table) requires a second, is undebatable and unamendable; it needs a majority vote and cannot be reconsidered. A motion which has just been taken from the table cannot be forthwith tabled again until some debate or other business has intervened.

When a motion may be taken from the table. It can be proposed either at the same session the motion was tabled, or at the next session in bodies that meet regularly at least quarterly. After the next session, the motion to take from the table becomes extinct, and it cannot be entertained. In other words, a motion which is voted tabled (table refers to the secretary) remains alive in the secretary's records for the duration of the present session and the next session; thereafter, the original motion which was tabled is said to be dead; hence, the motion to take it from the table expires with it and cannot be proposed after the next session, because there is nothing to take from the table. After the next session, the original motion can be reintroduced at any meeting.

Note: Tabled motions in conventions or annual meetings die upon final adjournment; but they can be reintroduced or refiled at the next annual meeting or convention.

How proposed and entertained

MEMBER (when no other business is pending): "Mr. Chairman, I move that we take from the table the motion to buy a new desk, which was laid on the table earlier at this meeting [or, the last meeting]." (Seconded.)

CHAIR: "It has been moved and seconded to take from the table the motion to buy a new desk, which was tabled earlier at this meeting." (Since it is undebatable and unamendable, he puts it to a vote; thus:) "Those in favor of taking the motion from the table will say aye; those opposed will say no. The ayes have it, and the motion is taken from the table." (Since it was ordered taken from the table, the question is now automatically restored before the body for further action, and the Chair then properly describes the situation thus:) "The question now before

---

KEY QUIZ

Q. Is this motion secondable? *A.* Yes.
Q. Is it debatable? *A.* No.
Q. Is it amendable? *A.* No.
Q. What vote adopts it? *A.* Majority.
Q. When can it be proposed? *A.* When no other business is pending.
Q. What class of motion is it? *A.* Restoratory.
Q. Can it be reconsidered? *A.* No.
Q. When can business be taken from the table? *A.* Either at the same session at which it was tabled or at the next session in bodies which meet as frequently as quarterly.
Q. Who can propose this motion? *A.* Anyone.

the body is on the motion to buy a new desk. Is there any discussion on this motion?" (After discussion it is put to vote, and it is voted either to buy the desk or not to buy it.)

Chapter 11
INCIDENTAL MAIN MOTIONS

There is a class of motions in parliamentary law and procedure known as incidental main motions. They can be also referred to as quasi-main motions (*quasi*, Latin for "as if").

They are called incidental main motions because they can be used in a dual role — depending upon the sense in which they are employed.

Incidental main motions are in the nature of and are treated exactly like main motions (except as otherwise shown in their specific treatment in the text). They pertain to some previous or present action taken by the body, or which propose future action, as shown in the following illustrations (among conceivable others such as to accept a resignation, to take the sense of the assembly on a question, etc.). Being in the nature of main motions, they yield to motions of higher rank — just as all main motions do.

Action on committee reports. Whatsoever the action, as when moving to accept the report, it will necessarily pertain or be incidental to a previous action of the body in designating the committee, from which a report may be expected, including reports of delegates and all officers' reports.

Action on the bylaws. Whatsoever the action, whether in amending or revising them, it will necessarily be incidental or pertinent to some existing governing rule previously acted on and adopted at some meeting by the body.

Action on the minutes. Whatsoever the action, whether in accepting or omitting the reading, it will necessarily concern the acts of record of the doings of the body of a previous meeting.

Nominations. But only if the subject matter, namely the slate or ticket, is not actually pending before the body; if the slate or ticket is pending before the body, then further nominations are equivalent to amendments to the ticket or slate; hence, further nominations in such a case are in the nature of the subsidiary motion to amend, and not incidental main motions.

Methods of voting. That is, motions suggesting how the vote on a motion shall be taken — as by secret ballot, roll call, etc., provided the subject or question to be taken up is not actually pending before the body; if the question is pending, then such methods of voting when proposed are incidental motions and not incidental main motions.

Appointment of committees. Provided the question or subject to be taken up by the committee is not actually before the body; if it is, then this motion is the subsidiary motion to refer, and not the incidental main motion.

Fix a time to which to adjourn. Provided no other business is before the body when proposed; if other business is pending, it is the privileged motion, not the incidental main motion.

Adjourn. Provided it specifies a future time for adjourning and not immediate adjournment; or when the assembly holds the first meeting of its existence, or the last meeting of its career and has no other governing rule or provision for reassembling or convening again; if the above exceptions are not contemplated in the motion, to adjourn is always the privileged motion.

Recess. But only if it specifies a future time, or is proposed when no other business is before the body; otherwise it is the privileged motion to recess, not the incidental main motion to recess.

Limit or extend debate. But not if other business is before the body when it is proposed; if other business is pending, it is the subsidiary motion.

Postpone. But not if other business is pending at the time it is proposed, as when it is proposed to *postpone* carrying out a previously decided motion to a *later* time.

Refer. But not if other business is before the body at the time, as when a question previously decided, such as to build a new clubhouse, is now being referred to a special committee with instructions to report at the next meeting.

Amend. As when you amend bylaws. Proposed amendments to the bylaws (constitution or standing rules) are in the nature of incidental main motions, since the bylaw (or constitution, or rule) is not actually before the body when you seek to amend it; the proposed amendment to them is pending, instead; hence, in all such cases, an amendment to the bylaws is in the nature of an incidental main motion or when you amend some question or motion previously adopted. An example: the body has previously adopted a motion "to buy a new state flag." The motion did not specify the price at which to buy it, and now it is desired to amend that motion by adding the words "at a cost not to exceed fifty dollars." In all similar cases, the motion to amend is the incidental main motion, and not the subsidiary motion to amend.

Suspend the rules. Provided that the question for whose benefit the suspension is sought is not actually before the body.

Other types of incidental main motions, in addition to the fourteen just enumerated are the following: to discharge a committee; to take the sense of the assembly pro or con on a question; to instruct the secretary to cast one ballot for a nominee or a proposition; to impeach, suspend or expel; to reconsider, rescind or ratify when no other business is pending; to postpone indefinitely (when no other business is pending); all reports of officers, boards and committees of any kind; votes of confidence (or of no confidence); motions to censure or to commend or compliment; motions like "I move the adoption [or, rejection] of the motion," or "I move that we proceed to take the vote on the motion before us"; and many, many more.

Note: All bylaws, and this includes constitutions and standing rules, and all the sections, paragraphs, provisions and clauses under them, are properly classified as original *main* motions at the time they are originally proposed for adoption as bylaws or as a constitution; but after their adoption they assume the status of standing laws or bylaws, or standing constitution, and thereafter, when a bylaw or constitutional provision is sought to be changed or amended in any way, such motions are technically termed incidental main motions.

Chapter 12
RENEWAL OF MOTIONS

1. *Renewal of main motions and resolutions.* A main motion or resolution which has been defeated cannot be renewed (offered again) during the same whole session, unless it is materially changed. But the vote on it can be reconsidered. Such defeated question can, however, be reintroduced at any future new session.

2. *Renewal of subsidiary motions.* Five of the seven subsidiary motions; namely: to lay on the table, the previous question, to limit or extend debate, to postpone to a definite time, and to refer to a committee, can be renewed on the same question at the same meeting if reasonable time has elapsed since they were last defeated, or after progress in business or debate, or when other motions or business have intervened. The same amendment to the same question cannot be renewed during the same session; but the vote on it can be reconsidered. The motion to postpone indefinitely cannot be renewed on the same motion, but an affirmative vote on such postponement can be reconsidered.

3. *Renewal of privileged motions.* The motion to fix an adjourned meeting cannot be renewed, but its vote can be reconsidered. The motions to adjourn and to recess can be renewed provided reasonable time has elapsed since they were last defeated, or after other motions or business have intervened. The same question of privilege cannot be renewed at the same meeting. A call for the orders of the day, if lost, is not renewable after disposal of the pending motions.

4. *Renewal of incidental motions.* The following incidental motions are not renewable if they relate to the same point: appeal, point of order, suspend the rules, for the same purpose, or objection to the consideration of the question.

5. *Renewal of restoratory motions.* The motions to reconsider, rescind and ratify cannot be renewed. The motion to take from the table can be renewed when other business has been transacted since its last defeat.

6. *Renewal of withdrawn motions.* A withdrawn motion can be renewed at the same meeting; and all previous notices that have been withdrawn at the same meeting may also be renewed at that same meeting, either by the same person or any other.

Distinction between whole meeting and parts thereof. The words session and meeting are synonymous terms. Any distinction between them depends upon the organization's bylaws; namely:

(1) If the bylaws designate the body's gatherings as "meetings" (as in "meetings shall be held monthly," or "special meetings may be called by the president," or "the annual meeting shall be held in June"), the bylaws make each such meeting a *whole* meeting; and if additional

gatherings of it under the same *call* for that meeting are needed to be held (as in convention or annual meeting), all such continued or additional assemblages of it are correctly known as sittings or sessions (or parts) of the same *whole* meeting (just like the calendar, which makes a week the whole week; and each part of that week is a day).

(2) If the bylaws designate the body's gatherings as "sessions" (as in "regular sessions shall be held twice a month," or "special sessions may be called by the president," or "the convention session [or annual session] shall be held in June"), each such session is made a *whole* session by the bylaws; and if additional assemblages of that session are needed to be held, then such continued or additional assemblages of it are properly referred to as sittings or meetings of that same whole session.

Note: The same rule would apply if the bylaws call the body's meetings or sessions "sittings," in which case the sitting's additional assemblages would be called meetings or sessions (or parts) of that same whole sitting.

Why the foregoing distinction is important. It aids enlightened parliamentary practice to recognize the rights that can be exercised during additional or continued sittings of a meeting or session, as discussed just above.

For instance, in conventions and annual meetings holding a five-day session, for instance, (*a*) you can "take from the table," up to adjournment of the whole session, any question which was tabled at a previous sitting of that session; (*b*) you can postpone from one sitting to the next therein any pending question, and then strategically take it up at the sitting most serviceable for your purposes; (*c*) a main question which is defeated at any sitting of the convention session cannot be renewed or proposed again at any other sitting of the session, although, of course, the question can be reconsidered therein; (*d*) if a main motion is voted *indefinitely* postponed at any sitting, that question is killed outright and cannot be made to be pending before the body again at that session unless its postponement has first been voted reconsidered.

Chapter 13

MOTIONS GROUPED BY RULES AND FUNCTIONS

Motions which do not require a second

A point of order.
A question of information.
A parliamentary inquiry.
A request of any kind.
Nominations for office, unless required by law or rule.
To rise to a question of privilege.
To doubt a quorum.
To doubt a vote (or "call for a division").
To fill a blank.
To call for the orders of the day.
To object to the consideration of a question.
To withdraw one's motion (unless it is not before the body).
Committee reports (or resolutions, recommendations, amendments, or any proposals or substitutes). The same is true of boards.

Motions which are not debatable

All five privileged motions: to fix a time to which to adjourn, to adjourn, to recess, to rise to a question of privilege, and to call for the orders of the day.

Three of the seven subsidiary motions: to lay on the table, the previous question, and to limit or extend debate.

Close or reopen nominations.

Close or reopen polls.

Amend or reconsider an undebatable motion.

Point of order, information, inquiry, clarification.

Doubt the vote or quorum.

Dispense with (omit) the reading of the minutes.

All the incidental motions except appeals and consideration by paragraph.

To take from the table.

To suspend the rules.

Motions which cannot be amended

Three of the seven subsidiary motions: lay on the table, previous question, postpone indefinitely.

Three of the five privileged motions: to adjourn, to rise to a question of privilege, and to call for the orders of the day.

Reconsider.

Take from the table.

The following incidental motions: point of order, parliamentary inquiry, information, appeal, suspend the rules, division of the assembly, objection to consideration of a question, to read from paper or manuscript, withdrawing a motion, withdrawing a second, filling a blank, requests of any kind, doubting a quorum.

A secondary amendment.

Motions which require a $\frac{2}{3}$ vote

Two of the seven subsidiary motions: previous question and limit or extend debate.

Close nominations, the polls, or discussion.

Amend or revise the constitution or bylaws, provided previous notice has been given.

Amend, revise or otherwise modify a standing rule, program or schedule of business unless previous notice was given.

Rescind, or repeal, unless previous notice was given.

Suspend the rules.

Object to the consideration of a question.

Take up a question out of its proper order.

Make a special order of business.

Discharge a special committee, unless previous notice to do so was given.

Advance or retard the time previously designated, or fixed, for adjourning or recessing or for taking up a special order of business.

Expulsion of members.

Correction (amendment) of *adopted* minutes if proposed in any session except the one in which they were first adopted.

Motions which require a unanimous vote

Any motion, proceeding or request whatsoever (provided it does not violate the bylaws) that the body cares to allow even though it is out of order when proposed, *if* there is unanimous consent; that is, if there is not a single objector.

Motions which cannot be reconsidered

One of the subsidiary motions: to lay on the table.

Four of the five privileged motions: adjourn, recess, rise to a question of privilege, call for the orders of the day.

Two of the restoratory motions: to reconsider, and to take from the table. Reconsideration.

The following incidental motions: point of order, parliamentary inquiry, information, suspend the rules, close nominations or the polls, division of a question, doubting the vote (division of the assembly), withdraw a second, requests of any kind, doubting a quorum.

Any main motion or vote remaining unexecuted after adjournment of the session in which it was adopted.

Motions (votes) which cannot be reconsidered if the affirmative side prevails (they can be reconsidered if the negative side prevails)

An adopted amendment or revision of the constitution or bylaws. That is, if an amendment to the bylaws is defeated, it can be reconsidered; but if carried, it cannot be reconsidered.

Election to membership or to office, if the member is present and does not refuse (or if the member, though absent, has been officially notified and does not decline).

Acceptance of a resignation, if the resigner is present and does not withdraw it.

To discharge a committee, if the committee has not actually taken up consideration of the question for which it was formed.

The following incidental motions: reopen nominations or the polls, object to the consideration of a question, withdraw a motion, consider by paragraph.

The following restoratory motions: rescind, ratify.

Motion (votes) which cannot be reconsidered if the negative side prevails (it can be reconsidered only if the affirmative side prevails)

To postpone indefinitely.

Motion which cannot be reconsidered after a motion under it has been put to vote

Previous question.

Motions which cannot be rescinded

A motion which has been carried out (executed).

A vote on the election of a member to office or into the organization, or on his expulsion or resignation or transfer, provided (in all four cases) that the member concerned either is present or has been officially notified of the action taken.

A motion involving a contractual obligation between the organization and another party, if the other party has been formally or officially notified of the action taken.

A motion which has been moved to be reconsidered and entered in the minutes.

Motions which cannot be renewed (proposed again) at the same session

A defeated main motion.
Adoption of an amendment to the bylaws or revision of the bylaws.
Amendments (same amendments) to a motion.
Appeal from a decision of the Chair (same appeal).
Point of order (same point).
Reconsideration of the same question.
Objection to the consideration of the same question.
Suspension of the rules for the same purpose.

Motions which cannot be withdrawn

Quorum.
Reconsider when too late for others to move it.
Any given previous notice except during same meeting at which given.

Motions which can interrupt a speaker (unless the organization's bylaws or rules specify otherwise)

A proper point of order.
A point of no quorum (doubting or challenging the quorum).
A proper question of privilege.
A call for the orders of the day.

Motions which cannot interrupt a speaker without his consent, but which may interrupt a pending proceeding

An appeal from the decision of the Chair.
A parliamentary inquiry or a request for clarification.
A question (point) of information.
Giving previous notice of reconsideration or rescission.
Objection to the consideration of original main questions.
A motion to divide a complex question.
Giving notice to amend or revise the bylaws.

Motions the Chair may ask to be put in writing

Main motions; resolutions; all amendments and substitutes; instructions to committees; points of order; appeals; questions of privilege; or, in general, any lengthy or unclear motion or proceeding.

Dual-function motions (which open to debate both themselves and the pending main motion simultaneously)

"Dual-function" is not the name of a separate class of motions, but merely a convenient descriptive term by which four motions in parliamentary law can be referred to as a group, distinguished by a special rule exclusively applicable to them. The four dual-function motions are:

To postpone indefinitely;
To reconsider;

To rescind;
To ratify.
(Note the letter *p* and the three *r*'s.)

The effect of these motions, when proposed, is special and exceptional: each of the four automatically opens to debate both the motion itself and the main motion which it concerns — a function not allowable to other motions. This is the exception to the general rule that debate shall be confined to the pending motion.

Example: Thus, if a main motion "to go on record in favor of a five-cent carfare" (which is debatable) is pending before the body and the motion "to postpone it indefinitely" is then proposed (which is also debatable), both motions can be discussed, mentioned or referred to at the same time, if desired.

How transacted. Below is an illustration of how a speaker can discuss or refer to such two motions in the course of debate (a right not permitted to members except in connection with these four dual-function motions).

MEMBER: "Mr. Chairman, I am in favor of the motion to postpone the question indefinitely [he is debating *postponement*], and I hope that postponement will prevail. A five-cent carfare in this day and age [he is now discussing the *main* motion for a five-cent fare] is ridiculous, and I sincerely trust that postponement [he is discussing *postponement* now] will prevail. The main motion for a five-cent fare is but an idle and useless gesture [he is discussing the *main* motion] and its adoption would only make us look ridiculous in the eyes of the railway trustees, and, I might say, also in the eyes of the intelligent public. Therefore, I trust that the motion to postpone indefinitely [back to *postponement*] will be adopted."

The same procedure is followed when it is moved to *reconsider* a main motion, or to *rescind* one already passed, or to *ratify* some action taken without authority from the body, or to ratify some action which requires the body's approval.

On all other proceedings debate is expected to be confined to the immediately pending question.

Chapter 14

CONSTITUTION AND BYLAWS

I. NATURE OF CONSTITUTION AND BYLAWS

Origin and meaning of terms. *Constitution* is Latin, for *cum* (con), meaning "with," "together," and *statuere* (to establish); it connotes the primary or more firmly established law. *Bylaw*, originally *bye*, Danish for "town" connotes secondary or more flexible law.

Constitution and bylaws are virtually synonymous terms. Normally, the constitution contains the basic or more permanent provisions, such as name of the organization, its objects, types of membership, etc. The bylaws import the more elastic or expandable and changeable provisions, such as the amount of dues, number of delegates to conventions, etc. An organization has inherent power to originate or adopt bylaws for its government.

Most organizations have bylaws only. Earlier organizations cherished this slight distinction between constitution and bylaws, and kept them separate. But most organizations today have bylaws only. New organizations today may adopt a constitution only, no bylaws; or bylaws only, no constitution; or they may have a combined instrument, constitution *and* bylaws, as the organization chooses. In this manual, "bylaws" also means "constitution" and their legal equivalents such as rules, regulations, canons, etc.

Advantages of bylaws only. (1) The single instrument eliminates conflict in rules between the two. (2) It eliminates confusion to members when proposing amendments thereto. (3) There is nothing which can be contained in the constitution that the bylaws cannot also contain. (4) The bylaws can provide for and safeguard the perpetuity of the organization as well as can the constitution, if previous notice and a $\frac{2}{3}$ vote is required to make changes.

Advantages of both constitution and bylaws. (1) The constitution contains the organic law and the more permanent provisions. (2) The constitution lets the bylaws contain the less essential provisions. (3) This safeguards and perpetuates the life of the organization.

To combine into one unit. To combine the constitution and bylaws into one unit, simply follow the amending process prescribed by each instrument for its amendment, then adopt the combined one as the whole and only one.

What vote needed to pass. It requires only a *majority* vote to adopt a set of bylaws in the beginning; but once these bylaws have been adopted, they automatically become standing laws or bylaws, and thereafter they can be amended at future meetings only in the manner specified in the bylaws, which is usually by a $\frac{2}{3}$ vote, provided notice of the proposed amendment has been given to the members in the call for the meeting. Check your bylaws.

When bylaws take effect. Bylaws take effect immediately upon their adoption, unless (a) it is otherwise specified or clearly understood at the time of their adoption, or (b) unless the bylaws provide differently, as, for instance, "These bylaws [or, this bylaw] shall take effect following adjournment of the session," or "in thirty days from passage," or "January 1," etc.

If there is no rule. If a rule needed for deciding any situation or proceeding is not contained in the organization's bylaws or parliamentary authority, the assembly has inherent power to create its own rule or provision — if it is not inconsistent with the organization's purposes or the existing rules of a superior body.

If there is conflict in rules. If there is conflict in the organization's laws, those contained in the constitution (or in a higher body) supersede those of the bylaws (or in a lower, subordinate, body.)

Seven fundamental subjects. There are *seven* fundamental subjects that should be contained in the bylaws. Each such subject occupies a separate article, which can be divided into as many subsections and paragraphs as desired.

The seven fundamental subjects (besides the preamble, if any) are arranged in the following logical order: name, object(s), membership, officers, meetings, parliamentary authority, amendments to bylaws.

Other articles, as desired, can be incorporated. Bylaws of some organizations contain scores of articles and hundreds of sections.

Contents of the Articles

Article I. Name. Give the organization a name or style of name.

Article II. Object(s). State its object (purpose or principles).

Article III. Membership. Prescribe qualifications for membership; class of membership, as active, associate, honorary, etc.; how admitted; vote required; dues; procedure and grounds for expulsion from membership; and anything else logically pertaining to membership.

Article IV. Officers. First list necessary officers in their proper order; give their title, qualifications, duties, term of office, manner of election, how vacancies are to be filled, procedure and grounds for censure and removal from office; and anything else pertaining to the officers. Next, describe the executive committee or board, its composition, powers, meetings, etc. Then set up standing committees, such as membership, relief, publicity, house committee, etc. Authorize method of selection or appointment of other committees; and, finally, provide for representation by delegates or deputies to conventions, etc.

Article V. Meetings. State kinds of meeting, as regular, special, and by whom called, where held, quorum, etc.

Article VI. Parliamentary authority. To supplement or add to the rules contained in the organization's bylaws, and thus provide against inadequacies or unresourcefulness in them, every organization should adopt a reliable manual of parliamentary law as additional authority for settling questions of procedure not covered by its own rules.

Adopt this manual, if you like it or deem it efficient and serviceable, as your organization's parliamentary authority, and incorporate it in your bylaws for the settlement of questions of procedure and in the interest of enlightened, orderly, and equitable parliamentary practice.

The form of the provision adopting a manual can be phrased in the following or similar language: (1) "The rules contained in . . . [naming manual] shall govern all proceedings of the organization." Or, (2) "The rules contained in . . . [naming manual] shall govern in all cases to which they are applicable and in which they are not inconsistent with these bylaws and special rules." (This is the better form.)

Article VII. Amendments to bylaws. Specify how the bylaws may be amended, such as: "These bylaws may be amended at any regular or special meeting by a $\frac{2}{3}$ vote of the members present and voting, provided previous notice shall have been given in the call for the meeting."

Additional articles can be incorporated. The seven fundamental topics constitute the *minimum* provisions that should be embodied in a set of bylaws. Others can be added as desired. There is no limit either to the number of subjects that can be included in a set of bylaws or the number of articles or sections into which the individual topics can be subdivided. Each organization decides this for itself. For example, additional separate articles and sections can be incorporated covering trial of members, conventions, resignations, etc.

Note: A convenient way to remember the order and contents of the seven fundamental subjects which make up an acceptable set of bylaws is by the first letter of each subject and the catchword NO-MOM-PA.

Logic of their order. The logic of the order of the seven essential topics is necessarily based on the fact that the organization (1) must first have a *name*; (2) it is created or founded for a definite *object* or purpose; then (3) *members* are accepted or taken in from whom (4) *officers* are elected (5) to guide and transact the business of the *meetings* in (6) orderly manner or according to proper form or *parliamentary authority;* and finally (7) its bylaws can be changed or *amended* as the growth, expansion and needs of the organization may require or warrant from time to time.

When amendments to bylaws are prohibited. When organizations bar amendments to their bylaws for a period of years, (as for two years or five), or when they can be amended only in even-number or in odd-number years, a safety provision should nevertheless be contained in the bylaws authorizing amendments in case of emergency; thus: "Amendments to these bylaws may be enacted when passed by unanimous [or, three-fourths] vote of the ruling body," or similar words.

Right to shorten or to abolish term of office. Since it is the body itself that creates its own bylaws, it has the right to change them (with notice to all members) at any time and in any way it chooses. Hence the body can thus shorten or abolish altogether a term of office or any officer's tenure of office before it has been fully served, and thus either reduce the occupant's tenure, or legislate him out of office altogether (unless it is expressly specified, at the time, that the incumbent officer may continue in office until the next election, or as the bylaw may otherwise provide or specify).

The same rule applies to prevailing salaries, or existing benefits or privileges, under the bylaws. Hence, if a bylaw is enacted either reducing or abolishing them, such salaries, benefits and privileges are likewise reduced, or are immediately extinguished or terminated.

Note: Since the body can abolish an office, or any officer's tenure of office (and thus immediately oust him as its occupant), then if the president, or any other officer, is grossly incompetent, defiant, or abusive and obnoxious, instead of impeaching him outright, or bringing charges to remove him from office (a step usually regarded as personal and hateful by him and his followers), it may sometimes be more strategic to amend the bylaws *abolishing* the term of office he holds (a step regarded as less "personal"), and thus minimize the likelihood of a serious factional split in the organization. But neither step, ouster by impeachment or ouster by bylaw amendment, should be undertaken unless at least a good ⅔ vote will back it up at the meeting.

Vacancy by removal from office. If a removal from office creates a vacancy, the vacancy is then filled as the *bylaws* provide. If there is no such provision in the bylaws, the vacancy is filled by special election at any meeting (regular or special), with due notice thereof to all members.

Emergency administration. It is advisable for organizations having state- or nation-wide membership to incorporate a special provision in the bylaws automatically providing for an emergency administration of the affairs of the organization in the event of grave emergencies, such as war, catastrophes of nature, or other extraordinary condition, so that the organization can automatically continue to function with minimum delay or handicap in the face of, for instance, curtailed, forbidden or impossible travel, gas ration and other emergency restrictions usually encountered in time of war, disaster, etc.

Types of emergency provisions. Authorizing voting by mail and/or empowering a smaller group or body within the organization to act and to carry on the functions and duties of a convention, for instance, are two points which experience has shown should be included in the bylaws as special emergency provisions. These can be phrased somewhat as follows:

(1) "Notwithstanding anything to the contrary in the bylaws, when, because of war or other grave disaster or extraordinary emergency or act of God, or of operation or force of law, the holding of the annual convention is made impracticable, all the functions, powers and duties of the said convention shall be and are hereby vested in . . ." (naming smaller group, as the Supreme Lodge, National Council of Administration, Executive Board, etc.) hereinafter called "Ruling Body."

(2) "In the event travel is forbidden or curtailed to a prohibitive extent, voting by mail for purposes of electing officers, amending the bylaws and performing such other essential functions as are required of a convention, shall be and are hereby authorized, and the Ruling Body is hereby empowered to prescribe full and appropriate procedure for the purposes hereof." Or, "In the event of such emergency, all the powers, functions and duties of the convention shall be referred to the subordinate bodies [lodges, chapters, etc.] to be decided by them by mail, or as the Ruling Body may otherwise prescribe."

When the emergency ends, all emergency powers also end.

Standing rules. Standing rules are merely previously adopted *main* motions, which have *continuing* effect, just like bylaws, which also have continuing effect until they are amended, modified or rescinded. Hence, standing rules are amendable, suspendable and rescindable by a *majority* vote if previous notice has been given at a previous meeting or in the call for the meeting; or by a $\frac{2}{3}$ vote without such previous notice, or by a majority vote of the *membership*, and in a convention or annual meeting by a *majority* vote of the *registered* delegates.

Examples of standing rules: House rules; election or convention rules; fixed annual charity donations; and any and all other effective motions, rules, orders or decisions of the body. All adopted *motions* of the assembly remain continually in force, regardless of succeeding administrations in office, until they have been modified, executed or rescinded.

II. CHANGING THE BYLAWS

Before taking up the precise procedure for revising a set of bylaws, a few useful observations will be helpful to a better grasp and understanding of the subject.

Distinction between "amend" and "revise." The term "amend" is properly used when referring to changing the bylaws in part and not in their entirety; the term "revise" or "revising" is accurately used when referring to changing any part or the entire set of bylaws. The former is called "amendment(s) to the bylaws," and the latter "revision of the bylaws." Bylaws and constitution are, as previously noted, synonymous terms.

Two essential differences. There are two essential differences between amending bylaws and revising them:

(1) In *amending* a set of bylaws, only those particular provisions can be changed which are proposed to be amended; the rest of them stand as they are. But in a *revision* of the bylaws, any and every provision from beginning to end can be affected or changed, just as in drafting an original set of bylaws for a new organization. In revision it is not required to give notice for each individual provision.

(2) No restriction whatsoever can limit the degree or extent of change that can be made in a proposed revision, whereas in amending a particular provision of the bylaws, no change or modification can be made which is greater than what the proposed amendment authorizes, or which is less than what the existing bylaw provides. To illustrate: if the existing bylaws provide that "Dues shall be six dollars a year" and notice was given at the last session to *amend* the bylaw to make it nine dollars a year, changes in the proposed amendment, if any, are limited only to sums between six dollars and nine dollars. It cannot be less than six dollars or more than nine dollars because absent members have no knowledge of any sums other than the *minimum* sum contained in the existing bylaw, namely six dollars, and the *maximum* sum contained in the proposed amendment, namely nine dollars. But if notice was given at the last meeting to *revise* the bylaws at the next meeting, the provision relating to the dues can be changed without limitation; it can be amended to one dollar a year, or fifteen dollars, or dues can be done away with altogether.

The same rule would apply if a bylaw change involved increase or decrease in the number of vice presidents (for instance), or delegates, or districts, etc., or other prevailing limitations which the bylaws may prescribe.

Revising the Bylaws

Notice for revision of bylaws. Notice for revising a set of bylaws must be given in the same manner as for amending a bylaw; namely, at the preceding meeting and in the call thereof. When notice to revise the bylaws is given, notice is automatically served to all members that they can expect any kind of change, even to the extent of drafting a completely new set. In view of this fact, a committee on revision of the bylaws should be appointed. A motion similar to the following can be proposed:

MEMBER: "Mr. Chairman, I have long felt our bylaws are deficient and outmoded. Therefore, I move that the bylaws be revised and the Chair be authorized to appoint a committee of five members as a revising committee." (It is seconded, restated by the Chair, debated pro and con, and put to vote; and if carried by a *majority* vote, the Chair appoints five members as a committee on revision.)

Note: It is not necessary to pass a formal motion in order to authorize a revision of the bylaws; the mere giving of notice thereof at the meeting and/or in the call for the meeting is sufficient notice. But it is good strategy to adopt such a motion and thus have the support of the body. Whether notice to revise the bylaws is by a formal vote of the body or is simply given by a member, the bylaws are nevertheless open to revision at the next meeting.

Revision procedure. If a committee on revision has been appointed, the procedure at the next meeting is as follows:

The chairman reports on each article or section of the proposed revision, beginning with the first one.

Each such article or section is then automatically open to debate and amendment before each subsequent article or section can be considered.

However, no vote is, or should be, taken on adopting *separately* each article or section so considered; only amendments *to* them, if any are proposed, are voted on, which, however, require only a majority vote; but the vote on adopting the proposed revision, as thus amended by the assembly, requires a $\frac{2}{3}$ vote.

The reason individual articles or sections are not put to vote for adoption separately is that changes or amendments made in subsequent articles may require changes in an article or section previously adopted, and such changes cannot be made, strictly speaking, because once a bylaw provision is adopted it immediately goes into effect and cannot be amended at the same meeting. Further, an affirmative vote on a bylaw provision can be neither reconsidered nor rescinded except by unanimous consent at the time.

Therefore, as each article or section is discussed and separately amended, it should not be put to vote for final adoption until the end, when all articles and sections have been considered and suitably amended. A single vote is then taken on the adoption of the entire instrument.

If the proposed revision is adopted, it cannot be again amended at the same session, except by unanimous consent and provided no one has left the room. But if the revision is defeated, the vote on it can be reconsidered, and such reconsideration throws the revision open to debate and amendment as before the vote on it.

Final vote on revision can be delayed. While ordinarily the vote on adopting a bylaw or revision is taken immediately after the proposed amendment or revision has been discussed and suitably amended, the assembly by a majority vote can, when necessary, proceed *only* to consider the proposed revision and to discuss and perfect it by amendments, and to have the final vote for its adoption taken at a later time. When that time arrives, if there is no further debate and if no further amendments are proposed to the bylaw or to the revision, the vote is then finally taken and the result announced accordingly. The motion to effect this step may be phrased as follows:

MEMBER: "Mr. Chairman, I move that we now proceed only to consider and amend the proposed revision of the bylaws, but that we delay the final vote on its adoption until [for instance] just prior to adjournment of the meeting [or, convention]."

If this is adopted by a *majority* vote, the assembly can proceed with full freedom to amend the proposed revision, and when it has been completed and satisfactorily perfected it is automatically set aside and is not voted on (and it still remains amendable) until just prior to adjournment of the session or such other time as agreed. However, the body can adopt separately any immediately desired or necessary provision of a proposed revision so as to govern *in the meantime.*

Until a new set of bylaws has actually been voted and adopted to replace the old bylaws, the old bylaws are still in full force and effect, and they continue to govern the organization.

When the chairman of the committee on revision is ready to report for the committee, it is advisable for him to confer with the presiding officer, so that between them they may decide on the best method of presenting each article and section of the revision for consideration and action. The two leaders must necessarily work together as a team, the Chair directing and guiding the proceeding, and the committee chairman reporting it, and explaining it when necessary.

It is important to bear in mind that in a revision, all the action is centered upon the articles of the proposed *revision*, not on the *existing* bylaws; that is, the proposed revised set of bylaws is what is pending before the body and not the present set of bylaws; hence, every amendment which is proposed should concern only the contents of the proposed revision, not the existing bylaws. The existing bylaws may, however, be referred to for comparison.

The correct procedure for reporting a revision of a set of bylaws is shown in the following section. The best method depends upon how much time is available to the members for thorough comprehension of the contents of the proposed revision and for comparison with the existing bylaws, and also upon the mood of the assembly, time of day, kind of weather, or other possible pressure, interference or concern. Here is one method (the most elementary) of revising the bylaws.

How transacted. The committee chairman begins by reading first each article of the existing bylaws and then reading the corresponding proposed revision of the same, pausing immediately after that for the Chair to submit the proposed revision of this article to discussion and amendment, after which both the committee chairman and Chair continue the identical procedure for each and every subsequent article, until all articles of the proposed revision have been thus considered, following which the vote is finally taken on adopting the proposed revision as amended in its entirety.

Note: It requires only a majority vote to *amend* a pending revision (or a pending bylaw provision), but when the revision (or a proposed bylaw provision) is put to a vote for *final* adoption, such final adoption requires a ⅔ vote.

CHAIR: "The Chair now recognizes the chairman of the committee on revision of the bylaws, Mr. Bright."

BRIGHT (after a brief word on the arduous work involved, and complimenting his committee): "Mr. Chairman, Article I of the existing bylaws provides as follows: 'Name. The name of this organization shall be the Chicago Parliamentary Law Club.' The proposed revision also reads: 'Name. The name of this organization shall be the Chicago Parliamentary Law Club.' No change has been proposed." (He pauses for the Chair formally to state the proceeding for the information of the members; thus:)

CHAIR: "Article I of the proposed revision is exactly the same as that of the existing bylaw. No change has been made by the committee. Is there any discussion or are there any amendments proposed to this article before proceeding to the next?"

MEMBER A: "Mr. Chairman, I move to amend the revised article by striking out the word 'Law' and inserting the word 'Practice,' so that if my amendment is carried the revised article as amended will read: 'Name. The name of this organization shall be the Chicago Parliamentary Practice Club.' " (Seconded.)

Note: Observe that what the Chair does now is to state simply what is actually transpiring before the body.

CHAIR: "It has been moved and seconded to amend the revised article by striking out the word 'Law' and inserting in place thereof the word 'Practice.' Is there discussion on the amendment?" (After discussion, if any, it is put to vote and defeated, say, and the Chair continues:) "The noes have it and the word 'Law' is not struck out. Are there any further amendments to the revised article before proceeding to the next article? (No response.) There being none, the next article is in order." (No vote is taken on adopting Article I right now.)

BRIGHT: "Article II of the existing bylaws reads as follows: 'Object. The object shall be to acquire a knowledge of parliamentary law and skill in its application.' No change is made."

CHAIR: "Article II of the proposed revision is exactly the same as that of the existing bylaw. No change has been made. Before taking up the next article of the revision, is there any discussion on or amendment to Article II of the revision?"

MEMBER B: "Mr. Chairman, I move to amend Article II of the revision by adding at the end thereof the words 'under a competent instructor.' " (Seconded.)

CHAIR: "It is moved and seconded to amend Article II of the proposed revision by adding at the end thereof the words 'under a competent instructor.' Is there any discussion?" (After debate he puts it to vote, and the words "under a competent instructor" are adopted by a majority vote, and the Chair describes the action; thus:)

CHAIR: "The ayes have it, and the amendment to add the words 'under a competent instructor' is *adopted*. The question now before the body is on Article II of the revision *as amended*, namely: 'Object. The object shall be to acquire a knowledge of parliamentary law and skill in its application under a competent instructor.' Are there any further amendments proposed to this article before taking up the next? There being none, Mr. Bright will continue." (Article II as amended is not put to vote for final adoption right now.)

BRIGHT: "Article III of the existing *bylaws* reads . . . , and Article III of the *revision* reads . . . , the only change made is . . .". (It is open to further amendments, as before.)

CHAIR: "The only change made in the article of the revision from the existing bylaws is . . ." Before taking up Article IV of the revision is there any discussion or amendments on Article III? [Pause.] There being none, Mr. Bright will please continue."

BRIGHT: "Article IV of the existing bylaws provides . . . , and Article IV of the proposed revision declares . . . The only change is . . ."

CHAIR: "You have heard Mr. Bright's notation of the change made. If there are no amendments, Mr. Bright will continue."

BRIGHT: "Article V says . . ." etc. And he continues exactly as in the preceding articles until all articles of the revision have been read through, compared, discussed or amended, after which he moves their adoption in toto, and the Chair admonishes the assembly:

Chair: "Before the vote is taken on adopting the entire set of the proposed revised bylaws, are there any amendments proposed to any article anywhere in the proposed revision as thus far amended? If there are any amendments, now is the time to introduce them, and not after its adoption."

Member X: "Mr. Chairman, is it in order to propose an amendment to Article X of the proposed revision?"

Chair: "Yes, certainly." (And it is acted on, if germane.)

Member Y: "Mr. Chairman, can we refer back to Article VII of the revision for an amendment to it?"

Chair: "Yes; state your amendment." (And it is acted on.) "Are there any further amendments proposed anywhere in the body of the revision or is there *reconsideration* of any action already taken thereon before the vote is taken? There being none, the Chair will put the proposed revision, as amended, to vote. A two-thirds vote is required under our bylaws to adopt a proposed revision as the new bylaws. Those in favor of the proposed revision will rise and stand until counted, and the tellers will return the count." (Count taken.) "Eight-nine. Be seated. Those opposed will rise. Eleven. Be seated. There being two-thirds in favor of the revision, the affirmative has it and the proposed revision is adopted in place of the old bylaws." The new set goes into effect at once, unless previously otherwise specified.

Note: In nearly all cases of revision, experience has shown that the assembly is slow at first to comprehend and appreciate its correct practice, but very quickly thereafter it grasps it with intelligence and full understanding. Hence in the latter case the strategy for expediting the revision (if time is short) can be varied, if need be, and accelerated, as sound judgment may dictate.

Other methods of revision. (a) Read through the first two or three articles of both the existing bylaws and the corresponding articles of revision, as shown above; then, when the assembly appears capable of readily following the procedure, read only each article of the proposed revision and not the corresponding article of the existing bylaw, but always pointing out the change in the revision from the original bylaw, if any.

(b) Take up the revision page by page, reading each article through and pointing out the changes made, if any, without reading the original bylaws on that page, and then continuing to consider amendments to one article at a time on that page until every page has thus been considered and amended.

(c) Without actually reading any article of the revision or the existing bylaws, but commencing at the beginning, point out, in informal conversational language, article by article or page by page exactly where and what changes have been made in the proposed revision from the existing bylaws, and consider any amendments to them.

(d) If the revision and original bylaws are printed or typewritten, and copies can be supplied to each member, suggest that the members study the revision overnight, or give them reasonable time in which to study both sets (if there is time for either). When action thereon is taken up, without reading any article of the revision or of the existing bylaws (unless called for by the members), the Chair asks: "Are there any amendments to the revision, or any questions thereon, and if so, on what page?"

(e) Adopt in place of the above methods any other method desired.

The method of procedure suggested above is subject to the approval of the body. Usually the procedure suggested by the Chair and the chairman on revision is adopted. Such approval, if put to a vote, needs only a majority vote.

Note: If the presiding officer, or the committee chairman, is not the best qualified person to carry out the procedure of a revision effectively, the vice president or other experienced member can be designated to preside or to report in the place of either, as the case may be. It is sound practice to invite and accept assistance, thus eagerly and unselfishly promoting organizational efficiency.

Adopted revision replaces old bylaws. The moment a proposed revision is adopted in the place of the old bylaws, all provisions, articles, sections and paragraphs of the old bylaws become automatically null and void (unless otherwise expressly provided), and they are of no further force or effect; and the new bylaws in whatever form, even if they are found to be in some respects imperfect or incomplete, are nevertheless substituted for the old and they then govern the organization. Any inconsistencies in them are changed in due form in subsequent sessions.

Thus if, after their adoption, the new bylaws omitted some provision, or excluded a provision (such as annual dues for which there *was* a provision in the old bylaws), the old bylaw does not automatically govern, strictly speaking; such omission must be rectified by proposal in the form of an amendment in due course, at a subsequent meeting. (See the note below). Hence, exercise great care when revising to embody in the proposed revision all the needful provisions of the old set.

Note: Where such omissions occur, such as in the case of omitting the dues, simply adopt a motion under new business at any meeting fixing the amount of dues, which motion then becomes a standing rule and requires payment of dues until the sum is later duly incorporated as a provision of the bylaws in due course.

Consideration from sitting to sitting. If the assembly meets *daily,* as in a convention, and consideration of the revision is not completed during one sitting or the same day, the consideration continues at the first sitting of the body on the next business day, unless it is otherwise ordered or agreed to.

But if the assembly does *not* meet daily, the interrupted consideration of the revision is resumed under unfinished business at the next regular meeting or session, unless otherwise ordered.

Amending the Bylaws

Basic Rules. Notice to amend the bylaws must be given in the manner authorized in the bylaws. If there is no governing bylaw and a member gives previous notice at a meeting, such notice is sufficient.

The *proposed* amendment when pending is debatable; it is also amendable, being open to primary and secondary amendments, when need be, just like any other pending main motion, because a proposed amendment to the bylaws is itself a main motion (technically an incidental main motion).

It requires a $\frac{2}{3}$ vote when it is finally put to a vote for adoption as a bylaw, but amendments to the proposed amendment requires only a majority vote.

An *affirmative* vote on an adopted amendment to the bylaws may not be reconsidered (except by unanimous consent), because the moment it is carried it takes effect at once, unless it is otherwise agreed at the time, or the bylaws specify to the contrary in any case. But a *negative* vote on it may be reconsidered.

Bylaws can be amended just like any other motion, namely, by adding words to it, or by inserting words, or by striking out words, or by striking out and inserting words, or by substitution.

Amendments to a pending proposed *bylaw* amendment can be reconsidered regardless of which side prevails, just as you can reconsider an amendment to a pending *main* motion regardless of which side prevails.

A proposed bylaw amendment is subject to all the subsidiary motions. Hence it can be tabled, or postponed to a later time within the same session (as in a convention or annual meeting); or it can be postponed to the next session; or it can be tabled or postponed from session to session each time it is taken up for consideration, if so desired.

Bylaws amended in three ways: (1) They are amended precisely as authorized in the bylaws and in no other manner. (2) If no method or notice for their amendment is specified in the bylaws, then they can be amended by a $\frac{2}{3}$ vote at any regular or special meeting, provided notice of the proposed amendment was given at the previous meeting or in the call for the meeting, or both. Or, (3) They may be amended by a majority vote of the organization's total membership at any regular or special meeting without previous notice, and by a majority vote of the total registered voting delegates in conventions or annual meetings. Bylaws not amended in one of these three ways are invalid.

Notice to amend. Giving notice to amend is not debatable. Such notice cannot be tabled or postponed. It can be withdrawn at the same meeting, in which case any other member who so desires can give the same notice; but it cannot be withdrawn at the next (the amending) meeting except by unanimous consent, because it would be too late then for others to move it to advantage.

Amending amendments. Amendments to bylaws are amendable by the same processes or methods as main motions; namely: by adding to them, or by inserting, or by striking out, or by striking out and inserting, or by substituting.

To give notice of proposed amendment. Notice to amend the bylaws is normally given in three ways: (1) In the mode prescribed in the bylaws; (2) by a motion in writing signed by preferably two members (the proposer and a seconder) but one will do; or (3) by merely announcing, at the meeting, notice to amend the bylaws, which is then included in the call of the meeting; thus:

(1) (*In writing*) "Proposed Amendment to the Bylaws: Amend Section 4 of Article III of the bylaws by striking out (under annual dues) the words 'five dollars' and inserting 'seven dollars.' "

[Signed] Member A, Member B

(2) (*Orally*) "Mr. Chairman, I give notice to amend Section 4 of Article III by striking out the words 'five dollars' and inserting in place thereof the words 'seven dollars.' "

In each case the Chair states the proposed motion to amend or the notice of the proposed action and directs: "The secretary will take notice of the proposed amendment which will be acted on at the next meeting," or he may say: "The Chair is in receipt of your notice; it will be included in the call of the meeting."

How notice is incorporated in the call. The secretary incorporates in the call of the meeting a statement of the proposed amendment somewhat thus:

"Action will be taken at this meeting on a proposed amendment to the bylaws striking out from Section 4, Article III, the words 'five dollars' and inserting in place thereof the words 'seven dollars,' so that if adopted the proposed amendment will read as follows: 'Section 4. DUES. The dues for active members shall be seven dollars a year.' " (Giving notice to amend the bylaws is *not* a debatable stage, nor amendable or votable stage. This is done at the next meeting.)

Procedure at the next meeting. Under unfinished business at the next meeting, consideration of the proposed amendment to the bylaws for which due notice was given in the call or at the previous meeting is taken up; thus:

CHAIR (to secretary): "Is there any unfinished business?"

SECRETARY: "Yes; a motion to amend the provision of the bylaws relating to annual dues." (He reads it.)

CHAIR (formally informing the assembly): "Under unfinished business, there is a proposed amendment to the bylaws regarding a change in the annual dues. The question now before the body is on the adoption of the proposed amendment to strike out the words 'five dollars' and insert in place thereof the words 'seven dollars.' " (After debate, if any, it is put to vote, a $\frac{2}{3}$ vote being required, thus:)

CHAIR: "Those in favor of the proposed amendment will rise. Forty-three. Be seated. Those opposed will rise. Sixteen. Be seated. There being two-thirds in favor, the affirmative has it and the proposed amendment is adopted."

Note: Amendments to bylaws are taken up under unfinished business unless otherwise ordered, but if they are bypassed they are actable under new business. All proposed amendments to bylaws are in the nature of main motions, hence subject to all the subsidiary motions (p. 47). Hence you can amend them, postpone them, or table them to kill them, or you can keep postponing or tabling them from meeting to meeting and thus keep them alive for any desired reason; or you can adopt or reject any proposed bylaw amendment in the first instance.

What vote needed. It requires a $\frac{2}{3}$ vote to adopt a *proposed* amendment as part of the bylaws, because the act of adoption is a final act; but only a majority vote is necessary to amend the pending proposed amendment itself, because the act of amending a proposed amendment is merely a perfective act preliminary to its final adoption as a bylaw.

Limitation in amending an amendment. No amendments to a pending proposed amendment are in order which propose a change greater or less than the range covered in the existing bylaw and the proposed amendment. To illustrate: Supposing an existing bylaw calls for annual dues of five dollars and a proposed amendment substitutes the amount seven dollars. It is not in order to amend the amendment to an amount less than five dollars or more than seven dollars.

Bylaws should be read to members. A copy of the bylaws should be furnished to the members, where possible, or be read to them once a year or so for their information and government. Where this is impracticable, the bylaws or a condensed summary of essential contents thereof should be communicated to the membership in some other way.

Increase in dues; reduction. If the bylaws are amended to increase the annual dues, the increase does not apply to those who had already paid their dues; and when dues are reduced, those who had paid are entitled to a refund, unless, in *either* case, it was clearly understood or specified to the contrary at the time.

III. A Practice Model for Revision of Existing Bylaws

The Existing Bylaws	The Proposed Revision
The existing bylaws are never open to debate or amendment during the transaction of a revision, but may be referred to when need be for comparison purposes.	The revised bylaws under this column are the only provisions which are open to debate and amendment when the revision of the existing bylaws is being transacted.

Note: The organization's existing bylaws are shown under column 1 purely for purposes of comparison with the proposed revised bylaws under column 2. Read across. Read 1 with 1, 2 with 2, and so on.

ARTICLE I. Name	ARTICLE I. Name
Sec. 1. The name of this Club shall be the New York City Parliamentary Law Club.	*Sec. 1.* The name of this Club shall be the Manhattan Parliamentary Law Club.

Now, using correct parliamentary language and forms, proceed to amend the *proposed* revised article in column 2 by striking out "Manhattan" and inserting "New York City," thus disapproving the proposed revised name and retaining the existing name. Then, whether this amendment prevails or not, without taking a direct vote on adopting Article 1 of the revision at this stage (thus leaving it still open to further debate and amendment until all the articles have been similarly separately discussed and amended), proceed to Article II.

ARTICLE II. Object	ARTICLE II. Object
Sec. 1. The object shall be to acquire a knowledge of parliamentary law and orderly procedure.	*Sec. 1.* The object shall be to acquire a knowledge of parliamentary law and skill in its application.

Proceed to amend Article 2 of the revision in column 2 by adding the word 'under a competent instructor.' Use correct parliamentary language and forms. Whether the amendment prevails or not, if no further amendments are proposed to the same article, without taking a final vote on adopting it at this stage (thus leaving it still open to further debate and amendment until a single vote is taken on adopting the whole revised set after all articles have been similarly discussed and amended), proceed to Article III.

ARTICLE III. Members	ARTICLE III. Members
Sec. 1. Any adult person who is interested in the object shall be eligible to join.	*Sec. 1.* Any adult male interested in the object shall be eligible for membership.
Sec. 2. The dues shall be ten dollars a year.	*Sec. 2.* The dues shall be fifteen dollars annually.

Take each section of the revised bylaws separately. First, try to amend Section 1 of the revision by striking out the word "male." Use proper language and forms. Whether this prevails or not, if there is no further discussion on this section and no other amendments, without taking a final vote on its adoption at this stage, proceed to Section 2. Try to amend it by changing the sum "fifteen" dollars to another sum. Then, as in the previous section, when there is no more debate and no other amendments, without adopting Article III as yet, proceed to Article IV.

ARTICLE IV. Officers	ARTICLE IV. Officers
Sec. 1. The officers shall be a president, a vice president, a treasurer, a clerk, and three members as a board of directors.	*Sec. 1.* The officers shall be a president, two vice presidents, a secretary, a treasurer, a parliamentarian, and five directors.

Now amend the revision of Article IV in any way desired. If, say, it is desired to retain the original article (under column 1) as is, in preference to the revised article, the correct way to accomplish it is to (a) move to "strike out Article IV of the revision and insert in place thereof the following article," using words identical to those contained in the existing article; or (b) move to "substitute for the proposed article the words of the existing article." Adoption of either motion does not mean that the existing bylaw is nullified or bereft of the words in it, but only that words identical to those contained in the original article have also been inserted in or substituted for the *proposed* article so as to be adopted *with* the revision. After perfecting the above proposed article with amendments, if any, without taking a final vote on Article IV as amended or substituted, proceed to the next article, Article V.

ARTICLE V. Meetings	ARTICLE V. Meetings
Sec. 1. Regular meetings shall be held on Monday of each week, October through May.	*Sec. 1.* Regular meetings shall be held each Monday, excepting a holiday, October through May.
Sec. 2. The last meeting in May shall be the annual meeting for the purpose of electing officers and committees, and for any other business legally coming before it.	*Sec. 2.* The annual meeting shall be held the third Monday in May or the last Monday in May if the previous Monday is a holiday, and shall be *only* for the purpose of electing officers and standing committees.
Sec. 3. When a meeting falls on a holiday, the meeting so scheduled shall be held on the subsequent Monday.	*Sec. 3.* Special meetings shall be called . . . etc.

Again, as before, proceed to discuss and amend, if need be, any part of the proposed article of revision beginning with Section 1. When perfected as desired, without a final vote being taken on its adoption at this stage, proceed to consider Article VI.

ARTICLE VI. Manual

Sec. 1. The rules contained in A's Manual of Parliamentary Law shall govern the proceedings in all cases not covered by our own rules or bylaws. A manual on parliamentary law shall be furnished each officer.

ARTICLE VI. Manual

Sec. 1. The rules contained in D's Manual of Parliamentary Law shall govern in all cases not covered by the bylaws. Each new president shall be furnished with a manual upon his installation to office.

As in previous articles, proceed to amend this article of the revision in any way desired, after which, without adopting the article at this stage, proceed as before to the next article of revision, Article VII.

ARTICLE VII. Amendments

Sec. 1. These bylaws may be amended at any regular meeting by a two-thirds vote of those present and voting, provided previous notice has been given to all members.

Sec. 2. A revision of the bylaws shall be ordered when requested in writing by not less than fifteen members, provided that at least three of them are current or past officers.

ARTICLE VII. Amendments

Sec. 1. These bylaws may be amended by a two-thirds vote at any regular or special meeting provided seven days notice thereof shall have previously been given.

Sec. 2. Revised bylaws shall not go into effect until after final adjournment and shall be open to further debate and amendment at any time prior to adjournment.

When through with the revision, the committee chairman says:

REVISION COMMITTEE CHAIRMAN: "Mr. Chairman, this completes the revision. By direction of the committee on revision, I move its adoption in place of the existing bylaws."

CHAIR: "The committee on revision has completed its report. The question now before the body is on the adoption of the proposed revision, as amended, in place of the existing bylaws. A single vote will be taken now on adopting the entire revision. A two-thirds vote is required under the bylaws. Before it is put to vote, however, members have the right to propose further amendments to any part of the proposed revision, or to reconsider any action already taken thereon. Are there any further amendments? If so, now is the time to make them. [No response.] There being no further amendments, the Chair will put the proposed *revised* bylaws as amended to vote. Those in favor of the adoption of the revised bylaws will rise and stand until counted." (He counts 82.) "Eighty-two. Be seated. Those opposed will now rise." (No one rising, he says:) "None." He then declares the vote, thus:

CHAIR: "Eighty-two members having risen in favor, and none against, there is a two-thirds vote [a unanimous vote includes a two-thirds vote], and the revised bylaws have been adopted in the place of the old [or, the existing] bylaws." And this concludes the proceeding of revision.

Note: If the proposed revision is *defeated*, it can be reconsidered. In any event the old (or existing) bylaws are still in force and continue to govern. They are open to amendment during the same session if so desired, by virtue of the notice that had been given for their revision. Therefore, undesirable individual provisions of the existing bylaws can be struck out, and new or more desirable provisions than those previously defeated with the revision can be incorporated in their place, *provided* that these new provisions are finally adopted by a ⅔ vote, and *provided also* that the revision has first been reconsidered, so as to release its provisions for presentation and adoption as separate amendments to the existing bylaws.

IV. Model Set of Bylaws

There is no limit to the number of articles or sections that can be included in a set of bylaws. Each organization decides this for itself to meet its own needs.

In large organizations. Some large organizations have greater needs and requirements; and they include a great number of bylaw articles; thus:

1. Name.
2. Location of headquarters.
3. Nonprofit, nonsectarian and nonpolitical.
4. Members. Classes of membership: active, honorary, etc.
5. Eligibility or qualifications for membership.
6. Voting on new members.
7. Dues. Amount, when payable.
8. Officers. Their nomination, election, eligibility, vote required to elect, term of office, duties, oath of office, etc.
9. Resignation from office.
10. Filling vacancies.
11. Penalty for absenteeism.
12. Grounds for removal.
13. Salary, compensation per diem, etc.
14. Immediate past president.
15. Meetings. Regular, special, annual.
16. Quorum.
17. Order of business.
18. Executive board; standing and special committees.
19. Composition, meetings, duties, powers, their election or appointment.
20. Resignation from membership.
21. Reinstatement.
22. Annual convention. Election of delegates, etc.
23. Assessments, fines.
24. Installation of officers or of new members.
25. Limiting expenditures.
26. Ladies auxiliary.
27. Parliamentary manual.
28. Amendments to bylaws.

Model bylaws. The object in including the provisions shown below is to enable a new organization, club or society to select and use any parts deemed desirable for incorporation in a set of bylaws, varying them to suit any particular purpose.

Article I. Name

Sec. 1. The name of this organization shall be the A Club.

Article II. Object.

Sec. 1. The object of the Club shall be:
(*a*) To inculcate in young men and women traits of leadership;
(*b*) To inspire in them active and useful participation in civic affairs and acceptance of the responsibilities of citizenship;

(c) To enable its members to acquire thorough knowledge of parliamentary law and its proper practice;

(d) To afford opportunities for self-expression, debate and public speaking;

(e) To inspire a desire for study of management and control of organizational procedures and civic programs;

(f) To instruct its members in the fundamental traits of self-discipline, self-confidence and self-government for the attainment of leadership and distinction in moral, intellectual and civic accomplishments; and

(g) To do all other things necessary and appropriate for the advancement of these objects and the welfare of its members.

Article III. Members.

Sec. 1. Any person, recommended by two members, upon subscribing to its objects and paying the annual dues, may apply for membership in the Club.

Sec. 2. Applicants shall be elected by a two-thirds vote.

Sec. 3. The annual dues shall be five dollars ($5), payable in advance, on or before the first week in January of each year.

Sec. 4. The masculine pronoun "he" connotes also the feminine "she."

Article IV. Officers.

Sec. 1. The officers of this Club shall be a president, a first vice president, a second vice president, a recording secretary, a corresponding secretary, a treasurer, an assistant treasurer, a chaplain and a parliamentarian.

Sec. 2. The officers shall be elected at the annual meeting at the second meeting in May, and shall hold office for one year and until their successors are elected and duly qualified.

Sec. 3. In the event of a vacancy in the office of president or first vice president, the Club shall fill the vacancy at the next regular meeting or at a special meeting called for the purpose, with due notice thereof to all members in either case.

Sec. 4. In the event of a vacancy in office other than president or first vice president, the executive board shall forthwith fill such vacancy.

Sec. 5. An officer who has served more than half of the *term* of office shall be regarded as having served that term.

Sec. 6. No officer who has served a term of office shall succeed himself in the same office.

Sec. 7. All officers who have been legally elected to office shall be regarded as past officers of that office, regardless of the length of time they may have served in the office, except one who was expelled.

Sec. 8. The *immediate* past president, having served the full, or more than half of, the term of his office shall be a member of the executive board and a delegate at the Club's annual convention with full vote and a voice therein only for the year then ensuing.

Sec. 9. There shall be no substitute for an *immediate* past president, and the resignation or death of the immediate past president who has been given the status provided under Sec. 8 shall terminate his status, and no vacancy shall be deemed to have occurred thereby which the board might fill.

Article V. Duties of Officers.

Sec. 1. The president shall preside at all meetings of the Club and of the executive board. He shall appoint the chairman of each standing committee, the other members thereof to be nominated from the floor. He shall be ex-officio member of all committees except the Nominating Committee and the Grievance Committee. He shall appoint such special committees as may be authorized by the body, and shall render a condensed annual report. He shall obey all lawful orders of the body and be thoroughly familiar with the Club's bylaws and the rules of parliamentary law and procedure.

Sec. 2. The first vice president shall assume and perform the duties of the president in the absence or disability of the president. In the event of the resignation or death of the president he shall become president for the unexpired term. He shall be thoroughly familiar with the bylaws and the rules of parliamentary law, and shall present a brief annual report.

Sec. 3. The second vice president shall assume and perform the duties of first vice president in the absence or disability of the first vice president, and in the event of the resignation or death of the first vice president he shall become first vice president for the unexpired term. In the absence or disability of the president and first vice president, he shall perform the duties of president. He shall be thoroughly familiar with the bylaws and the rules of parliamentary law; and shall present a brief annual report.

Sec. 4. The recording secretary shall keep accurate record of the minutes of all meetings of the Club and executive board. He shall keep a full and up-to-date roster, shall call the roll of officers and members when so required, shall notify officers, delegates and committees of their election or appointment, and shall assist the president in the preparation of the order of business to be considered at each meeting. He shall present a brief annual report.

Sec. 5. The corresponding secretary shall send out proper notices of all meetings of the Club and the executive board at least five days in advance, and shall conduct all correspondence, unless otherwise provided or ordered.

Sec. 6. The treasurer shall be the custodian of the Club's funds, except as may otherwise be provided or ordered. He shall deposit the same in such banking institution as the executive board shall authorize, and the account shall be in the Club's name. He shall be a member ex-officio of the Finance Committee, and shall render an annual report, and a report at such other times as the Club may authorize.

Sec. 7. The assistant treasurer shall assist the treasurer and shall, in his absence, perform the duties of the treasurer.

Sec. 8. The chaplain shall open and close the meetings of the Club with prayer. He shall be chairman of the Sick and Relief Committee, and shall render a condensed annual report.

Sec. 9. The parliamentarian shall be well versed in parliamentary law and in its correct practice, and shall advise the presiding officer of the Club and its members on their respective parliamentary rights when so requested or directed.

Sec. 10. All officers shall have the right to vote and to debate questions the same as any other member.

Sec. 11. The president, or one who presides in the president's absence, shall avoid taking sides in debate with the members on questions before the Club unless he first surrenders the chair. The president, or one presiding in his absence, need not surrender the chair to debate an appeal from his decision on any motion; nor shall he be required to surrender the chair when debating questions at executive board meetings.

Sec. 12. In the absence of the president and vice presidents, the recording secretary shall take the chair, call the meeting to order and preside until a chairman pro-tem has been elected. But on the appearance of the president or a vice president, the secretary or the chairman pro-tem, as the case may be, shall cease to preside and the president or vice president shall take over.

Sec. 13. All officers of the Club shall take the following oath of office at the time of their election, or, in the necessary absence of any officer at the time, at a later time.

Oath of Office

"I solemnly promise to abide by the rules, bylaws and regulations of the Club, and the lawful orders of the assembly. I further promise that I will perform the duties of my office to the best of my knowledge and ability."

Sec. 14. Officers shall assume their duties upon adjournment of the annual meeting in May.

Article VI. Executive Board.

Sec. 1. There shall be an executive board which shall consist of the nine officers, the immediate past president of the Club, the chairmen of the six standing committees, and five members who shall be elected thereto at the annual meeting.

Sec. 2. Eleven members shall constitute a quorum in the board.

Sec. 3. Regular meetings shall be held at least once a month, from September to the first meeting in May inclusive.

Sec. 4. Special meetings of the board may be called by the president, and shall be called by him at the written request of seven members of the board. No business other than that for which a special meeting is called shall be transacted except by unanimous consent.

Sec. 5. The board may make its own rules and bylaws not in conflict with those of the Club.

Sec. 6. The board shall fill vacancies occurring within its membership and in any office except that of the president and first vice president.

Sec. 7. The board shall also fill vacancies in standing committees, except a vacancy in their chairmen which shall be filled by the president.

Sec. 8. The Board shall be the Grievance Committee, and shall have original jurisdiction and plenary power to settle and adjudicate all grievances and charges from which there shall be no appeal. All such matters shall be decided by a two-thirds vote of the entire board membership.

Sec. 9. All votes of the board relating to grievances or charges for suspension or expulsion from office or membership shall be by ballot. All other votes shall be by not less than a majority of the members present and voting, a quorum being present, and may be decided by any form of voting.

Sec. 10. The board shall, at the annual meeting in May, present the Club's budget for the ensuing year, which shall be open to amendment and debate. The budget shall be approved by two-thirds vote of the Club members present and voting thereon.

Sec. 11. The board shall have power to fix the compensation of officers and for guest speakers and instructors.

Sec. 12. The board shall have power to recommend to the Club any proposals, including amendments to these bylaws. The Club shall then decide these proposals in due course of proceeding. The board's own recommendations on all matters shall be taken up under new business, unless otherwise ordered by a two-thirds vote of the Club members present and voting.

Sec. 13. The board shall carry out all lawful orders and instructions of the Club.

Article VII. Standing Committees.

Sec. 1. There shall be the following standing committees: Membership, Nominating, Parliamentary Law, Public Speaking, Politics, and Publicity.

Sec. 2. Standing committees shall be composed of three members.

Sec. 3. The president shall appoint the chairman of each standing committee. The other two members shall be appointed by the executive board.

Sec. 4. Standing committees shall serve for one year.

Sec. 5. All decisions of a standing committee shall be by majority vote. A vacancy in any standing committee shall be filled forthwith by the appointer.

Sec. 6. The Membership Committee shall procure applications for membership, collect the annual dues from all applicants, and promptly present the applications for a vote at the next meeting of the Club.

Sec. 7. The Nominating Committee shall, at the second meeting in April, present the name of one candidate for each office, following which additional nominations may be made from the floor. Further nominations may also be made from the floor at the first meeting in May. After such meeting further nominations shall not be permitted and the election shall then take place at the annual meeting in May. Members may vote for any eligible person at the annual meeting even though not previously nominated as provided herein.

Sec. 8. The Committee on Parliamentary Law shall instruct the meetings in various phases of parliamentary law and practice.

Sec. 9. The Committee on Public Speaking shall devise means of affording professional instruction in oratory and public speaking.

Sec. 10. The Committee on Politics shall devise means of affording professional lectures on city government, town government, and state and federal government.

Sec. 11. The Publicity Committee shall publicize the efforts of the Club toward the attainments of its objects.

Sec. 12. Special committees may be appointed by the president, or by or under the authority of the Club by majority vote in any case.

Sec. 13. The Club may, by majority vote, go into committee of the whole for any purpose whatever, including a purpose to demonstrate the operation of proper parliamentary practice and the orderly discussion and disposition of questions before it.

Sec. 14. The Club may, by a two-thirds vote, hold an open meeting

once a year to which the public, interested in parliamentary practice and
public speaking, may be invited, under such conditions and at such time
as the executive board may determine.

Article VIII. Meetings.

Sec. 1. Regular meetings of this Club shall be held on the first and
third Wednesday of each month from September to May inclusive. If
such meeting falls on a holiday, then it shall be held on the next day not
a holiday.

Sec. 2. Special meetings may be called by the president, or they may
be called jointly by the president and the executive board; and they shall
be called by the president upon the written request of eleven members
of the Club or of seven executive board members.

Sec. 3. The annual meeting shall be held at the second meeting in
May, and shall be for the purpose of electing the Club's officers and for
the election of five executive board members, and for such other business
as may properly come before the meeting under the Club's regular order
of business.

Sec. 4. The quorum shall consist of twenty-one members.

Article IX. Elections.

Sec. 1. All elections at the annual meeting shall be by ballot.

Sec. 2. The officers shall be elected by majority vote.

Sec. 3. The five executive board members shall be elected by a plurality
vote.

Sec. 4. The election shall take place under unfinished business, unless
otherwise ordered by a $\frac{2}{3}$ vote.

Sec. 5. In the event of failure to elect any officer by majority vote,
further balloting on that office shall continue until a majority vote has
been attained.

Sec. 6. In the event of a tie vote in the election of executive board
members the election thereon shall be decided by lot.

Article X. Order of Business.

Sec. 1. The order of business in regular meetings of the Club, except
its annual meeting, shall be as follows:

  (1) Call to order by the president
  (2) Prayer
  (3) Reading of the minutes and their approval
  (4) Reading of communications and correspondence
  (5) Treasurer's report, bills
  (6) Executive board report
  (7) Standing committee chairmen's reports
  (8) Special committee reports
  (9) Applications for membership
  (10) Unfinished business
  (11) New business
  (12) Good of the Club, comments, constructive criticism
  (13) Announcement of functions, dates or events
  (14) Adjournment
  (15) Social or instruction hour

Sec. 2. The order of business at the annual meeting shall be as follows:

(1) Call to order by the president.
(2) Prayer.
(3) Pledge of Allegiance.
(4) Reading of the minutes and their approval.
(5) Summary of communications and correspondence.
(6) Annual reports of:
    (*a*) The president and vice president
    (*b*) The secretaries, recording and corresponding
    (*c*) Auditor's-treasurer's report.
    (*d*) The chaplain.
    (*e*) The parliamentarian
    (*f*) The executive board
    (*g*) The chairman of standing committees
    (*h*) The chairmen of special committees
    (*i*) Unfinished business
    (*j*) Election of officers and executive board
    (*k*) Installation
    (*l*) Adjournment
    (*m*) Refreshment hour. Collation.

Sec. 3. The order of business as listed under Sections 1 and 2 may be changed by a $\frac{2}{3}$ vote. The social hour, item 15 of Section 1 and the refreshment hour and collation, item (m) of Section 2 shall not be changed.

Article XI. Parliamentary Authority.

Sec. 1. The rules contained in . . . [name of manual] shall be the parliamentary authority in all cases not covered by these bylaws.

Article XII. Amendments to Bylaws.

Sec. 1. These bylaws may be amended at any regular *or* special meeting by a $\frac{2}{3}$ vote of the members present and voting, provided notice, including the subject, of the proposed amendment has been given in the call for the meeting.

V. THE LANDRUM-GRIFFIN LAW

This law is correctly called the Labor-Management Reporting and Disclosure Act. It was passed by the Eighty-sixth Congress of the United States.

Purpose of the Landrum-Griffin Law. Quoting from its preamble, the general purpose of the act is "to provide for the reporting and disclosure of certain financial transactions and administrative practices of labor organizations and employers, to prevent abuses in the administration of trusteeships by labor organizations, to provide standards with respect to the election of officers of labor organizations, and for other purposes." Following is a sampling from this bill of rights for labor organizations.

Sec. 101. (a) (1) *Equal Rights.* Every member of a labor organization shall have equal rights and privileges to nominate candidates, to vote in elections or referendums, to attend membership meetings, and to participate in the deliberations and voting upon the business of such meetings, subject to reasonable rules and regulations in such organization's constitution and bylaws.

(2) *Freedom of speech and assembly.* Every member of a labor organization shall have the right to meet and assemble freely; to express any views, arguments, or opinions; and to express at meetings of the labor organization his views upon candidates in an election of the labor organization or upon any business properly before the meeting, subject to the organization's established and reasonable *rules* pertaining to the *conduct* of meetings.

(3) *Dues, Initiation Fees, and Assessments.* Except in the case of a federation of national or international labor organizations, the rates of dues and initiation fees payable by members of any labor organization in effect on the date of enactment of this Act shall not be increased, and no general or special assessment shall be levied upon such members except:

(*A*) in the case of a local labor organization, (1) by majority vote by secret ballot . . . at any membership meeting . . . or (2) by majority vote . . . in a membership referendum conducted by secret ballot; or (*B*) in the case of a labor organization, other than a local labor organization or a federation of national or international labor organizations, (1) by majority vote of the delegates . . . at a regular convention, or at a special convention . . . or (2) by majority vote . . . voting in a membership referendum conducted by secret ballot.

(4) *Protection of the Right to Sue.* No labor organization shall limit the right of any member thereof to institute an action in any court . . . irrespective of whether or not the labor organization or its officers are named defendants . . . , provided that any such member may be required to exhaust reasonable hearing procedures . . . within such organization, before instituting legal proceedings against such organizations or any officer thereof.

(5) *Safeguards Against Improper Disciplinary Action.* No member of any labor organization may be fined, suspended, expelled, or otherwise disciplined except for nonpayment of dues by such organization or by any officer thereof unless such member has been (a) served with written specific charges; (b) given a reasonable time to prepare his defense; (3) afforded a full and fair hearing.

Sec. 102. *Civil Enforcement.* Any person whose rights secured by the provisions of this title have been infringed by any violation (of it) may bring a civil action in a district court of the United States for such relief (including injunctions) as may be appropriate.

Sec. 201. (*a*) *Report of Labor Organizations.* Every labor organization shall adopt a constitution and bylaws and shall file a copy thereof with the Secretary, together with a report, duly signed, containing the following information:

(1) name of the organization, its mailing address or addresses.

(2) the name and title of each of its officers.

(3) the initiation fee or fees required.

(4) the regular dues or fees or other periodic payments.

(5) detailed statements . . . showing (*a*) qualifications for or restrictions on membership, (*b*) levying of assessments, (*c*) insurance or other benefit plans, (*d*) authorization for disbursement of funds of the labor organization, (*e*) audit of transactions . . . (*f*) the calling of regular and special meetings, (*g*) the selection of officers and stewards . . . (*h*) discipline or removal of officers . . . (*i*) imposition of fines, suspensions, and

expulsions ... (*j*) authorization for bargaining demands, (*k*) ratification of contract terms, (*l*) authorization for strikes, and (*m*) issuance of work permits.

(*b*) (Note: A financial report, duly signed, is also required to be filed annually with the Secretary disclosing its financial condition and operation for its preceding fiscal year, such as:)

(1) assets and liabilities; (2) receipts of any kind; (3) salary, allowances and other direct or indirect disbursements to each officer and each employee who, during such fiscal year, received more than $10,000 ... (4) direct and indirect loans to any officer ... which aggregated more than $250 during the fiscal year ... (5) direct and indirect loans to any business enterprise, and (6) other disbursements made by the organization including the purposes thereof.

Sec. 203. (*a*) *Report of Employers.* Every employer who in any fiscal year made:

(1) any payment or loan ... of money ... to any labor organization or officer ... or (2) any payment ... to any of his employees ... for the purpose of persuading other employees to exercise or not to exercise ... the right to organize and bargain collectively ... or (3) any expenditure ... (whose object) directly or indirectly, is to interfere with, restrain or coerce employees in the exercise of the right to organize and bargain collectively ... or (4) any agreement ... with a labor relations consultant or other independent contractor ... (whose object), directly or indirectly, is to persuade employees to exercise or not to exercise ... the right to organize and bargain collectively ... or (5) any payment, including reimbursed expenses, pursuant to an agreement or arrangement described under 4 above, shall file with the Secretary a report, duly signed, showing in detail the date and amount of such payment ... and the name, address and position, if any, in any firm or labor organization ... and a full explanation ... of all such payments ... agreements, or arrangements.

Sec. 209. *Criminal Provisions.* Any person who willfully violates this (Act) shall be fined not more than $10,000 or imprisonment for not more than one year, or both.

Sec. 304. *Enforcement.* Upon written complaint of any member or subordinate body of a labor organization alleging that such organization has violated the provisions (of this Act, excepting Trusteeships) the Secretary shall investigate the complaint, etc.

Sec. 401. (*a*) *Elections; Terms of Office; Election Procedures.* Every national or international labor organization, except a federation (thereof), shall elect its officers not less often than once every five years either by secret ballot ... or at a convention of delegates chosen by secret ballot.

(*b*) Every local labor organization shall elect its officers not less often than once every three years by secret ballot.

(*c*) [This paragraph gives all candidates for office equal right to access and use of lists of members in aid of such candidacies.]

(*d*) Officers of intermediate bodies, such as general committees, system boards, joint boards, or joint councils, shall be elected not less often than every four years by secret ballot.

(*e*) [This paragraph grants to every member equal rights to nominate for office, be eligible to be candidate and to hold office — subject to section 504, below — and to vote for or support any candidates, without being subject to penalty, discipline, interference, or reprisal, etc.; no member whose dues have been withheld by his employer for payment to his organization shall be declared ineligible to vote or to be candidate for office.]

(*f*) [This paragraph provides that elections shall be conducted in accordance with the constitution and bylaws; ballots and other papers of the election shall be preserved for one year.]

(*g*) No moneys received by way of dues, assessments, etc., shall be used to promote any candidacies for office.

(*h*) [This paragraph authorizes members to invoke adequate remedies for the removal, by secret ballot, of an elected officer guilty of serious misconduct, if the organization's constitution and bylaws do not provide adequate procedure for such removal.]

(*i*) The Secretary shall promulgate rules . . . prescribing minimum standards and procedures for determining the adequacy of the removal procedures referred to in the preceding paragraph (*h*).

Sec. 504. *Prohibition Against Certain Persons Holding Office.* (*a*) No person who is or has been a member of the Communist Party or who has been convicted of, or served any part of a prison term resulting from his conviction of, robbery, bribery, extortion, embezzlement, grand larceny, burglary, arson, violation of narcotic laws, murder, rape, assault with intent to kill, assault which inflicts grievous bodily injury, or a violation of title II or III of this Act, or conspiracy to commit any such crimes, shall serve:

(1) as an officer, director, trustee, member of the executive board, business agent, manager, organizer, etc., other than as an employee exclusively clerical or custodial, or (2) as labor relations consultant, and also as stated under (1) above.

No labor organization or officer thereof shall knowingly permit any person to assume or hold any office or paid position in violation of this subsection (504, above).

Sec. 609. *Prohibition on Certain Discipline by Labor Organizations.* It shall be unlawful for any labor organization, or any officer, agent, shop steward, or other representative of a labor organization, or any employee thereof, to fine, suspend, expel, or to otherwise discipline any of its members for exercising any right to which he is entitled under the provisions of this Act.

Chapter 15
COURT CITATIONS

This chapter contains references on some essential rights of the members. Sources of citations numbered in superscript are on pages 343–347.

Definition of meeting. In parliamentary law, a meeting is an assembly of persons for the purpose of discussing and acting on matters in which they have a common interest.

Meeting and quorum synonymous. The terms "meeting" and "quorum" are synonymous. Where there is no legal quorum there is no legal meeting.[1]

Definition of member and membership. Supreme courts define a member as "a person who has united with or has been duly chosen to form a part of an organization or body"; and "membership in an organization implies not only the enjoyment of its privileges but also subjection to the rules governing it." [2]

By whom called. In order to constitute the acts of a meeting valid it must have been called by one authorized to call it. Hence an officer who has been expelled, removed or who seceded, or whose resignation has become effective, is not competent to call a meeting, and any business transacted under his call or name is null and void.[3]

Meetings should be called by those authorized to do so under the rules or laws of the organization, or according to usage therein. If the president is authorized to call a meeting, then in his absence or disqualification the vice president calls it. When it is prescribed who shall call it, no other person or officer may call it. If it is not prescribed who may call it, a majority of the board or executive committee may do so. If there is no rule or law, bylaw or custom and usage for calling a meeting, then whoever is entrusted with the management and control of the organization's affairs may call it.[4]

Notice of meetings. When notice of meetings is required by rule or law, all the members must be notified; and in the case of a special meeting they should be notified of the purpose thereof, especially if business of an unusual character is to be transacted therein.[5]

If notice of a meeting is not *required*, but the time and place thereof are specified in the organization's rules or bylaws, or are fixed by custom or usage, then a notice of the meeting is not necessary (but it is recommended).[6]

When the time or manner of giving notice is prescribed, it is essential that notice be given in the mode prescribed. If no length of time is prescribed, then reasonable notice must be given.[7]

Notice by publication, by posting or by personal service, where so prescribed, is good notice, if complied with as prescribed.[8]

Waiver of notice. Where the required notice of a meeting has not been given or the notice given was insufficient or defective in any essential respect, if all the members appear at the meeting and participate without objection, it will be deemed a waiver by each member of any defect in or failure of notice, and hence acts done at such meeting would then be valid.[9]

Quorum. It is a well established parliamentary rule that a quorum must be present in order to transact business, or to validate (ratify) some action.[10]

Members can make the point of "no quorum" whenever evident, and for that purpose they can interrupt a speaker at any time.[11]

If the absence of a quorum is not noticed or is not raised when an act is done or is not raised immediately after its completion, a quorum is presumed to have been present.[12]

Presence of nonmembers at meetings. The presence of nonmembers at a meeting will not invalidate the acts of such meeting if they did not vote.[13]

Conduct of meeting. Unless the organization prescribes the manner in which its meetings shall be conducted, the commonly accepted rules in use for deliberative bodies can be resorted to in considering the regularity of the proceedings; but the fact that strict parliamentary usages are not observed will not necessarily invalidate the proceedings; regularity is presumed in the absence of a showing to the contrary.[14]

Presiding officer's role. Basically, questions must be put to vote by the proper officer, otherwise the vote taken will be ineffectual.[15]

But the presiding officer of an organization cannot prevent the transaction of business either by leaving the meeting or by refusing to put a motion, which is in order and which is duly made and seconded, to a vote; and in case of such refusal, the vice president may properly put the motion, although the president is still in the room.[16]

The proper way to take exception to obnoxious rulings of presiding officers is by an appeal to the body.[17]

The president has no power to adjourn the meeting against the wishes of the assembly. The power to adjourn resides in the members present, and not in the officers or officials who are authorized to call the meeting, unless otherwise expressly provided.[18]

Withdrawal of members from a meeting. Members may not be forced to remain in the meeting against their will. Hence they can depart prior to adjournment. If enough depart (though sometimes wrongfully) and the quorum is thereby reduced below the number required to do business, the point of "no quorum," if raised, prevents further business. But regardless of how many withdraw from a meeting, those remaining may continue to do business if they have a quorum present at the time.[19]

Members who attend a meeting and then voluntarily withdraw are in no better position than those who voluntarily absent themselves from the meeting.[20]

Where any portion of the members withdraw from the meeting and then organize another meeting in their own interest, the acts of such meeting are null and void.[21]

Termination of membership by secession, expulsion or resignation When a person ceases to be a member of the organization, whether it be by voluntary separation, secession or expulsion, his interest in the funds and property of the organization likewise ceases. This rule applies even when a number of persons secede in a body, even if they constitute a majority, or even when they organize a separate organization under the same name.[22]

In such cases of separation or secession the remaining members and only they are entitled to retain in the organization its entire funds and property, so long as they continue to keep the organization alive and to adhere to its purposes. Hence the members remaining loyal have the right to elect their own officers and to recover all the organization funds and property carried away by the seceding or rebellious members.[23]

Adjourned meetings. The body has the right to adjourn its sittings from day to day, or week to week, etc., so as to complete as much business as possible prior to the convening of the next regular or stated meeting.

Any business which would have been proper to consider at the original meeting may be considered and acted on at an adjourned meeting thereof.

Members are bound to take notice of adjourned meetings and to be present at the time and place of such meeting.[24]

Resignation is a motion. A resignation from membership or from office is a main motion (precisely, an incidental main motion); and when a motion is made "to accept the resignation" a second is required; it is debatable and amendable, and is subject to subsidiary, privileged and apt incidental motions.

Mode of resignation. If no particular mode of resignation is prescribed, no particular mode is necessary to tender the resignation. It can be in writing or oral, and it can be sent in or presented in person at any meeting.[25]

Mode of acceptance. If no specific mode of acceptance is prescribed, no formal mode is necessary.[26]

Language of resignation. It is not necessary that any special phrase or words be used in a resignation. It is sufficient if the language shows a clear intent to resign.[27]

To whom tendered. A resignation from membership is properly tendered to the organization itself (usually the secretary). A resignation from appointive office is tendered to the president, and one from elective office to the body authorized to fill the vacancy (usually to the assembly itself, but to the board if the board is authorized to fill it).[28]

Unauthorized tender. If the organization's laws provide that a resignation shall be tendered to the person or body having the power to fill the vacancy, a resignation tendered to an unauthorized person or body is null and void.[29]

Types of resignation. There are three types of resignation: (1) immediate — intended to take effect at once; (2) prospective (or future) — submitted to take effect *not* immediately but at a definite future time; and (3) conditional — tendered to take effect only upon the condition imposed by it.[30]

Examples of conditional resignation. (1) "I hereby resign as member, *in the event* I am transferred to another State"; (2) "I submit my resignation as Secretary *in case* I am elected senator in the forthcoming state election."

Rules governing conditional resignation. Unless the laws of the organization provide to the contrary, the rules stated below govern:

(1) If a resignation imposes a condition, such resignation does not take effect until after the condition has occurred; and until it has occurred, there is no parting from membership and no surrender of the office.[31]

(2) In the meantime, the conditional resignation cannot be accepted, since it would violate the condition imposed; and if it is accepted (through misadvice, misunderstanding or anxiety) the acceptance is null and void.[32]

(3) Until the condition imposed by a resignation occurs, the resigner can withdraw it by communicating it to the body entitled to receive it any time before occurrence of the condition, even if the resignation was accepted in the meantime.[33]

(4) In a conditional resignation the member still retains his membership, and the officer still occupies his office. Hence, no vacancy per se

results in office from a conditional resignation, and therefore an election cannot be held to choose a successor before occurrence of the condition; and if a premature election is held and a successor is chosen, the action taken is deemed null and void, and the chosen successor does not acquire legal possession of the office.[34]

Prospective (or future) resignation. The rules that govern a conditional resignation (as stated above), also govern a prospective (future) resignation; namely: (a) a prospective resignation, submitted to take effect at a definite time, does not take effect prior to the specified time; (b) until the time specified by it has elapsed, a prospective resignation cannot be accepted, as it would violate the terms of the resignation; (c) the resigner can withdraw his resignation at any time prior to the specified time; and (d) in a prospective resignation, as in a conditional one, no vacancy *per se* results, and there is no vacancy to fill prior to the specified time (unless a vacancy occurs in the meantime due to the resigner's disability, death, etc.).[35]

Examples of prospective resignation. (1) "I am resigning from membership, effective the end of the year"; (2) "I tender my resignation as treasurer, same to take effect two weeks from this date"; (3) "I announce herewith my resignation as business manager, effective the first of next month (naming it)."

Immediate resignation. Some examples of immediate resignation: (1) "I hereby resign as vice president, to take effect immediately [at once, forthwith, etc.]"; (2) "I resign as member effective upon receipt hereof."

Immediate resignation from membership. Unless otherwise prescribed in the organization's laws, the rules stated below govern immediate resignation from membership:

(1) A member who is not in arrears in his dues or other financial obligations, and is not under charges for suspension or expulsion, may resign his membership whenever he pleases, by duly communicating such intention to the organization (secretary). Such resignation, unless withdrawn on or before it reaches the organization's headquarters, or before it is presented or read at the meeting, or even before it has been voted on by the body, becomes effective immediately upon its acceptance (if acceptance is required by organization rule, otherwise whether it is accepted or not is immaterial after the sitting has adjourned).[36]

(2) A member who thus resigns while in good standing does not incur additional dues, assessments or other pecuniary obligations accruing after termination of his membership.[37]

(3) Where the resigning member is in financial arrears, or is under charges, the organization is not under obligation to accept the resignation, in which case the member continues to be further liable for accruing dues or other financial indebtedness (upon which he may be sued; or he can be expelled, although, at times, and in order to avoid disunity, notoriety or undue hardship, the organization can waive such indebtedness or drop the charges against any of its members; or it can just simply accept the resignation and then remove or expunge the resigner's name from the roster of membership).[38]

Resignation from office. Unless an organization rule or bylaw otherwise governs, the rules stated below apply to immediate resignation from office:

(1) No one can be compelled to continue in office against his will.[39]

(2) An officer may resign his office without the consent of the appointing (or electing) power.[40]

Compensation in office. If a term of office in the organization's laws is "until his successor has qualified," and the office is salaried, the officer thus holding over is entitled to the compensation of the office up to the day a successor has duly qualified.[41]

The compensation of officers can be changed, increased, decreased or even abolished altogether during their tenure, unless prohibited by law.[42]

Wrongful removal from office or membership. An officer of the organization who has been wrongfully dispossessed from his office, or a member who has been wrongfully suspended, expelled or otherwise illegally ousted from membership, may sue the organization for any damages that he has thereby sustained.[43]

It is not necessary for the dispossessed officer or member to resort to violence or forcible collision with those preventing him from occupying or exercising the duties of the office (or of his membership); nor will his failure to keep up clamor or constant quarrel for reinstatement of his office or membership, or to take immediate legal proceedings, work an abandonment of his claim.[44]

Note: All that a wrongfully dispossessed officer or member need immediately do is (*a*) to rise and voice his protest if present at the meeting; then/or (*b*) for the record, to write promptly to the ousting body and stress his rightful claim; then (*c*) to follow up his claim thereafter (if he so desires) by appeal to the organization's higher body (supreme lodge, or convention, etc.), or to pursue it in courts thereafter (if good judgment so suggests) after first exhausting all means of remedy specified in the organization's laws.

Acquiescence in wrongful removal. If the officer who has been wrongfully removed from office (or a member from membership) acquiesces in, or is indifferent to, such ouster and makes no protest, or takes no steps to vindicate his claim, he is considered as having abandoned all claims.[45]

Expulsion. Where the bylaws provide for the expulsion of a member on specified grounds, he may not be expelled for any other cause.[46]

But where there are no specified grounds in the bylaws for the suspension or expulsion of a member, the right to expel or suspend can include any acts or omissions which the organization deems injurious to the association and its good name, as well as for false charges against its officers or members.[47]

Trial of members. A member cannot be tried for another or different offense than that with which he has been charged.[48]

A trial procedure is valid, although informal in character, provided it is conducted fairly; any procedure resulting in a fair trial is permissible.[49]

Steps to be taken. Before a member may be suspended or expelled for cause, he must (*a*) be given notice of the proceeding, and of the time and place thereof; (*b*) he must be served with written specific charges; (*c*) he must be given reasonable time to prepare his defense; and (*d*) he must be afforded a full and fair hearing.[50]

Resignations tabled. If the resignation of a member is laid on the table and is not taken up, it automatically takes effect when the time for taking it from the table has expired; that is, if A's resignation has not been duly withdrawn, and is not taken from the table during the session at which it was tabled, or before the close of the next session (in organizations having sessions at least as frequently as quarterly), the resignation automatically becomes final therein.

Resignations postponed definitely. Where a resignation is postponed definitely (to the next meeting, in organizations which meet at least quarterly), and is not withdrawn before adjournment of the said next meeting (session), the resignation then becomes effective. If the organization meets less frequently than quarterly, a resignation, unless withdrawn prior to adjournment of the current or present session becomes effective upon adjournment of the session.

Resignations postponed indefinitely. If a resignation is voted postponed indefinitely it takes effect immediately when voted so postponed. And if its such postponement is not reconsidered so as to allow it to be withdrawn or be otherwise disposed of at the session, then it becomes effective upon adjournment of the session, whether the body meets regularly more frequently than quarterly or less frequently than quarterly.

Resignations voted accepted. A resignation which is voted accepted takes effect immediately, unless it is otherwise provided at the time. No resignation may be reconsidered after the body votes to accept it, except by unanimous consent.

Will of the assembly. An assembly expresses its will, decision or stand on a question by finally voting upon it. The proper way to ascertain the wishes of the assembly is by a vote of some kind.[51]

When not otherwise prescribed by the laws of the organization, the vote on a question, duly put, may be taken by any method under general parliamentary practice.[52]

Majority vote adopts. Where a legal quorum is present, a proposition is carried by a majority of the votes actually cast, or by such number greater than a majority that the proposition or motion may require under the laws or bylaws of the organization.[53]

Announcing the vote. It is the duty of the presiding officer to announce the vote correctly and according to the fact. The erroneous declaration of the vote by the Chair cannot have the effect of nullifying the act of the members.[54]

A misannouncement of the vote by the presiding officer is ineffectual, and is not binding.[55]

Refusal of members present to vote. If the meeting is duly assembled and there is a quorum, members who do not vote when they might are bound by the result.[56]

Hence, where a quorum is present a question is carried if it receives the required vote for its adoption (whether it be majority or $\frac{2}{3}$), although some of the members refuse to vote.[57]

The word "present" when used alone (as distinguished from "present and voting") includes every member physically present.[58]

Status of suspended members. As distinguished from a member who has been expelled, "a suspended member is still a member of the organization"; that is, his suspension "does *not* terminate his *membership* in the organization; it merely deprives him temporarily of the exercise of *certain rights*" therein.[59]

Since the mere suspension of a member does not terminate his membership, he continues to be liable for dues, fines and assessments accruing during the period of his suspension.[60]

Members cannot be compelled to vote. It is the duty of every member to vote (unless he has a *direct* personal or pecuniary interest), but no member can be compelled by the body to vote. "It has been found impracticable" (declares Rule VIII, 1. §658, U. S. House of Representatives) "to enforce a provision requiring every member to vote."

Time and place of elections. Time and place and due notice thereof are of the substance of any election, and it is essential to the validity of an election that it be held at the time and place prescribed; and if it is not so held, the eligibility of the candidate voted for will not help the matter.[61]

But a slight change in the voting place does not render an election void where it was in all other respects regular and was conducted according to law, and no one was prevented from voting at such election on account of the change (as where the voting place was changed to another room or place next door to the other, or nearby, because of better or more comfortable facilities, etc.).[62]

Candidates lacking nomination. The fact that a person has not been nominated as a candidate does not render him ineligible to office (in any club, society or organization), or preclude the voters from voting for him, or invalidate the votes so cast.[63]

Hence, the right of the members to vote for any person eligible for office whether he has been nominated or not has been recognized, as by requiring blank lines for the writing in, or pasting in (by "sticker") any other name(s) in their place.[64]

But where a law or bylaw declares that "no one shall be elected to an office except that he be first nominated in the manner provided" (or "votes cast for an unnominated member shall be void," or similar language), then such provision renders an unnominated person ineligible to be elected to office.[65]

Credentials. In conventions, after the temporary organization has been effected, the question as to who are accredited delegates entitled to vote is properly submitted to the committee on credentials. But such committee may properly refuse to *determine* which of two contesting delegations is entitled to be seated, and leave the question for the determination of the convention.[66]

If an election result is challenged on the ground that illegal votes were cast, the burden is on the challenger to show (*a*) not only that the votes had been cast, and (*b*) that they were illegal, but also (*c*) that they were cast for the contestee, or winning candidate, and (*d*) that they were sufficient in number to change the result of the election.[67]

Vote and ballot distinguished. While these words can sometimes be used synonymously, a "ballot" is the instrument by which the voter expresses his choice on candidates or questions, and his "vote" is his choice or preference thereon.[68]

Indication of voter's choice on ballots. Ballots are not treated as void which appear to have been innocently made as the result of awkwardness, inattention, ignorance, mistake or physical infirmity, if the lawful *intent* of the voter can be ascertained.[69]

Except in those cases in which statutes, bylaws or rules specify that the voter *must* observe the markings *as prescribed* on the ballot and which expressly *prohibit* the counting of ballots not marked as specified, all other cases recognize that the *intent* of the voter is the prime consideration in determining the validity of the ballot; but his intent must be determined by an inspection of the ballot itself.[70]

Where there is no certain way of ascertaining the voter's choice, the ballot is defective as to *that* choice or office and is not counted.[71]

No ballot should be rejected for any technical error which does not make it impossible to determine the voter's choice.[72]

Allowances must be made for infirmity of sight, unsteadiness of hand, inability to write well or make straight lines.[73]

A ballot does not count where a cross has been marked and then covered by marks of erasure.[74]

Lines which intersect and cross even slightly within the proper circle or square constitute a cross, no particular form of cross being required.[75]

Lines of the cross that are wavering as if made by an unsteady hand do not invalidate the ballot.[76]

A mark that is made like a T is regarded as a cross.[77]

Where, instead of making the cross, the voter blackens the whole face of the squares with a lead pencil, etc., the ballot is void.[78]

Position of cross or mark. To count the ballot, the cross should be fairly in the place designated; yet, where it is clear that the voter made an honest attempt to conform by marking it in the proper place, although with more or less imperfect success, the ballot should be counted.[79]

Where the laws or instructions *require* the voter to mark his ballot in the circle at the head of one of the columns, *or* within the space opposite the candidate's name, a cross mark elsewhere is insufficient.[80]

When the voter makes the cross mark in the circle, as required, and erases no name thereon, the vote is counted for the entire ticket.[81]

If he places the cross in the circle, and then he also marks a cross in the *square* opposite one or more candidates under the circle group, or erases any names under it, the cross in the circle is nullified and the vote in such case counts only for those individual names having the cross mark, or for those not erased.   (See next paragraph.)

If his ballot is marked with a cross on the *first name* under a *circle* in a column having a *group* of names, the vote is counted only for the name so *marked*, although probably he intended to vote for the entire ticket.[82]

If the cross is partly within and partly outside the square, the vote is counted; the intent is clear.[83]

Ballots marked with a cross to the right of the name, not in the voting space left for the purpose, but in a vacant space immediately after the name, is counted, except where the laws or rules require the cross to be placed in the square "and in no other place." [84]

But where a law or rule merely *directs* that cross marks shall be made opposite the names of candidates for whom the voter desires to vote, it is immaterial on which side the cross marks are made.[85]

A ballot marked on the back is not counted.[86]

Pasters or stickers. If the bylaws or rules prohibit the use of pasters or stickers at elections, their use is invalid.[87]

But when the laws or rules provide for stickers, (or do not prohibit them) voters can use stickers for the insertion of names not on the ballot, and a cross mark after the name is not necessary.[88]

Writing in names. When an elector desires to vote for a person whose name is not on the ballot, he can do so by writing in his name on the line left blank in the appropriate place, and a cross is not actually essential, the intention being obvious.[89]

When a voter erases the name of a candidate and writes in the name of another, the vote is good for the candidate whose name is written in.[90]

Names misspelled. If the voter's intention can be determined, it cannot be defeated by the fact that the name of the candidate for whom he intends to vote is misspelled, or a wrong initial used, or some other or slightly different name of like or similar pronunciation has been written.[91]

Erasures. The erasure of a candidate's name is regarded as a proper manner of expressing the voter's intent not to vote for such candidate.[92]

An erasure of a candidate's name destroys the effect of a cross opposite it.[93]

Double or conflicting marking. A ballot marked with a cross mark opposite the names of two opposing candidates for the same office is void as to that office, but it is properly counted for other candidates if otherwise correctly marked.[94]

A ballot having a cross in a party (or group) circle but with the name of a candidate of that party marked out is void as to him but not as to the others.[95]

A *general* designation by the marking of a ballot with a cross at the head of the ticket or group, indicating the intention to vote for all its candidates, is controlled by a *particular* designation by the marking of crosses opposite the names of part of the candidates under the party emblem, or group, and ballots so marked cannot be counted for any of the candidates opposite whose name no cross appears; it counts only for those opposite whose name a cross appears.[96]

A ballot on which a name has been written in opposite a printed name without erasing the printed names is counted in favor of the person whose name is so written in.[97]

Split ticket. The only way to vote a split ticket is to make cross marks in voting spaces opposite the candidates for whom the elector desires to vote.[98]

Identification or distinguishing marks on ballots. Laws, rules or bylaws and express instructions which prohibit the placing of distinguishing marks for the purpose of identification upon the ballot and which prescribe that ballots which contain such marks will *not* be counted are binding on the voter.[99]

But a ballot is not rejected on account of slight irregularity in the marking, unless it is clear the voter intended it as a mark of identification.[100]

But where there is no *express* rule or law forbidding or outlawing marks of identification, the ballots are counted in all cases, if otherwise valid. Hence, no attention is paid to any identification marks or any witticisms, wisecracks, or improper remarks written upon any ballot. It is the vote that counts.

Extra crosses. Ballots are not rejected if they are marked with heavy cross, or heavy cross extending outside the square or circle, or *inside* of them with the arms of the cross a whole inch outside of them, or two crosses for a candidate instead of one, making a double cross or a cluster of crosses, a cross in a party or group circle, or three crosses opposite the name of a candidate, or a cross after the name of a candidate written in, or a cross inside a circle or square and a cross outside of it.[101]

Opening and closing of polls. An election is not void because the polls were kept open after the hour for closing, in the absence of evidence that any votes were cast after that hour, or that sufficient votes were cast after that hour to change the result.[102]

Delay in opening the polls which thus *prevents* electors from voting is grounds for invalidating the election.[103]

A vote cast *before* the opening of the polls is void.[104]

Also, the reception of a vote after the polls have been *closed* at the proper time is void.[105]

But ballots cast and accepted after premature closing of polls are counted.[106]

Temporary closing of the polls for an hour spent at dinner by the election officers and then reopening the polls does not invalidate the election where it appears no fraud was practiced and no substantial right violated.[107]

If a person votes twice, or casts two ballots, when he is only entitled to vote once, or to one vote, then *both* votes are rejected.[108]

A voter is not allowed to repeat his vote because he violated the law in *casting* the first one.[109]

Voting by ballot. A vote by ballot is complete when the voter deposits his legally prepared ballot in the ballot box.[110]

Count of votes. An election is not invalid because the election officers began to *count* the votes before the close of the polls.[111]

In the absence of fraud, the action of the election officers in removing the ballots and counting them elsewhere does not void an election or require the rejection of any ballots.[112]

A ballot regular in form picked up from the floor cannot be counted if not shown to have actually been in the ballot box.[113]

The last ballot in the ballot box, if legal in form, cannot be rejected merely because there is one more ballot in the box than there are counted voters.[114]

If two or more *separate* ballots are found so folded together as to present the appearance of a single ballot, they must be laid aside until the count of the ballots is completed, then, after comparing the count and names of the electors on the lists, it appears that the two ballots thus folded together were cast by one elector, they must both be rejected.[115]

Recount. Where the entry of the total votes in the different columns opposite an office on the tally sheet do not balance with the total of ballots voted at the polling place, the ballots must be recounted for such office.[116]

Preservation or disposition of ballots. Organizations have inherent right to provide for the preservation of ballots in a locked and sealed box or in a sealed envelope, paper bag, or package for a certain period of time after the election, and for their destruction at the end of such period, if no contest has been instituted.[117]

The custodian of the ballot container may not permit it to be opened or be inspected by any person or for any purpose except in case of a contest, and he is not required to destroy the ballots after expiration of the time fixed for their destruction if they are needed in the event of such contest.[118]

Majority vote. Plurality vote. It is fundamental that no one can be declared elected (and no measure or question can be declared carried) unless he or it receives a majority vote (or a plurality vote where *so* authorized) of the legal votes cast.[119]

The fact that a majority (or a plurality) of the votes cast are cast for an ineligible candidate does not entitle the candidate receiving "the next highest number of votes" to be declared elected.[120]

In such case, the voters have failed to make a choice, and they proceed to vote again.[121]

Religious Corporations

Definition of a religious society. A religious society is an assembly or body of persons who usually meet in some stated place for the worship of God and for religious instruction. This includes all religious societies and congregations, without regard to their being incorporated, and may or may not include a church or spiritual body.[122]

Religious corporation defined. A religious corporation is one whose purposes are directly and manifestly ancillary or auxiliary to divine worship or religious teaching; it is not necessarily a church in the common acceptation of the term, or even a religious society.[123]

Certificate and charter. The filing for certificate of incorporation or for charter must be substantially followed as statutory law may require. Many provisions in the charter are not necessary, since they can be contained in the body's bylaws.[124]

The most essential points for inclusion in the certificate are: (1) name; (2) objects or purposes; (3) place of meeting (city and state); (4) its duration or term of existence; (5) membership; (6) officers (give the minimum number; add more in the bylaws); (7) provide for right to acquire property; (8) prohibit diversion of funds of original donors (if so desired); (9) prohibit admission of members not of the religious sect of the incorporators; and add such other points as may be desired.[125]

Acceptance of charter. Legal acceptance of the proposed charter can be effected by majority vote at a meeting regularly held for the purpose.[126]

Change and amendment of charter. A charter may be surrendered at any time and a new one accepted; or it may be amended from time to time, provided such amendment does not alter the original principles or violate the fundamental law of the church.[127]

"Corporation" and "church" distinguished. The corporation and church are distinct bodies, the objects of one being temporal, and those of the other spiritual. The former acquires the rights and powers of a corporation for certain purposes, without losing its sectarian and denominational characteristics.[128]

Constitution and bylaws. When a written constitution or bylaws have been adopted, it is the embodiment of the terms of the compact by which the society is to be governed.[129]

In all cases, when the constitution or bylaws require *notice* for changes or amendments thereto, a change made without giving such notice is not binding.[130]

Withdrawal, expulsion, resignation. The continuance of a member with a religious society is purely voluntary and he may withdraw when he wishes; he may also resign.

And when he is expelled, the member's further rights in the property or beneficial interest therein are to be determined by its constitution and bylaws.[131]

Meetings. It is essential to the validity of its decisions and wishes, that the society's meetings shall be legally held meetings in conformity with its laws.[132]

Elections. Officers must be elected in accordance with and in the manner prescribed by its laws.[133]

A religious society having power to make rules and bylaws for its government may make bylaws regulating the mode of conducting elections and the forms of ballots. But if there is no such bylaw, then a long established custom or usage will govern.[134]

Quorum. If the laws or bylaws prescribe no quorum, but the roster of membership is definite, a majority of that total membership is legal quorum; if there is no roster of definite membership, then a majority of those who happen to be present at any time constitute a quorum; and if the quorum is fixed, as 10% or 20%, or 45 members, or 70 members, then that quorum governs.[135]

Entitled to vote. Every member of a religious society is entitled to vote until he voluntarily withdraws or is expelled.[136]

Officers. The rules of the society control the election of officers and trustees, unless otherwise prescribed.[137]

Duration of office. If the term of office is not limited in point of time, an officer continues in office until he is succeeded, removed, withdrawn from the church or society, or if he joins another denomination.[138]

Proper court proceeding. The proper remedy to test an officer's right to exercise the office is by the proceeding of *quo warranto:* and to restore officers wrongfully removed, a writ of *mandamus* is the proceeding.[139]

Acquiring and holding property. A religious society, incorporated or not, can acquire and hold property.[140]

Control, use and disposition of property. The members of a religious society may, as a general rule, control and direct the disposition of its property, unless otherwise specified, provided it is done conformably to the principles and laws of the church or to the charter of the corporation.[141]

Pewholders. Pewholders merely have the right to use the pew subject to any limitations or provisions relating to them, usually limited to the exclusive occupancy thereof for public worship and during the time the church is open for church services.[142]

They cannot remove or convert the pew to other use.[143]

Church tribunals, judicial or legislative supervision. When a person becomes a member of a church, he does so upon the condition of submission to its ecclesiastical jurisdiction; and however much he may be dissatisfied with the exercise of that jurisdiction, he has no right to invoke the supervisory power of a civil court, so long as none of his civil rights are involved.[144]

All questions relating to faith, practice, doctrine and discipline of the church belong to the ecclesiastical tribunal.[145]

All matters within the province of church courts or tribunals and their decisions and proceedings are respected by civil courts.[146]

Division of society. The separation or secession of part of the members from a church does not destroy the identity of the church, nor lessen the rights of those adhering to the organization. And the fact that the minister also secedes does not alter the rule.[147]

But the members seceding from a church thereby forfeit all rights to the church property, and the courts, when called upon, will award the property, and all rights pertaining thereto, to those who continue to adhere to the doctrine, tenets and rules of the church as they existed before the division, or, in case it is a denominational church, to those recognized by the highest judicatory of the denomination, as being the church or congregation.[148]

Seceders from a church who form a new organization cannot acquire any right to the church property by adopting the name of the original organization.[149]

         *   *   *

Impeachment of officers. To "impeach" a person means to accuse him, to bring an accusation against him.[150]

If your bylaws provide a method of impeachment, then follow the procedure prescribed therein.[151]

Failure to qualify for office. Unless it is expressly otherwise provided, a failure to qualify for an office does not create a vacancy in the office.[152] Hence, the *same* body has to hold another election to choose one who is qualified.

But where a law or bylaw provides that a vacancy shall exist in such event, then a vacancy exists for failure to qualify[153]; and in such case, it is filled by the party (board or president) having authority to fill vacancies.

Indefinite tenure. Where the term of an officer is not fixed by law or rule, the officer is regarded as holding office at the *will* of the appointing or electing power.[154] Usually, in such case, he holds office up to a year; but the body can hold the election whenever it pleases, which can be sooner or later, with due notice thereof.

A prior enactment relative to the term of office must give way to a later provision with which it is in conflict, notwithstanding the fact that such first act is brought forward without a change in a revision of the laws.[155]

Where officers are elected at the same time to fill *terms* of varying length, and there is no bylaw or rule indicating a method of determining *which* officers are elected for the *longer* term, the fact that one of the officers receives a larger number of votes does not (necessarily) entitle him to the longer period; instead, an agreement between the officers is a proper method of deciding the question.[156]

Jurisdiction of incoming officers. All business which naturally belongs to the *first* day of the official term of the incoming officers is within the jurisdiction of the incoming officers, although there may be some delay during the day in qualifying and assuming official duties. Hence, the outgoing officers cannot act on matters properly falling on or coming up for attention *that* day.[157]

Changing term of office. Where a law prescribes a term of office, the assembly has power through regular amending process, to amend it by changing the term of office even during the term of an incumbent.[158]

If a law is passed by the body extending the term of office (say from one year to two years), the incumbent of the office continues only for the time to which the law was originally limited, unless it is expressly provided that the incumbent may continue for the extended period.[159]

Where a successor to an incumbent has been legally chosen and duly qualified, at that moment the right of the incumbent to hold over ceases, and does not revive upon the death of his successor before the commencement of the latter's term.[160]

Duty to continue in office. When the laws provide that incumbent officers shall hold over until their successors are legally chosen and duly qualified, such a law imposes upon an incumbent the duty of continuing in office after expiration of his term.[161]

The holding over does not change the length of the term of office, but merely shortens the term of his successor.[162]

Vacancy in office. An office is vacant in the eye of the law if it is unoccupied by a *legally* qualified incumbent who has a lawful right to continue therein until the happening of some future event.[163]

On the other hand, an office is not vacant so long as it is *supplied*, in the manner *provided* by the constitution or bylaws with an incumbent who is legally qualified to exercise the powers and perform the duties which appertain to it.[164]

"Sufficient cause" for removal. "Cause" which is sufficient to authorize removal from office means legal cause. A bylaw authorizing the removal of an officer for sufficient cause, contemplates a cause relating to the administration of his office, affecting the rights and interests of the members, or which shows that he is not a fit or proper person to perform the duties.[165]

Offenses during prior term. Offenses committed by an officer during a *previous* term of office are not good grounds for removal from the office he *presently* holds. But where the officer is his own successor to the office, he may be removed for acts done in his preceding term.[166]

Derivation of "bylaw." When the Danes acquired possession of a shire or town in England, each such township was called a "bye," and as they enacted laws of their own they were called "bylaws," or town laws.[167]

History of "constitution." The term "constitution" was promulgated by the Crown, or sovereign ruler, having the force of law, and resembling the character of modern statutes, such as are enacted by the Congress and the state legislatures. (*Stubbs Constitutional History*, Eng., Third Ed., sec. 140)

A constitution is defined as that "fundamental law of a State which contains the principles on which government is founded, regulates the division of sovereign powers, and directs to what persons each of these power is to be entrusted and the manner of its exercise." [168]

The purpose of a constitution (as contrasted with bylaws) is to prescribe the permanent framework and a uniform system of government of a nation or other sovereign state.[169]

Constitution a misnomer. Since the word "constitution" is the proper or appropriate term for use only by *nations* and *sovereign* states, the use of the term "constitution" in deliberative bodies (as in "constitution and bylaws," or simply "constitution") is, strictly speaking, only a bylaw under the inappropriate name, "constitution." [170] Hence, "constitution" in clubs, societies and organizations is a misnomer; but it is common usage.

Interpretation of bylaws. The primary object in the interpretation of bylaws is to ascertain and give effect to the intention of the framers thereof.[171]

In their interpretation the same principles obtain which govern the interpretation of statutes and contracts.[172]

It is a familiar and well-settled rule that a subsequent statute or bylaw, revising or amending the subject matter of a former one, and evidently intended as a substitute for it, although it contains no express words to that effect, operates to repeal the former to the extent to which its provisions are revised and supplied.[173]

Where there is such revision or amendment, there need not (but there can) be express words of repeal.[174]

Speaking generally, the bylaws of associations, clubs, societies and other like organizations are not scrutinized closely by the courts, nor are they interfered with, unless there has been an abuse of discretion and a clear, unreasonable and arbitrary invasion of private rights.[175]

Bylaws subject to charter. If an organization possesses a charter, and its charter provides sufficiently for the government of the body, bylaws are unnecessary even where the charter confers upon it the power to adopt bylaws.[176]

And subject to its charter, articles, or certificate of incorporation, every organization has inherent power to make all necessary and legal bylaws, rules and regulations for its government, although such power may not be expressly conferred in its charter, or in the statutes or laws of its creation.[177]

By whom adopted. Unless the organization's laws have vested the power of making bylaws in some particular board or body, it can be exercised only by the constituent body; namely: the members. Hence, bylaws cannot be *adopted* by the board of directors or trustees or by other officers, unless specially so authorized (but they may recommend bylaws).[178]

Ratification of bylaws. Where bylaws are adopted by the wrong body, as by a board of directors, managers or trustees, when in fact the bylaws vest the power solely in the members or stockholders, or vice versa, the subsequent ratification thereof in proper form by the proper body is equivalent to the passing or adoption of the bylaws by such body in the first instance, and therefore they are valid bylaws.[179]

If the charter or bylaws require that a bylaw adopted by the directors or trustees must be confirmed by the stockholders or members, or vice versa, compliance therewith is essential; a substantial compliance is sufficient.[180]

Quorum necessary to enact bylaws. Where bylaws are enacted by a body, there must be a quorum present to constitute the bylaw valid.[181]

If the bylaws authorize the board of directors to make bylaws, a majority of that body at least is necessary and sufficient for a quorum; and by the act of the majority in legal meeting assembled, the bylaws become binding upon the organization or corporation, the act of the majority being the act of all, unless a greater vote is required for such acts by the charter, statute, or bylaws.[182]

Power to amend or repeal. A body which is expressly or impliedly authorized to make such bylaws as may be necessary to attain the objects for which it is created, has power to amend, modify, limit, or repeal such bylaws from time to time, when deemed necessary to carry out such objects, unless its charter, articles, or certificate of incorporation, or its constitution or bylaws otherwise provide.[183]

Mode of amendment or repeal. In amending or repealing a bylaw it is necessary to comply substantially with the formalities, if any, prescribed by the mandatory provisions of the charter, governing statute, or articles of incorporation, or by the constitution or bylaws in force at the time where these are binding on the body making the change.[184]

Notice of amendment. Notice of proposed amendments to the organization's laws must be given as specified in any case.[185]

Implied repeal by new bylaws. A bylaw is impliedly repealed by a new bylaw which is so inconsistent therewith that both cannot stand, and the adoption of a new bylaw covering the same grounds as the former one, and intended for the same purpose, impliedly repeals and supersedes the earlier bylaw, so that any penalties imposed by the earlier, or other provisions therein, but omitted from the later bylaw, no longer apply.[186]

Bylaws contrary to general law. Bylaws must not be contrary to the law of the land, whether common, statutory, or constitutional, or to public policy or good morals.[187]

Operation of laws retroactively. A bylaw which creates new penalties or punitive burdens and which attempts to operate retroactively is void.[188]

But a bylaw which does not disturb vested rights or existing contract terms (or, in general, which confers benefits) can operate retrospectively.[189]

Disqualification to vote by direct interest. If a deliberative body has adopted a bylaw to the effect that no member immediately interested in a proposition shall vote thereon, such rule is binding on the members. The general rule at common law is that members are disqualified to act on propositions in which they have a direct personal or pecuniary interest. Hence, such members are not counted in the quorum at the time the action is taking place, and they may not vote on the matter involved.[190]

Indirect interest. Members having no interest other than that which is common to every member are not disqualified to vote on a proposition affecting the members (such as voting themselves a salary, or per diem expense, or voting a sum of money to pay for a catered supper for themselves, etc.).[191]

Business Corporations

Definition of a corporation. A corporation is an association or a collection of natural persons, chartered by act of the legislature to accomplish some purpose, pecuniary, ideal or governmental, united together and having continuous succession to maintain or carry on some kind of business or undertaking like a natural person." [192]

Other definitions. "A corporation is an immortal being"; "an artificial being, invisible, intangible, and existing only in contemplation of law"; an "artificial person created by the legislature"; "a body of individuals created by law, united under a common name, and having succession while it shall exist; it is the creature of the law of its creation." [193]

Origin and history. The nature of corporations was known to the Greeks as early as the time of Solon (638–558 B.C.), who permitted such "associations whether for purposes of mere affection, of business, or of devotion," subject only to the condition that their purposes should not be contrary to the general law of the land.[194]

But corporations were recognized by the Romans at an earlier date, for, according to Plutarch, they were introduced by Numa Pompilius, the second legendary king of Rome (715–672 B.C.), who, finding upon his succession that Rome "was torn to pieces by the two rival factions of Sabines and Romans, thought it a prudent and politic measure to subdivide these two into many smaller ones, by instituting separate societies of every manual trade and profession." [195]

The Romans established corporations in Britain after its conquest, and subsequently such bodies were established and recognized by English law for various purposes — municipal, charitable, and purely private.[196]

Various corporations were also created thereafter, both public and private, in the American colonies by the English kings or parliaments; and since the independence of the United States, (1776), corporations of every conceivable nature, kind and purpose have been and are constantly being established under legislative enactment of the States and of the United States.

General corporate powers. The general powers of corporations are: (1) perpetual succession; (2) to sue and to be sued, and to receive and to grant, by their corporate name; (3) to purchase, hold, mortgage and convey real and personal property; (4) to have a corporate seal, and (5) to make bylaws.[197]

The only essential attribute of a corporation is the capacity to exist and to act, within the powers granted to it, as a legal entity apart from the individuals who compose its members; and this is the characteristic which distinguishes a corporation from other associations.[198]

Incorporators and members. Constitutional and statutory provisions as to who may become incorporators, stockholders or members of corporations must be observed; no one can become so who is excluded or who does not come within the terms prescribed.[199]

Members and stockholders. A stockholder is one who holds stock in a corporation or joint-stock company by virtue of holding one or more shares of stock. The term is used synonymously with "shareholder," and also with "member." [200]

Directors and officers. A corporation possesses implied power to elect directors and other suitable officers and agents to direct and govern its affairs and to conduct its business. [201]

The power to elect directors or trustees of a corporation belongs exclusively to the members or stockholders, unless otherwise provided by the organic law of the corporation. [202]

It is generally provided by statute or charter that directors shall be elected by the stockholders. [203]

The directors of a corporation, in the absence of express authority, have no valid power to fill vacancies in the board. [204]

The right of stockholders to elect directors extends to filling a vacancy therein, unless by statute or charter the right to fill a vacancy in the board is conferred on the board itself. [205]

Authorizing the board of directors to fill vacancies in directorships does not apply to the filling of newly created directorships. [206]

Calling and notice of election. Where the giving of notice of a meeting for the election of directors is required by statute, charter, or bylaw, a failure to give the notice required or a failure to give it for the required time or in the required mode renders the election of directors at such meeting illegal, unless all the stockholders expressly waive the requirements or are present and consent to the holding of the election. [207]

Author's note: Forms for annual and special meetings. Following are the forms usually used to notify stockholders for annual and special meetings, with the proxy form in each case.

(1) Notice of Annual Meeting

The annual meeting of stockholders of B Corporation will be held at (place, city and state), on (date, year), at (hour), for the election of directors and for such other business as may properly come before the meeting.

So that we may complete arrangements for those who plan to attend the (year) Annual Stockholders' Meeting, please mail this RSVP card today.

SIGNED: _____A.I.P. Secretary

Proxy for Annual Meeting

Know All Men By These Presents:

That I do hereby constitute and appoint (name) attorney and agent for me and in my name, place and stead to vote as my proxy at the annual meeting of stockholders of B Corporation, to be held at (place, city and state), on (date, year), at (time), or at any adjournment thereof, according to the number of votes I shall be entitled to vote if then personally present.

In witness whereof, I have hereunto set my hand and seal, on this (day) of (month), (year).

WITNESS: _____   SIGNED: _____ (L.S.)

(2) Notice of Special Meeting

A Special Meeting of Stockholders of X Corporation will be held at (place, city, state), on (day, month, year) at (hour), for the following purpose:

To consider and take action upon a proposed merger of X Corporation, a New Jersey Corporation, with and into U. S. S. Company, all as described in the attached Proxy Statement, dated (month, date, year), and in the Joint Agreement of Merger, dated (month, date, year), attached as Exhibit I to the Proxy Statement, enclosed herewith.

You are requested to sign the enclosed proxy and mail same promptly in the return envelope provided. Shares cannot be voted at the meeting unless the owner of record is present to vote or is represented by proxy.

BY ORDER OF THE BOARD OF DIRECTORS,

_____, Secretary.

Proxy for Special Meeting

The undersigned hereby appoints A, B and C, or any of them, as proxies, to vote on behalf of the undersigned at the special meeting of stockholders of X Corporation on (day, hour, month, year), and any adjournments of the said special meeting.

DATED_____   SIGNED_____

Note: No particular form of words is necessary to appoint or constitute a proxy, nor is it necessary to be executed with any particular formality, except where specially so required. Hence, compare the more formal proxy under (1) above, with the less formal proxy under (2) given just above.

The president. Aside from his position as presiding officer of the board of directors and of the stockholders when convened in general meeting, the president of a corporation has, by virtue of his office, merely, no greater power than that of any director. Whatever authority he has must be expressly conferred upon him by statute, charter or bylaw or the board of directors or be implied from express powers granted to him, or by usage or custom, or the nature of the company's business.[208]

He may be, and frequently is made the chief executive officer of the company and is invested with broad general powers.[209]

He is without power, however, to do an act which is beyond the objects of the corporation, or which has the effect of overruling or revoking the action of the directors.[210]

The vice president. The vice president of the ordinary corporation performs the duties and functions of the president in the latter's absence, disability, or death. In some large corporations the bylaws provide for several vice presidents and authorize all of them to perform any duties which the president or the board of directors may assign to them.[211]

The treasurer. The treasurer of a corporation is the custodian of its funds.[212]

The secretary. The secretary of a corporation makes and keeps its records and he is custodian of the corporate seal. Acts pertaining to the office of secretary need not be performed by him personally in order to be binding: they may be performed by another under his direction or under the direction of the corporation or by a secretary *pro tem* in his absence.[213]

Directors holding over. The directors of a corporation who hold over must perform the duties assigned by law with the same fidelity as regularly elected officers.[214]

Responsibility of officers. The relation of all officers of a corporation to it is fiduciary, and they must at all times act in good faith and unselfishly toward the corporation.[215]

An officer is but the agent of his corporation, and in all transactions in which its interests are involved he must act for it with unselfish singleness of purpose.[216]

Legal definition of proxy. Proxy is defined by supreme courts as "an *authority* or power to *do* a certain thing." [217]

Authority of proxy. A person can confer on his proxy any power which he himself possesses. He may also give him secret instructions as to voting upon particular questions.[218]

But a proxy is ineffectual when it is contrary to law or public policy.[219]

Where the proxy is duly appointed and he acts within the scope of the proxy, the person authorizing the proxy is bound by his appointee's acts, including his errors or mistakes.[220]

When the appointer sends his appointee to a meeting, the proxy may do anything at that meeting necessary to a full and complete exercise of the appointer's right to vote at such meeting. This includes the right to take the vote by ballot, or to adjourn (and, hence, he may also vote on other ordinary parliamentary motions, such as to refer, postpone, reconsider etc., when necessary or when deemed appropriate and advantageous to the overall object or purpose of the proxy).[221]

Presence of principal. A proxy cannot vote when the member or stockholder himself is present and votes. He can vote only in the principal's absence.[222]

Where the authority conferred upon a proxy is limited to a designated or special purpose, a vote for another and different purpose is ineffective.[223]

A proxy in the usual, ordinary form confers authority to act only at the meeting then in contemplation, and in any adjourned-meetings of the same; hence, it may not be voted at another or different meeting held under a *new call*.[224]

A proxy's unauthorized acts may be ratified by his appointer, and such ratification is equivalent to previous authority.[225]

Revocation of proxy. According to the weight of authority, a proxy only to vote stock may be revoked at any time, notwithstanding any agreement that it shall be irrevocable.[226]

The sale in the meantime by a stockholder of his shares in a corporation or company automatically revokes any proxies made or given to vote in respect of such shares.[227]

And a proxy is also revoked where the party giving it attends the election in person, or gives subsequent proxy.[228]

Hence, a proxy cannot vote when the owner of the stock arrives late or is present and votes.[229]

Effect of motive or interest. Whatever rights the stockholders may have to control the affairs or management of the corporation or to dictate its policies may be exercised by the holders of a majority of the shares of stock.[230]

On the principle that a man has the right to do as he pleases with his own property, the motive which governs a stockholder in voting is not ordinarily a subject of judicial inquiry.[231]

However, the majority stockholders are bound not to act fraudulently or in bad faith, or beyond the powers or purposes of the corporation.[232]

When the majority stockholders violate their obligations in this respect, the minority stockholders are entitled to appeal to a court of equity for relief.[233]

But where the acts of the majority stockholders are not fraudulent, or they are not *ultra vires* or beyond the powers of the corporation, the minority or dissenting stockholders have no ground of complaint, and a court of equity will not interfere with corporate action or management on their application.

Every corporation is bound to the will, and is dominated by the will, of the majority stockholders. But so long as this domination is not exercised unlawfully or inequitably, courts are powerless to interfere.[234]

Chapter 16
PARLIAMENTARY PRINCIPLES IN ACTION
An Entire Meeting in Drill Form

This chapter, presented in drill form, consists of interesting proceedings, conceivable parliamentary interruptions, and some uncommon proceedings that can properly occur in the conduct of meetings of deliberative bodies. It is designed to illustrate the rule involved in each instance and the appropriate parliamentary language and forms to be used in conducting the proceeding.

The rules illustrated are applicable in all organizations holding meetings at least as frequently as quarterly (weekly, monthly, etc.), as in city councils that meet weekly, and in fraternal orders, labor organizations, veterans' associations, women's clubs and auxiliaries, etc., that usually meet once or twice each month. These methods of procedure apply to their conventions or annual meetings as well.

Mastery of language, forms and rules illustrated herein (all of which are authentic and authoritative, and in accord with long-established parliamentary and legislative usage and practice) will add immensely to your knowledge of parliamentary law, and to your poise, self-confidence and parliamentary skill.

Read the drill aloud. Observe the rule involved and the steps taken to cope with situations.

Preparatory warning

CHAIR (striking one firm rap with gavel): "The Chair is about to call the meeting to order. The officers will take their respective stations and all members will please be seated."

This done, the Chair then *calls* the meeting to order; thus:

Call to order

CHAIR: "The meeting will come to order."

INSIDE SENTINEL (unexpectedly): "Mr. President!"

CHAIR: "Inside Sentinel!"

SENTINEL: "His Honor the Mayor has just arrived."

CHAIR (informing his assembly officially): "The Chair has just been informed that the Mayor, who is to address the meeting, has just arrived. The Chair appoints Mr. X and Mrs. Y to escort the Mayor to the platfrom, at the Chair's right. Inside Sentinel, you will admit His Honor, Mayor Z."

As the Mayor and the president shake hands on the platform, the president (very considerately) asks the Mayor privately: "When would you like to address the meeting?" Reply: "Immediately, if I may, as I am scheduled to address the PTA half an hour from now." The Chair then makes the introduction at once.

Introduction of guest speaker

CHAIR: "Ladies and Gentlemen, at our last meeting it was unanimously voted to invite the mayor of our city to address this meeting. Our guest speaker hardly needs an introduction, for he is also a past president of this lodge. It is therefore a privilege and a pleasure for me to present to you His Honor, Mayor Z." The Mayor then addresses the meeting.

After the Mayor's address and his departure from the hall, the Chair proceeds with the customary opening formalities; thus:

Opening ceremonies, absence of quorum

CHAIR: "The chaplain will now invoke prayer." (All rise.)

MEMBER A: "Mr. President. I question the presence of a quorum."

CHAIR: "Under the rules of parliamentary law (and also in the Congress of the United States), prayer does not require a quorum. A quorum is also not necessary for other preliminary formalities such as the pledge of allegiance, examination of dues cards and taking the secret password."

After prayer and the chaplain's return to his station, the Chair continues:

CHAIR: "The members will remain standing for the pledge of allegiance." (This done, he continues:) "The sergeant-at-arms will examine the dues cards and the secret password from all present." (The sergeant-at-arms is aided by the treasurer.) This done, the Chair seats the members and takes up the agenda.

Presence of quorum, minutes

CHAIR: "A quorum is now present. The first business in order under our order of business is the reading of the minutes. The secretary will please read the minutes of the last meeting."

MEMBER B: "Mr. President, I move that the reading be omitted."

CHAIR: "It is moved and seconded to dispense with the reading of the minutes. As this motion is not debatable, the Chair will put it to a vote. A majority vote is required. Those in favor of dispensing with the reading of the minutes will say aye." (Response.) "Those opposed will say no." (Response.) "The noes have it. The secretary will read the minutes."

SECRETARY: (Reads and completes the reading, following which:)

CHAIR: "Are there any corrections?" (Silence follows; then:)

MEMBER C: "Mr. President, I move that we accept the minutes."

CHAIR: "It is moved and seconded to accept the minutes as read." (He pauses two or three seconds for possible corrections; then he continues): "Those in favor will say aye; those opposed will say no; the ayes have it, and the minutes are accepted as read."

Unanimous consent, suspension of rules, motion to rescind

CHAIR: "The next business in order is the treasurer's report."

MEMBER D: "Mr. President, at our last meeting two weeks ago we adopted the special committee's recommendation to buy the adjoining lot for club parking. I would like to move to rescind that recommendation. Is it in order to do so now?"

CHAIR: "No, not now; but it would be in order when business of that class is reached; namely, when we reach reports of special committees." (The Chair pursues the order of business. He repeats:)

CHAIR: "The treasurer's report is the next business in order."

TREASURER: (Reads and completes his report.)

CHAIR: "Are there any questions on the treasurer's report?"

MEMBER E: "Mr. President, why $350 for the downtown club office instead of the usual $300 monthly rental?"

TREASURER: "Mr. President, the rent was raised $50 a month."

CHAIR: "If there are no further questions on the treasurer's report," (he pauses two or three seconds, and then:) "we will now take up the next business in order which is . . ." (interrupted by member F).

MEMBER F: "Mr. President, I rise to a point of order."

CHAIR: "The member will state the point of order."

MEMBER F: "We have not voted to accept the treasurer's report."

CHAIR: "Under the rules, it is not necessary to vote to accept the treasurer's report, since we have no way of determining the accuracy of the items in the treasurer's report; we have an auditing committee for the purpose."

MEMBER F: "But we have always been doing it, and I would like to have the practice continued in the present instance, too."

CHAIR (understandingly): "If you wish to move to accept the report of the treasurer, the Chair will entertain your motion."

MEMBER F: "I so move." (Seconded.)

CHAIR: "It is moved and sec–" (interrupted by Member G).

MEMBER G: "Mr. President, a question of parliamentary inquiry."

CHAIR: "The member will state the parliamentary inquiry."

MEMBER G: "Since, as I understand it, to accept the treasurer's report is to approve it, what happens if a sum of money or other item that we thus approved is found afterward to be wrong or false?"

CHAIR: "In such case, it is within the power of the assembly to correct the error whenever it is noticed, and the fact that we thus approved an erroneous or false entry in the treasurer's report in any instance does not relieve the treasurer of responsibility for accurate accounting for each item. The question now is on the acceptance of the treasurer's report." (He puts it to a vote and, as usual, it is voted accepted. The Chair pursues the order of business.)

CHAIR: "The next business in order is the report of the executive committee, Mr. C, chairman . . ." (interrupted by member H).

MEMBER H: "Mr. President, I wish to . . ." (Chair interrupts him).

CHAIR: "For what purpose do you rise? You are not a member of the executive committee, are you?"

MEMBER H: "No; but I wish to make a motion. Is it in order?"

CHAIR: "It depends. The member will state the motion first."

MEMBER H: "Under new business at the last meeting two weeks ago, we adopted a motion to authorize the house chairman to engage a contractor to convert the Club's extra stockroom into a service kitchen, at a cost not to exceed $3,000. First, I want to ask the House chairman..." (interrupted by the Chair).

CHAIR: "The Chair cannot permit any inquiries on the subject of the service kitchen right now, because that question is not before the body. The question before the body is on the report of the executive committee."

MEMBER H: "Yes, I know, Mr. President; but I am leading up to the question of the service kitchen, which I propose to bring canonically before the body for further consideration by appropriate motion that can supersede the executive committee report."

CHAIR: "In that case, the Chair will hear your motion."

MEMBER H: "First, I wish to ask the house chairman through the Chair: has he engaged a contractor?"

CHAIR: "The Chair recognizes the house chairman for a reply."

HOUSE CHAIRMAN: "Mr. President, in answer to the member's inquiry, I regret to say that I have not engaged any contractor and I have done nothing at all about it, because I was on vacation the last two weeks; I just got back."

MEMBER H: "Mr. President, in that case I move to *rescind* the motion concerning the service kitchen which we adopted under the category of new business at the last meeting." (Seconded.)

CHAIR: "Under the rules, the motion to rescind a question originally adopted under a certain category is in order only when business of the same class, or business under that same category, has been reached; namely, in this case, under the category of *new* business."

Note: Observe that although Member H did not succeed in outwitting the president when he proposed his motion to rescind which the Chair properly ruled *not* in order for the reason he gave, Member H apparently knows his parliamentary law, as shown below, and he is attempting to reach the category of new business before its regular turn. He now uses two methods for the purpose, methods not often resorted to (or known) in ordinary assemblies; thus:

MEMBER H: "Mr. President, a question of parliamentary inquiry."

CHAIR: "The member will state it."

MEMBER H: "Is it in order for me to ask *unanimous consent* to act on the rescission of the motion we passed under new business?"

CHAIR: "Yes."

MEMBER H: "Then, Mr. President, I ask unanimous consent to have my motion to rescind acted on now."

CHAIR: "Mr. H asks unanimous consent to have rescission of the service kitchen question acted on now. Is there any objection?"

VOICE: "I object." (*Any* member can object.)

CHAIR: "There being objection, unanimous consent is denied."

MEMBER H (again): "Mr. President, a further inquiry."

CHAIR: "The member will state his further inquiry."

MEMBER H: "Is it in order, after refusal of unanimous consent, to move to suspend the rules for the purpose of having action taken on the rescission?"

CHAIR: "It is. The motion to suspend the rules requires a two-thirds vote."

MEMBER H: "Then, Mr. President, I move to suspend the rules." (Seconded.)

CHAIR: "It is moved and seconded to suspend the rules in order to take action upon the motion to rescind. As suspension is not debatable or amendable, the Chair will put it to a vote. Those in favor of suspension will raise their right hand. Forty-four hands. Hands down. Those opposed will raise their right hand. Twenty. Hands down. There being two-thirds in favor, the rules are suspended and the Chair now recognizes Mr. H."

MEMBER H (using tact): "Mr. President, I wish to thank the members for granting me suspension of the rules. I now move to rescind the motion adopted under the category of new business at the last meeting authorizing the treasurer to engage a contractor for the conversion of a stockroom into a Club service kitchen."

CHAIR: "It is moved and seconded . . ." (repeating the above motion). "Is there any discussion on the motion to rescind?"

After debate on the rescission *and* on the merits of the service kitchen question, which the motion to rescind automatically opens to debate, the Chair is about to put it to a vote, when:

MEMBER I: "Mr. Chairman, what vote is needed to adopt the motion to rescind?"

CHAIR: "In this case, a $\frac{2}{3}$ vote is required to rescind, since previous notice of intention was *not* given at the last meeting, or in the call for this meeting. If such notice had been given, only a majority vote would now be required." (The Chair then puts the motion to rescind to a vote.)

CHAIR: "Those in favor of the motion to rescind will raise their right hand; forty-six, hands down. Those opposed will raise their right hand; eighteen, hands down. There being two-thirds in favor, the affirmative has it and the motion authorizing the construction of a service kitchen is rescinded."

The Chair now resumes the regular order of business at the point previously interrupted; thus:

CHAIR: "The next business in order is the report of the executive committee. The Chair now recognizes its vice chairman, Mr. J, as Chairman C is not in the room."

Executive committee report, tablement, reconsideration

MEMBER J: "Mr. President, at its last meeting the executive committee voted to recommend that . . ." (gives his report, then he concludes:) "Therefore, by direction of the executive committee, I move the adoption of its recommendation; namely: that we award $100 to the member who brings in the largest number of new members during our membership drive the next three months."

CHAIR: "It is moved to adopt the recommendation of the executive committee. Is there any debate?"

MEMBER K: "A point of order, Mr. President."

CHAIR: "The member will state the point of order."

MEMBER K: "The recommendation has not been seconded."

CHAIR: "The point of order is not well taken, as recommendations or motions of committees and boards do not require a second. Is there any discussion on the recommendation?"

MEMBER L: "Mr. President, I move that the executive committee's recommendation be laid on the table." (Seconded.)

CHAIR: "It is moved and seconded to lay on the table the executive committee's recommendation. As the motion to lay on the table is not debatable or amendable, the Chair will put it to a vote. Those in favor of tabling the recommendation will say aye; those opposed will say no. The ayes have it, and the recommendation is laid on the table.''

MEMBER M: "Mr. President, I move to reconsider the tablement."

CHAIR: "Under the rules, the motion to lay on the table is not subject to reconsideration.''

Note: It is the only *subsidiary* motion (p. 47) that cannot be reconsidered: the others can be.

Reports, unfinished business, indefinite postponement

CHAIR: "The next business in order is reports of standing committees." (Reports, if any, are then made and are disposed of in due course of proceeding.)

CHAIR: "The next business in order is reports of special committees." (Reports, if any, are disposed of in due course.)

CHAIR: Next, special orders.'' (Turning to the secretary, the Chair asks:) "Are there any special orders, Mr. Secretary?''

SECRETARY: "No.''

CHAIR: "Now, unfinished business. Is there any unfinished business, Mr. Secretary?''

SECRETARY: "Mr. President, a parliamentary inquiry, first.''

CHAIR: "The Secretary will state his inquiry.''

SECRETARY: "In the call for this meeting, as we all know, notice has been given of a motion to assess the members one dollar a month for the next six months, to accumulate a Home Fund. My inquiry is: Is this motion to assess actable under unfinished business now, or under new business?''

CHAIR: "It is actable under unfinished business, since previous notice to assess was given in the call for this meeting.''

SECRETARY: "Then, Mr. President, under unfinished business a motion to assess the members one dollar each for the next six months is pending.''

CHAIR: "The question now before the body, under unfinished business, is the motion to assess the members. Is there any debate?''

MEMBER N: "Mr. President, I move that the motion to assess the members be postponed indefinitely." (Seconded.)

CHAIR: "It is moved and seconded to postpone indefinitely the motion to assess the members. Is there debate on the postponement?'' (After debate, if any, the vote:) "There being no further debate, those in favor of indefinite postponement will say aye." (Response.) "Those opposed will say no.'' (Response.) "The ayes have it, and the motion to assess is indefinitely postponed.''

Main motion, reconsideration

CHAIR: "The next business in order is new business.''

MEMBER O: "Mr. Chairman, I move that we go on record in favor of holding the Olympic Games every two years instead of four." (Seconded.)

CHAIR: "It has been moved and seconded that this organization go on record in favor of holding Olympic Games every two years. Is there any debate on the motion?'' (After debate, the vote:) "Those in favor of the motion will say aye; those opposed will say no. The noes have it, and the motion is rejected.''

MEMBER O: "Mr. President, I move reconsideration of the motion.''

CHAIR: "Did you vote on the prevailing side [the negative]?''

MEMBER O: "Yes."

MEMBER P: "Mr. President, with all due respect to Mr. O, I did *not* hear him vote with the prevailing side. I thought I heard him vote with the losing side, the *ayes.*"

CHAIR (tactfully): "Did the Chair hear you correctly, Mr. O, that you voted with the prevailing side, namely, you voted *no?*"

MEMBER O: "I *did* vote with the prevailing side. I intentionally voted no, in order to qualify to move reconsideration in case my motion was defeated."

CHAIR: "The Chair thinks that Mr. O qualifies to move reconsideration on the strength of his claim that he did vote with the prevailing side. The general rule is [also the rule in the U. S. House of Representatives] that a member claiming that he voted on the prevailing side is given the benefit of the doubt in *all* cases except when the record of a roll call vote shows otherwise. Since in this case the vote was by voice, the reconsideration is in order. Is the reconsideration seconded?"

VOICE: "I second it."

CHAIR: "It is moved and seconded to reconsider the vote on the motion in favor of biennial instead of quadrennial Olympic Games, which was just defeated. Is there debate on reconsideration?" (After debate, the vote:) "Those in favor of reconsideration will say aye." (Response:) "Those opposed will say no." (Response:) "The ayes have it and the motion to reconsider is carried. The question now is on the original motion, namely, that we go on record as favoring holding Olympic Games every two years instead of quadrennially. Is there any further discussion on this motion?" (After discussion pro and con, the Chair is about to put the question to a vote, when:)

MEMBER Q: "Mr. President, I move to table the question."

CHAIR: "It is moved and seconded that the question be tabled. As the motion to lay on the table is neither debatable nor amendable, the Chair will put it to a vote. Those in favor of tabling the motion will say aye." (Response.) "Those opposed will say no." (Response.) "The ayes have it and the question is tabled."

Further illustration of reconsideration

CHAIR (continuing): "Is there further new business?"

MEMBER R: "Mr. President, I move that we buy twenty tickets to the testimonial dinner for Senator X." (Seconded.)

MEMBER S: "Mr. President, a point of order."

CHAIR: "The member will state the point of order."

MEMBER S: "I believe our bylaws prohibit buying tickets to testimonial dinners of politicians."

CHAIR: "There is no such bylaw provision. An attempt was made last year to adopt such a bylaw but it was rejected. The question now before the body is to purchase twenty tickets to the testimonial dinner. Is there any debate?" (After debate, the vote:) "Those in favor of the motion will say aye; those opposed will say no. The ayes have it."

MEMBER T: "Mr. President, a question of parliamentary inquiry."

CHAIR: "The member will state his inquiry."

MEMBER T: "I intend to move to reconsider the vote just taken on buying twenty tickets to the testimonial dinner, but I don't believe I have enough votes right now to attempt to reverse the vote. My inquiry is: Up to *when* have I the right to move to reconsider?"

CHAIR: "Until adjournment of this meeting." (The Chair continues:) "Is there any further new business?"

Other business is then transacted during the next half hour. In the meantime, three more members have come in, and member T has been talking to each one of them; then:

MEMBER T: "Mr. President, about half an hour ago we adopted a motion to buy twenty testimonial dinner tickets. I now move to reconsider that motion. I voted with the prevailing side." (Seconded.)

CHAIR: "It has been moved and seconded to reconsider the vote on the motion to buy twenty tickets to the testimonial dinner. Is there any discussion on the motion to reconsider?"

MEMBER U: "Mr. President, now I've heard and seen everything! Mr. T waited until some of the members who voted in favor of buying the tickets left the meeting; and in addition, he must have telephoned the three members who came to the meeting a few minutes ago to come and help him put over his reconsideration. I am opposed to the reconsideration, and I hope it will be rejected."

Note: At this point, member T can rise to a question of privilege and assail Member U for engaging in reference to personalities and in the impugnation of his motives; but he shrewdly refrains, conceivably because (a) he does not want to confuse the issue or to delay putting his reconsideration over as quickly as possible; or (b) he prefers to let this attack upon his motives appear to be an injustice to him; or (c) he feels that the president knows his parliamentary law and will admonish member U accordingly on such improprieties. The Chair does this.

CHAIR (looking in the direction of U, says to him by way of warning): "It is highly improper and unparliamentary for any member to engage in reference to personalities or to assail or impugn the motives of another member in the course of proceedings, or to suggest that a member is using insidious tactics, when all he does is to exercise his basic parliamentary rights. A member has the right, under the rules, to move to reconsider a question either immediately after the vote thereon has been taken, or when he has sufficient votes at a later time prior to adjournment of the meeting. Improper motives should therefore never be assigned to members who are exercising their rights" (or similar words).

MEMBER T: "Mr. President . . ." (interrupted by member U).

MEMBER U: "Mr. President, I . . ." (interrupted by the Chair).

CHAIR (addressing Mr. T): "Do you yield the floor to Mr. U?"

MEMBER T (looking in U's direction): "Well . . . yes; I yield for a *question* only."

MEMBER U: "Mr. President, I don't want to ask a question."

MEMBER T: "Mr. President, reserving the right not to yield the floor, may I ask through the Chair why, then, does Mr. U want me to yield the floor to him?"

MEMBER U: "Mr. President, I feel that I should make an apology at this time."

CHAIR (to member T): "Do you yield the floor to Mr. U?"

MEMBER T: "Gladly, for that purpose." (Note that T cleverly restricts the yielding for *apology* only, so as not to lose the floor altogether.)

CHAIR: "The Chair recognizes Mr. U for the purpose stated."

MEMBER U: "Mr. President, I regret that in the heat of debate I impugned Mr. T's motives, and I apologize." (Applause.)

MEMBER T: "Mr. President, I appreciate Mr. U's magnanimity and his sense of fairness." (Applause.)

CHAIR: "Is there further discussion on the motion to reconsider the vote on the motion to buy twenty testimonial dinner tickets we adopted a short while ago?" (After debate, the vote:) "Those in favor of reconsideration say aye." (Response.) "Those opposed will say no." (Response.) "The ayes have it."

MEMBER U: "Mr. President, I doubt the vote."

CHAIR: "The vote has been doubted. Those in favor of the motion to reconsider will raise their right hand. Thirty-six hands; hands down. Those opposed will raise their right hand. Ten; hands down. The affirmative has it; the motion to reconsider is carried. The question now before the body is on the original main motion, namely, to buy twenty tickets to Senator X's testimonial banquet. Is there any further debate on this motion?" (After further debate, if any, the vote:) "Those in favor of buying the tickets will say aye; those opposed will say no. The noes have it, and the motion to buy the tickets is lost."

MEMBER U: "Mr. President, I doubt the vote."

CHAIR: "The vote has been doubted. Those in favor of buying the tickets will rise and stand until counted. Thirty; please be seated. Those opposed to buying these tickets will rise and stand until counted. Thirty-six; be seated. The negative has it, and the motion to buy twenty tickets is defeated."

Take from the table, motion to amend

CHAIR: "Is there any further new business?"

MEMBER C: "Mr. President, a question of parliamentary inquiry."

CHAIR: "The member will state the inquiry."

MEMBER C: "Under the category of reports earlier at this meeting, we voted to table the executive committee's recommendation to give $100 to the member who brings in the largest number of new members during our membership drive. My inquiry is: Is it in order to move to take from the table, under the category of new business, the executive committee's report which was voted tabled when we were operating under the category of reports?"

CHAIR: "It *is* in order to move to take from the table the executive committee's report. Under the rules, if a report or other piece of business operating under its own category has been voted tabled, and is not taken from the table before completion of that category, then it can be taken from the table by a majority vote under either unfinished business or new business."

MEMBER C: "In that case, Mr. President, I move now to take from the table the recommendation of the executive committee to give $100 to the member who brings in the largest number of new members during our membership drive." (Seconded.)

CHAIR: "It is moved and seconded to take from the table the executive committee's recommendation concerning the membership drive. As the motion to take from the table is neither debatable nor amendable, the Chair will put it to vote. Those in favor of taking it from the table will say aye." (Response.) "Those opposed will say no." (Response.)

"The ayes have it, and the recommendation has been taken from the table. The question now before the body is the recommendation. Is there any discussion thereon?"

MEMBER V: "Mr. President, why not include under the $100 award reinstatements as well as new members. It is just as important to get reinstatements of lapsed memberships as it is to get new members."

CHAIR: "Then, are you proposing an *amendment* to the executive committee's recommendation to that effect? Is that your intent?"

MEMBER V: "Certainly!"

CHAIR: "Then, will you make it in the form of an amendment?"

MEMBER V: "Mr. President, I'm just a new member, and I don't know the technical forms of parliamentary practice and procedure; and besides, if I may say so, I think it is the Chair's duty to express the member's clear intent in the form of the proper motion."

CHAIR (addressing Mr. V): "If the Chair may say so, you are quite right that the Chair should, if he can, put into form of a motion the clear intent of a member's words relating to a proceeding, as in this case, and the Chair will do so; but it is for the reason that you are a new member, and a progressive one, that the Chair suggested that you acquire, as early as possible, the correct parliamentary forms for *proposing* the proper motion. If the Chair may be pardoned, if you will look under 'Amendments' in your parliamentary manual you will see how easy it is to acquire the forms for proposing amendments to motions."

MEMBER V: "Thank you, Mr. President, for your encouragement. As a matter of fact, I did read the proper amending forms in my manual the other night, and I think I now remember them. Therefore, I wish now to propose my amendment properly. Will the Chair please restate the executive committee's recommendation?"

CHAIR: "The secretary will read the recommendation."

SECRETARY (reading it): "To award $100 to the member who brings in the largest number of new members during our membership drive."

MEMBER V: "Mr. President, I move to amend the recommendation by inserting the words 'or reinstatements' after the words 'new members.' " (Applause by the assembly. Amendment is seconded.)

CHAIR: "It has been moved and seconded to amend the executive committee's recommendation by inserting the words 'or reinstatements' after the words 'new members.' Is there any discussion on Mr. V's amendment?" (After discussion, if any, the vote:) "Those in favor of the amendment will say aye." (Response.) "Those opposed will say no." (Response.) "The ayes have it, and the amendment is adopted. The question now before the assembly is on the executive committee's recommendation as amended. Is there any debate?" (After debate, if any, the vote:) "Those in favor of the recommendation as amended will say aye; those opposed will say no; the ayes have it, and the executive committee's recommendation, as amended, has been adopted. Is there any further new business?"

Main motion, amendment, reconsideration

MEMBER W: "Mr. President, I move that we have a bowling team." (Seconded.)

CHAIR: "It is moved and seconded to have a bowling team."

MEMBER A: "Mr. President, I move to amend the motion by adding at the end of the motion the words 'to bowl once each week for the next ten weeks.' " (Seconded.)

CHAIR: "It is moved and seconded to amend the motion by adding at the end thereof the words 'to bowl once each week during the next ten weeks.' Is there any discussion on the amendment?" (Then:) "Those in favor of the amendment will say aye; those opposed will say no. The ayes have it, and the amendment is carried. The question now is on the main motion as amended."

MEMBER B: "Mr. President, can that amendment be reconsidered?"

CHAIR: "Yes."

MEMBER B: "I so move!" (Seconded.)

CHAIR: "It is moved and seconded to reconsider the vote of the amendment just adopted. Is there debate on the reconsideration?" (After debate:) "Those in favor of the reconsideration of the amendment will say aye; those opposed will say no." The ayes have it, and reconsideration is adopted. The question now before the body is again on the *amendment* to add to the main motion the words 'to bowl once each week during the next *ten* weeks.' Is there any further debate?"

MEMBER C: "Mr. President, can I amend the amendment?"

CHAIR: "Yes; a secondary amendment is in order."

MEMBER C: "I move to amend the *primary* amendment, by striking out the word 'ten,' and inserting in its place the word 'twelve.' "

CHAIR: "It is moved and seconded to amend the primary amendment by striking out the word 'ten' and inserting in place thereof the word 'twelve.' Is there any debate on the *secondary* amendment?" (After debate, if any, the vote:) "Those in favor of the secondary amendment will say aye; those opposed will say no. The ayes have it, and the secondary amendment is carried. The question now is on the *primary* amendment as amended." (After debate:) "Those in favor of the primary amendment will say aye; those opposed will say no. The ayes have it, and the primary amendment is carried. The question now is on the main motion as amended, which is: That we have a bowling team, to bowl once each week during the next twelve weeks. Is there any discussion on the pending main motion?" (After discussion:) "Those in favor will say aye. Those opposed will say no. The ayes have it, and the motion as amended is adopted." (The Chair continues:) "Is there any further new business?"

Oath, previous question, recess

MEMBER D: "Mr. President, I move the adoption of the following resolution: *Resolved*, That our delegates to the national convention be instructed to vote as a unit for the candidacy of Mr. W for national secretary." (Seconded.)

CHAIR: "It is moved *and* seconded to adopt the resolution just read. Is there any discussion on the resolution?"

MEMBER D: "I hope my resolution . . ." (interrupted by the Chair).

CHAIR (to Mr. D): "Will the member suspend his debate, so that the Chair may administer the oath of office to our vice president-elect who just came in, and who did not take the oath of office at installation because he was ill?"

MEMBER D: "Mr. President, with all due respect to you and our uninstalled vice president, I should not be interrupted for the administration of any oath."

CHAIR: "The Chair will respectfully inform the member that the administration of the oath to officers-elect or to newly elected members presents a proper question of privilege, and hence it can interrupt a speaker and temporarily it suspends a pending business."

MEMBER D: (Sits.)

CHAIR: "The sergeant-at-arms will escort the vice president-elect before me [or, before the rostrum] for the administration of his oath of office." (This done, the Chair resumes business at the point of interruption, and reassigns the floor to member D who was interrupted; thus:)

CHAIR: "The Chair now recognizes member D."

MEMBER D (concluding his debate): "Therefore I hope, Mr. President, that my resolution will be adopted."

MEMBER E: "Mr. President, I move the previous question." (Seconded.)

CHAIR: "It has been moved and seconded to adopt the previous question; that is [he may elucidate], to shut off further discussion, and amendments, on the pending resolution. Under the rules, this motion requires a two-thirds vote for adoption."

MEMBER F: "Mr. President, I move we recess for ten minutes." (Seconded.)

CHAIR: "It has been moved and seconded to take a ten-minute recess. As the motion to recess is not debatable if it is proposed while another motion is pending, as in the present instance, the Chair will put the motion to recess to a vote. Those in favor of a recess will say aye; those opposed will say no. The ayes have it, and the assembly will be in recess for ten minutes."

After the recess, the Chair reconvenes the assembly; thus:

CHAIR: "The meeting will now come to order. Just before recessing [he properly informs the body], there was pending before the assembly the following business: a resolution to instruct the delegates to vote as a unit for the candidacy of Mr. W: and also pending was the previous question on the resolution. The first vote will be on the motion to order [or, adopt] the previous question. It requires a two-thirds vote. Those in favor of ordering the previous question will raise their right hand. Fifty-one; hands down. Those opposed will raise their right hand. Eleven; hands down. There being two-thirds in favor, the previous question is ordered, and there is to be no further discussion on the resolution."

Note: While the adoption of the previous question prohibits further discussion, it does not prohibit "points of clarification" or other strictly pertinent inquiries by the members so they may know what they are voting on.

CHAIR: "The Chair will now put the *resolution* to a vote. Those in favor will say aye; those opposed will say no. The ayes have it, and the resolution is adopted." (The Chair continues:) "Is there any further new business?"

Previous notice to amend the bylaws

MEMBER G: "Mr. President, a parliamentary inquiry."

CHAIR: "The member will state the parliamentary inquiry."

MEMBER G: "I would like to give previous notice of an amendment to our bylaws. Can I give such notice under the category of new business?"

CHAIR: "Previous notice of a proposed amendment to the bylaws can be given under *any* category of business, provided no member is speaking at the time, or with a speaker's consent. Since, at the moment, no one has the floor in debate, notice of your proposed amendment is in order."

MEMBER G (reading it): "I hereby give notice to amend Article Four, Section One, of the bylaws, by inserting appropriately therein the words 'and a second vice president' after the words 'a vice president,' so that the said section, if thus amended, will read: 'Section One. The officers of this Club shall be a president, a first *and a second* vice president, a secretary, and a treasurer.'" (Member G hands the written notice to the president, who says:)

CHAIR: "The Chair is in receipt of your notice to amend the bylaws. The secretary will take due notice thereof and will include it in the call for the next meeting as required by Article Nine."

Main motion, resolution

CHAIR: "Is there further new business?"

MEMBER H: "Mr. President, I move we donate fifty dollars to X charity."

CHAIR: "It is moved and seconded to . . ." (repeats the motion). "Is there any discussion on the motion?"

MEMBER I: "Mr. President, our United States senator will be in our city the day we have our next meeting. I therefore move the adoption of the following resolution: *Resolved*, That Senator Y be invited to address our next meeting."

CHAIR: "The resolution is not in order at the present time, because there is another main motion before the body, 'to donate fifty dollars to X charity.' After the main motion has been disposed of, you may then offer your resolution. Under the rules, only one main motion at a time may be pending."

MEMBER I: "But I didn't offer another main motion; I offered a resolution."

CHAIR: "Resolution is another word for main motion. They are synonymous terms for all practical purposes. As a matter of fact [he can add, purely from the instructional standpoint], both legally and legislatively, as well as parliamentarily, the word 'resolution' is the pure term for 'main motion.'"

The Chair proceeds to transact the pending main motion; thus:

CHAIR: "The question before the body is on the motion to donate fifty dollars to X charity." (After debate, the vote:) "Those in favor of the motion will say aye. Those opposed will say no. The ayes have it. Is there any further new business?"

MEMBER I: "Mr. Chairman, I now move the adoption of the following resolution: *Resolved*, that Senator Y be invited to address our next meeting." (Seconded, put to vote and adopted.)

Amending a previously adopted motion

MEMBER J: "Mr. President, at the last meeting, you may remember, we passed the following motion: 'to authorize the treasurer to buy a new television from ABC & Co.'"

CHAIR: "Yes; please proceed."

MEMBER J: "I would like to amend that adopted motion. Can I?"

CHAIR: "Certainly; please present your amendment."

MEMBER J: "First, I would like to ask if the TV has been purchased."

CHAIR (to treasurer): "Have you bought or ordered the TV?"

TREASURER: "No, I haven't yet; I haven't had time."

MEMBER J: "Mr. President, in that case I move to amend that previously adopted motion by adding at the end thereof the words 'at a cost not to exceed $150.' "   (Seconded.)

MEMBERS K, L, M, and O (rising and shouting excitedly): "Point of order!" "Point of order!"

CHAIR: "The Chair can recognize but one member at a time. The Chair will recognize first Mr. K. What is your point of order?"

MEMBER K: "You can't amend a main motion which is not actually pending before the body! That's my point of order!"

MEMBERS L, M and O (calling out from their seats): "That's my point of order, too!"

CHAIR (striking once firmly with the gavel, implying order): "The point of order is *not* well taken. It is perfectly in order to amend a main motion which was previously adopted, even though that motion is not actually before the body, provided that the motion is still alive and still executable, as in the case with the television. Hence, you can amend the motion by adding words to it, or by inserting words, or striking out words from it (even all its words), or by striking out and inserting. In other words, a member has the right to amend the contents of a previously adopted main motion in any way he desires provided that the motion is still alive, and the proposed amendment to it is germane, as in this instance."

MEMBER K: "Mr. President, can you give us a parallel example?"

CHAIR: "Yes. A bylaw is an excellent parallel. For example: Article Three, Section Three, of our bylaws states that the annual dues shall be ten dollars, payable in January.

"The Chair now asks Mr. K: When this provision was first adopted as a bylaw, was it not proposed originally as a main motion; namely: that the annual dues be ten dollars, payable in January?"

MEMBER K: "Yes, of course."

CHAIR: "Then, is not that bylaw provision actually a 'previously adopted' main motion, except that it is now called a bylaw?"

MEMBER K: "Yes, certainly."

CHAIR: "Can that standing bylaw be amended?"

MEMBER K: "Yes; we often amend standing bylaws."

CHAIR: "When you amend it, is that bylaw actually pending before the body at the time?"

MEMBER K: "No."

CHAIR: "Even though that bylaw is not actually before the body, is it still *alive*, and still *effective?*"

MEMBER K: "It certainly is. It still obliges me to pay annual dues."

CHAIR: "Can you amend the bylaw, then, so as to make the annual dues five dollars or fifteen dollars, instead of ten dollars, or amend it by changing the month?"

MEMBER K: "Yes to both questions."

CHAIR: "And can you amend the bylaw by striking it out altogether, so as *not* to have to pay annual dues?"

MEMBER K: "Yes, if the body will so vote."

CHAIR: "Coming, now, to the standing main motion we previously adopted at the last meeting, authorizing the treasurer to buy a brand-new TV from ABC and Co., which has *not* yet been purchased, is not that motion still *alive?*"

MEMBER K: "Yes; it is a previously adopted main motion which is still alive, just like a live bylaw."

CHAIR: "Then, can that motion be amended, even though it is not actually before the body, as by specifying the *kind* of television, or by striking out the words 'from ABC and Co.' and inserting in place thereof the words 'from XYZ and Co.,' or by rescinding the whole motion altogether so as not to buy television at this time?"

MEMBER K: "Yes, it is clear to me now. The body can amend a previously adopted question which is still alive, just as it can amend a live bylaw."

CHAIR: "Then is Mr. J's amendment, adding the words 'at a cost not to exceed $150' to the previously adopted main motion to buy a TV, in order?"

MEMBER K: "Yes, it is in order."

CHAIR: "The Chair thanks the assembly for its patience in our explanation of the operation of the process of amending a previously adopted motion. The question now before the body is on Mr. J's amendment, to add to that motion the words 'at a cost not to exceed $150.' Is there any debate on this amendment?"

MEMBER L: "What vote is required to adopt this amendment?"

CHAIR: "The rule is as follows: It requires a $\frac{2}{3}$ vote to amend a main motion which was passed, as in this case, at a *previous* session of the body when previous notice of intention to amend it was not given; but if previous notice has been given, or if the previously adopted motion was passed at the *same* session, only a majority vote is required to amend it." (The Chair continues:)

"There being no further debate on this amendment, the Chair will put it to a vote. Those in favor of the amendment, adding the words 'at a cost not to exceed $150,' will raise their right hand. Forty-eight; hands down. Those opposed will raise their right hand. Twelve; hands down. There being two-thirds in favor, the affirmative has it and the amendment to the previously adopted main motion is adopted." (The Chair continues:)

CHAIR: "Is there any further new business?"

MEMBER M: "A point of order, Mr. President. We only acted on the amendment; we have not yet voted on the previously adopted main motion as we just *amended* it."

CHAIR: "The point of order is not well taken. A previously adopted motion which is still alive and still executable is not put to a vote for readoption when an amendment has been made to it — just as in the case of a previously adopted bylaw, which is not put to a vote for readoption when an amendment has been made to it. It is only when a motion is actually pending before the body that it is put to vote *as amended* after an amendment has been made to it."

Note: An amendment to something previously adopted is not the subsidiary motion to amend (p. 68). Instead, it is a *quasi-main* motion, also called *incidental main* motion.

CHAIR (continues): "The Chair requests the first vice president to preside. Mr. X, will you take the chair?"

VICE PRESIDENT (taking the chair): "Any further new business?"

MEMBER N: "Mr. President, I move we buy a new piano."

Note: When presiding, a vice president is addressed by the same title as the organization's regular presiding officer, whatever be his title.

VICE PRESIDENT: "It is moved and seconded to buy a new piano. Is there any discussion?" (After which the vote:) "Those in favor will say aye; those opposed will say no. The ayes have it. Is there any further new business to come before the meeting?"

MEMBER O: "Mr. President, I move that this organization go on record in favor of having a twelve-inning all-star baseball game, instead of the traditional nine-inning game, and that there be no extra innings beyond the twelve innings, in case of a tie game."

VICE PRESIDENT: "Will the member repeat his motion?" (The motion is repeated, or the secretary reads it, and the Chair continues:) "Is there any discussion on this motion?" (After much discussion, the vote:) "Those in favor of the motion will say aye; those opposed will say no. The noes have it, and the motion is lost. Is there any further new business?" (Silence follows, then he advises:) "If there is no further new business," (he pauses) "a motion to adjourn is in order."

MEMBER W: "Mr. *President*, I move we adjourn." (Seconded.)

VICE PRESIDENT: "It is moved and seconded to adjourn." (He pauses two or three seconds, just in case, then he continues:) "Those in favor will say aye; those opposed will say no. The ayes have it, and the meeting is adjourned."

Chapter 17
NOMINATIONS AND ELECTIONS
I. NOMINATIONS

Basic rules. Nominations do not require a second, except by custom or by special rule of the assembly.

Nominations are voted on in the order in which they were made unless it is otherwise decided before nominations commence or unless the bylaws differently provide. Usually, when the vote is taken by printed ballot, the names of the nominees under each office are arranged alphabetically, regardless of the order in which they were nominated; but by a majority vote, the position each name is to occupy on the ballot can be decided in advance by drawing lots or by coin, if it is so voted. When the names of nominees are written on the blackboard they are listed in the order nominated.

Who can be nominated. Any member may be nominated and elected to office whether he is present or not, unless the body's rules specify to the contrary.

A member has the right to nominate himself for office.

Unless there is a *bylaw* provision specifying that a member who is in arrears in dues shall not be nominated for office or be elected to office, and unless he has been suspended from membership, he is still in possession of all his rights in the assembly. Hence he may still be nominated and be elected to office. A member may hold more than one office in an organization unless this is prohibited by bylaw or rule. When thus barred, a nominee need not resign from his office until after the election results have been announced, when he can then choose which office he will hold.

Origin of the word "candidate." The term "candidate" is from the Latin *candidus,* meaning white. In ancient Rome, candidates for public office clothed themselves in a white tunic as a symbolic gesture of clean and honest government.

Distinction between candidate and nominee. One who seeks an office is a candidate. When the candidate's name is put in nomination as required by rule or law, he is then a nominee.

Who can nominate. Only one who has the right to make motions can make a nomination.

Member can nominate only one candidate. When a board or committee of several members is to be elected, no member may nominate more than one candidate. Hence he cannot say, for example, "I nominate A, B, and C as three of the five committee members." He can only nominate one. But if, after nominating the one, no other member cares to make a further nomination, he can nominate a second candidate, etc.

Nominees do not leave room. Nominees are never required to leave the meeting room during nominations, elections, or when election votes are being counted.

Propriety in nomination. When nominating to office in the organization, nominators should confine their nominating speech strictly to the virtues and capabilities of their own nominees. They should avoid ridicule or criticism of competing nominees. It is unfair, unfraternal and unparliamentary to thus engage in personalities, as this can lead to excitement of personal feeling and resentment among the members.

Declining nomination. If a member declines nomination or withdraws as nominee, his name is not included in the slate.

If acceptance of nominations is required under the organizations rules or laws, this must be observed. If acceptance of a nomination is not required by express rule or a bylaw, a candidate cannot be compelled to state whether he accepts. If he does not expressly decline, he impliedly accepts; this is so even if he says, "I do not choose to say I accept or not," or "I am not saying one way or the other." If no rule or law requires him to accept, he can remain noncommittal. It is then up to the body to vote for him or not.

A nomination is *declined* (properly speaking), not resigned. But after a person is elected to membership or office he *resigns* his membership or office, not declines.

When nominations close. If nominations are ordered closed in any meeting preceding the electing meeting, such closure is not carried over to the electing meeting. Hence further nominations are always in order up to the moment of proceeding to the election. Hence if a bylaw reads: "The election shall be held in December," and nothing is said about when nominations may be made, nominations can be made (a) just before the election is to take place, or (b) at any meeting before December if the body so chooses, provided due notice thereof is in the call for the meeting.

If a rule or bylaw asserts that "Nominations shall be made at [a certain] meeting *only*," nominations made in any other meeting are out of order.

Note: The word "only" merely prevents *nominations* from being made in any other meeting; it does not prevent members from *voting*, just the same, for a member not previously nominated unless a bylaw says that "Those not previously nominated shall not be voted on."

Nominating committee. A nominating committee can be either a standing committee (to observe and judge the capabilities and fitness of members for future office), or a temporary committee specially appointed or elected in advance of an election. (Your bylaws should embody full nominating processes to cover your own needs.) The terms "nominating committee" and "committee on nominations" are synonymous, but the latter is the more formal and precise name.

Generally speaking, nominating committees should make sure beforehand that their nominees will accept nomination and the office.

Nominations made by the committee cannot be amended by the body, as by striking out any nominee's name; instead, additional nominations to those of the committee can be proposed.

The president should never serve on a nominating committee; and a nominee should not serve as teller. But if either one does so (innocently, or helpfully as is sometimes done, or when no one at all objects at the time), this in itself is not illegal.

Nominating committees automatically expire with their report; but they are revived when need be.

Nominating committee report and minority report. Where the nominating committee reports a slate of nominees and their names are written on the blackboard, the names of a minority slate proposed by dissenting members of the committee are also entitled to be written on the blackboard; and the body then elects from either slate, as well as from other names, if any, nominated from the floor.

When committee nominates two members or slates. A nominating committee may nominate two members for the same office (as when two are equally gifted and able). And if a nominating committee is empowered or instructed to present two slates (as is at times the case), it can nominate the same person for the same office on both slates.

If a nominating committee is empowered by a bylaw or is instructed by the body to present two slates, and if the nominating committee presents only one ticket or slate, then further nominations are in order from the floor in the meeting itself. If the committee fails to submit any slate, the assembly itself may nominate if it is too late to designate another committee.

Committee members eligible. Members of a nominating committee are eligible for office just like any other member; therefore, they can nominate one or more of their number. If any are nominated who are unfit, simply do not vote for them.

Members can suggest nominations. Members have the right to communicate to the nominating committee or to appear before it to recommend their choice of candidates for any office, but the committee is not bound to follow these suggestions.

Nominating by ballot. The process of nominations by ballot is merely a method by which members may nominate in secrecy instead of in the open. Such a process is merely a "feeler" for guidance, and members can still vote for whomever they please afterward.

Additional nominations from the floor. Additional nominations are always in order after the nominating committee makes its report, until nominations are closed or except where bylaws prohibit it. Additional nominations are made from the floor after the committee has presented its ticket, thus:

CHAIR: "For president the committee has nominated Mr. A. Are there further nominations for the office of president?" (Additional nominations can then be proposed. Nominations can never be closed right away. They should remain open until all who wish to nominate have had a chance to do so, after which the Chair continues:)

CHAIR: "The next office is that of vice president. The committee has nominated Mr. B. Are there further nominations?" (And so on to the end of the slate.)

The Chair's role. As each additional nomination to that of the committee is proposed, the Chair states it thus: "Mr. X has been nominated," (and if no one rises to nominate further he continues:) "Are there further nominations?"

Can move to accept the slate. It is in order to move to accept the nominating committee's slate in its entirety or such parts of it as have no competing nominees, even if a secret ballot is required, provided no one objects.

Printed ballots. Nominating committees attend to having the names printed on ballots. If there is no nominating committee, the secretary does it, unless otherwise ordered.

The committee's nominees for each office are listed first under each office, alphabetically, followed by any others who have been nominated from the floor.

A member not nominated may be elected. Unless otherwise expressly prescribed, unnominated members may be elected to office if they receive the necessary vote at the election.

But if the bylaws or rules state that "only those previously nominated shall be voted on [or, shall be elected,]" or similar language, then the election of unnominated members is invalid.

II. ELECTIONS

Your bylaws should contain reasonably full election rules and election processes drawn from past experience at your elections.

How to Interpret the Vote Cast

Read across the page. Read (a) with (a), (b) with (b), (c) with (c), (d) with (d) from left to right under column 1 and 2.

COLUMN 1	COLUMN 2
(a) If the bylaws read that a question shall be decided by: a majority vote; or a majority of those voting; or a majority of the vote cast; or a majority of the members present and voting; or a majority of the body	(a) The language is interpreted to mean: a majority of the votes actually cast (ignoring blanks), regardless of how many votes are cast, even if 100 are present and only 10 members vote, or 5, or only 1, a quorum being present.
(b) If the bylaws read that a question shall be decided by: a majority of those present; or a majority of those present and qualified, or those present and entitled, or those who are eligible to vote	(b) The language is interpreted to mean: a majority of those present, who must be counted; a majority in such cases consists of more than half of the members present who have a vote.
(c) If the bylaws read that a question shall be decided by: a majority of the whole body (or of the membership), or a majority of the organization	(c) The language is interpreted to mean: a majority of the whole number of the organization's members, both present and absent.
(d) If the bylaws read that a question shall be decided by: a plurality vote (as in national and state elections and, sometimes, in conventions)	(d) The language is interpreted to mean: the most votes; that is, whoever receives the most votes, without regard to majority.

The same rule of interpretation governs and is applied to questions requiring a $\frac{2}{3}$ vote (of those "present" or those "voting").

In every such case, just simply interpret what the words plainly say and clearly mean.

Some basic rules. "Number of votes cast" means the total number of votes cast for each individual office without regard to the number cast for any other office.

In all cases, election to each separate office is decided by the number of votes cast for each office *separately*. It is both illegal and irrational to attempt to decide election to office by the total number of votes cast for all the offices and then divide the result by the number of offices involved in order to determine whether a nominee received a majority of the votes cast — thus compelling the nominees to share each other's votes:

Tellers can vote in elections. Candidates or nominees can vote for themselves.

If there is no conclusive election on the first ballot voting, members who arrive late may vote on the second ballot.

The presence of nonmembers who do not vote does not invalidate the results of an election.

If a member has not paid his dues, he may still vote unless he has been suspended from membership, or unless a bylaw says he may not.

If the Chair is a candidate for reelection, he is not obliged to surrender the Chair unless he prefers to, or the bylaws say he must.

One vote when holding two positions. A member holding two positions in the assembly, such as secretary and treasurer, each of which has a vote, nevertheless casts only one vote unless the bylaws or the organization's customs say otherwise.

A delegate to a convention who at the convention is elected a convention officer casts only one vote unless convention rules or established custom say otherwise.

Amend objectionable or inadequate bylaws. The language of the bylaws must be strictly construed and adhered to. If the existing wording or language of the bylaw providing for determining questions such as election of officers is in any way undesirable, the proper remedy is to amend the bylaws and change the language to suit. Until such a change is legally made, the existing provisions — good, bad, or indifferent — strictly govern.

But by majority vote, in an emergency, the body can always decide for itself the meaning of ambiguous or contested words, phrases or provisions.

To emphasize: Never go to an election unless (1) you know by what vote officers are elected, and (2) whether they can be elected by a majority of those *voting* or of those *present* (and thus be enabled to apply the rule of legal election). Also (3) look up by what vote amendments to your bylaws are adoptable, whether by ⅔ of those *voting* or of those *present*. Ask to see the bylaws; you have that right. The life of an organization depends on the legal election of its officers, and the legal enactment of its bylaws.

The force of custom. Custom has the force of law in voting procedure as in other areas, until it is ordered stopped by action of the body. To be adopted, motion to discontinue an established custom requires a ⅔ vote without notice or a majority vote with notice. Following are two examples in which the force of custom applies:

1. An organization has no bylaw authorizing voting by mail on elections, but it has been the usual custom for years to accept absentee ballots from members unable to attend the election meeting. At a certain election a motion is made to "ignore and throw out all absentee ballots received in this election." Such a motion is out of order because the absent members followed the customary practice in good faith and in the expectation that their absentee ballots would be given full credit.

2. The bylaws of an organization read, "Notice of meetings shall be mailed by the secretary to all members," but instead of mailing such notices, the secretary has for years been placing the notice in the members' pigeonholes at the clubhouse. At a certain contested election, member C is elected president over the opposition's candidate, and the opposition contends that "The election of C as president is void because tonight's meeting notices were not mailed to the members as required by the bylaws." However, the election of C is valid, because the bylaw has been continuously ignored for years and may not be suddenly and unexpectedly

invoked to invalidate an election and thus disfranchise members at this election.

Note: Custom has the status of a standing rule, and a standing rule may be discontinued by a ⅔ vote without previous notice, or by majority vote with notice.

Voting continues until decisive. If the vote on elections requiring a majority of a ⅔ vote is not conclusive, voting must continue until a final decision is reached, even if this may require hours, days, or weeks.

Useful bylaw clause. To expedite election processes, adopt a clause: "If no one receives a majority of the votes cast, the name receiving the lowest number of votes on each ballot shall be excluded in further balloting."

Adjournment before ballots counted. If a meeting having election of officers adjourns before the ballots are counted and a tie vote results or the result is otherwise indecisive, the election is resumed under unfinished business at the next meeting unless ordered taken up sooner.

When elections take effect. If a candidate is present when elected and does not decline, his election takes effect immediately; if he is absent and on being notified of this election he does not decline, his election also takes effect immediately. When the election has become effective, it is too late to reconsider the vote. If the candidate declines acceptance, further nominations for that office are open and another election is held as prescribed in the bylaws.

In all cases, elected officers assume office upon their election unless it is otherwise voted or is differently prescribed in the bylaws or by custom (as when the bylaws state "they shall assume office after adjournment," or "in April," etc.)

When two persons serve one term. If, due to resignation or death, etc., more than one person served in a term of office, the person serving more than half the term is credited with the whole for all purposes.

An *example* of how this might be applied: Suppose the bylaws read, "Elections shall be held every two years," and "No one shall be eligible for reelection to succeed himself in the office he holds." The president of this organization resigns after 11 months and a successor is chosen who fills the office for the remainder of the term. The president who resigned would then be eligible for election in the next term, because he served less than half of the term of two years.

Special election. If the bylaws contain no provision for holding a special election to fill a vacancy, such election may be held at any regular meeting with due prior notice thereof. A special election is also known as a by-election.

Use of the Ballot

When vote by ballot is required. If bylaws require that the vote on a question shall be taken by ballot or secret ballot, if the vote is taken in any other manner the question is not considered as having been legally decided, even if the vote thereon is unanimous, because the bylaws cannot be ignored, suspended, or violated, even by a unanimous vote. Hence if there is objection, the vote is deemed invalid, and the vote on the proceeding or question should be taken all over again in the manner prescribed by the bylaws. Objection to such illegality, however, must be raised at the time the vote is taken.

However, since the above contingency usually occurs at election of officers where there is but one candidate for an office, in the interest of orderly procedure and legality of action, an appropriate provision should be inserted in the bylaws (under election of officers), validating such election; thus:

(1) "In the event there is but a single nominee for an office, the secretary shall cast one ballot for such nominee." Or, (2) "A secret ballot shall not be required when there is but one nominee for an office." Or, (3) "A secret ballot may be waived [or, omitted] if no one objects," or similar words.

Procedure in casting one ballot. When the casting of a single ballot by the secretary is prescribed, the secretary should actually mark the ballot in favor of the nominee or write out the name, as the case may be, and, rising in his place, say: "I hereby cast one ballot for Member X for treasurer," and hands the ballot or paper to the Chair who makes the formal announcement.

If the bylaws prescribe election by ballot and the secretary casts a ballot for a sole nominee for an office when not so authorized by the by-laws, the vote is not necessarily invalid; it depends on the bylaws.

If the bylaws provide that the election shall be "by a majority of the votes *cast*." and the secretary's vote is the *only* vote cast (all other members voluntarily abstaining from voting, say), since *one* is a majority of one vote cast, the election is valid.

But if the bylaws specify a "majority of the members *present*," and 50 members are present, since a majority of 50 is 26, the fact that the secretary's vote was the only vote cast does not constitute valid election of the candidate, because one vote out of 50 members present is not a majority of those present, regardless of the fact that the secretary was unanimously ordered to cast one ballot for the candidate.

Hence, alert leaders can challenge it. But if no one does so, because *all* present favor the nominee, then the vote may be deemed valid.

Committee of tellers. When the vote on elections is to be by ballot, the Chair appoints a committee of tellers comprising a representative of each major or principal candidate, and such additional members as may be deemed necessary to expedite and safeguard the election and the ballots. Nominees should not be appointed tellers. The Chair says:

CHAIR: "The Chair appoints the following committee as tellers: A, B, C, D, and E. They will distribute, collect and count the ballots, and report thereon to the Chair."

The first named member acts as chairman of the committee.

When it appears that all members have voted and before the polls are ordered closed, the Chair asks:

CHAIR: "Have all members voted who wish to do so?" (If there is then no further vote casting, and no formal motion is made to close the polls, the Chair declares:) "The polls are now closed; the tellers will collect the ballots, count them, and report back to the meeting.'

The tellers thereupon withdraw from the meeting room to some convenient place and there count the ballots.

When the committee is ready to report to the body, the committee chairman says:

COMMITTEE CHAIRMAN (addressing the Chair): "Mr. President, the result of the vote is as follows: Number of votes cast, 91; necessary for election, 46; Mr. X received 47; Mr. Y received 31; Mr. Z received 13."

The report, signed by all the tellers agreeing to it, is then handed to the Chair who formally announces the result, repeating the figures.

Note: When crediting votes to candidates, as the votes are called the tellers mark them in vertical lines, thus: Candidate A: | | | | , and every fifth vote crosses each set of four votes; thus: ⊥⊦⊢⊤ .

The Results: Majority, Plurality

A majority vote elects. It is an established rule of parliamentary law that elections shall be decided by a majority vote because the majority rules, and until a majority has been attained, the question has not been legally decided. This is true even if the bylaws are silent, because a majority is always understood. A majority vote means more than half of the votes cast at a legal meeting with quorum.

Plurality vote. To avoid lack of final or decisive votes, the bylaws can be amended to specify or provide for a plurality vote instead of a majority, if desired, thus legalizing the election of one who receives less than a majority of the votes but more votes than any other candidate.

Difference between majority and plurality. "Majority" means a number greater than half. Thus, six is a majority of ten; 11 is a majority of 20; and 36 is a majority of 70. A person has a plurality vote if he has more votes than any other person. Thus, if A receives 17 votes, B 11, C 6, and D 5, A with 17 votes has a plurality vote.

To decide deadlocks. To deal with possible tie votes or deadlocks in such cases, the bylaws should also specify that in the event of a tie vote for a final choice, the candidates (or their representatives or nominator shall decide the result by lot, or by coin.

If the bylaws are silent, to minimize deadlocks and tie votes a motion can be adopted in advance of a vote, or proceeding, prescribing a determining method, thus:

(1) "Mr Chairman, I move that in the event no candidate receives a majority vote on the first ballot, all names except those having the three highest votes (or four, or five, etc.) shall be eliminated from further ballots." Or,

(2) "Madam President, I move that in the event a tie vote results in the final ballot, the candidates or their nominator or designated representative shall determine the result by lot or coin," or "The Chair may cast a *second* ballot to decide it."

Note: Bylaws of some organizations now give the president an extra vote to be cast only in case of a tie, even though he voted previously.

Majority vote

Majority vote. If the bylaws state that officers or directors shall be elected by majority vote, it means more than half of the votes actually cast (not counting either the "blanks" or the members not voting), a quorum being present.

Hence, under a bylaw requiring a majority, if (say) 100 members are present at the election, and A receives 40 votes, B 30 votes, C 20 votes and there are three "blanks," since the three blanks are not counted and the seven members who did not vote also are not counted, a majority of the 90 true votes cast is 46 votes. Since neither A, B nor C received a majority vote as required by the bylaw, no one is elected. The assembly failed to make a choice; therefore, the assembly proceeds to vote again (and again, when need be) until one of the nominees receives more than half of the votes cast.

Note: At times, assemblies vote dozens of times before a choice is made; and in some cases they vote more than one hundred times. In a city council election in Massachusetts 114 votes were taken before a choice was finally made for president of the council. In a national political convention the delegates voted 103 times before a choice was made of the nomination of President of the United States.

Majority of the members present. If the organization's laws or bylaws provide that officers or directors shall be elected by majority vote of the members *present,*" it means more than half of all members physically present at the meeting, whether they vote or not. They must be counted.

Hence, under a bylaw requiring a majority of the members present, if 100 members are present a majority in such a case means a more than half of the members present, in this case 51. In order to be elected under such bylaw a member must receive at least 51 votes.

Irregularities and Illegalities

Votes not provided for on ballot. A ballot cast for someone not previously nominated is valid unless the bylaws specify that votes cast for unnominated members are void.

A *Write-in* candidate who receives a majority vote may be elected over the candidate whose name is printed on the ballot even if the printed name is not crossed out. The intent of the voter is clear and unmistakable in such a case.

Sticker labels are legal votes unless prohibited by rule or bylaw.

"Bullet" votes are legal unless bylaws prohibit them. A bullet vote is a vote cast for only one nominee when more than one nominee is supposed to be voted for. An example would be: Three directors are to be elected, and a faction or member decides to vote for a favorite one of them only.

If a ballot has been marked for *more than the prescribed number* of candidates, the ballot is *void.* For example, if five candidates are to be voted for out of a larger group, a ballot on which seven are marked is void, because it is impossible to know which two to eliminate.

Crediting votes. A vote should be credited to the person for whom it is evidently intended. For instance: if candidate Thompson's name is written as "Thomson," or "Tomson," the vote is evidently intended for him and is credited to Thompson. When in doubt, the committee returns to the meeting room, informs the Chair of the fact and obtains further instructions.

Unclear marking of ballots. On Australian ballots where the symbol X signifies the voter's choice, if the cross happens to come about midway between two names, the vote is credited to the candidate in whose square the two diagonal lines of the X actually *cross.* If the X is so crossed that it is impossible to credit the vote to either candidate, the vote is void.

Australian ballots are usually marked by a cross (X). But if they are marked uniformly by some other method, as by a check mark (√), or by "yes," or "O," or "OK," etc., the votes so marked are valid provided they are so marked throughout the ballot. If they are mixed, only those bearing the commonly accepted X mark (or other mark or designation specially authorized) are valid votes, and the others are void.

Blank ballots. Blank ballots (ballots with no name written on them, or formal Australian ballots with no name marked) are not counted as part of the total number of votes cast; they are not ballots, but blanks; they are reported, however, purely as information.

If two ballots are folded together, both of them are rejected as fraudulent votes and are not credited to the candidate for whom they were cast; such fraud vitiates or nullifies the votes so cast, as only one ballot should have been cast, but they are reported and included in the total number of votes cast as *one* vote.

However, if one ballot is folded with a *blank* ballot, the ballot is good and the vote counts; there is no fraud.

Extra illegal ballots. In an election in which more votes are cast than the number of members voting, the results are not invalid unless the number extra is enough to affect the results. To illustrate: If 57 members are present at an election and all vote, but 59 ballots are cast, of which A received 31 and B received 28, the results are nevertheless valid because even without two extra votes which may have been cast for him, A would still win.

Partial election may be void. If the vote for officers is correct in all respects except that in the case of the group of directors, for example, more directors were elected than the number of positions to be filled, the entire election is not void. Only the vote on directors is void and must be cast again; the vote on the officers stands.

Vote by unanimous acclamation. If the bylaws specify that election shall be by roll call or secret ballot, and a vote on one or more unopposed candidates is taken by unanimous acclamation and thunderous applause instead, such an election is legal if no one objects.

Challenging election results. If fraud or illegalities are claimed on elections, only those offices are voted on again as are challenged, not the entire slate. No claim or challenge is in order unless (a) it is specific and (b) is raised before adjournment.

To avoid illegal elections. To make certain that an election which requires a majority vote (or a majority of those present and voting, which is the same thing) is legal, it should be remembered that all the votes cast must be counted; that is: all which have a name on them, regardless of whose name it is, member or nonmember, must be reported in the *total* number of votes cast, but not those without a name on them (called blanks). Blanks are ignored.

Example of inconclusive election. If election results were as follows: S receiving 32 votes, P receiving 31 votes, M receiving one vote, R (a suspended member) receiving one vote (which has to be included in the total number of votes cast), and three blanks being cast; then, in such case, no nominee had received a majority of the votes cast (in this instance a majority of 65 votes being 33), and no one is legally elected.

The election is inconclusive, and another ballot must then be taken and voting must continue until one of the nominees receives a majority of the votes cast (blanks are not votes; hence they do not count as votes, they are ignored).

Inconclusive election should be challenged. Many such or similar inconclusive elections are at times accepted as final and conclusive, when in fact they are not; but the "losing" nominee and his supporters allow the election to be forfeited to the opposing candidate because of their unfamiliarity with the basic parliamentary right to question an inconclusive or invalid election and thus continue the balloting until a nominee has been duly elected by majority vote.

How inconclusive elections are reported. If the result of an election is inconclusive because no one received the required majority vote, the result is reported to the body as follows:

TELLER: "Mr. Chairman, the result of the vote cast for president is as follows: Number of votes cast (not counting blanks), 65; necessary for election, 33; Mr. S received 32; Mr. P received 31; Mr. M received one; Mr. R. [suspended member] received one.

"There were [he can add] three *blanks* which, under the rules, are not counted or included in the total votes cast." (Teller hands result, if in writing, to the Chair who repeats the vote cast and announces the result formally; thus:)

CHAIR: "Number of votes cast, 65; necessary for election, 33; Mr. S received 32 votes; Mr. P, 31; and Mr. M, one; there was one void vote cast for R, who has been suspended; and there were three blanks which, under the rules, are not counted as part of the total vote. The legal total vote cast is 65. Since no one of the candidates received the required majority of the votes cast (which is 33), the election is not conclusive; therefore, the assembly will proceed to vote for president again."

When it becomes too late to nullify an illegal election. Until the president-elect or other officer of an illegal election actually takes possession of the office — that is, prior to the time when he is supposed to assume the duties of his office as provided in the bylaws, or before he actually enters into his duties if the bylaws do not specify time — an illegal election may be vacated or voided. It is too late to nullify it after adjournment or after assumption of the office, or when too late to convene a legal meeting to correct it. And if such illegalities occur in conventions or annual meetings in which the opposition slept on its rights, good sense allows them to stand as legal acts after the body has adjourned, on the ground that "procedural misfeasance" or parliamentary wrongfulness cannot be allowed to call another convention.

Recount. Your bylaws should contain full election laws and procedure to cover cases that have arisen in the past and are likely to reoccur; or make them standing rules or convention rules instead. If your bylaws do not prescribe a recount procedure on any issue, the major candidates in issue can agree on one.

Destroying the ballots. To avoid tampering or meddling with the ballots, as soon as the result has been announced and accepted as final the ballots should be immediately ordered destroyed, or, in any event, before adjournment. A recount of the vote, if necessary, can be ordered before their destruction. Usually, nothing can be gained from having the ballots impounded (ordered held over) until another meeting, unless a motion or request is made to that effect, or fraud or irregularities are claimed.

Chapter 18
OFFICERS AND THEIR DUTIES
I. DUTIES AND LIMITATIONS OF EACH OFFICE

It is the duty of all officers to obey the bylaws and rules and to obey and execute all lawful orders of the body, else they betray their trust. Officers, like the members, can participate in all proceedings and can debate and vote on all questions except that they cannot participate in debate with the members while presiding in the main body.

President

Also referred to in some organizations as chairman, the Chair, speaker, moderator, etc.

Duties. 1. To know parliamentary law and procedure and the organization's rules and bylaws.

2. To call the meeting to order; to preside and to maintain order throughout the proceedings.

3. To direct the business of the assembly and to control the conduct of the members.

4. To announce and take up each piece of business in proper turn unless otherwise voted, and to entertain every admissible motion.

5. To assign the floor to those properly entitled to it.

6. To ignore no one who seeks the floor, and, when several rise to claim the floor at the same time, to patiently counsel them that but one member at a time can be recognized and to explain that in due course the floor will be assigned to each in turn (unless debate is voted closed).

7. To entertain and repeat all motions properly coming before the assembly; to permit no one to debate them before they are seconded and stated; to make sure the rules of debate are followed; to put motions to vote properly and to announce the result distinctly.

8. To enforce the rules of decorum and discipline.

9. To decide points of order and to answer all questions of parliamentary inquiry. He is expected to know parliamentary procedure.

10. To entertain all legitimate appeals.

11. To adjourn or recess a meeting in the event of uncontrollable disorder or other exigency menacing the safety, health, integrity or property (S-H-I-P) of the members or the organization.

12. To stand (1) when he first convenes and when he adjourns a meeting; (2) when he addresses the body; (3) when he puts a motion to vote; (4) when he discusses an appeal from his decision; (5) when he speaks on a point of order or answers a question of parliamentary inquiry. At other times he may sit or not, as good judgment may suggest.

13. To refrain from discussing (in the main body, but not in board or in committee) a motion while presiding, unless he first surrenders the chair; but he need not surrender the chair if no one objects to his speaking.

14. To be absolutely fair and impartial, and calm but firm.

15. To refer to himself as "the Chair," or "the president," etc., in preference to "I." Thus: "The Chair appoints," not "I appoint"; "The Chair now recognizes," not "I recognize."

16. To permit the vice president to put motions to vote if he himself has a direct personal or pecuniary interest.

17. To state motions in the language in which the members propose them, unless he is sure he can improve on the wording (but he must not change their sense or meaning); to require lengthy or complicated motions to be submitted in writing before he will entertain them.

18. To vote with the members when the vote is taken by ballot, and to vote last on a roll call; but he cannot cast two votes (to the members' one) unless the bylaws so authorize (as some bylaws now do to prevent hopeless deadlocks) or by unanimous consent of the body.

19. To protect the assembly and the speakers from annoyance and frivolous, obstructive and dilatory tactics.

20. To perform such other duties as are prescribed in the bylaws. (Look up your bylaws.)

21. To encourage or assign the floor to new or timid members who seldom speak, if they show signs of a desire to participate in the proceedings, in preference to veteran and experienced members.

22. To authenticate by his signature the minutes of each meeting, when necessary, and other acts, orders and proceedings.

23. To enlighten and guide the assembly impartially, and to avoid taking sides while presiding.

24. (a) To recognize members entitled to the floor; (b) to state (repeat) and put to vote all motions duly moved; (c) to announce the result of the vote in all cases; (d) to entertain legitimate appeals from his decision; (e) to declare or announce what the assembly's will (decision) is on questions determined by it; and (f) to obey the assembly's orders and commands.

Note: Repeated failure to exercise the duties of his office, especially the basic duties contained in the preceding paragraph, can subject a president to censure by majority vote, or removal from office by a $\frac{2}{3}$ vote.

Privileges. 1. To give reasons for his decision (that is, to debate) an appeal from his rulings without leaving the chair.

2. To vote on any motion members can vote on, or to vote for himself for office if he wishes to do so.

3. To debate motions in the main body just like any other member, if he so desires, provided he surrenders the chair, which he does not resume while the question on which he spoke is still before the body.

4. To exercise informally such prudent leadership and initiative (without strict compliance with the rules) as in the exercise of sound judgment no one would be likely to object to — as when suggesting cessation of further debate, or allowing only one or two more speakers on each side of the question, or taking some other necessary routine or informal action as would expedite accomplishment of business — but to instantly desist if anyone objects, or put it to a vote for approval.

5. To preside during nominations and elections even if he is a candidate, unless he cares to leave the chair.

6. He may call upon a vice president to preside at any time.

Vice President

The vice president automatically becomes president in the case of the removal of the president from office, or of his death, resignation, or inability to discharge the powers and duties of said office, unless the bylaws provide to the contrary.

When the vice president becomes thus vested with the office of president by virtue of the bylaws, the assembly cannot proceed to elect someone else as president. He serves for the remainder of the term. A vice president is a "standby" president. He should therefore know all the duties of the president's office, and especially he should know parliamentary procedure.

Recording Officer

Also referred to in some organizations as secretary, clerk, recorder, scribe, etc.

Duties. 1. To call a meeting to order in the absence of a duly authorized presiding officer and to preside pending the election of one.

2. To maintain a complete and up-to-date roll of the membership and to call the roll thereof when ordered to do so.

3. To read the minutes of meetings and other papers or documents.

4. To have custody of all documents and papers of the assembly.

5. To keep temporary notes or records of the progress of a proceeding during the course of the meeting.

6. To maintain and incorporate in permanent form a true record of the proceedings.

7. To record the proceedings (what is done) and not the debate (what is said), and also to record a proposer's name.

8. To provide the Chair with the order of business and a list of all committees.

9. To prepare and turn over to committee chairmen all papers and copies of motions voted referred to them, together with the names of their respective committees.

10. To aid the Chair in every way possible.

11. To know the bylaws.

12. To authenticate by his signature all minutes, records, etc.

13. To do all other things incidental to the office.

Note: He does not send out notices of meetings, or communications ordered sent out by the organization, or any correspondence, if the assembly has a corresponding secretary; if there is no corresponding secretary, then the recording secretary performs all these things.

Privileges. He may propose motions, second, debate and vote on them just like any other member when he so desires, and no one may object to his doing so.

Corresponding Secretary

The corresponding secretary has charge of all general correspondence of the organization, but not that properly belonging to or relating to some other officer, or to a board or committee, unless he is requested to conduct their correspondence or the body so directs in any instance, as is often done. The corresponding secretary also has the duty to send out notices of all meetings. He can participate in all proceedings.

Treasurer

Also known in some organizations as finance officer, financial secretary, quartermaster, etc.

Duties. 1. He is custodian of all funds not otherwise allocated.

2. He deposits all monies in an account, separate from his own, in the organization's name, and he never commingles the two.

3. He should be prepared to give a statement of the condition of the treasury at each meeting. Technically this is called a report. Such statements are given purely for the information of the members at meetings and need not be put to vote to be accepted or adopted, because this would be certifying to their accuracy and completeness without proper audit.

4. He puts out monies on vote of the body, or as he may be authorized by the bylaws.

5. His books, vouchers, and records can be audited either by an auditing committee of members or by a certified public accountant.

6. Such audits can be made quarterly, semiannually or annually, or as desired.

7. He makes an annual report, and if it has been previously audited, the vote for its final approval or adoption is taken not on his report but on the auditor's or auditing committee's report, which, when adopted, automatically also adopts the report of the treasurer without additional action; thus:

CHAIR: "The question now before the assembly is on the adoption of the auditor's [or, auditing committee's] report relating to the annual report of the treasurer. Are there any questions on the report? Those in favor of its adoption will say aye; those opposed will say no; the ayes have it, and the report is accepted."

The auditor's report is secondable and debatable, but it is unamendable, except for errors. A majority vote adopts it. It can be reconsidered; and questions on it may always be asked.

If there is no auditor's or auditing committee's report and no other procedure is prescribed for accepting such annual report. the treasurer's report is considered for acceptance or rejection on its own merits.

Parliamentarian

A parliamentarian is one who is versed in parliamentary law and procedure. He is appointed primarily to advise the presiding officer on questions of parliamentary law and procedure, thus helping to safeguard the rights and privileges of all the members equally, and to help transact the business of the assembly legally and efficiently. The parliamentarian should be strictly nonpartisan at all times.

By whom appointed. The parliamentarian can be appointed in any one of the following ways: (1) by the Chair with the prior consent or subsequent approval of the executive board or the body itself; (2) by the executive board; (3) by vote of the body or (4) as otherwise provided in the bylaws.

When introduced. The parliamentarian may be introduced just before the business portion of the program begins. It is useful to the members to know that a competent parliamentarian has been appointed to help guide the proceedings legally and impartially, and to know that a parliamentary expert is available to advise them when necessary on their parliamentary rights. The parliamentarian is usually assigned a seat near the presiding officer for convenient consultation. After he is introduced, he is referred to as "the parliamentarian." If he is not a member, he has no vote; if he is, he may vote upon any and all questions.

Addressed through the Chair. Questions or inquiries intended for the parliamentarian should be addressed to him through the Chair, because the Chair and not the parliamentarian is the presiding officer. The parliamentarian, in turn, communicates with or answers the members' inquiries through the Chair; that is, he tells the Chair what the answer should be and the Chair declares it formally. When the Chair knows the answer to a rule or inquiry, the parliamentarian need not be asked to answer it; the Chair himself gives the answer directly. The parliamentarian answers only such inquiries or questions from the floor as the Chair relays to him, unless a different intent is indicated; and he does not speak in the assembly except when requested to do so either by the Chair or by the body, such as if he were asked to explain a phase of a question in which the Chair is not sufficiently versed.

Opinion and ruling distinguished. Opinion is advice; ruling is a decision. The parliamentarian gives the opinion (advice), and the Chair the ruling (decision). The Chair or the assembly may ask advice of the parliamentarian on any question, but they are not obliged to follow the advice. Appeals can be taken only from the decision of the Chair, not from that of the parliamentarian. Thus, if the parliamentarian is asked by the Chair or by the body for an opinion on a question which is given openly to the body, such opinion cannot be appealed from until the Chair has adopted it as his decision and has announced it as such.

May point out errors to the Chair. When serious errors in the conduct of business are noticed, the parliamentarian may call them to the attention of the Chair in the manner previously agreed between him and the Chair, for the parliamentarian is essentially an advisor, not a reformer.

The engagement or appointment of a parliamentarian is strongly urged upon every organization, especially for district, state and national conventions and other large assemblies.

Executive Secretary

If the organization has an executive secretary he usually has charge of the office of the organization, and he executes the orders of both the organization and the board of directors, unless otherwise provided. He is also secretary of the board and the executive committee, if there is one.

Other Officers

Additional officers, elected or appointed, can be assigned such duties as the organization may prescribe. Such officers might be chaplain, warden, and sentinel or guard. If no special duties are drafted or prescribed in the bylaws or special rules, the following convenient form can be adopted therein: "He shall perform such duties as pertain to his office."

II. TERM OF OFFICE

Installation and oath. If officers are required by law or by the bylaws to take an oath of office, one who has not taken the oath is not regarded as having duly qualified. If installation or induction into office is also prescribed by law or a bylaw, such installation is also necessary. But if, in either case, the oath or installation has not been observed regularly, the law presumes that one who is in actual possession of the office has duly qualified. Whenever need be, the oath can be administered or the installation held belatedly.

Term of first officers of new organization. Officers who are elected at the first election of a newly established organization serve until the first annual meeting thereafter, unless a longer or a different term is specified in the bylaws or a different intention was clearly understood at the time.

Succession of office: vice presidents. The vice president is a standby president in every case, and he automatically becomes president for the balance of the term in the event of the president's resignation, death, etc., unless the bylaws specify that the vacancy shall be filled otherwise.

If the bylaws state that "in the event of the president's resignation, removal, [etc.], the vice president shall become president for the unexpired term," then the second vice president automatically becomes first vice president, the third becomes second, etc.; and the vacancy then to be filled is the lowest ranking vice presidency.

If there are several vice presidents without designation of rank (as in simply "there shall be four vice presidents") and there is dispute as to how to determine their rank for succession to office, or as to who should preside by virtue of rank, then (a) refer to the records or minutes of the meeting at which they were elected, and whoever received the highest vote is properly regarded as first vice president, the next highest the second, etc.; but (b) if the record does not disclose their vote, then the name which is listed first therein is the first vice president, the next name the second, etc. Rank in the above instances is not determined by alphabetical order unless the minutes so disclose.

Distinction between president-elect and president elect. A president-elect (with hyphen) is the organization's *newly elected president* who has not yet been formally installed in office. A president elect (no hyphen) is an officer chosen at the previous election, and is the organization's *pre-elected next president.* He will automatically occupy the office of president once the incumbent president's prescribed term expires. The office of president elect is next in rank below that of president and is above that of vice president. The president elect, rather than the vice president(s), presides when the president vacates the chair. In the event of the incumbent president's resignation, removal, disability, death, etc., the president elect completes the unexpired term unless the bylaws specify otherwise.

Officers holding over into new term. In organizations, an officer "holding over" is one who holds his office after its expiration either (a) because a bylaw expressly empowers him to hold over, as when it provides that "officers shall hold over until their successors are elected and qualified," or (b) because of some unforeseen happening (as when the legal successor resigns or dies, etc.), the incumbent officer is prevailed upon to hold over.

Holding over applies as follows: Some organizations' bylaws specify (a) that "Officers shall hold over until their successors are elected and qualified," or installed; or (b) that they "shall serve for one year or until their successors are elected and qualified." In such cases the incumbent officers automatically continue in office by right of the bylaw, and no vacancy results. This is so because the legal period of holding over is as much a continuing part of their tenure of office as the period of the original tenure fixed by the bylaw — just as an adjourned meeting is a continuing part of the original meeting.

Therefore, when the body having original power to elect fails to elect a successor, or it cannot hold the intended election for any reason, such failure to elect does not produce vacancies in office which can be filled by the board or president. The bylaw in effect *extends* tenure until the same original body conducts the intended election at another time. The body thereafter convenes another meeting as promptly as feasible, and proceeds then to conduct the election.

Note: All such holdover officers are in all respects continuing *legal* officers, being regarded as *de jure* officers. *De Jure* is Latin for "by right," therefore, by right of the bylaw.

When there is a vacancy to be filled. A vacancy *does* result (which another body that has the power, such as the board or the president can fill) if a holdover officer resigns or dies while he is a holdover officer, or if he resigns or dies before a delayed election takes place.

In some organizations the bylaws do not expressly empower incumbent officers to hold over, but on the contrary limit tenure of office, as when they say (a) "Officers shall serve until the next annual election [or, annual meeting]," or (b) "until their successors are elected," or (c) "until the end of their respective term," — or other like provision denoting automatic cessation of their tenure. In such cases the incumbent officers automatically go out of office at the specified time.

Therefore, in such a case, if the body having original power to elect successors fails to elect or to hold its intended meeting to elect, such failure to elect produces vacancies in office which the body having that power (board or president as the case may be), can then proceed to fill. All vacancies, by whomever filled, are for the unexpired term.

Note: If, after the expiration of his legal term, and in cases where no bylaw empowers him to continue in office as holdover, an officer is prevailed upon to hold over for the time being, such officer is then regarded as a *de facto* officer, as distinguished from a *de jure* officer. (*De facto* is Latin for "in fact" or "in effect.") The legal acts of a de facto officer are as valid as though he were an officer de jure; hence, a de facto officer may be referred to as a quasi-de jure officer, or in the nature of a de jure officer.

Resignation. A resignation from *elective* office or position can be withdrawn prior to its acceptance by the body having power to accept it, provided notice of such withdrawal is communicated to the body any time *before* the body acts on it at a legal meeting, regular or special. A resignation from *appointive* position becomes automatically acceptable upon its receipt by the appointer.

If the resignation is conditional or prospective (to take place at a specified future time), the recipient of the resignation, elective or appointive, is without power to accept it before occurrence of the condition or of the effective date, as this would violate the terms of the resignation.

An undated resignation, or one which allows the appointing authority to set the date, or an unconditional resignation (one which does not impose any condition or future time) becomes effective upon its receipt or upon its acceptance.

Rules of resignation. 1. A resignation is not effective, even though a successor has been chosen, if transmitted or presented without authority.

2. If a resignation is required to be in writing by organization law or rule, an oral resignation is not effectual.

3. If the resigner is present at the meeting, he can present his own resignation therein; he can move to accept it; he can debate it; he can vote upon it. (He is, after all, still a member.)

4. If the resigner is present and his resignation is accepted, the acceptance cannot be reconsidered except by unanimous consent.

5. If delegates and alternates have been chosen and any one of the delegates resigns, the first alternate succeeds him; if another delegate resigns, the second alternate succeeds him, etc.

6. The resignation of a member of a committee is submitted to the appointing power (president or chairman, if he did the appointing), or to the board (if it appointed him), or to the body (if elected by the body).

7. An officer who resigns before expiration of his term is not required or expected to submit an annual report, as this would be premature; but he can make memoranda for his successor to incorporate in the annual report.

8. If a resignation has been laid on the table (which is sometimes done as a courtesy to the resigner to give him an opportunity to change his mind, or so he can be prevailed upon to withdraw it), such resignation takes effect when the time for taking it from the table has expired, if it was not previously withdrawn.

9. One who submits a conditional or prospective resignation has the right to withdraw it at any time prior to occurrence of the condition or contingency; and after withdrawing it, he can resubmit it, if he wants to, with new conditions.

Note: When you feign resignation but are not really serious about resigning, make your resignation effective at a future day, week or month; then you can withdraw it if need be prior to that time.

10. Since a conditional or prospective resignation legally can be withdrawn at any time before occurrence of the imposed condition or of any other limitation or restriction made by it, the appointing or electing authority is, in effect, put on notice that it should first make sure the resigner has not withdrawn his resignation before proceeding to choose a successor.

The disappearing officer. An officer or committeeman who abandons the duties of his post or who has disappeared and is not heard from, can be removed by the electing or appointing power unless the bylaws specify otherwise.

Abolition of office. The assembly or authority which possesses the power to create an office or position has, in the absence of superior law to the contrary, the implied power to abolish the office or position.

An officer accepting office does so subject to the possibility that his duties may be increased or diminished, or his term of office may be shortened or the office itself even abolished altogether.

The abolition, through canonical processes, of any office or position in the organization automatically terminates the right of the incumbent officer to exercise the duties of the office, *unless* at the time he is excluded by express terms or express agreement.

Note: If an officer in the organization seriously neglects his official duties or is obnoxious, incompetent or dictatorial, or is chargeable with fraud, bribery or conspiracy, etc., it may sometimes be more prudent to abolish his *term* of office through the orderly process of a bylaw *amendment*, and thus legislate him promptly out of office, than to institute impeachment and removal proceedings against him and cause internal dissension.

Where removal from office of an officer is accomplished through abolition of his term of office, or of the office itself, the body can reestablish the same in due course thereafter, and then proceed to elect to fill it. In such a case, the officer who was thus removed *can* be a candidate thereto, if he is still a member and no express penalty was previously imposed upon him so as to make him ineligible for the same or any other office.

Past officers. If a bylaw defines a past officer, then it is only one who qualified under that definition who can be called a past officer, as in this case: "A past president is one who, having been elected and installed, has served to the end of his term, or ceased to hold office by reason of consolidation of lodges, or of death before expiration of his term, or one who resigns his office to enter active duty in the Armed Forces." A president who does not qualify fully under such definition may not properly be referred to as a "past president" in this organization; he should be referred to in some other way.

But if no bylaw defines a past officer, then anyone who was duly elected and qualified to serve a term of office, or who shared the term with another due to resignation, death, etc., is known as a past officer, regardless of how long he served, if at all, just so long as he was duly chosen and qualified. Thus if A is elected and installed to a two-year term, and he dies just as he is about to thank the assembly, if B is then duly elected and he resigns after serving two months, and C is then elected and finishes the term, all three, A, B, C, are known as past presidents by virtue of having been duly elected.

Note: Two Presidents of the United States shared a term of office in more than six instances, due to death, etc. All who shared a term are designated as ex-Presidents. President William H. Harrison, for instance, served only 31 days of his four-year term in 1841. He is nevertheless reckoned as the Ninth President of the United States.

Immediate or junior past officers. Immediate or junior past officer status, such as immediate or junior past president, automatically ceases when the next election has intervened. Each intervening election extinguishes the continuity of the status of each outgoing junior or immediate past president. If under the organization's bylaws a junior past president is made a member of the board by reason of such status, and he resigns or dies during his tenure, no vacancy occurs, and the authority having general power to appoint a successor for the unexpired term in any office may not elect or appoint anyone, because the bylaws reserve such tenure on the board only for one who emerges as a junior past president at each subsequent election.

Chapter 19
DISCIPLINE OF MEMBERS AND OFFICERS
I. VOTE OF NO CONFIDENCE (S, D, A, M)

Test vote of trust. Motions for a vote of confidence or of no confidence, where practiced by virtue of a nation's laws, or under an organization's bylaws, are test votes to express whether the membership has trust in the policies, program or official conduct of the administration in power.

Basic rules. The motion for a vote of confidence or no confidence is an incidental main motion. It requires a second and is debatable and amendable. A majority vote adopts it unless the organization bylaws otherwise provide. It may be tabled, postponed, etc., and yields to subsidiary, privileged, and apt incidental motions (pp. 47–48). It can take the form of a question of privilege. The vote is final and may not be reconsidered.

Two types. There are two kinds of confidence motions: a vote of confidence and a vote of *no* confidence. Both are subject to the same rules.

How used. A motion for a vote of *no* confidence is proposed by opponents of the administration in power when they feel they may be able to swing enough votes (majority) to win a no confidence vote, and thereby discredit the administration's program and policies.

A motion for a vote of confidence is proposed by the supporters of the administration (and sometimes it is purposely proposed by them) when they feel sure they have the necessary votes to win a vote of confidence, and thus beat the complaining opposition to the punch, and bar it, thereafter, from proposing its intended vote of no confidence upon the same question or issue.

Effect of vote of no confidence. In ordinary assemblies (fraternal orders, labor organizations, veterans' associations, women's clubs, etc.), a vote of no confidence is mere disapproval of the program, acts, or policies of some officer or the board, etc. It indicates that the leadership is losing its grip or is falling in disfavor with the membership. It is in the nature of a black mark and is almost equivalent to a vote of censure but without its sting. It amounts to nothing more, unless the organization's laws provide to the contrary in any way.

Hence, in such organizations as the above, a vote of no confidence does

---

KEY QUIZ

Q. Is a vote of confidence a motion? *A.* Yes; it is a main motion; precisely, an incidental main motion.

Q. Does it require a second? *A.* Yes.

Q. Is it debatable? *A.* Yes.

Q. Is it amendable? *A.* Yes.

Q. What vote adopts a motion for a vote of confidence? *A.* Majority, unless the assembly's laws prescribe to the contrary.

Q. Can it be reconsidered? *A.* No; the vote is final either way.

Q. Can it be tabled, postponed, etc.? *A.* Yes; it yields to all the subsidiary, privileged, and apt incidental motions (pp. 47, 48).

not, in the absence of express bylaw or rule, compel resignation or ousting from office or position, whereas in the government of nations a vote of no confidence can, under their express laws, bring about resignations and new election.

II. CENSURE (S, D, A, M)

Nature of censure. Instead of suspending or expelling an officer or member for violation of its bylaws or rules, or its orders and instructions, or for misconduct in office or disorderly conduct at meetings, or for offensive words in debate, or for unethical acts, etc., the assembly may censure him when this seems a more judicious step. Censure expresses the assembly's indignation, and is a lighter form of pronounced punishment. It is a reprimand, aimed at reformation of the person and prevention of further offending acts. It is the warning voice of suspension, removal, or expulsion.

Note: Under Art. 1, sec. 5, second paragraph of the Constitution of the United States, each House may "punish its members for disorderly behavior, and, with the concurrence of two-thirds, expel a member." Thus the two methods of punishment therein are by censure and expulsion, censure being a lighter form of punishment.

Both the U. S. Senate and House of Representatives use the term "censure." The General Assembly of the United Nations uses "condemnation" in place of "censure."

Basic rules. The motion to censure is an incidental main motion which requires a second. It is debatable and amendable and is subject to all the subsidiary motions and apt incidental motions (pp. 47–48). A majority vote, quorum being present, adopts it. The vote on a motion to censure is final and may not be reconsidered. No person may be censured a second time for the same offense, and, normally, censure should not apply to more than one person at a time. The best interests of the assembly require that the reasons for censure not be recounted. The offender himself may not vote on the motion. A vote by secret ballot is advisable.

Censure of an officer or member may not be inflicted by the presiding officer except by vote of the assembly.

When members have resigned pending proceedings for censure, the assembly has nevertheless the right to proceed with the motion to censure.

When introduced. While censure is normally introduced under new business, it may also be presented under the good of the order.

Previous notice. Previous notice is not necessary in order to act on a censure; but if previous notice is given, it should not name the member or the reason for the censure in the call for the meeting, so as to avoid defamation and slander. If previous notice was given, censure is introduced under unfinished business.

Grounds for censure of members. Regarded as serious grounds for censure are: persistent violation of the rules; assaults on the floor; slanderous or insulting remarks such as calling a member "liar" or "thief," etc.; disorderly conduct; reference to personalities; misconduct in office; neglect of duty; disobedience to instructions by delegates or committees; threats to hurt a member of the organization; defrauding or cheating the

KEY QUIZ

Q. Does a motion or resolution to censure need a second? *A.* Yes.
Q. Is it debatable? *A.* Yes.
Q. Is it amendable? *A.* Yes.
Q. What vote adopts a motion to censure? *A.* Majority vote.
Q. Can it be reconsidered? *A.* No; the vote is final either way.
Q. May a person be censured a second time for the same act or offense?
A. No.
Q. What class of motion is it? *A.* Main motion (precisely speaking, an incidental main motion).
Q. Can it be tabled, postponed, amended, etc.? *A.* Yes; it is subject to all the subsidiary motions and to apt incidental ones.
Q. What method of voting is best? *A.* Secret ballot.
Q. May the offender vote on it? *A.* No; he is disqualified from voting on it.
Q. If the offending officer or member persists in violating the rules, or persists in his misconduct, what happens? *A.* Suspension, removal from office or expulsion may follow.

---

organization; bribery; conspiracy; larceny; misuse of funds; false charges and accusations; divulging the secret password; violation of the oath; disloyalty; secession; vilification of a member or of the presiding officer or the organization; willful destruction of organization property; absenteeism; and many others.

Grounds for censure of presiding officers. Serious grounds for censure against presiding officers (presidents, chairmen, etc.) are, in general: arrogation or assumption by the presiding officer of dictatorial powers — powers not conferred upon him by law — by which he harasses, embarrasses and humiliates members; or, specifically: (1) he refuses to recognize members entitled to the floor; (2) he refuses to accept and to put canonical motions to vote; (3) he refuses to entertain appropriate appeals from his decision; (4) he ignores proper points of order; (5) he disobeys the bylaws and the rules of order; (6) he disobeys the assembly's will and substitutes his own; (7) he denies to members the proper exercise of their constitutional or parliamentary rights.

How Censure Is Proposed and Entertained

If the censure is made against the president, it is put to vote by the vice president, and if he declines it is put by the secretary. If neither one is present or is willing to entertain it, it is put to vote by the maker of the motion. Robert prescribes a similar rule (*Rules of Order*, p. 238).

Censuring a member. Under new business, X takes the floor.

Mr. X: "Mr. President, before making a motion to censure, may I call to the attention of the members the fact that Brother F has been coming to the meetings intoxicated of late and disturbing the meetings, thereby violating Article Five under Conduct of Members. Mr. President, the interests and dignity of the organization require that we now show our disapproval of such conduct. I therefore move that Brother F be censured." (Seconded.)

Chair: "It is moved and seconded to censure Brother F. Is there any discussion?"

Mr. Q: "Mr. President, I move to table the motion." (Seconded.)

Chair: "It is moved and seconded to table the motion to censure.

Those in favor of tabling the motion will say aye; those opposed will say no; the noes have it. Is there further debate?" (After debate, the censure is put to vote, the Chair continuing:) "Those in favor . . ." (interrupted by member S).

Mr. S: "Mr. President, I move that the vote be by ballot."

Chair: "It is moved and seconded that the vote of censure be taken by ballot. Those in favor of a secret ballot will say aye; those opposed will say no; the ayes have it, and the vote will be by secret ballot.

"The question before the assembly is to censure Brother F for the reason stated. Those in favor of censure will vote yes; those opposed will vote no. The tellers will distribute and collect the ballots and report to the body." (This is done, with this result, the Chair saying:) "On the motion to censure, seventy-three members voted yes, twelve members voted no. The affirmative has it, and the vote of censure is adopted."

Note: At this point the Chair, in ordinary meetings such as fraternal orders, labor organizations, veterans' associations, etc., should strongly stress to the offender the meaning of a censure vote, somewhat thus:

Chair (addressing the offender by name): "Brother F, you have been censured by vote of the assembly. A censure indicates the assembly's resentment of your conduct at meetings. A censure is a warning. It is the warning voice of suspension or expulsion. Please take due notice thereof and govern yourself accordingly," or parallel words of warning. (Compare the above note with the one below).

Note: In legislative bodies like the U. S. House of Representatives, whose system of parliamentary procedure ranks second to none, and from which all state legislatures, city councils, etc., have taken most of their prevailing rules, after the House of Representatives has voted censure, the offender "is brought to the bar [before the Speaker's rostrum] by the Sergeant-at-Arms to be censured," whereupon "censure is inflicted by the Speaker" (*U. S. House Rules and Manual,* § 63).

At that moment, the Speaker says: "You [naming the offender] have been censured"; or "You have merited," or "You have incurred the censure of the House," and the matter ends right there if no additional penalty is included in the vote of the censure.

In one year, the Congress censured two of its members. In the Senate, one senator was censured for alleged misuse of campaign funds. The House of Representatives censured a congressman for alleged misuse of his committee's funds. In the United Nations, the Security Council refused to censure (*condemn* was the word used) a member nation for alleged acts of aggression on another member nation.

Censuring an officer. An officer is censured in the same manner as any other member, as just shown; thus:

Member Y: "Mr. President, shortages of small sums of money in the treasurer's books from time to time have got to stop. Rather than bring charges for removal from office at this time, I move that we proceed to censure the treasurer." (Seconded.)

Chair: "It is moved and seconded to censure the treasurer. Is there any debate on the motion to censure?" (As before, after debate by any member, including the treasurer, the Chair puts the censure to vote and declares the result accordingly.)

If the officer is censured, the Chair immediately addresses him by name and says: "Mr. So-and-so, you have been censured by the body. A censure is a warning. Take due notice thereof and govern your office accordingly" (or similar words). The Chair then proceeds to other business.

Censuring the presiding officer. Very commonly, members ask what they can do about a president who refuses to give members the floor; or who is a dictator; or who ignores points of order and appeals; or who will not put legitimate motions to vote; or who opposes everyone in debate; or who rejects proper amendments; or who is otherwise ignorant of parliamentary law, does not heed the assembly's orders, adjourns the meetings against the assembly's will, etc.

The president can be censured in the same manner as is any other member. All you have to do is to introduce under new business a motion "to censure the president," and have your supporters at the meeting to vote for it. You need only a majority vote to pass a vote of censure. But be sure the president deserves censure, and that a very large majority can be relied upon to support the vote of censure.

The motion or resolution to censure the president is addressed to, and is entertained and put to vote by the vice president, and not by the president himself (an exception to the rule). If the vice president declines, the secretary entertains it. If both of them decline or are absent, the maker of the motion conducts the censure, from the floor rather than from the platform. If the vice president or secretary conducts it, he does so from his station, and not from the president's station. The president can debate the censure, but he may not vote on it. The process of censuring the president, if canonically and faithfully adhered to, is carried out in the following manner:

MEMBER X (under new business and addressing *first* the president by way of preliminary information to him and to the body): "Mr. President, I am about to propose a resolution of censure against the president [or, against you], which I have a right to do. As you well know, Mr. President, under our parliamentary authority [Demeter's *Manual*, citing this page; or Robert's *Rules of Order*, page 238: or other such parliamentary authority], when a motion is made to condemn or censure the president, the motion is addressed to, and is entertained by, the vice president."

Member X now turns to the vice president, and, addressing him as "vice president" and not as "chairman," or "president," since a censure is merely a warning and not a proceeding that removes the president from the chair, says:

MEMBER X: "Mr. Vice President."

VICE PRESIDENT: "Mr. X."

MR. X: "I move the adoption of the following resolution of censure:

"Whereas, The president [omit his name] has repeatedly denied to the members the proper exercise of their parliamentary rights — refusing them the floor, ignoring proper amendments, points of order and appeals, and otherwise disobeying the assembly's orders and the rules of order; and

"Whereas, He has been arrogant, abusive and obnoxious; and

"Whereas, Such conduct is against the best interests of the organization and the rights and dignity of the members; be it therefore

"*Resolved*, That the president be censured." (Seconded.)

VICE PRESIDENT: "It is moved and seconded to censure the president Is there any discussion on the resolution of censure?" (After discussion pro and con by members, including the president, and after the vote is taken by ballot, the vice president says:)

VICE PRESIDENT: "On this vote of censure one hundred seven members voted yes, and nineteen voted no. The vote of censure is adopted." He then faces the president, and addressing him *by name*, says:

VICE PRESIDENT: "Mr. Mean, you have been censured by the assembly for the reasons contained in the resolution. I now return to you the presidingship." And this ends this instance of censure. The president then takes up the next business in order (since a simple censure is a mere warning).

If misconduct of an officer persists. If, after the vote of censure, the president persists in being obnoxious or arrogant, then, if need be, (A) bring charges against him for neglect of duty as presiding officer, or (B) abolish his term of office by amending the bylaws with due notice to all members. A $\frac{2}{3}$ vote is needed in either case. Step B is often preferable, since it can be a less turbulent and divisive proceeding.

If a $\frac{2}{3}$ vote is attained in either case, the president or any other elective officer is automatically dropped from office. The resulting vacancy is then filled by the authority having power to fill vacancies under the by-law. If no one else is expressly authorized to fill any vacancy, then the body fills it in due course.

Using the "good of the order." Nearly all organizations have a "good of the order" category. Under it, anyone is entitled to voice complaints, suggestions and constructive criticism and thus attempt in good faith to rectify wrongs, and thus, perhaps, make unnecessary later censures, impeachments, etc., as, for instance:

(1) MEMBER A: "Mr. President, under the good of the order, I wish to point out that one or two members habitually come to the meetings in an intoxicated condition, causing distress and annoyance to many of us. This is becoming increasingly intolerable. I hope this situation will stop."

(2) MEMBER B: "Mr. President, under the good of the order is the best spot I know of to air any complaints we may have. We paid our annual dues three months ago. Why haven't we received our dues cards yet?"

(3) MEMBER C: "Mr. President, at each one of the last two meetings the treasurer could not account for certain small expenditures. We feel that this situation should be quickly corrected."

(4) MEMBER D: "Mr. President, with all due respect to the Chair, many of us feel that the Chair, in refusing repeatedly to give certain members the floor, and in turning down proper amendments, points of order, appeals, etc., displays incompetence as a presiding officer. Under the good of the order, many of us wish to voice our displeasure."

III. IMPEACHMENT (S, D, $\frac{2}{3}$, R)

If your organization's laws provide a method of impeachment, then follow the method prescribed therein.

Legal definition. To impeach a person is to accuse him, to bring an accusation against him.

Basic rules. A motion to impeach (usually an officer, for gross misconduct or for such grounds as may be specified in the organization's laws) is a main motion, precisely known as an incidental main motion. As such, it requires a second, and it is debatable and amendable; it needs a $\frac{2}{3}$ vote to convict, but only a majority vote to put the accused on trial. A decision or finding *favorable* to the accused may not be reconsidered, but an *unfavorable* decision can be reconsidered. The motion to impeach yields to all the subsidiary, privileged and incidental motions.

Origin of impeachment. Historically, the device of impeachment is a British invention (now in disuse in England).

Under English law, both Houses of Parliament (House of Commons and House of Lords, equivalent to the House of Representatives and the Senate of the United States respectively) have a hand in impeachments.

Charges against a public official are started and are considered first by the House of Commons; and if approved therein as constituting sufficient grounds, the charges are then sent to the House of Lords where the actual trial on the charges is held, and the final verdict is rendered there. But if the charges are deemed insufficient, they are dropped.

Impeachment in the United States. Following the British example, the constitutions of Virginia (1776) and Massachusetts (in 1780) and other states thereafter, adopted the impeachment doctrine.

Then the Constitution of the United States (1787) also incorporated an impeachment provision, under which both Houses of the Congress have a hand in it, as in the British Parliament. The U. S. Constitution specifies the grounds upon which impeachment may be based; namely:

"The president, vice president, and all civil officers of the United States, shall be removed from office on impeachment for, and conviction of, treason, bribery, or other high crimes and misdemeanors." (Art. 2, sec. 4).

The Constitution then gives each House of the Congress a share in the impeachment proceeding, namely:

(1) "The House of Representatives shall have the sole power of impeachment." (Art. 1, sec. 2)

(2) "The Senate shall have the sole power to try all impeachments" (Art. 1, sec. 3)

Thus, each House of Congress can share in the disposition of an impeachment proceeding; to wit: (1) the impeachment (the charges or accusation) must be introduced in the House of Representatives, and if approved there by majority vote they are then sent to the Senate where

---

KEY QUIZ

Q. Is impeachment a motion? *A.* Yes; it is a main motion.

Q. Is it debatable? *A.* Yes.

Q. Does it require a second? *A.* Yes.

Q. Is it amendable? *A.* Yes.

Q. What vote adopts or approves the impeachment? *A.* It requires a majority vote to approve the accusation and to proceed to put a person on trial, but a $\frac{2}{3}$ vote to convict him.

Q. Can the impeachment be reconsidered? *A.* If the impeachment or accusation is approved, or the accused is convicted, the vote can be reconsidered; but if the accused is not impeached or he is acquitted, the vote may not be reconsidered.

---

the actual trial of the accused is held (the Senate in effect sits as a court), and the Senate renders the final verdict for or against the accused person.

Note: The legislative impeachment (which is merely an accusation or a statement of charges) may be likened to a proceeding (*a*) before a grand jury, seeking indictment of a person, or (*b*) in the nature of a proceeding for "probable cause" in a hearing before a judge. If the grand jury returns an indictment or the judge finds probable cause, a formal trial is then held; otherwise the proceeding is dropped.

The vote on legislative impeachment. In the Congress, a majority vote is necessary to sustain the accusation or impeachment of a person in the House of Representatives; but a ⅔ vote of the members present is necessary in the Senate to convict, or to adjudge the impeached person guilty of the offense charged (Art. 1, sec. 3).

Impeachment in ordinary societies. Ordinary assemblies, like fraternal orders, associations, clubs and other organizations, do not meet daily as do the Congress of the United States and state legislatures. Therefore, when charges for the impeachment of a person are made in ordinary assemblies, the impeachment is usually decided in the same sitting or session, since these organizations are not reconvened until, usually, two weeks or a month later. Hence, when the word "impeachment" is used in such organizations it means trial of the accused on the charges or accusation against him. (Look up "trial of members," or "grievances" or "charges against members" in your bylaws. In the event your organization does not contain any such provisions, see "Trial of Members," the next section in this chapter.)

Maneuvering impeachment for quick defeat. Since a motion or proposal to impeach is a main motion, and main motions *yield* to the subsidiary, privileged and apt incidental motions, then whenever the impeachment charges seem to you to be frivolous, mischievous, unreasonable or otherwise unnecessary, you and a fair-minded assembly can administer a quick defeat to the charges by voting to postpone them indefinitely or table them, etc., in an attempt to suppress or get rid of them at the very beginning. All you need is a majority vote to eliminate further consideration of the charges if you move to postpone them indefinitely or to table them (even from meeting to meeting, or session to session).

Illustration of killing impeachment. Assume charges for impeachment pending against a vice president before the body, now being discussed pro and con:

MEMBER A: "Mr. President, these charges are preposterous, sheer fabrications against the member, motivated by personal reasons; I therefore move to postpone them indefinitely."

CHAIR: "It is moved and seconded to postpone indefinitely the pending charges. Is there any discussion on such postponement?"

After debate, the vote is taken thereon. If a majority votes to postpone them indefinitely, the charges are dismissed or are eliminated from that session. If postponement is rejected, the assembly proceeds to trial.

IV. TRIAL OF MEMBERS AND OFFICERS

If the bylaws specify the grounds upon which, or the manner in which, or by whom a member or an officer may be suspended, expelled from membership, or removed from office, the bylaws must be strictly followed, otherwise the action will be invalid. If the bylaws prescribe a hearing or trial for such member or officer, and he has not been served with written specific charges or given a reasonable time to prepare his defense, or he has not been afforded a full and fair trial or has not been heard or tried by the body specified in the bylaws, any action taken thereon will be illegal and void.

Rules for trial. In general, a member of the organization may be placed on trial for just cause in accordance with the organization's bylaws and the following rules:

1. Only the body against which the offense has been committed has jurisidction, and hence authority, to try the offending member.

2. If the bylaws specify that for certain offenses an officer or member may be suspended, expelled, or removed from office by his lodge, chapter, or local, etc., no superior body such as at the district or national level has legal power to intervene.

3. Bylaws specifying that an officer or member may be placed on trial upon the written complaint of a certain number of members or chapters must be strictly complied with or the trial is not legal.

4. Charges shall be put in writing and must be preferred or instituted strictly as specified in the organization's bylaws and before the body having jurisdiction, and based on such specific grounds as the bylaws may prescribe or impliedly authorize. All charges must be specific, with times, places, and acts adequately stated with full particulars; otherwise the charges may be rejected as insufficient.

5. If charges are dismissed as insufficient, they may be refiled when properly executed at any later time.

6. The accused should always be allowed to choose his own counsel for his attorney, whether or not the attorney is a member of the organization.

Note: Some organizations specify that the accused shall have as attorney someone who is a member of the organization. Such a requirement is unreasonable because the organization may not have any members who are attorneys, or the only attorney in the membership could be one of the accusers or even the organization's prosecutor. Such a demanding bylaw should be repealed.

If bylaws do not provide for trial. If there are no bylaws relative to trial of members, the body has authority to draw up or adopt a set of rules for the trial, or the body can authorize a committee to draft a set of rules.

Due notice. Reasonable notice, or the notice required by the bylaws, should always be given the accused, and ordinarily it should be given by registered letter, with receipt therefor requested. Where this is impracticable, notice of the charges may be handed him in the presence of two members of the organization. The accused must be given the opportunity to be heard and to have counsel.

If the accused is missing. If the accused absconds or stays away from trial he may still be tried if he was given due notice. Trial in absentia is valid, if it is valid in all other respects.

By whom conducted. The trial can be conducted for the organization by such member as may be authorized in the bylaws; but if no one is so authorized, then the assembly can designate the member or members (not more than two) who are to conduct or be concerned with the trial.

The conduct of the trial on behalf of the accused should be left in all cases up to the accused to decide, and he may select one or two persons or an attorney to defend him. It can be limited to just one person or attorney in either case, or to not more than two, as the body may decide for both sides.

By whom heard. The complaint or charge can, by vote of the body, be first heard before a committee or board, or a single impartial person or member, unless differently authorized in the bylaws. Or it may, and usually is, heard by the body itself.

Who gives the verdict. The final verdict in all cases is rendered by the body itself unless the bylaws otherwise specify. The vote is taken by secret ballot.

Conduct of the trial

1. The complaint or accusation is heard first. The charges are read by the secretary, committee, or counsel for the organization, as the case may be. The organization witnesses, if any, are then heard one at a time.

2. The accused or his attorney has the right to cross-examine or question these witnesses.

3. The accused is then heard, including any witnesses he may have. The accused cannot be compelled to testify.

4. The counsel or attorney for the organization can then cross-examine or question the accused and his witnesses.

5. The attorney or counsel for the accused, or the accused himself (in the absence of counsel) then argues the case in his behalf, explaining or commenting on the evidence and testimony produced during the trial, and makes his final plea or recommendation.

6. The counsel or attorney for the organization then completes the case by presenting his argument, commenting on or explaining the testimony or evidence heard by the body, and makes his recommendation on the disposition of the charges.

7. The accused now withdraws from the room, but not his counsel if he is a member of the organization.

8. The vote is then taken by secret ballot. All members can vote who are entitled to be in the room when the vote is taken. A majority vote convicts for a minor offense, and a $\frac{2}{3}$ vote for a major offense. What constitutes a minor or major violation or offense is determined by vote of the body if it is not covered by the bylaws. Normally, a vote of censure or reprimand requires majority vote, and suspension or expulsion a $\frac{2}{3}$ vote.

9. The Chair appoints a fair and impartial committee to distribute, collect, and count the ballots, and report the result to the Chair. The verdict is announced by the Chair.

10. There is no appeal from the decision of the body unless an appeal for redress to a higher body or some other form of appeal is specifically authorized in the bylaws. An appeal might also be taken under the law of the land in certain instances.

Questioning of participants by members. Members of the assembly cannot directly ask questions of the accused, the complainant, or any of the witnesses. They do have the right, however, unless otherwise agreed, to submit during the course of the trial questions in writing to be put to the contending parties or their witnesses. Such questions are submitted to the Chair. Questions need not be signed, but only voting members may submit them.

The Chair does not ask the questions himself, but hands them to counsel who asks them. The presiding officer in a deliberative body (as distinguished from the presiding judge in a law court trial) should never directly question witnesses except in writing through counsel.

When members can discuss the case. Members of the body have the right to discuss any and every phase of the case touched on in the course of the trial, and to speak pro or con on the merits of the accusation, just as they may discuss any other question before the body, and thus condemn, justify, or otherwise express their feelings on the question.

Hence, the accusation is open to general discussion, except where the previous question (shutting off further discussion at any stage of the proceeding) is adopted by a ⅔ vote.

The accused should not be present during general discussion or voting, nor is his counsel permitted to be in the room if he is not a member. Witnesses who are not members are also excluded.

Rules of such debate. An accusation is a main motion (precisely, an incidental main motion); hence it is subject to all the subsidiary and privileged motions (p. 47), and, therefore, it can be tabled, postponed, or postponed indefinitely, etc.

Verdict. A finding of *not guilty* stands as final, and it may not be reconsidered. The accused may not be tried a second time upon the same charges.

Chapter 20
BOARDS AND COMMITTEES

Boards and committees are created to assist the assembly in achieving the business of the organization.

They are of three kinds: 1) boards, 2) standing committees, and 3) special (also called "select" or "ad hoc" committees.)

Examples of boards. Boards of directors, trustees, managers, governors, overseers, executive boards, executive committees, councils of administration, etc.

Examples of standing committees. Membership committee, house, by-laws, program, initiation, reception, relief, publicity, ways and means, grievance.

Examples of special committees. Committees chosen to perform some temporary or special function, after completion of which they automatically expire, such as a committee to conduct a bridge party, a dance, a raffle, or to escort the mayor into the hall, to notify the governor of his election as honorary member, etc.

Ad hoc committees. Another name for a special committee is an ad hoc committee. The term *ad hoc* (Latin for "for this") means "for this purpose," or "for this particular matter." Hence, when a member says

"I move that a committee ad hoc be appointed," it is equivalent to "I move that a special committee be appointed for the purpose."

Caucus means "meeting." It is strictly a political term, and is used only in political parties, and not in *other* bodies. "Caucus" is a meeting of a political party or faction to decide on policies or candidates.

I. BOARDS

Composition of boards. The board is usually composed of the organization's officers (president, vice presidents, etc.), those specifically chosen as directors and chairmen of committees, and such others as may be authorized. Directors are usually elected when the officers are elected, or so many of them as the terms thereof expire from time to time.

Boards have no valid power to fill vacancies within their own body, unless it is expressly conferred upon them, because the power of the assembly to elect a board impliedly confers the right to fill vacancies occurring in the board.

A person who claims to be a member of the board but who has not been duly elected by the method prescribed in the organization's laws is without right or title to the office.

Newly created directorships. Vacancies occurring in newly created directorships, for which no provision for filling has been made in the rules or bylaws, may be filled by the body (board or president as the case may be) having general power to fill vacancies.

When boards can transact business. The board possesses authority to act as a board only when it holds legal meetings. If the members act or give their consent separately, and not as a board, the action is not deemed binding, strictly speaking, unless it is approved or ratified at a legal meeting thereof afterward.

A board may not transact business while the assembly is in session, unless expressly so authorized.

Authority of boards. A board is brought into existence by vote of the assembly or by a bylaw, and has only such powers, functions and duties as are conferred by or specified in the bylaws of the organization or the bylaws of the board itself when approved by the body. The object of choosing boards is to vest functions in them which they are to carry out between sessions of the body, or as may otherwise be provided.

What powers or functions the board can carry out independently of the body depends on the bylaws. If there is conflict or misunderstanding as to what the actual authority of the board is, it should be clarified, and when necessary, the bylaws should be amended to remove all doubt by granting or taking away authority, as the case may be.

Boards cannot suspend, amend, repeal or otherwise change any act of a higher body (convention, assembly, etc.) except by express bylaw; and they cannot delegate their constitutional powers to another to perform; but they can designate subcommittees, investigators, etc.

Unlimited power possible. A board can be given unlimited power by the assembly or by enactment of a bylaw to that effect, as by authorizing it to hear grievances, with full power to dispose of them; fix or vary the dues; transact all business of the organization until the next convention or between sessions of the body; approve the minutes of a meeting of the organization or the minutes of its conventions, etc.

Body can ratify unauthorized action. If a board exceeds its authority but its act is not illegal, the body may ratify it if it so chooses, or it can disaffirm it.

Limitations of power. A board may not reduce or add to prohibitions fixed in the bylaws. It cannot create an office in the organization, unless expressly so authorized. It cannot censure or otherwise punish any one of its members. Instead, it can propose such action before the assembly. Any action taken by a board not expressly authorized by a bylaw may be reversed by the assembly.

Force of a board's action. Acts of the board which have been adopted (motions, resolutions, recommendations, etc.), or which have been ratified by the assembly, continue in force until actually carried out, regardless of time; but until they are carried out they can be amended, if desired, or be rescinded altogether at any meeting.

Force of custom. If no law or bylaw specifies to the contrary or restricts the board members to a different method, acts done or consent given by its members separately according to custom, usage or long practice are valid.

Records. The minutes of a board are not usually read at meetings of the body, unless customary, but the chairman of the board reports to the body at fixed times. A nonmember of the board has not the right to examine the board's minutes except with its consent or by order of the assembly. If a board refuses to read its minutes to the main body or to have them inspected by it, then the body may, by majority vote, order their reading or their inspection.

Boards are supposed to submit an annual report.

How board business is transacted

CHAIR: "The board meeting is about to be called to order; the members will please take their seats." (This done, he then calls it to order; thus:) "The meeting will now come to order." (He might then explain:) "The printed order of business will not be ready for this board meeting, but it will be at the next meeting. The order of business at this meeting will be as follows:

1. Reading of the minutes of the previous meeting,
2. Reports of board officers and committee chairmen,
3. Reports of special committees,
4. Special orders (business postponed to a special hour),
5. Unfinished business,
6. New business, and
7. Good of the organization."

Note: An easy way to remember the above standard order is by the first letter of each business in order: R. R. R/S, U, N. G.

CHAIR (continuing): "The first business in order is the reading of the minutes of the last board meeting. Will the secretary please read the minutes?"

SECRETARY: (Reads the minutes.)

CHAIR: "Are there any corrections?" (Hearing none, he says:) "There being none, the minutes stand approved as read."

CHAIR: "The next business in order is reports of officers of the board." (He then renders his report, if any, and asks:) "Are there any questions on my report as president?" (If he concludes his report with a recommendation, he may move its adoption; thus:) "I move we appropriate five hundred dollars for [such-and-such] purpose." (He then asks:) "Is there any discussion?" (After which the vote:) "Those in favor will say aye; those opposed will say no; the ayes have it." (He continues:) "Does the vice president have a report?"

VICE PRESIDENT: "I have a brief report" (and he renders it, with or without recommendations, as the case may be); or "I have no report."

CHAIR (continues): "Next, the secretary's report."

SECRETARY: (Makes his report, if any, with or without recommendations, as the case may be.)

CHAIR: "Now the treasurer's report."

TREASURER: (Gives his report.)

CHAIR: "Next, reports of the chairmen of committees, and, first, the chairman of committee A." (The chairmen of each committee present their reports, and then the Chair continues:)

CHAIR: "The next business in order is reports of special committees; first, the chairman of special committee X." (Following which the Chair proceeds:) "Now, the report of special committee Y." (And so on until all reports have been made. The Chair continues:)

CHAIR: "The next business in order is special orders." (He turns to the secretary and asks:) "Are there any special orders for this meeting?"

SECRETARY: "Yes; a motion to authorize the treasurer to negotiate for the purchase of the adjoining lot for club parking was postponed to this meeting to be acted on at this time."

CHAIR: "As the motion to negotiate was duly made and seconded at the last meeting, it is now automatically before you. Is there any discussion?"

TREASURER: "Mr. President, I regret to say that the lot in question was sold to Z Insurance Company one hour before I made contact with the owner. As the motion is now useless, I move that it be postponed indefinitely." (Seconded.)

CHAIR: "It is moved and seconded to postpone indefinitely the motion for further negotiations thereon. Is there any discussion?" (After which the vote:) "Those in favor of indefinite postponement will say aye; those opposed will say no; the ayes have it, and the motion for further negotiations is indefinitely postponed, and the authority to negotiate further is therefore abolished."

CHAIR (continuing): "The next business in order is unfinished business." (Turning to the secretary he asks:) "Is there any unfinished business?"

SECRETARY: "No."

CHAIR: "The next business in order is new business. Is there any new business?" (If silence follows, the Chair can prompt:) "If there is any new business, now is the time to propose it." (After which the Chair continues:)

CHAIR: "The last business in order is the good of the organization. Is there anything to come under this category?"

DIRECTOR A: "Mr. President, the assistant treasurer has been absent the last two meetings. Under the good of the order I suggest (I don't want to make a formal motion) that the secretary contact him and find out the reason; otherwise I will invoke Article X, under which it is provided that the seat of a director absenting himself without valid excuse for three successive meetings may be declared vacant and that the board shall fill the vacancy."

CHAIR: "If there is no objection [pausing a couple of seconds, for possible objection], the secretary will please contact him. . . . Is there anything further under the good of the organization? . . . If not, a motion to adjourn is in order," or, "There being nothing further [pause], the meeting is adjourned. The next board meeting will be held the second Wednesday of next month."

Informal/formal conduct of business. In boards, as in committees, business is usually acted on informally, unless their membership is very large, or, in any event, unless the meeting determines otherwise.

Hence, where a board meeting transacts its business informally it is not necessary for a member to rise to make a motion, or to wait for recognition (or for his motion to be seconded) before he may speak on it, or before he may speak on another's motion; and a member may speak as often therein as he may choose (in turn with other members wishing to speak on a question).

This is so because motions to limit debate or for the previous question (to shut off debate) may not be entertained in a board or committee meeting which allows informal conduct of business, except by unanimous consent.

When business in a board is conducted informally, the presiding officer has all and the same rights therein as any other member. Hence the presiding officer may make motions (as in the preceding paragraph), debate them, etc., without having to rise or to surrender the chair. All subsidiary motions (p. 47) can be entertained in board and committee meetings except to limit or close debate. A board may, at any stage of its proceedings, order that the remainder of its business be thereafter conducted formally, instead of informally, or vice versa.

II. COMMITTEES

Committees are "the eye, the ear, the hand, and often the brain of the assembly" — Ex-Speaker Thomas B. Reed, U. S. House of Representatives.

Basic rules. A majority of the total membership of the committee constitutes a quorum for the transaction of business, unless a rule or a bylaw specifies otherwise. In committee, motions to stop or limit debate are not entertainable except by unanimous consent. A motion to reconsider can be proposed by anyone who did not actually vote with the losing side (that is, it can be proposed by one who voted with the prevailing side, or who was absent or who failed to vote when the vote was originally taken). Committees can propose amendments and "substitutes" both to resolutions and to proposed bylaw amendments coming before them.

Minutes. Committees need not keep formal minutes, although it may be done when deemed useful.

Roll of committee membership. The name, address and telephone number of each member of a committee, together with all papers, documents, information or other data bearing on the subject or question to be considered by the committee should be supplied the committee chairman by the organization secretary; and upon its discharge, or on completion of its work, the committee returns all papers, books or documents to the organization.

Kinds and composition of committees. There are two general types of committees: (1) committees for action, and (2) committees for deliberation, investigation, or recommendation. A committee which is appointed merely to carry out some action previously approved or adopted by the body should consist of but a small number of members who are thoroughly in accord with the motion adopted; committees chosen to investigate, recommend or deliberate on a matter should be large and representative of the various groups, parties or factions in the organization. Such procedure obviates delay and assures greater cooperation and accomplishment of business. Committees of the latter class should be composed of an odd number of members in order to minimize tie votes.

Ex officio members. Sometimes a member of the assembly is made ex officio member of a committee by virtue of his office (as where the treasurer is made ex officio member of the finance committee, or the parliamentarian is made ex officio member of the rules committee, or the president is made ex officio member of all committees).

In all such cases, the ex officio member has the same privileges of membership as any member of the committee, including the right to vote, unless it is expressly provided to the contrary in any respect, and he is counted in the quorum, except a president who is made ex officio member of *all* committees (who is not counted in the quorum). If a nonmember is made ex officio member of a board or committee by reason of his special talent, he has all and the same privileges therein as any other member, including the right to make motions, to speak and to vote but he has none of the obligations of membership, such as dues, assessments, etc. Ex officio members who have full rights in board or committee are counted in the quorum.

No one can be a member ex officio except by virtue of a bylaw, special rule or express vote of the assembly; and when an ex officio member ceases to hold the office, his ex officio status is automatically terminated therein. An ex officio member can be elected to any office on the board or committee, and he can be appointed to serve on any subcommittee thereof. He cannot vote in any other board or committee of which he is not an ex officio member.

Note: Ex officio is Latin for "from office," or by virtue of office.

Ex officio committee officers. One who is made chairman ex officio of a committee is authorized to preside therein; if he is absent, a chairman pro tem is chosen to preside. If the president is the ex officio member, the vice president does not have the right to attend meetings in the place of the absent president.

Committees with "full power." When it is desired to appoint a committee and at the same time give it full power to transact the question referred to it, the words "with power" or "with full power" or other appropriate phrase can be used in the motion of appointment.

When a committee is thus authorized, the question referred to it can be carried out without further authority from the body. But the body has the right, in its meetings, to amend or otherwise modify its previous action and to amend or repeal any proposal, action or decision of the committee not yet actually carried out or executed by it. In other words, the body can take away from, as well as add to, a committee's powers or the duties granted to it.

Members' right to express opinion. Members have the right to appear before, or to communicate to, a committee their stand or attitude on questions before it.

How chairman is appointed. Chairmen of committees and boards can be designated as such by vote of the body, as when a motion is made to "refer the question to a committee of three, of which Mr. A shall be chairman." In other cases a chairman is designated by the president, if so authorized by the body, as when it is moved to appoint a committee of three, whose chairman shall be designated by the president. When designating or appointing a committee, the first-named member acts as chairman and he convenes the committee; he continues as chairman, in such case, unless the committee at its meeting chooses to elect a chairman, which they have a right to do.

Rights of chairmen. Chairmen of boards and committees have all and the same rights, and they can exercise all and the same rights the other members can exercise therein. Hence, they can make motions, take part in debate and vote on any and every motion the same as other members. This they may do without leaving the chair. A board or committee is not the main body; hence its chairman can participate in all proceedings without being required to surrender the gavel to the vice president, unless he wishes to do so at the time.

If chairman fails to call meeting. On failure to convene a committee meeting after demand therefor, any two members may call a meeting with due notice to all its members. The committee is then in legal session; and if a quorum is present, it can transact business. If the regular chairman of the committee is absent, the vice chairman presides; otherwise a chairman pro tem is chosen to preside.

Committees are informally conducted. The formalities required in the assembly are not always observed in committee. For instance:

In committees and small boards members need not rise to propose motions or to speak in debate; motions need not be seconded; there is no limit to the number of times a member can speak on motions in turn with others who desire to speak. Frequently, the formality of a vote is omitted where committee or board sentiment is apparent.

The chair can propose and debate motions at meeting of small boards (or at meetings of boards which are being conducted informally), and he can *vote* thereon as freely as any other member without surrendering the chair.

If the committee or the board is large, the formal rules of the assembly are supposed to be observed.

Committee deliberations are secret. Deliberations in committee are supposed to be secret and confidential. Therefore, no reference or comment should be made in the main body as to what transpired in committee. Only such matters can be openly discussed in the main body as are contained or mentioned in the report. The object of secrecy is to protect full and free expression in committee. Who openly voted pro and con on a question in committee may be revealed and commented on (unless it was voted in committee to the contrary), but not what was said by members or how members acted or reacted.

Amendments to referred matters. If the body votes to refer to a committee a motion which has amendments pending, and the committee reports back a further amendment, the amendments of the body are considered first in the assembly because they were proposed first, then the amendment of the committee, and finally the referred motion as thus amended.

But if the motion when referred to the committee does not have amendments and the committee recommends amendments, the committee's amendments are considered first by the body, then any other amendments, after which the vote is taken on the original matter referred to the committee as thus amended or not.

In other words, action in the assembly is first taken on the amendment, if any, that was first proposed to the referred question, whether it was proposed first by the body or by the committee, and then further amendments can be proposed, and finally the original matter referred to the committee is put to vote either as amended, if it was amended, or as is, if the amendments are defeated.

The executive session. The term "executive session" means "deliberation in private." It is a popular and common legislative term.

To "go into executive session" therefore means to "deliberate on a matter in private session" — after the matter, or question, has been heard, as when a legislative or other committee, which has conducted an open hearing on a question and has concluded it, then goes into "executive session" to deliberate on the question and to come to a decision thereon.

Hence, when chairmen of committees say, "the committee will now go into executive session," this is the signal for noncommittee members to withdraw from the room so that the committee can privately deliberate on a question; it is equivalent to the motion to adjourn (or, in committee of the whole, to rise and report). Any body or committee except a committee of the whole can go into executive session to safeguard its proceedings.

Adjourned meetings of committees. When a committee adjourns and designates an adjourned (continued) meeting to another day on which to meet, it is not required that additional notice of the adjourned meeting be mailed, but it is a good reminder by which to try to convene all the members. If no next meeting is so designated, notice is again given when it is to be again convened.

Resignations from committees. Resignations from committee are addressed to the appointing power; thus, if the Chair originally made the appointments, resignations are addressed to the Chair; if the assembly originally elected members on a committee, resigning members address their resignation to the organization. Vacancies in committees resulting from resignations are filled by the same appointing power, unless differently stated in the bylaws.

Expiration of committees. Boards and standing committees expire as provided by the bylaws. But elected special committees do not necessarily expire with the year, administration or term; they expire when their assignment has been accomplished, or when custom otherwise permits. Appointed committees automatically expire when the appointing power expires.

A special committee (such as a committee to conduct a raffle or hold an outing) ceases to exist as soon as its final report has been rendered. In such a case, no motion to discharge the committee need be proposed, because the committee automatically ceases to function, but the motion is popular and it can be entertained. Nominating committees expire in the same way unless otherwise warranted.

Subcommittees. Boards, standing committees and special committees can appoint subcommittees from their own number to study, investigate or pass on a certain matter. A subcommittee is a division of the committee, usually appointed by the committee for some specific purpose. All such subcommittees report to the committee, not to the main body. The term subcommittee is incorrect if it is not composed of members of the committee which appoints the subcommittee.

Standing Committees

Standing committees are in the nature of permanent committees — committees which function all through the year, term or session. Standing committees are usually named in the bylaws, and their functions, powers and duties specified therein. If the bylaws do not specify standing committees, then standing committees are those which prevailing custom has recognized as such, or such as the assembly may create. Standing committees make an annual report.

Overlapping terms of office. Standing committees, like boards of directors, can be constituted so that term of office of a certain number of their membership will automatically expire at the end of the term (as in the Senate of the United States wherein the tenure of only one-third of its members expires at the end of the six-year term).

If boards or standing committees are constituted so that the tenure of (for instance) one-third of the members expires each year (or every two years, etc.), after each such year the board or committee elects new officers, chooses new committees, and enacts or reenacts any rules desired, in the same manner as if the entire board or committee has been reelected; and all business left unfinished theretofore falls to the ground, but any part thereof can be reproposed for consideration by the re-formed board at any time desired.

A useful provision for setting up a division of membership of a newly created board or standing committee is as follows:

"I move that the three of the nine directors [or, committeemen] receiving the most votes shall serve for three years; the three receiving the next largest numbers shall serve for two years; and the next three for one year [or any other tenure desired]; and upon expiration of the term of a member thereof his successor shall be chosen to fill the established term."

Seniority. Seniority dates from the beginning of a member's last *uninterrupted* service as a member, regardless of previous terms or interrupted service. A ranking committee member who ended connection with his committee by reason of suspension, expulsion, failure of reelection, etc., upon his return to the committee automatically takes rank at the foot of the committee because his continuity of committee tenure has been broken.

III. COMMITTEE REPORTS

Basic rules. Committee and board resolutions, recommendations, of motions do not require a second if moved for adoption by a member or the committee. If the committee member neglects to move their adoption, any member may move their adoption, in which case a second is then required.

When committees propose motions or recommendations of any kind, the Chair need not ask for or wait for a second; instead, the Chair at once states the committee's proposal as though it has been seconded; thus: "It is moved and seconded to adopt the committee's recommendation; is there any discussion?"

Minority reports on motions, recommendations, resolutions, or a slate of nominees, require a second, since they are not *the* committee's proposals.

Note: Committees can be referred to as either "who" or "which." When submitting reports, if invited guests or officials are at the Chair's station or rostrum, reporting members address the presiding officer only, not the guests or officials. Simply say: "Mr. Chairman!"

The words "report," "recommendation" and "motion" in the course of the proceeding are often apt synonyms. All are treated as main motions.

If body's chairman spoke in committee. The president, when speaking in a committee, speaks not as the organization's presiding officer but as a member of the organization. He is not disqualified from presiding when the question on which he spoke in committee is before the body.

Premature reports. Reports called for or given prior to schedule can be prematurely acted on, provided (a) no one objects, or (b) the rules are suspended for the purpose, or (c) their scheduled time is ordered (voted) changed by a $\frac{2}{3}$ vote.

Three kinds of committees. All the purposes for which committees are chosen fall into three general classes: committees for action, committees for study or investigation, and committees for recommendation.

Committees for action. A committee for action is one which is chosen to carry out some specific decision or action previously voted by the body, as when it has been voted to buy a new desk for the secretary and a committee is appointed to buy it. In such a case, the reporting member of the committee merely reports the purchase at the next meeting, and makes no motion — nor is any motion necessary — to accept the report of the committee. The fact of the purchase speaks for itself, and that ends the matter. All reports of this type are acted on in the same manner. If, notwithstanding this, a member moves to accept the report of the committee, the motion is in order, even though it is time-consuming, since the proceeding encourages participation in the deliberations.

Committees for study or investigation. If the motion originally appointing the committee empowers it merely to investigate, study or deliberate on a question, and nothing more, then the sole function of the committee is to report only the facts or data pertaining to the question and nothing more; in such a case the reporting chairman does not move adoption of the report and does not make any recommendation. The facts speak for themselves. It is up to the assembly, strictly speaking, to decide what further action shall be taken, after disclosure of the facts. This kind of committee sometimes makes a recommendation on its *own* initiative.

Committees for recommendation. When a committee is empowered to consider a question and also to report recommendation, the function of the committee is to consider the question from all angles and to report its recommendation for the passage or defeat of the question.

In all cases of a recommendation, if the question originates in (is first suggested or proposed by) the committee, the chairman of the committee moves the adoption of the committee's recommendation, and the question is stated by the Chair on "the adoption of the committee's recommendation," which, if adopted, also adopts the subject matter of the recommendation. But if the question on which a recommendation is made originated with (was first proposed in and referred by) the assembly, the Chair states as the question before the house not the recommendation of the committee, but the question originally referred to the committee.

Thus, if a motion "to buy a new radio" has been referred to the committee and the committee recommends its adoption, the question before the body, correctly speaking, is stated on "the adoption of the motion to buy a new radio," not on the adoption of the committee's recommendation, because the committee did not originate the question to buy a radio — the assembly did; hence, the recommendation of the committee in such a case serves merely as influence in behalf of the question. But if the committee had been appointed "to consider the advisability of buying a new radio and to report appropriate recommendation," and the committee reports a recommendation to buy a new radio, then the question before the house would be "on the recommendation of the committee to buy a new radio," which is open to debate and amendment, just like any other main question.

Only wrong facts are amendable in reports. You cannot amend any committee report unless its *facts* are wrong (such as wrong names, wrong sums, dates, distances, ages, etc.); thus: "Mr. Chairman, the applicant's name is Adams, not Adamson"; "His age is listed as thirty-three and it should be thirty-eight"; "He is a graduate of Yale, not Dartmouth," etc. Such misinformation in the report can be amended (corrected).

Recommendations can be amended. You can amend any recommendation or motion in the report which is moved for adoption; thus: "Mr. Chairman, your committee recommends that we paint the club exterior for six hundred dollars," or "that we donate one hundred dollars to charity X," or "that we buy a new flag, a gavel and a Bible," etc. You can amend a recommendation in a committee report just like any other recommendation before the assembly.

Favorable and unfavorable recommendations. Committee recommendations can be either favorable or unfavorable. The technical procedure for acting on unfavorable recommendations is slightly different from that of favorable ones; thus:

Action on favorable recommendations

CHAIR: "Is the committee to whom was referred the motion to build a new clubhouse ready to report?"

COMMITTEE CHAIRMAN: "Mr. Chairman, the committee to which was referred the question to build a new clubhouse submits the following report: The committee held five meetings. It consulted three architects and two builders. This is a good time to build. The committee therefore unanimously recommends that we build a new clubhouse."

CHAIR: "You have heard the favorable report [or, recommendation] of the committee. The question now before the body is on the original main motion referred to the committee, namely, to build a new clubhouse." (And after amendment and debate, if any, the motion is put to vote and is adopted or defeated.)

All other motions originally proposed in the assembly and referred to a committee are treated, if favorably reported back, in the manner just shown.

Action on unfavorable recommendations

CHAIR: "Is the committee ready to report?"

COMMITTEE CHAIRMAN: "Mr. Chairman, the committee's task was not an easy one. Seven meetings were held since its appointment, and, I am glad to say, no member missed a committee meeting. We consulted architects, builders, looked into prices, etc. As a result, the committee is of the opinion that this is not a proper time to build a new clubhouse. Therefore, the committee recommends that the motion to build a new clubhouse not be adopted [or, that it be rejected]."

CHAIR: "You have heard the unfavorable report [or, recommendation] of the committee. The question now before the house [note carefully the language used on unfavorable recommendations] is on the original motion to build a new clubhouse, the recommendation of the committee to the contrary notwithstanding. Is there any discussion on the motion to build a new club house?" After discussion or amendments, if any, the motion is put to vote and it is voted to build or not to build. The words "the recommendation of the committee to the contrary notwithstanding" serve to indicate, for the information of the body, the attitude of the committee on the motion given; hence, if these words are inadvertently or conveniently omitted from the motion when stated by the Chair (as is nearly always done except in legislatures) it would make no difference whatsoever. Similar procedure and action follow all other unfavorable recommendations.

Practical method of acting on committee reports. Where the necessary technical knowledge in acting on recommendations in the reports of committees as shown in the last section is lacking, here is a practical yet authoritative method of acting on such committee reports (this form has legislative authority and sanction, being used in state legislatures):

CHAIR: "Is the committee on [such-and-such] matter prepared to report?"

COMMITTEE CHAIRMAN: "Mr. Chairman, the committee appointed to do . . . [specifies] reports . . . [states committee's attitude]." Or, "The committee to whom [or, to which] was referred the matter of . . . [naming it] recommends . . . [favorably or unfavorably]."

CHAIR: "The question is on the acceptance of the report of the committee. Is there any discussion on the motion to accept the report of the committee?" (After discussion and amendments, if any, the motion to accept is put to vote, and it is then voted to accept or not to accept whatever the committee reported.)

In other words, instead of acting on reports of the committee in the technical manner illustrated earlier, the equivalent form of the technical procedure is to move "to accept the report of the committee," by which is meant that the recommendation of the committee, whether it be favorable or unfavorable, is thereby approved, and that ends it.

To defend a report on the floor. The member designated to present and defend the committee's report should be fortified with necessary arguments in support of the committee's report. Therefore, the member chosen to report should be thoroughly familiar and in accord with the contents of the report. Committee members should be alert, and should be prepared to rise to engage in debate and assist the reporting member when necessary, and to enlighten the body in defense of the committee's report whenever the report is attacked or weakened on the floor of the meeting. Members of the committee can be "planted" in advance in strategic locations in the hall in order to thus draw backing and neighborly sentiment for their side. The opposition can employ the same strategy.

When the committee faces unexpectedly strong opposition by an apparent majority, it may, if it appears expedient, move to recommit the report and afterward modify it in committee to improve it or to meet the demands of the majority. To recommit may be proposed by anyone.

Note: All reports that are made by boards and committees are in the nature of incidental main motions; they are subject to the same rules (S, D, A, M, R) as main or principal motions. Hence they can be amended, postponed, recommitted, and tabled, and debate thereon can be limited, etc.

Committee amendments on top of the assembly's amendments. If a question when referred to a committee has amendments pending and the committee reports back a further amendment, then when the question is transacted before the body, the amendments that were pending are acted on first (that is, debated, amended, and voted on), and then the amendment of the committee; thus:

COMMITTEE CHAIRMAN: "Mr. Chairman, the committee to whom was referred the main motion to build a new clubhouse, and the pending amendment 'in Washington, D. C.,' recommends that the motion be further amended by adding the words 'provided the cost does not exceed one hundred thousand dollars,' and as thus amended, the motion with its pending amendment be adopted."

CHAIR: "The first question is on the adoption of the motion's pending amendment to add the words "in Washington, D. C." (Put to vote and adopted; then he proceeds:) "The question now is on the adoption of the committee's amendment to add the words 'provided the cost does not exceed one hundred thousand dollars.' " This amendment is then put to a vote, after which the main motion as amended is put to a vote in due course.

Amendments of assembly on top of committee amendments. If a question when referred to a committee does not carry any amendments with it, and the committee decides to report out an amendment, when the question is transacted before the body the amendment of the committee is disposed of first, then further amendments can be proposed by the body; thus:

COMMITTEE CHAIRMAN: "Mr. Chairman, the committee to whom was referred the motion to build a new clubhouse for one hundred thousand dollars recommends that the motion be amended by striking out one hundred thousand dollars and inserting eighty-five thousand dollars, and that, as thus amended, the motion be adopted." (He can add:) "Therefore, by direction of the committee, I move to amend the motion by striking out the words 'one hundred thousand dollars' and inserting in place thereof the words 'eighty-five thousand dollars.'"

CHAIR: "You have heard the amendment proposed by the committee. The question is on its adoption." (He puts it to vote, and after it is out of the way, the original motion is then open to further amendments, after which the Chair puts it to a vote as amended or not in due course.)

When only one primary amendment is pending on a question before the body, a germane secondary amendment is always in order irrespective of whether it is proposed on top of a committee amendment or on one of the assembly — just like on main motions.

Majority report. The report of the committee is frequently referred to as the majority report to distinguish it from a minority report. Precisely speaking, however, the majority report is properly known as committee report.

Form of majority report. The language used in reporting for the committee can be as follows: "The committee to whom [or, to which; both are correct] was referred [such-and-such] question, respectfully reports as follows . . ." (citing the conclusion or recommendation on the question considered). The report may, when befitting, end thus: "Respectfully submitted." It is signed. The word "Respectfully" is not required, but is courteous.

By whom signed. Usually, all members concurring in it sign the report of the committee, or they can authorize the chairman to sign alone; his title, "Chairman," appears on the report after his name, when he signs it alone. But when all names appear on the report, the word "Chairman" is usually omitted, it being understood that the first name is that of the chairman, thus eliminating distinction among members engaged in the same task.

Chairman's name at the top. When committee names are listed on a report, the chairman's name belongs always at the top of the list, never at the bottom (it is unparliamentary and an act of false modesty to list the chairman's name at the end). All reports in the Congress, in parliaments, in state legislatures and well-governed assemblies list the chairman's name first, then the others.

Minority report. A minority report of dissenting members is as natural and logical as a dissenting opinion of a member in an assembly. Hard feeling is therefore as out of place in the one as it is in the other case.

If committee's chairman is of minority. The chairman of the committee usually makes the committee's report. But if he is not in favor of the report, the committee appoints another member who *is* in favor of it to make the report.

Form of minority report. The language of a minority report is as follows: "The undersigned members not agreeing with the views of the majority respectfully submit the following minority report . . . [citing it]."

Minority report treated as substitute. The most efficient method of considering a minority report is to move to substitute the minority report for the report of the committee.

In other words, whoever is placed in charge of the minority report should be on guard to note when the majority report of the committee is called for, and as soon as it is stated by the Chair he should rise at once and move to substitute the minority report for the report of the committee. (If this is not *then* done, its precious advantage is sidestepped and confusion will follow.) Such motion is then treated as a motion to substitute. Note the timing of the minority in proposing their motion to substitute:

CHAIR: "Is the committee which was appointed to consider the advisability of constructing a new clubhouse ready to report?"

COMMITTEE CHAIRMAN: "Mr. President, the committee considered the matter and has come to a favorable conclusion. Therefore, on behalf [or, by direction] of the committee, I move that we construct a new clubhouse at a cost not to exceed $175,000." (A second is not necessary on committee motions, recommendations or reports, but the Chair may state them as though seconded; thus:)

CHAIR: "It has been moved and seconded that we construct a new clubhouse at a cost not to exceed $175,000. Is there any discussion on the committee's motion?"

MINORITY MEMBER: "Mr. Chairman, I move to *substitute* for the committee's majority motion the following motion of the minority, namely, that the sum of eleven thousand dollars be appropriated from the general fund to remodel and repair our present quarters."

CHAIR: "It has been moved and seconded to substitute for the committee's majority motion the substitute motion of the minority" (repeating the above substitute).

After debate or amendments on the majority's motion first, the minority's substitute is then open to debate and amendment. When ready for the vote, the substitute motion is put to a vote first, because it is in the nature of an amendment. If the substitute is adopted, it replaces the committee's motion in due course, just like any other substitute amendment. But if the substitute is defeated, the committee's motion is then put to a vote in due course for adoption or rejection.

Alternative: Treat minority report as amendment. Another way of considering a minority motion besides *substituting* it for the majority's motion is to amend the *majority* recommendation by striking it out in its entirety and inserting in its place the *minority's* report. The minority's such proposal is then transacted as an amendment, and not as a substitute. This is a more direct or more practical way; thus:

COMMITTEE CHAIRMAN: "Mr. President, by direction of the committee I move acceptance of its report, namely, to construct a new clubhouse for $175,000."

CHAIR: "It has been moved and seconded that . . . [repeats the motion]. Is there any discussion on the majority report?"

MINORITY MEMBER: "Mr. President, two of the seven members of the committee do not agree with the views of the majority, and wish to submit a minority report. Therefore, I move to *amend* the majority report [to construct a new clubhouse, etc.] by striking it out in its entirety and inserting in place thereof the words "to remodel and repair the clubhouse for $11,000.'" (Seconded.)

CHAIR: "It is moved and seconded to amend the pending motion by striking it out in its entirety and inserting in lieu thereof the minority's amendment 'to remodel and repair the clubhouse for $11,000.'" (This amendment is then put to vote and adopted or defeat d in due course.)

Chairman thanks the committee. Upon completion of their assignment or their tenure of service, the Chair expresses to the committee his appreciation and the assembly's for a job well done.

IV. INFORMAL CONSIDERATION

Assemblies with 13 or fewer members in attendance almost invariably conduct business informally. Those with more than 13 members present are supposed to conduct business formally. But they may conduct all their proceedings and transact business either way, regardless of the number of members present, if no objection is made.

Limitations of informal consideration. Considering a piece of business informally does not mean that members can avoid doing things the right way at meetings, or that they can disregard or ignore propriety of language, or conduct; or that members are thereby "licensed" to do and say whatever they wish. They must still obtain the floor in turn with the other members wishing to take the floor, and still discuss the main motion germanely and without reference to personalities; and still amend the pending question correctly and appropriately; and all this because there is no easier or surer way to deliberate upon and to transact a piece of business than by observance of the rules and proprieties of parliamentary etiquette.

Object of informal consideration. The object of considering a question informally is to permit the members to discuss the question at issue and amendments to it with greater freedom than the formal rules of the assembly allow — the same as in a committee of the whole, but with these important differences:

(1) The permanent presiding officer himself presides in the informal consideration of a question, whereas in a committee of the whole the permanent presiding officer surrenders the chair to another to preside.

(2) In informal consideration of a question any and all subsidiary motions may be proposed on the pending question, whereas in a committee of the whole only *one* of the subsidiary motions can be proposed: to amend the pending main question.

(3) In informal consideration the members are at liberty to debate only the pending question and its amendments, as many times and for as long as they wish, in turn with one another, but the motion to postpone and to refer may not be debated therein more than two times or longer

than ten minutes each time, whereas in a committee of the whole the motions to postpone and refer cannot be entertained at all.

Two methods of informal consideration. The same rules apply to both.

(1) Without first proposing the question formally, members can start discussing the question, although the question is not yet actually pending before the body. When the question has been fully discussed and amended, a motion is then made to adopt it, and the vote is formally taken and the result announced. And this ends it.

(2) The question is *first* proposed, as for example: "Mr. Chairman, I move that we consider informally [or, I move informal consideration of] the motion to sell our clubhouse." The Chair states it when seconded and asks: "Is there any discussion on the informal consideration of the question to sell the clubhouse?" Members then can discuss the motion, in turn with one another, as many times and for as long each time as desired, until the question has been sufficiently debated, or up to a point where it is voted to end further debate, which can be proposed at any time. The question is then put to a vote. And this ends the consideration.

V. COMMITTEE OF THE WHOLE (S, D, A, M, R)

Instead of referring or transferring a question to a committee, the assembly has the power, by a majority vote, to act as a committee itself; that is, it has the right to constitute itself into a "committee of the whole" (meaning the entire or whole body) for the purpose of considering any desired question.

Form of the motion. The old English form of the motion is: "That the house do now resolve itself into a Committee of the Whole to take into consideration . . ." (naming it). The modern form is: "That the body [or, assembly] constitute itself a committee of the whole to consider . . ." (naming it). Another or a simpler form is "That we go into a committee of the whole." Or, "I move to refer . . . [a pending question] to a committee of the whole."

Why go into committee of the whole. While the body has the right to go into a committee of the whole to consider any question whatsoever, from a specific standpoint it would ordinarily do so (a) because the question to be considered is of extremely compelling or unusual nature: or (b) because the question is one of great importance or urgency and a decision must be arrived at while the body is still in session; or (c) to afford the members greater freedom in debate.

The primary reason for going into such committee is to obtain greater freedom in the discussion of urgent or engrossing questions. That is, since members, while the body is in formal session, may not speak more than the prescribed number of times or length of debate on a question if anyone objects to more times, to make it possible for members to consider a question with the freedom of an ordinary committee and to discuss a question many times if they so desire, in rightful turn with the other members, parliamentary law invented the proceeding known as "committee of the whole." This proceeding is frequently used in legislative bodies, but rarely resorted to in ordinary assemblies.

How transacted. As soon as it has been voted to "go into a committee of the whole," unless it is otherwise specified in the bylaws or is practiced differently by custom and usage, the organization's presiding officer designates another member to act as chairman of the committee of the whole, and the following steps or proceedings take place:

(1) The presiding officer of the organization then surrenders the gavel and his chair to the chairman, and takes a seat either among the members, or remains on the platform or near the rostrum.

(2) The chairman then calls the committee to order, and states the question or proposition which the body authorized the committee to consider; thus: "The committee of the whole will be in order. The question before the committee is . . . [stating it, or it is read by the secretary]. Is there any debate?" Members may then debate it.

(3) When the committee's task or assignment has been completed, and it wishes to make its report to the main body, a motion is made "to rise and report" (equivalent to adjourning the committee).

(4) The moment the motion to rise and report is carried, the regular presiding officer immediately takes the gavel and resumes presiding over the main body.

(5) It is then the duty of the committee chairman to report for the committee, just as is done by chairmen of other committees; namely: (a) the committee can recommend adoption or rejection of the proposition or subject assigned to it to consider; (b) it can recommend amendments to it or propose a substitute amendment to it, just as other committees may do; or (c) if it has come to no decision for or against the subject referred to it, then it so reports to the body; and it may ask leave to reconvene.

Motions that cannot be acted on. Committees of the whole cannot appoint subcommittees and cannot go into executive (secret) session — all other committees can.

Motions that can be acted on. The following motions or proceedings are in order in a committee of the whole:

1. To vote to recommend the adoption or rejection of the question referred to it (just as is done in other committees).

2. To recommend amendments to the question (or a substitute motion in place of it, as other committees do).

3. To rise and report (the equivalent of to adjourn; "rise and report" is the technical form).

4. And the following incidental motions: (a) an appeal from the decision of the Chair; (b) doubting the presence of a quorum; (c) doubting the vote on a question; (d) a point of order, or point of clarification; (e) a parliamentary inquiry; (f) a question of information; and (g) a secret ballot (but not a roll call).

In other words, the body, when acting as a committee of the whole, may, strictly speaking, transact only the motions or proceedings mentioned just above, except in cases where the organization's laws specify to the contrary or as they may otherwise provide.

Hence it is not in order in committee of the whole to entertain any privileged motion (p. 47), such as to recess, call for the orders of the day, etc., or to entertain any subsidiary motion (p. 47) excepting amendments to the pending proposition or question.

Authority to make exceptions. However, when the need arises in the course of the committee's proceedings for proposing some motion not allowed by the above rules, the committee of the whole must receive authority from the body, which may be done either (a) while the *body* is in session and prior to constituting itself as a committee of the whole, or (b) while the *committee* of the whole is in session, by voting to rise and report (that is, to adjourn), and then apply to the body for further authority or greater rights in any respect desired. Upon obtaining from the body such further authority or greater rights, the body then reconstitutes itself as a committee of the whole and continues its sitting.

The committee can repeat the process of applying for additional powers or authority from the body whenever the exigency arises in the course of its proceedings.

Action by the body. If the committee chairman reports out the proposition without any amendments, the presiding officer states as the question before the assembly the original question "as was" when referred to the committee of the whole, which is then open to debate and amendment, and the body votes upon it in due course.

If the chairman reports back an amendment to it, the amendment is then acted on by the body, following which the body acts upon the question as amended (or as further amended by the body).

If the chairman reports back a substitute to the original proposition or subject, the Chair applies the substitute procedure to it, and the substitute is voted adopted or rejected in due course.

If the chairman reports back or recommends rejection of the subject referred to it, the body can accept the rejection of the report or recommendation of the chairman, or it may amend it to suit and then adopt it, notwithstanding the committee's recommendation to the contrary.

Records. The organization's secretary does not keep minutes of the proceedings of a committee of the whole. He records only the fact of the reference of the question to the committee, the committee's report thereon to the body, and the action on it taken by the body after the committee of the whole has made its report.

Secrecy. One notable advantage in going into a committee of the whole is the secrecy of its proceedings. This is especially true in public bodies such as legislatures, city councils, etc., because only the members comprising the committee can be present, and any others who are non-members or who have no business with the committee are excluded from its deliberations.

Quorum in committee of the whole. The quorum of a committee of the whole is the same as in the assembly, unless otherwise prescribed by rule, bylaw or long established custom and usage. When a quorum is lacking, at any time, and the fact is disclosed or challenged, the committee terminates its sitting, reports the fact to the assembly, and the assembly then takes such action as it deems necessary and proper.

Chair of body may restore order. Whenever a committee of the whole becomes disorderly or its chairman is unable to bring it under control, the assembly's presiding officer has inherent power to step in, take the gavel from the chairman and attempt to restore order, or dissolve the committee, thus: "The committee of the whole is hereby dissolved on account of disorder." (Such dissolution does not thereby also dissolve or adjourn the assembly. Instead, the presiding officer calls the assembly to order, admonishes it discreetly and then hands the gavel back to the committee chairman.)

Illustration of committee of the whole. The procedure in creating a committee of the whole body and the committee's subsequent proceedings are substantially as follows — for which purpose assume the following main question being debated before the assembly: "That this organization join the World Federation of Law and Order."

PRESIDENT: "Is there any further debate on this question?"

MEMBER A: "Mr. President, this is an extremely important question, and it is conceivable that members may want to discuss its merits more times or at a greater length than the formal rules of the assembly permit.

"Therefore, I move that we go into a committee of the whole to consider this question."

PRESIDENT: "Is there a second to the motion?"

VOICES: "I second the motion."

PRESIDENT: "It has been moved and seconded that the assembly go into a committee of the whole to consider the pending question. Is there any discussion on this motion?" (After discussion thereon, the vote follows:)

PRESIDENT: "Those in favor of going into a committee of the whole will say aye; those opposed will say no. The ayes have it, and the assembly will now go into a committee of the whole."

The Chair then designates a chairman for the committee. He says:

PRESIDENT: "The Chair appoints Mr. Lodge as chairman of the committee of the whole." (Hands him the gavel and leaves the chair.)

CHAIRMAN LODGE (who now assumes the chair): "The question before the committee is that we join the World Federation of Law and Order. Is there any debate?" (After considerable debate, Member B obtains the floor and makes the following motion:)

MEMBER B: "Mr. Chairman, I move to *table* the question." (Seconded.)

CHAIRMAN: "The motion just proposed is out of order, because under the rules, the motion to lay on the table cannot be entertained in a committee of the whole. Is there further discussion on the pending question?" (When discussion on the question appears to have ended, the Chair can say:) "If there is no further discussion, the Chair will put the question to vote." (Instead of the Chair himself thus expediting it, a member can move to "recommend adoption of the question," which is then put to vote in due course.)

The committee is now ready to rise and report; hence the following procedure ("rise and report" means adjourn):

MEMBER C: "Mr. Chairman, I move that the committee rise and report."

VOICES: "I second it."

CHAIRMAN: "It has been moved and seconded that the committee rise and report." (Put to vote and adopted; thus:) "The ayes have it, and the motion is adopted." (Whereupon the permanent presiding officer immediately advances to the chair, takes back the gavel and resumes presiding, pausing until the committee chairman has returned to his seat and, if the committee chairman does not address the Chair first for recognition, the Chair himself says:)

CHAIRMAN: "The Chair now recognizes Mr. Lodge, chairman of the committee of the whole."

LODGE: "Mr. President, the committee of the whole has had under consideration the question that this organization join the World Federation of Law and Order. The committee recommends [or, voted to recommend] that the question be adopted." (Sits.)

PRESIDENT (purely by way of preliminary information to the body prior to formal action on the question): "You have heard the favorable report [or, recommendation] of the committee of the whole. The question is on the adoption of the original question; namely . . . [repeats original motion]. Is there further discussion on the question?" (It is open to further discussion and amendment by the body because it is a main motion; and then the vote:) "Those in favor of the motion," etc. "Those opposed," etc. "The ayes have it, and the question is adopted, and this organization will join," etc.

In more formal bodies, as in legislatures, where the direct words "you" and "your" are not permitted, the Chair (in transacting the proceeding illustrated just above) omits the phrase "You have heard the favorable report [or, recommendation] of the committee," and directly says: "The question is on the motion that this organization join . . . " etc., which is then put to vote.

Quasi-committee of the whole. This proceeding, popular in the U. S. Senate, is scarcely ever used in ordinary assemblies, whereas a straight "committee of the whole" and "informal consideration" are not uncommon practices in organizations.

When the body decides to consider a question in a quasi-committee of the whole, the permanent presiding officer does not surrender the chair to another to preside. Instead, he himself presides — as is the case in informal consideration, but unlike in a committee of the whole, in which he would surrender the chair to another to preside.

The question considered in a quasi-committee of the whole is open to debate and amendment, and the members may speak in turn as often and for as long as they desire on the question, just as is done in a committee of the whole, and it is then put to a final vote.

Note: The word *quasi* (Lat.) means "as if." Hence a member can say "I move that we sit as a quasi-committee," or "I move that the assembly, convention, annual meeting, etc. sit as if in committee of the whole."

VI. PUBLIC HEARINGS

Basic rules. Public hearings before committees (or boards, commissions, etc., whether they be of the legislature, city council, school committee, selectmen, etc.) are governed by the committee's rules.

Speakers give their name and residence to the committee, and they address all their remarks on pending matters to the committee and not to the audience or spectators in the committee room. Committee members can ask questions of all speakers.

Recording the proceedings. The clerk or secretary records the name and address of all speakers appearing before the committee. An efficient clerk also records briefly the gist of their arguments or testimony before the committee (which the committee members can afterward use in the main body in debate on the question).

Members of the committee can also keep a memorandum of the arguments advanced by speakers for their information, and for use thereof whenever need be outside the organization (as guest speakers before interested groups, PTAs, leagues of voters, etc.)

Maintaining order. Observance of order and decorum is essential, and when seriously breached or threatened, the chairman admonishes the offenders, and, when necessary, may exclude them from the hearing room; or he may take such further steps as in sound judgment he and the committee may deem expedient or appropriate.

Affirmative and negative side. The affirmative side is heard first, one speaker at a time, then the negative side.

Procedure at public hearings. The procedure at public hearings is substantially as follows:

CHAIRMAN: "The hearing will be in order. The first matter [question, proposition, etc.] before this committee is . . . [states it]. First, are there any speakers for the affirmative?"

MR. A: "Mr. Chairman and members of the committee, my name is [states it] and my address is [gives it]. I am wholeheartedly in favor of the question." (He then gives his reasons and sits.)

CHAIRMAN: "Are there further speakers for the affirmative?"

MRS. B: "Mr. Chairman, I am Mrs. A. B. of 123 First Street. I urge the committee to act favorably upon this matter for the following reasons: in the first place, . . .; in the second place, . . ." etc. (She resumes her seat.)

Chairman continues the same process; and when the affirmative side has been heard he says:

CHAIRMAN: "If there are no further speakers for the affirmative, the negative side will now be heard."

MR. C: "Mr. Chairman and members of the committee. I am opposed to this question . . ." (interrupted by the chairman).

CHAIR: "Will you please state your name and address?"

MR. C: "I beg the committee's pardon. My name is . . . and my address is . . . I am opposed to the question because . . ." (he gives reasons, after which he returns to his seat).

CHAIR: "Are there any other speakers for the negative side?"

MISS D: "Mr. Chairman and ladies and gentlemen of the committee, my name is . . . , and my address . . . ; I wish to speak against this proposal . . ." (She gives reasons, and then returns to her seat).

CHAIRMAN: "Are there any others who wish to speak?" (When there is no response he says:) "Both sides having been heard, the hearing on this matter is closed," or, "The committee will now go into executive session," or, "The committee will now take up the next matter before the committee, which is [names it]."

Executive committee session. When the committee chairman says, "The committee will now go into executive session," it is the signal for all present to depart from the meeting room except members of the

committee and such others as have been invited to be present by the
committee.

Chapter 21
CONVENTIONS AND ANNUAL MEETINGS

All the rules applicable to convention procedure (including convention
rules) also govern annual meetings. All sittings of the convention session
or annual meeting constitute a single whole session or meeting under
that call.

Convention business may not commence or continue until it has been
duly organized.

What business can be considered. If the bylaws provide for an annua
meeting and a special or particular business is prescribed in the call for
that meeting, the business of the meeting is strictly that prescribed in
the call of the meeting or in the bylaws and no other.

Thus, if the bylaws prescribe that "The annual meeting shall be for
the purpose of (1) electing officers, (2) choosing standing committees,
and (3) electing three national delegates," the business of the meeting is
confined strictly to those three matters; but if the bylaws read that "The
annual meeting shall be for the purpose of (1) electing officers, (2) choosing standing committees, (3) electing three national delegates, and
(4) any other business that may properly come before it," then, in addition to the election of officers and delegates and the selection of standing
committees, any other business within the scope and objects of the
organization can be transacted, except business that requires but does
not have previous notice.

The permissive clause. If the clause "and for such other business as
may legally come before the said meeting" is not a part of the bylaw
providing for the annual meeting, other business than election of officers,
committees and delegates could not be acted on at the annual meeting;
but the permissive clause "and any other business," etc., allows the
transaction of further business besides that specified, provided it relates
to the objects, scope and purpose of the organization.

Note: If business other than that specified in the bylaws is proposed,unless
a point of order is raised to prevent it or unless it is reconsidered or rescinded
during the session, the action taken is considered legal and valid upon final
adjournment. But if the bylaws say: "Business not specified shall not be
acted on," then no unspecified business can be transacted. But if it is necessary to act on unpermitted business, move to ratify it at the next meeting.

Delegates and Alternates

Definition of delegate. In its parliamentary sense, a delegate is one
sent and empowered to *represent* and perform a duty for others — for his
lodge, chapter, council, post, local, unit, etc.

Definition of alternate. An alternate is one sent and authorized to take
the place of a delegate, if need be, in performing a duty.

Authority of delegates. Unless instructed otherwise, delegates can exercise full authority in the duty to be performed.

When delegates are under instructions. (1) If the organization (lodge, chapter, etc.) has a bylaw or standing rule requiring delegates to vote as instructed by the body, delegates elected under such compelling authority are automatically under legal obligation to obey the assembly's instructions. (2) If there is no such bylaw or rule, but delegates are elected with the prior understanding (or by prior order or adopted motion) that they will vote as instructed, such elected delegates are similarly under legal obligation to vote as the assembly may instruct them. (3) If there is no such compelling bylaw, rule or prior understanding, and after the election for delegates has been held a motion is adopted instructing the delegates about their vote at the convention, such belated instructions are purely recommendatory or advisory, and are not binding upon the delegates, who may ignore them with no risk of penalty, since their election was not predicated upon having to abide by any instructions. (4) Where there is no compelling bylaw or standing rule as to how delegates shall vote, and a motion is proposed or adopted before the election takes place instructing delegates as to their vote, if a nominee-delegate announces *before* the election that he will not be bound by instructions and the body nevertheless elects him as a delegate, such delegate is then not under legal obligation to abide by any given instructions.

Penalty for failure to obey instructions. If a delegate who is under legal obligation to obey instructions by virtue of a bylaw, standing rule or order of the assembly (as in instances 1 and 2 in the preceding paragraph) disobeys or violates imposed instructions, he may be penalized as the assembly may decide, as by censure, suspension or other penalty not barred by a bylaw.

Authority of alternates. An alternate can exercise the same authority, and to the same extent, as the delegate he replaces. In a convention or annual meeting, (1) the alternate takes the place of a delegate who is absent from the convention or from a sitting of a convention. (2) The alternate has no authority whatever to act when his delegate is present; he is silent. (3) If the alternate in the delegate's absence from a meeting casts his vote on a question, and the delegate upon his return disapproves, the delegate can reverse that vote, provided he does so *before* the voting on that question has ended, by casting it himself — as when there is a retake of the vote thereon, or the roll call on it has not ended, etc., but he cannot reverse that vote on a secret ballot if the alternate has already cast his vote or has parted with his ballot. (4) Alternates must register the same as the delegates before they can qualify to act as delegates. (5) Alternates usually sit in a separate section from that of the delegates. (6) If the delegate is chosen convention officer, such as chairman, secretary, etc., the alternate cannot assume the delegate's *office* when the delegate is absent from the room, nor may he act as delegate while the delegate occupies such office and is present in the room.

Unit rule. The unit rule, so called, used in conventions of many deliberative bodies in the United States, allows a delegation to cast its *entire* vote as the majority of its delegates shall decide, regardless of any preference the minority may have.

Therefore, when the unit rule has been canonically imposed upon a delegation by its lodge, chapter, post, local, unit or other authority, a majority of its delegates can cast the *entire* vote of the delegation for a nominee, or any issue, regardless of the number of its delegates absent or the number refusing to vote.

A Model Set of Convention Rules

Well-governed societies adopt convention rules for the guidance and orderly government of delegates, thus enabling them to achieve maximum business within the minimum time of the convention period. Adoption of these rules shall be the convention's first business in order. The set below can be enlarged upon or altered to suit.

1. The convention shall be composed of [state its composition].

2. All provisions of the constitution and bylaws shall govern, and are hereby incorporated by reference.

3. *Demeter's Manual* shall be the parliamentary authority in all cases not governed by the constitution and bylaws.

4. In cases where neither the constitution and bylaws nor said Manual cover a given question, the convention shall decide the same.

5. Delegates shall register promptly upon arrival and shall attend all sessions of the conventions.

6. The Credentials Committee shall report at the opening sitting, and periodically thereafter, or when directed to do so.

7. Addresses or greetings of officials and guest speakers shall take place [specify when].

8. Nominations of officers shall take place [state when].

9. Nominating speeches shall not exceed five minutes each, and not more than two seconding speeches of two minutes each shall be allowed.

10. Election of officers shall take place [state when].

11. In the event of a tie vote on election to any office, unless otherwise covered by the constitution and bylaws, the principal candidates in issue may, by mutual consent, and with the approval of the body, draw lots or flip a coin. Only those offices shall be affected as result in a tie.

12. The presiding officer shall enforce order and decorum at all times and shall require observance of same for the expeditious and orderly transaction of business.

13. No delegate shall be entitled to the floor unless he rises, addresses the presiding officer and gives his name and unit [post, chapter, lodge, state, etc.].

14. Debate shall be limited to five minutes a speaker. No delegate shall speak a second time to the same question the same day, if another delegate who has not spoken thereon rises and asks for the floor. No delegate shall speak more than twice on the same question if anyone objects.

15. All resolutions shall be in writing and shall be signed. Main motions shall be put in writing when the Chair so directs.

16. No motion shall be entertained by the Chair unless seconded, nor shall it be open to debate or amendment before the Chair has repeated it to the assembly.

17. Delegates shall rise to second motions in convention, and shall also rise when wishing to doubt or challenge the vote.

18. Roll call or secret ballot on any question shall not be taken except by majority vote of the convention, unless otherwise specifically authorized by existing rule, or unless by general consent.

19. On roll call, the presiding officer's name shall be called last [unless otherwise authorized by a bylaw or rule], and he may, *after* examining the result, vote or not on a question, as he may determine. But on a secret ballot he shall vote, if he wishes to, when the members also vote, not thereafter. He may cast the deciding vote on any question, provided he has not already voted on it [unless the bylaws otherwise specify].

20. The vote on a question, once commenced, shall not be interrupted, except only by a request that the question be restated or clarified by the Chair, so that members can vote intelligently on it.

21. A delegate may change his vote from one side of the question to the other, provided he rises and asks for the floor promptly as soon as the voting process ends and before the Chair declares, or is about to declare, the result on that question. A delegate may not change his vote if something or some act has intervened or been taken up after the voting process has ended on a question, even though the final result has not been determined or announced yet. If, for instance, tabulation of the vote is awaited, and guest speakers are heard or some business is transacted in the interim, or a recess is taken while the votes are being counted by the tellers, it is then too late to vote or to change one's vote.

22. Claims of fraud, illegalities or irregularities or other parliamentary misfeasance must be raised promptly and while the convention is in session. After final adjournment of the convention all such claims shall be ignored.

23. Appeals from decisions of the Chair should be based upon a point of order. The appeal shall be seconded. When an appeal is taken, the vote shall be put not on whether or not to sustain the member's appeal, but whether or not to sustain the decision of the Chair. If a majority of the votes cast disapproves the decision, then the Chair's decision is reversed, otherwise the decision stands in all cases; a tie vote sustains the decision of the Chair. The Chair can vote on appeals.

24. Not more than two amendments to any question shall be pending at one time; but after disposal of one or both of them, additional amendments may be proposed.

25. Motions and amendments shall be open to debate and amendment until put to vote, unless the previous question is ordered ending the debate before then.

26. Reconsideration in convention shall not be entertained unless proposed by one who voted with the prevailing side; it may be acted on either the same day the original question was acted on or on the very next working day — not counting days devoted only to socials, or exhibits, excursions, etc. To rescind applies thereafter. If reconsideration is defeated, to rescind shall not be in order at the same sitting. No question shall be reconsidered at the last sitting of the convention except by unanimous consent. The same question shall not be reconsidered more than once.

27. A bylaw which has been defeated can be reconsidered; but a bylaw which was adopted shall not be subject to reconsideration, regardless of when it is to go into effect, except by unanimous consent, because bylaws take effect upon their adoption, unless otherwise specified at the time or unless the bylaws otherwise prescribe.

28. Motions to lay on the table and the previous question shall be undebatable and unamendable. Motions to postpone, commit or recommit

are subject to both debate and amendment. All shall require a majority vote.

29. The convention may, to expedite business, limit equally the time for debate or the *number* of speakers for each side on a question, or the *total* time for debate thereon, by a ⅔ vote.

30. Officers' reports shall be signed and be read [state when].

31. Chairmen of committees may make partial reports during lull periods of the convention, unless otherwise ordered. Resolutions rejected by committees shall not be read to the convention unless asked for by their proposers or other members.

32. The motion to adjourn shall not be in order between sittings of the convention session; to recess shall be used instead. To adjourn shall be in order on the last convention sitting and shall be undebatable and un-amendable if other business is actually pending. To recess shall be undebatable if other business is actually pending at any time, but it is amendable at any time.

33. These rules shall be adopted by a majority vote; but they may be suspended, rescinded or amended after their adoption by a ⅔ vote.

Add any further rules your organization may need.

Transacting Resolutions in Conventions

Basic rules. Resolutions are debatable, amendable, and require a majority vote for adoption. They can be reconsidered. They are treated exactly like main motions because they are main motions and are subject to the same rules. Hence, they can be amended, postponed, tabled, recommitted (referred back to the same committee), etc.

Members have a right to take a rejected resolution to the floor of the convention unless barred in advance by a ⅔ vote of the convention.

The Chair should announce to the body when rejected resolutions may be taken up for consideration by the body.

Committee on Resolutions reports to the floor. In conventions, annual meetings or conferences of large organizations where action is swift and procedure rapid, resolutions which have been acted on by the Committee on Resolutions can be reported back on the floor of the convention in any number of ways — the best way being dependent on the time available, mood of the assembly, time of day, kind of weather, etc. But a quick and effective way is as follows:

Report only the favorable resolutions; that is, those recommended by the Committee for adoption, and those amended by the Committee, and no others; omit those rejected; thus:

CONVENTION CHAIRMAN: "The Chair will now call on the chairman of the Committee on Resolutions, Mr. Set."

RESOLUTIONS CHAIRMAN: "Mr. Chairman, for the information of the body, I should like to state that in order to expedite the business of the convention, only the resolutions favorably acted upon by the Committee will be reported on, and they will be put to vote collectively at the end in order to conserve time, unless there is objection. Afterward, members who wish to can call for any resolution not reported." (He pauses for possible objection, since this must meet with the approval of the body; and if no objection is then raised and no motion is made to consider them in a different manner, which the body can order by a majority vote, he continues:)

RESOLUTIONS CHAIRMAN: "Mr. Chairman, seventy-four resolutions in all were submitted to the committee, twelve of which have been approved. They are as follows:

"Resolution 1, submitted by Mr. A: *Resolved*, That this convention commends the courage of the Congress in . . ." etc. (The vote is not taken separately on each resolution; all will be voted on together at the end, as agreed just above.)

"Resolution 2, submitted by Mr. B: *Resolved*, That . . ." etc.

"Resolution 3, submitted by Mr. C: *Resolved*, That . . ." etc.

"Resolution 4, submitted by Mr. D, as amended by the committee: *Resolved*, That . . ." etc. (Committees can amend submitted resolutions.)

After each resolution is read, it is open to debate and amendment — just like any other main question before the assembly. The "whereases" need not be read unless asked for.

When all the favorable resolutions have been read, the Committee chairman moves their adoption collectively (if they were not previously voted on individually); thus:

RESOLUTIONS CHAIRMAN: "Mr. Chairman, by direction of the Committee on Resolutions, I move the adoption of the resolutions just read." (No second is necessary, since a committee recommends them, and the Chair puts them to vote collectively, thus:)

CONVENTION CHAIRMAN: "The question is on the adoption of the resolutions just read. Those in favor of their adoption will say aye; those opposed will say no. The ayes have it, and the resolutions are adopted."

Any resolution can be postponed, tabled, reconsidered, etc.

Procedure on rejected resolutions. As soon as the above vote has been completed, members whose resolutions have been rejected, or which have not been reported, can call up their resolution for action on the floor of the convention, thus:

MEMBER A: "Mr. Chairman, I call up the resolution which I submitted relating to the annexation of the Territory of [name] as a State." (No second is necessary merely to call it up.)

CONVENTION CHAIRMAN: "The chairman of the Committee on Resolutions will read the member's resolution."

COMMITEE CHAIRMAN (reading it): "*Resolved*, That it is the sense of this convention that the Territory of [name] be made a state of the United States." (At this stage, the author of the resolution should, strictly speaking, rise and move the adoption of his resolution — the Chair is not duty bound to do so himself — thus:)

MEMBER A: "Mr. Chairman, that's my resolution! I move its adoption." It must be seconded before it can be entertained.

CHAIR: "It has been moved and seconded to adopt the following resolution: *Resolved*, That it is the sense of this convention that the Territory of [name] be admitted as a state, the recommendation of the Committee on Resolutions to the contrary notwithstanding. Is there any discussion?" (And here he recognizes first the author of the resolution who speaks on his proposal; then he assigns the floor to the Resolutions chairman who defends the Committee's report and gives reasons for rejecting it, if he cares to do so, and then recognizes such other members as desire to discuss it, after which the vote is taken, thus:)

CHAIR: "Those in favor of the adoption of the resolution will say aye; those opposed will say no. The ayes [or, noes] have it, and the resolution is adopted [or, lost]." The same procedure is pursued for other resolutions rejected by the Committee.

Scheduling reporting of Committee's work. Resolutions can be reported after completion of the Committee's entire work, or they can be reported on as completed from meeting to meeting, as at the morning or afternoon meeting of the session, or from day to day, thus expediting the work not only of the Committee but also of the convention when there is a lull in, or lack of, other convention business. This procedure can also apply to reports of all other committees.

Releasing information to the press. After they have been passed by the floor of the convention, the most important or urgent resolutions should be reported first to the waiting press or reporters.

Chapter 22
PUBLIC COURTESIES AND CEREMONIES
I. OPENING CEREMONIES

Order of opening ceremonies. If the organization's program or agenda of ceremonial observance includes all or any of the following formalities: prayer, presentation of colors (flag), national anthem or pledge of allegiance, they are executed in the order mentioned: prayer should come first, then presentation of colors, then the national anthem, and then the pledge of allegiance or singing of "America," etc.

If it includes also a hymn, the hymn follows the assembly's prayer. (Formula: Ceremonies symbolic of God or Heaven properly belong next after prayer. Ceremonies symbolic of country or patriotism come after the national anthem. Ceremonies relating to the organization, such as secret password, "Alma Mater" song, collection, etc., are executed last.)

National anthem. If two organizations are meeting in different halls or different floors of the same building, as is at times the case, and one assembly plays the national anthem either live or via the public address system audible to the other assembly, the latter one does not join in the observance. The observance is not intended for them.

If the national anthem is played in an adjoining meeting room, and its audibility actually hampers or overcomes another organization's proceedings, the latter assembly need only suspend business momentarily; it does not join in the observance.

A Selection of Appropriate Prayers

1. *Opening a meeting:* "Almighty God, we thank Thee for bringing us together this day. Inspire us to worthy deeds and sound decisions, and direct us toward the attainment of our goal. We pray Thee to guide and inspire us that we may deliberate in unity and harmony. Amen."

2. *Organizing a new lodge, chapter, post, etc.:* "Heavenly Father, we gather here in Thy presence to do Thee honor. Bless, we beseech Thee, those who are gathered here to institute this society [club, organization, lodge, etc.]. Endow us with the spirit of progress and cooperation, and

inspire us to wise decisions, to the end that all our energies may not have been devoted in vain. Amen."

3. *Faction or Discord:* "Almighty God, continue us in our courage of conviction on all matters that come before us, but without division in our Christian feeling and amity for one another. We pray Thee to eradicate all discord from us, and to break down the barriers that divide us. Bridge the span of Thy contending children, that we may work together in full accord and understanding to the end that unity and cooperation shall reign. Amen."

4. *Acquisition of new members:* "Heavenly Father, Bearer of mankind, we thank Thee for the new strength Thou hast added [or, Thou art about to add] to our ranks through these new members; guide, protect and inspire them as Thou hast with others before them. Stimulate in them frequent attendance at meetings, ready participation in all our proceedings, and willing acceptance of the will and decision of the majority, to the end that all our efforts and labor will not have gone in vain. Amen."

5. *Installation of new officers:* "Almighty God, Ruler of the Universe, we beseech Thee to bless and protect our new officers, and to guide them to uplifting and proficient deeds. Help them to direct the course of our beloved Organization. Imbue them with a full sense of justice, and with the spirit of cooperation, loyalty and devotion to its cause. Continue them steadfast and true to their oath of office and to their obligation. Amen."

6. *Military organizations:* "Almighty God, Architect and Commander of the Universe, we thank Thee for Thy deliverance. We gratefully remember our heroic comrades who paid the supreme sacrifice that the Universe may dwell in peace. Strengthen, we beseech Thee, the ties of human relation throughout Thy domain, and inspire in all of us a firmer bond of brotherhood and understanding. We thank Thee for the security of our nation and for the protection of all our people from all source of danger. Amen."

7. *Adjournment:* "Almighty Father, Who seest over all, as we prepare to adjourn we thank Thee for the opportunity of joint deliberation and action witnessed during the course of this meeting [convention, conference, etc.]. We thank Thee for the measure of friendship and association with one another. Bless, O Lord, all who are gathered here prepared to go forth, and do Thou attend to their well-being until we again gather here. Amen."

II. OATH OF MEMBERSHIP

Model forms of oath or obligation of membership (especially for young people) can be as follows:

A concise form

PRESIDENT: "Candidates, you will place your left hand over your heart [pause]; your right hand raised to heaven [pause]; and repeat after me the following obligation of membership:

"I solemnly promise and swear [pause for candidates to repeat it], that I will obey the laws, rules and regulations [pause], of the Order of Parliamentarians [pause]. So help me God [pause]. You may now lower your hands."

A more elaborate form

PRESIDENT: "Candidates, you are about to take the obligation of membership in this great Order. Are you willing to receive it?"

CANDIDATES: "I am."

PRESIDENT: "You will place your left hand over your heart, your right hand raised to heaven, and repeat after me the following oath, giving your name where I give mine.

"In the presence of Almighty God [pause for repetition], I, [give name], do solemnly promise and swear [pause], that I will obey the laws [pause], and the rules and regulations of this Order [pause].

"I will familiarize myself at once [pause] with the Order's constitution and bylaws [pause].

"I will study my parliamentary law manual [pause] in order to improve myself in parliamentary law and practice [pause].

"I will endeavor to attend all meetings [pause] and will strive to increase our membership [pause] with candidates of good moral character [pause].

"I will never wrong, cheat or defraud [pause] this Order or any member thereof [pause].

"I will honor and respect [pause] the good name of every member [pause], and I will speak evil of no one [pause].

"I further promise [pause] that I will pay my dues promptly [pause], and I will cooperate for the good of the Order [pause].

"And when elected or appointed to office [pause], I will strive to perform my duties diligently [pause], faithfully [pause], and conscientiously [pause]. So help me God [pause]. You may lower your hands."

The president then congratulates the new members.

III. INTRODUCING OR PRESENTING A SPEAKER

Distinction between "introduction" and "presentation." A person whose name or fame is known or is expected to be known to an assembly (in a convention, banquet or installation, etc.) is presented, not introduced; and one whose name or fame is not known is introduced. To present is more flattering; use "present" when in doubt.

Keep it short. Lengthy introductions should be avoided. Introductions should be brief, forceful and to the point. Comments or remarks by presiding officers after a speaker has concluded his speech are usually superfluous. Except for a word such as "Thank you," or "Thank you, Mr. Jones for a fine address," further comments are unnecessary.

Simple forms. "It gives me great pleasure to present." "I am happy to introduce," "I have the honor to present," "It is a distinct privilege and honor," "I present," "I wish to introduce," "It is a rare privilege for me to . . ." etc.

The use of adjectives and adverbs in introductions or presentations is a good practice; they are effective and can often eliminate the need of lengthy speeches. *For example*:

Presenting a governor

TOASTMASTER: "The next speaker who has honored us with his presence here tonight is the distinguished first citizen of our state, an eminent leader of our party; a political figure whose administration has made him preeminent among the chief executives of our states, and which singles him out as positive presidential timber to be seriously reckoned with at the forthcoming national convention. Ladies and gentlemen — the very able, popular and magnetic governor of our fair state, John Jones [or His Excellency or the Honorable John Jones]."

Controlling speakers' length. To avoid embarrassment and to preserve assembly orderliness, presiding officers can regulate the length or order of speeches with the speakers in advance, or as they arrive. When a speaker exceeds the time limit or is long-winded, whisper to him or put a note before him, saying, for example, "One minute more."

IV. HOW TO ADDRESS THE ASSEMBLY

Order of importance. The presiding officer should not be ignored in the address. He should always be mentioned or addressed first. The clergy, if present, may be mentioned next, then the others collectively as "distinguished guests," or individually, if not more than three or four, as "Mr. Mayor, Senator A, Professor B, Doctor C, and Ladies and Gentlemen . . ."

Some examples. When numerous speakers or guests are seated at the head table, they are usually (though not necessarily) recognized by the speaker, thus:

"Mr. Chairman, Distinguished Guests, Ladies and Gentlemen . . ."

"Madam President, Governor A, Mayor B, Notable and Distinguished Guests. Ladies and Gentlemen . . ."

"Madam Toastmistress, Reverend Father [or Reverend Clergy if more than one are present], Invited Guests, Ladies and Gentlemen . . ."

"Comrade Commander, Distinguished Guests, Officers and Members of the Organization, Ladies and Gentlemen . . ."

"Mr. Supreme President, Members of the Supreme Lodge, Brothers, Sisters, and Ladies and Gentlemen . . ."

"Supreme Knight, Grand Knights and Brothers . . ."

"Supreme Chancellor, Officers and Members . . ."

Collectively addressed. If there is a long array or list of eminent speakers or guests it is best to address them collectively as Distinguished Guests or Honored Guests, and not individually; thus:

"Mr. Toastmaster, Distinguished Guests, Ladies and Gentlemen . . ."

Note to guest speakers: When you are unfamiliar with the proper title of the presiding officer at any gathering, and you made no effort to find out in advance, say "Chairman," "Mr. Chairman [or Madam Chairman], Ladies and Gentlemen . . ."

V. NOMINATION AND ELECTION SPEECHES

Nominating speech. As in the case of an introduction or presentation of a speaker, a nomination should ordinarily also be brief, forceful and to the point. Use of adjectives rather than lengthy remarks is preferable. For example:

NOMINATOR: "Mr. Chairman, it is a great privilege for me to place in nomination for chairman of this great convention a member who is extraordinarily gifted for just such a post. He is an attorney, for years a consultant parliamentarian for various clubs and organizations, and a man whose sense of justice, impartiality and fair play are unquestioned. In him we have a combination of a capable presiding officer and an expert parliamentarian. He is the ideal choice. It therefore gives me great pleasure to nominate for chairman of this convention Brother Smith."

To hold the interest of the assembly, the name of the candidate can be given at the end of the nominating speech. But for purposes of deliberate emphasis, the name of a nominee can be mentioned at the very outset, and is then intentionally repeated practically with every sentence or statement, thus:

"I have the honor to nominate Mr. A. Mr. A is [thus-and-so]. Mr. A stands for [thus-and-so]. Mr. A's magnificent past record is [thus-and-so]. Mr. A will do [thus-and-so, etc.]. I therefore proudly nominate and strongly recommend the election of Mr. A."

Speech acknowledging election. Upon being elected to office, such as chairman of a convention or of other assembly, a word of acknowledgment or appreciation is always in order, thus:

"At this time I wish to express my very sincere appreciation for the honor you have bestowed upon me. I shall do my best to deserve your confidence. Thank you."

Sometimes the successful chairman is escorted to the platform by the one who nominated him, and, in conventions with rival candidates and contentious election, as a sign of good sportsmanship he is escorted by his nominator and the losing candidate, the chairman saying: "The Chair will ask Mr. X [the nominator] and Mr. Z [unsuccessful candidate] to escort Mr. Y to the platform."

Occasionally, especially in spirited elections, in the interest of organization harmony and solidarity, the losing candidate or his representative moves to make the election unanimous. It is put to vote perfunctorily, or merely as a matter of form, and is invariably approved and is so recorded in the minutes. If a single member seriously objects, however, the motion for a unanimous vote is ignored and is not put to vote, because a single objection destroys unanimous consent, the Chair saying: "There being objection, the motion to make the election unanimous is not in order."

On taking the chair, the chairman elected thanks the assembly for his election. In peaceable assemblies he merely says:

CHAIR: "I wish to thank the assembly for electing me chairman. I shall do my best to carry out the business of the meeting creditably," or words of like nature.

In elections which waged a spirited campaign with one or more rival candidates in the field, the successful chairman's speech includes a promise of impartiality and fair play; thus:

CHAIRMAN: "I wish to thank the delegates for the honor they conferred upon me in electing me chairman of this great convention. It will be my firm purpose and intention to preside over the convention fairly and impartially and to protect the rights of all members equally."

VI. INSTALLATION RITUAL AND OATH OF OFFICE

In an organization which has no prescribed oath of office or installation ritual for the induction of its officers-elect, the following model of ritual and oath can be adopted, or varied to suit:

INSTALLING OFFICER (when all is in readiness): "Captain of the guard (or whatever his title), you will conduct the officers-elect before the altar (or 'before me') for their oath of office."

This is done, the captain conducting each officer separately before the altar (to the accompaniment of music, if any), or all the officers can be collectively directed to "assemble before the altar" (or before the installing officer), to expedite the ceremony.

CAPTAIN: "Mr. Installing Officer, the officers-elect are ready to take their oath of office." (Captain of the guard takes position immediately behind the officers.)

I.O.: (addressing officers-elect): "My Brothers [or, Comrades, or Officers-elect, etc.], you will raise your right hand; place your left hand over your heart [or, on the Holy Bible, altar, flag of our country, etc.]; pronounce your name where I pronounce mine; and repeat after me the following oath of office:"

Collective Oath of Office

"In the presence of Almighty God [pause for repetition], and the members here assembled [pause], I [give name in full], do solemnly promise and pledge [pause], that I will discharge the duties of my office [pause], to the best of my knowledge and ability. [Pause.]. *So help me God!*"

I.O.: "You may lower your hands. The assembly will please be seated." (Addressing the Captain of the Guard:) "Captain of the Guard, you will now conduct each officer, beginning with the president [or beginning with the vice president, leaving the president last] before me for his installation."

Each officer is then conducted before the station of the installing officer, who says:

President's Charge

I.O.: "My Brother, you have been elected president of this lodge [chapter, post, etc.]. It will be your duty to preside at meetings, and to enforce impartially the rules, laws and regulations of our Order. You will be ex officio member of all committees, except the nominating committee. It will be your duty to see that all officers perform the duties assigned to their respective office. You will thoroughly familiarize yourself with the rules of parliamentary procedure and our bylaws. I now present you with the gavel, symbol of your authority, and invest you with this jewel [if any] emblematic of your office, which I know you will wear with equal pleasure to yourself and honor to the Organization." (Or:) "It gives me great pleasure to present to you this gavel, emblematic of your authority and right to act officially in the capacity and office to which you have been elected." (He continues:) "I congratulate you upon your election. Captain of the guard, you will now escort the president to his station." (This is done.)

Each officer mentioned further on is similarly conducted before the station of the installing officer, and afterward to his own station.

In each case, the installing officer says: "Captain of the guard, you will now conduct [state name] before me for his installation."

Vice President's Charge

I.O.: "Brother Vice President, the office of vice president is an important post. It will be your duty to preside in the absence of the president, and, as such, to conduct the duties of the office justly and impartially. You will perform such other duties as are specifically prescribed in the bylaws. You will immediately familiarize yourself with the rules of parliamentary procedure and the bylaws. I congratulate you on your election." (The vice president is escorted to his station.)

Secretary's Charge

I.O.: "My Brother, the office of secretary is of supreme importance. It demands constant attention and involves much work. It will be your duty to record the minutes of all meetings and to send out all meeting notices; to conduct the Organization's correspondence; to submit the order of business to the president at each meeting; to keep a fair and impartial record of the proceedings; to collect all dues and assessments from the members which you will pay over to the treasurer and receive a receipt therefor. Your books and accounts shall be open to the inspection of the executive committee at reasonable times. And at the last regular meeting of the year, you will make an annual report. I congratulate you on your election." (He is then escorted to his station.)

Treasurer's Charge

I.O.: "My Brother, the office of treasurer is one of high trust. You are the custodian of all our funds, except those otherwise designated. It will be your duty to keep an accurate record of the same, and be ready to report thereon at each regular meeting for the information of the members. It will be a further duty of your office to submit your books and records to the examination of a certified public accountant, designated by the Lodge, once every six months. I congratulate you upon your election." (Treasurer is conducted to his station.)

Chaplain's Charge

I.O.: "My Brother, you have been elected to the office of chaplain. The office of chaplain is one of divine grace. It will be your duty to open and close the meetings with prayer. Through your office we beseech the blessing of Almighty God. Through your prayer we ask our Creator for courage and wisdom, for clear thought, guidance, and health. I congratulate you upon your election." (The chaplain is conducted to his station.)

Charge for Executive Board

I.O.: "My Brothers, you have been elected to the important office of executive directors [or other appropriate title]. You are worthy of the honor thus bestowed upon you. Your business experience, your zeal and loyalty to the Organization constitute you an admirable executive board of directors. It will be your duty to inspect the records of the secretary and the books of the treasurer semiannually and at such other times as the body may deem expedient and appropriate. You will also perform such other duties as are prescribed in the bylaws. My Brothers, I congratulate you upon your election." (They are directed to return to their seats or to follow the captain of the guard who formally escorts them to their places.)

Collective Charge. If the ceremony of installation starts late and there are speakers, or the hall is uncomfortable, or a storm is imminent, or other uneasiness or concern is apparent, instead of installing the officers individually, *all* can be installed collectively; thus:

I.O.: "My Brothers, by the authority vested in me, I now proclaim you duly installed in your respective offices. I congratulate you upon your election. You may now assume your station."

VII. PRESENTATION OF A GIFT OR TRIBUTE

Presentation speech. "Brother Smith, it has fallen to my happy lot to present you with a token of our esteem and appreciation for the able and progressive administration of the affairs of this lodge during the past year. This gift may not have great intrinsic value, but it does carry the best wishes and congratulations of your fellow-members. I know that it will bear witness to the year of your fine administration. I am very happy to present you with the past president's jewel."

Speech of acceptance. "Brother Stone, I want to thank you, and, through you, the members of the lodge for their gift of remembrance. I assure you that I shall always prize it. I will always remember the very pleasant days of my administration as president of this lodge, and the fine spirit of cooperation from the members."

VIII. CONFERRING HONORARY MEMBERSHIP AND OFFICE

Like colleges and universities which confer honorary degrees on individuals for distinguished or extraordinary services to the community, state or nation, or for other conspicuous attainments, clubs and organizations confer honorary membership and office on select individuals — members of the organization and nonmembers as well — for unusual or meritorious service.

Honorary memberships are conferred by authority of the bylaws or by vote of the body. They can be rescinded by a $\frac{2}{3}$ vote without previous notice, or by majority vote with notice.

Privileges and obligations. For nonmembers of the organization, honorary membership carries certain privileges but no obligations; thus, nonmembers elected to honorary membership have the right to attend meetings and to speak on motions, but not the right to propose, second or to vote on motions, unless expressly conferred upon them. They do not pay any assessments or annual dues, are not counted in the quorum, and are not subject to other obligations of the society. They may not hold office.

But members of the organization who have been elected to the additional honor of honorary membership within their own body have all the obligations and privileges of active members, unless expressly exempted therefrom; there is no change in their status, unless otherwise prescribed in the bylaws or in the motion creating the honorary membership. Hence, these members may be elected to any office or position of any kind, including delegate, honorary president or other office. No honorary member or officer may cast two votes where he holds an active office as well as an honorary one.

If an honorary member later becomes an active member, he retains the honorary status, but enjoys thereafter all the obligations and privileges of an active member.

Honorary membership can be conferred by a unanimous vote, or as the body may determine or the bylaws expressly authorize.

Chapter 23
PARLIAMENTARY POINTERS

Under the rules of parliamentary law the following proceedings govern in all cases to which they are applicable, unless the organization's laws or bylaws and rules otherwise specify:

1. Absent members cannot vote on questions unless voting by mail is permitted by a bylaw or standing rule. Absent members can be nominated and be elected to office or position in the organization. When present at meetings later, they can exercise all and the same rights as other members, and can vote on any and all questions, including minutes of meetings they did not attend.

2. Any member can *propose* any motion whatsoever when present, except the motions to reconsider and reconsider and enter in organizations whose bylaws or parliamentary authority specify that reconsideration may be proposed only by one who voted on the prevailing side.

3. Any member can *second* any motion except his own.

4. Members can vote on any and all motions except those in which they have a direct personal or pecuniary interest.

5. All officers can vote on any motion or question that members can vote on; this includes the presiding officer, unless barred by a bylaw.

6. Democratic self-government implies that the minority, however convinced of its own wisdom, consents to be ruled by the majority until in orderly process it can make itself the majority.

7. The *rights of members* at meetings and conventions are, in general, the ten tenets, or decalogue, listed here: (1) to receive notice of all meetings and all previous notices required to be given under the bylaws or rules; (2) to attend meetings, and to expect them to be opened reasonably promptly, within ten or fifteen minutes, a quorum being present; (3) to make motions and amendments, or to second them; (4) to debate motions which are debatable; (5) to vote on motions; (6) to apply motions of higher rank on pending motions; (7) to nominate and be nominated for office, and to elect or be elected to office; (8) to make inquiries, parliamentary or informational, and also necessary requests; (9) to enjoy reasonable quiet and peaceable attendance, free from abuse and from danger or menace to his safety, health and integrity; (10) and he has legal entitlement to his share in all of the organization's funds and property as long as he remains a member.

8. Varying roles of members: (1) When all is peaceful in the assembly, the members are the collective caretaker of the organization's needs. (2) When a member is charged with wrongdoing and they disapprove of his act, they are the district attorney. (3) If they condone it, they are defense attorney. (4) And when they cast their vote for conviction or acquittal, they are the judge and jury.

9. The principle of debate connotes *free discussion* before decisions are made and full *unity* afterward.

10. It is not improper to turn one's back to the chairman and face the members when speaking. This is common practice in legislatures. Do not address the members in the second person "you." Leave out "you."

11. Avoid shouting "I call for the question!" or "Question! Question!" It is discourteous. If you mean to end further debate, rise and simply

say "I move the previous question," or "I move we end the debate."

12. It is proper parliamentary etiquette to say "I beg the Chair's pardon" when called to order for disturbing the meeting or for other misconduct in assembly.

13. A "member in good standing" is defined by the Congress of the United States as one "who has fulfilled the requirements for membership and who neither has voluntarily withdrawn from membership nor has been expelled or suspended from membership after appropriate proceedings" (Public Law 86-257).

Note: Observe that no mention is made that *payment* of dues is necessary to constitute a person a "member in good standing"; under this definition, whether a member's dues have been paid or not he still has all the rights and privileges of membership, unless he is suspended by vote of the body on account of it, or unless he is expelled — just as, for instance, a person who has not paid his installments on his house or his automobile still has the house and still has the automobile, unless there is a foreclosure of the house or his automobile is repossessed.

But if a bylaw says, "If a member has not paid his dues by [a certain time] he shall be suspended from membership," then he is deprived of his rights, and may not debate, vote, or make motions. He is also subject to whatever other penalties (if any) the vote of suspension or the bylaw may specify in any case.

14. The president can preside at both nominations and elections even though he is himself a candidate, alone or with others. When he is sole nominee, out of a sense of delicacy (merely) he permits the vice president to put the question to vote. If this is overlooked and he himself puts the question to vote, it is not invalid. When he is to be sole recipient of a gift, honor or compliment the vice president usually puts the question to a vote.

15. The president is disqualified from presiding only when he wants to take sides in debate, or to argue with the members on a pending question, and also when the pending question is one which *he* proposed or seconded. He resumes presidingship when the question is no longer pending. When, however, no one objects to the president debating or presiding on such a pending question (which he could do by merely rising and saying, "Mr. President, I respectfully object to the president presiding on a motion he made," or, "on a matter on which he has spoken"), he retains the chair and the proceeding is perfectly proper and legal, because the body so consents.

16. The president has the right to debate as well as vote on an appeal from his decision and is not disqualified from presiding on account thereof, unless barred under the organization's rules.

17. When the president presides in *board* or *committee*, he is addressed as "chairman," unless a bylaw prescribes "president" as the proper title. When a vice president presides in the *assembly*, he is addressed as "president" (or whatever the constitutional title of the president is); if anyone other than a vice president so presides, he is addressed as "chairman." *Committee* chairmen can propose, debate, vote and participate in all committee proceedings, without surrendering the gavel or the chair.

18. A meeting which starts late (or if its presiding officer arrives late) is perfectly legal, if it is legal in all other respects. A late arriving president waits until the pending question (if any) is disposed of, before he takes the chair from one then presiding.

19. When presiding, the Chair should show no indication of partisan-ship.

20. Appeal is the only motion the Chair can debate without having to surrender the chair, unless, in either case, the bylaws otherwise prescribe.

21. If the presiding officer (president, chairman, etc.) is a regular con-stituent member of the body he can vote the same as any other member, if he is not limited by the bylaws in any way; hence he can vote to break a tie, or make a tie, or complete a $\frac{2}{3}$ vote on any question, except on elections.

22. A member is never told "You are out of order," unless he is dis-orderly. If his motion or amendment is out of order, the Chair should say so. Say: "The motion [or, your amendment] is out of order," etc.

23. A motion should never be ruled out of order if the presiding officer is at all in doubt.

24. Usually (but not necessarily) the Chair awaits a point of order from the floor before he himself applies points of order on improper motions.

25. Under "unfinished business" you can transact not only (1) motions postponed definitely from the last meeting, but also (2) proposed amend-ments to the bylaws or their revision, (3) motions to reconsider, rescind, or take from the table a question after its own category has been by-passed or gone unnoticed, (4) nominations and elections, unless otherwise scheduled, and (5) all questions arising out of having given previous notice at the last meeting, or in the call for the meeting, such as previous notice to assess members, or to appropriate a larger sum of money than a bylaw or rule allows.

26. Previous notice for any purpose is good notice when given (a) at the previous meeting, or (b) in the call, or (c) by mail to every member, or (d) strictly as prescribed in the bylaws. Giving previous notice is not a debatable stage, nor is it subject to tablement or postponement.

27. To *file* a paper, report, correspondence, record, request or petition, etc., is to leave it with the appropriate officer (usually the secretary or clerk) for preservation or action. The custodian who receives them en-dorses thereon the date of their reception with a notation or index of their contents; thus: "Ordered placed on file [or, filed]; date; contents: Report of Special Committee on Sale of Clubhouse."

28. Every proceeding in parliamentary law is called a motion. Amend-ments are motions; so are nominations, points of order, questions of privi-lege, and postponements — every proceeding. Never call any subsidiary motion an "amendment," but only the amendment itself (see p. 10 *now*). To table or to postpone is *not* an amendment.

29. When a proposition is offered to the body it is called a motion; when placed before the body by the Chair it becomes a question; when adopted, it becomes an order, vote or decision.

30. A motion is never said to be before the Chair; it is before the body.

31. "Maker" or "mover" of the motion or of the amendment are appropriate terms.

32. Say "I move," not "I move you." Say "Is the motion seconded?" not "Do I hear it seconded?" Say "Those in favor of the motion will say aye," and "Those opposed will say no," not "All in favor aye" and "Contrary-minded by the same sign." Say "The ayes have it," or "The noes have it," not "It's a vote and I so declare it."

Note: "It's a vote" should never be used *alone;* it does not indicate in the record which side prevailed. Simply say, "The *ayes* [or, *noes*] have it," or, "It's a vote; the ayes [or, noes] have it."

33. All motions require a second except those listed in the text (see p. 173). A member cannot second his own motion. If unseconded motions are adopted, the vote is valid and a second is implied after adoption.

34. Except where a recorded roll call vote shows differently, a member's insistent claim that he voted on the prevailing side is final and unchallengeable.

35. Members are supposed to know their rights and must not be sleeping on them at meetings and conventions. Hence, if wrong procedure (procedural misfeasance) results in illegal action, unless points of order are raised while the action is pending to prevent it, sound sense allows it to stand as legal after adjournment.

36. In parliamentary law, the following terms are in the nature of "parliamentary twins": (1) main motion and resolution; (2) amend and substitute; (3) refer and recommit; (4) limit and extend debate; (5) postpone definitely and postpone to a definite time; (6) lay on the table and take from the table; (7) question of general privilege and question of personal privilege; (8) adjourn and fix a day to which to adjourn; (9) reconsider and reconsider and enter; (10) rescind and expunge; (11) parliamentary inquiry and information; (12) constitution and bylaws; (13) amend and revise; (14) majority report and minority report.

37. A motion or resolution which conflicts with a bylaw or rule is out of order, and if it is adopted it is null and void, even if it carries the clause "This motion hereby repeals any bylaw contradicting it"; reason: a bylaw is superior in class to a motion. Hence, it is necessary first to repeal the bylaw, in due course.

38. But if a bylaw is adopted which conflicts with another bylaw, and it carries the proviso "This bylaw hereby repeals a conflicting bylaw," the new bylaw cancels out the old one; the intent is clear.

39. If a bylaw is adopted which is in conflict with a previously adopted motion or resolution, the bylaw automatically cancels that motion.

40. If a new motion is adopted which is in conflict with a motion previously adopted, and if the new motion carries the clause "This motion hereby repeals any conflicting other motion," the intent is clear: it cancels out the old one.

41. To give your motion a chance to win: (1) arrange for a second beforehand; (2) take the floor, and ask others to take the floor to speak in favor of it; (3) have your supporters at the meeting; (4) ask them to remain at the meeting to help you defend it and protect it to the end.

42. A virtually unknown advantage: By proposing a question in the form of a *resolution* with "whereases" (thus affording you opportunity to discuss it by virtue of its "whereases" *before* it has even been seconded or stated by the Chair), instead of proposing it as a straight main motion (which, under the rules, must first be seconded and stated by the Chair before you may discuss it), you thus bring out in debate your resolution's meritorious points so as to make the assembly immediately more receptive to your proposal. A question which is proposed in the form of a resolution has a notable advantage over one which is proposed in the form of a straight main motion.

To illustrate: "Mr. Chairman, I move the adoption of the following resolution." (Now observe that he is *debating* the resolution although it has not been seconded or stated.)

"Whereas, Our clubhouse was in a dilapidated condition when it was bought thirty-nine years ago, and it is in a deplorable and totally unimprovable condition today; and

"Whereas, We have some $300,000 now in our treasury; and

"Whereas, We need a larger meeting room and parking lot; be it

"*Resolved,* That we build a new clubhouse for $175,000."

CHAIR: "Is there a *second* to the resolution?" etc.

43. "Ballot" means "secret ballot." Both forms are authoritative. Courts say the advantages of voting by ballot are: (1) the voter conceals from every person how or for whom he voted; (2) the voting by ballot is the independence of the voter; (3) a ballot means secret ballot, the object being to guard and protect the voter against intimidation, and to reduce to a minimum the incentive to bribe him or to influence his vote.

44. "Ballot" comes from the Greek word *ballo*, meaning to cast, put in, throw. It was originally applied to voting in ancient Greece by casting a marble ball, pebble, shell or bean into a box in legislative and judicial bodies, and from this ancient practice our ballot box process has been derived, as well as the paper ballot, commonly known as Australian ballot.

45. The Australian Ballot was conceived by Francis S. Dutton, member of the South Australia legislature (1851–1865). It first became law in Victoria, then in Tasmania, New South Wales and New Zealand. In 1872 the British House of Commons adopted it, then Canada, Luxembourg, Italy and Norway. In the United States, the first states to adopt the Australian ballot system in elections were Massachusetts, Indiana, and Wisconsin.

46. If a quorum is present, a proposition is carried by a majority of the votes *cast* (or by such larger vote as may be required, such as two-thirds), even if some of the members present refuse to vote.

47. The Chair, if a member of the body, is counted in the quorum. He can doubt the quorum at any time, or the vote on a motion, and he can be an objector to granting unanimous consent in any case.

48. A quorum is essential to the validity of giving any "previous notice" which may be required under the organization's bylaws or its parliamentary authority, such as previous notice to amend the bylaws, or to rescind, etc.; if there is no quorum when previous notice is given, and no point of order is raised, the notice is good and it cannot be challenged after the meeting has adjourned.

49. Absent members cannot be voted present to fill a quorum or for any other purpose.

50. On a tie, majority is generally construed to mean the negative side.

51. A majority vote reconsiders a motion requiring a $\frac{2}{3}$ vote.

52. Where a bylaw, rule or vote of the body prescribes a $\frac{2}{3}$ vote to continue a meeting's business beyond a prescribed time and such vote is given, a *majority* is thereafter competent to adjourn from time to time as the necessities of the business may require.

53. Unanimous consent, whenever required, means that everyone in the assembly *must be* in favor; hence, a single dissenting vote destroys unanimity, and that ends it. General consent means, in effect, that if everyone is in favor, there will be no *need* to put the motion to a vote; but if

anyone opposes it, then it will be put to vote to decide it. The Chair asks: "Is there any objection to doing [thus-and-so]?" If no one then objects it is both a unanimous vote as well as a vote by general consent.

54. The Chair cannot have the vote taken by roll call or by secret ballot on motions except by majority vote of the body or where the rules so require.

55. The fact that illegal votes are cast (or more votes cast than members are present) does not invalidate the result if they do not affect the result in any way.

56. Nominations need no second, except where specifically required (persons are not proceedings). Seconding is purely complimentary. A member can nominate himself to office.

57. No member may nominate more than one person for a board or committee until others have their turn at nominating.

58. The term "office" implies a duty or duties to be performed.

59. If there is no bylaw or rule specifying how a vacancy in office or position shall be filled, the body or person having *original* power to elect or appoint fills the vacancy.

60. If the bylaws are duly amended *shortening* the terms of officers, the officers previously elected for a longer term now serve the shortened term unless it is expressly provided that the shortened term shall not apply to the incumbent officers. This is so because new bylaws go into effect as soon as adopted, unless otherwise specified at the time, or unless the bylaws otherwise prescribe.

61. If the bylaws are amended *lengthening* a term of office, the incumbent officer does not serve the longer term unless it is expressly so provided. (Compare with paragraph 60.)

62. If a bylaw is adopted *abolishing* an officer's term of office, the officer is automatically out of office; he is legislated out of his tenure.

63. If an office in the organization is abolished, the incumbent has no further right to compensation.

64. A member who legally serves in office, or who fills an office *more than half* of the term is credited with having served that term, regardless of whether he served the early part or the latter part of the term.

65. "Organization" presupposes recognition of order and obedience to duly constituted authority.

66. When the phrase "in ordinary assemblies" (fraternal orders, labor organizations, women's clubs, veterans' associations, etc.) is used herein, it is merely meant to distinguish these assemblies from state legislatures, the Congress, parliaments, etc.

67. No board or executive committee can repeal, rescind, reconsider or otherwise modify or change any act or vote of a superior body unless expressly so authorized by a bylaw.

68. Members who withdraw from the meeting or convention because of dissatisfaction or dissension hurt their own cause, since the remaining members can legally transact business if they have a quorum. Even the withdrawal of a majority of the members cannot prevent those who remain at the meeting from transacting business legally if the number of those who remain is not reduced to below the quorum.

69. If a group or faction withdraws from a meeting to break a quorum, or withdraws under a preconceived scheme to organize and run a separate meeting in their own interest, the acts done at such a separate meeting

are illegal. Members who attend a meeting and then voluntarily withdraw are in no better position than those who voluntarily absent themselves in the first instance.

70. Members seceding from the organization forfeit all rights to the organization's property. It may be stated in general that those who adhere to the trust, purposes and rules of the original organization are awarded the property by the courts, even though they constitute a minority of the members. Seceders or rebellious members who form a new organization cannot acquire any right to the organization's property by adopting the name of the original organization.

71. The person or body that issues a charter has authority to suspend it, revoke it or demand its surrender, according as the organization's laws may prescribe. In case of dissolution, surrender or forfeiture of the charter, all property of the forfeiting unit is disposed of as the organization's laws or bylaws specify.

72. The "floor" means any place inside the hall or meeting room. This includes the platform and balcony. Hence, if a bylaw says "Nominations shall be made from the floor," or "Anyone from the floor may make a motion," this does not mean that the member or delegate shall step down from the platform or come down from the balcony (in a crowded convention) to nominate or to make a motion, but may do so from his place, or from the nearest microphone.

73. "Privilege of the floor" means admission to the hall or meeting room. It does not mean recognition to speak or to vote (although members often erroneously apply it to mean recognition). Recognition is one thing, admission is quite another.

74. If members are directed to speak from the microphone, the fact that members or delegates have lined up at the microphone for recognition is no guarantee that they will be entitled to recognition when they actually reach the microphone. A member or delegate ahead of them might move the previous question, which would end debate if the previous question were carried. Members have the same parliamentary rights at the microphone as they have when they are in their seats. Hence, a member at the microphone who has prior recognition has the right to move to table the pending motion, or to postpone it, or to end the debate, etc. If it is not desired to table, postpone or close debate on a motion, vote it down or propose a motion that more members shall speak (stating how many). If two or more microphones are set up, members are recognized alternately from each one.

75. "Per diem" (by the day) is such amount of compensation as is authorized by law or by vote of the body. "Per diem" and salary, or compensation, are virtually synonymous terms.

76. Mileage is an allowance for traveling expenses at a certain rate per mile. It is calculated by the shortest route. If the bylaws do not prescribe (but do not forbid) a mileage rate, the assembly has power to authorize mileage payment on the spot.

77. "Ex post facto law," "bill of attainder," and "habeas corpus" play no role whatever under parliamentary law. They are provisions of the American Constitution (U. S. Constitution, Art. 1, sec. 9).

78. The most misinterpreted, misunderstood and misapplied proceedings in parliamentary practice are: (1) previous question, (2) question of privilege, (3) appeal, (4) point of order, and (5) reconsideration.

79. Outmoded or arbitrary parliamentary practice and procedure in organizations is uneducational, unenlightening and oppressive; it belongs in the past — with the oil lamp and the horse and buggy. Members are now more informed on parliamentary law than ever before and they expect its proper practice by their presiding officers.

80. To enable the members collectively to acquire the rules of order, have the Chair, judge advocate or parliamentarian read to them desired portions of the pages in this manual at any desired meeting. The results will prove amazing.

81. When an assembly or organization adopts a parliamentary law book for its government, such book is subordinate to the organization's or assembly's constitution, bylaws and special or standing rules. Hence, such adoption does not in any way affect, alter or otherwise disturb or impair any proceedings previously acted on by the body, or any rulings or decisions of its officers, committees, or parliamentarians and judge advocates. Such adoption begins to operate as a guiding authority on future proceedings from the day of its adoption; it does not operate retroactively.

82. "Seniority," or "seniority of membership" and like terms, means *length* of membership or service in the organization that prescribes it. *Seniority* means (and it dates from) the beginning of a person's *last uninterrupted* membership or service in the organization, regardless of previous membership or interrupted service therein. *Senior member* refers to one who has the last longest uninterrupted connection in any status or capacity, and senior *person* means the eldest in age — unless the bylaws state or specify plainly to the contrary.

83. Ten ways to wreck an organization

(1) Don't come to the meetings.

(2) If you do come, come late.

(3) If the weather does not suit you, don't think of coming.

(4) If you attend a meeting, find fault with the officers and the other members.

(5) Never accept an office, as it is easier to criticize than do things.

(6) Feel hurt if you are not appointed on a committee, but if you are, do not attend committee meetings.

(7) If asked by the Chair to give your opinion on some matter, tell him you have nothing to say; after the meeting tell everyone how things should be done.

(8) Do nothing more than is absolutely necessary, but when members roll up their sleeves and willingly and unselfishly use their ability to help the organization, say that the unit is run by a clique.

(9) Hold back your dues as long as possible, or don't pay them at all.

(10) Don't bother about getting new members; let someone else do it.

84. Parliamentary Entanglements.

The following sets of motions are designed to test your knowledge of the rules of order and your skill and ability to transact each proceeding in correct form and parliamentary language. Therefore, some of the motions contained in the sets are intentionally listed out of order, while others are given in their proper order. In each case the Chair entertains the motions proposed, provided it is in order, and does not entertain it if it is out of order.

Begin by calling the meeting to order in due form and transacting the minutes accurately. After this has been done, the Chair may say: "The next business in order is new business."

Now, commence each set by first proposing a main motion. The Chair is then supposed to entertain it *if* it is in order. Then the motion immediately above the main motion is proposed, which the Chair entertains *if* it is in order or does not entertain it if it is out of order.

The motion immediately above that is offered next, which the Chair again entertains or does not entertain, depending upon whether or not it is in order when proposed. The same procedure is followed until all the motions listed in each set have been proposed.

Now, the Chair puts to vote each motion then remaining before the house, beginning with the motion of highest rank. He announces as *adopted* those motions showing a cross (+) in the parentheses alongside the motion, and as *lost* those showing the minus sign (−) in the parentheses. Remember: voting does not commence until all motions of the set have been *proposed*.

Now, carry out the drill under each set. Start with the bottom motion in each set and work up. Propose each one in turn — upward. Review the rank of motions on pp. 10–11.

Set 1
Lay on the table (−)
MAIN MOTION (+)

Set 2
Postpone to next meeting (−)
MAIN MOTION (−)

Set 3
Recess
Adjourn (−)
MAIN MOTION (+)

Set 4
Previous question
Recess (−)
MAIN MOTION (+)

Set 5
Refer to committee
Previous question
Lay on the table (−)
MAIN MOTION (+)

Set 6
Amend the main motion
Postpone indefinitely
Limit debate to two minutes (+)
MAIN MOTION (+)

Set 7
Main motion (another one)
Recess for ten minutes (−)
Amend the main motion (+)
MAIN MOTION (+)

Set 8
Amend main motion
Lay on the table (+)
Refer to committee
MAIN MOTION

Set 9
Fix adjourned meeting (+)
Refer to committee
Postpone to next meeting
Take from table
Amend main motion (+)
MAIN MOTION (+)

Set 10
Lay on table
Adjourn (−)
Refer to committee
Recess (−)
Main motion (another one)
MAIN MOTION (−)

Note: If you can properly conduct the above sets, you can consider yourself a skillful presiding officer, capable of presiding efficiently over any assembly or convention, large or small, anywhere, anytime.

Chapter 24
FORMING TEMPORARY AND PERMANENT ORGANIZATIONS

I. HOW TO ORGANIZE A PERMANENT SOCIETY

Procedure at the first meeting:
(1) Call the meeting to order.
(2) Read the call of the meeting and explain the object.
(3) Elect a temporary chairman.
(4) Elect a temporary secretary.
(5) Adopt a motion or resolution making the organization permanent, thus: "Mr. Chairman, I move that we be organized into a club [or association or organization` to be known as . . . [naming it];" or "Mr. Chairman, I move the adoption of the following resolution: *Resolved*, That it is the sense of this meeting that we organize a club to be known as [naming it]." A majority vote adopts either method.
(6) Authorize the Chair to appoint a committee to be known as the committee on bylaws; or move that the body proceed to elect a committee to draft bylaws.
(7) Adopt such other motions as may needfully come before the body at this meeting, such as to issue a press release, or to appoint a publicity or public relations committee, nominating committee, membership committee, etc.
(8) Appoint a time for reconvening in order to adopt the bylaws, to elect officers, etc.
(9) Move to recess or adjourn.

Procedure at the second meeting (or third, if needed).
(1) Call the meeting to order.
(2) Read the minutes of the previous meeting.
(3) Call for the report on the bylaws, which can be discussed, and be amended article by article or section by section by a majority vote; but it is best not to vote on them individually by article or section until the entire set is discussed, amended and perfected (in case changes are indicated later in any of them).
(4) Now adopt the bylaws in their entirety, by a single vote. A majority vote only is required to adopt a set of bylaws for initial adoption, but a $\frac{2}{3}$ vote to amend thereafter.
(5) Collect the dues, giving receipts.
(6) Sign the bylaws (some organizations require this).
(7) Elect the permanent officers, boards, committees, etc.
(8) Transact any other necessary business.
(9) Adjourn.

Can be done in one sitting. The two outline meetings shown above can be combined into one sitting when necessary or expedient, and the order of business can then be varied as desired. A recess is taken in the interest of orderly procedure when signing the bylaws or collecting dues. Only those who paid their dues are entitled to vote, to elect officers, or be elected to office, unless a different intention governs.

Charter members. Those who attend the early organization meetings and who pay for and accept membership in the proposed organization are sometimes referred to as charter members or founders, but such title is purely complimentary or designatory, and not official. Only a bylaw or a motion to that effect can make it official. This can be done either during the organization period, or it can be done at any future time.

II. ORGANIZING A TEMPORARY GROUP

Preliminary action. When organizing a temporary meeting, the following preliminary steps should be considered.

Confer with and enlist the support of others interested in the same cause; decide on the time and place of meeting; draft the contents of the notice, and determine how it shall be given and by whom signed; designate one who will call the meeting to order, and who will explain the object of the meeting; decide who will be proposed for chairman and secretary, and who will nominate each one; prepare a suitable motion or resolution to effectuate the object of the meeting, and select those who will move and speak for its adoption.

Giving notice. Notice of a proposed temporary meeting can be given in various ways — by mail, telephone, newspaper publication, radio and TV announcement, public posting, etc.

The text of the notice may be given in the following or similar manner:

"A meeting of the residents of the Town of X will be held next Monday, February 1, (year), at 8:00 P.M. in Town Hall to protest against the failure to remove the snow from our streets this winter, and to take such further action as may be necessary and proper to safeguard the health, safety and convenience of the townspeople. Everyone is welcome." [Signed] A.B., C.D., and E.F.

Calling the meeting to order. When about to open the meeting, the one previously chosen to call it to order (preferably one of the signers of the call) raps for order and says:

TEMPORARY CHAIR: "The meeting will please come to order." (When all are seated, he, or whoever was previously chosen for the purpose, reads the call of the meeting, after which he explains the purpose of the meeting. He then continues:)

TEMPORARY CHAIR: "The first business in order is the election of a chairman. Nominations for chairman are now in order."

Nominating a chairman. At this point, the person previously designated to do so promptly rises (to get his nomination in ahead of others), and addressing the presiding officer, says:

MEMBER A: "Mr. Chairman, I rise at this time to nominate for chairman a prominent and esteemed member of our community. It gives me great pleasure to nominate Mr. Y." (Nominations do not need to be seconded.)

It is then the duty of the presiding officer to repeat the name of the person nominated. He says:

TEMPORARY CHAIR: "Mr. Y has been nominated." (He immediately asks:) "Are there further nominations for chairman?"

Nominations cannot be closed immediately; reasonable time (a few seconds) must be allowed others to nominate further, after which nominations are closed either (1) on the initiative of the Chair or (2) on motion of a member. A $\frac{2}{3}$ vote is necessary to close nominations if a formal vote is taken.

When no further nominations are proposed, the Chair says:

TEMPORARY CHAIR: "There being no further nominations, nominations are closed." (He puts the nomination to a vote; thus:) 'Those in favor of Mr. Y for chairman of this meeting will say aye. Those opposed will say no. The ayes have it and Mr. Y is elected chairman. He will please take the chair." Or, "The noes have it and Mr. Y is not elected; further nominations are therefore in order." (When there is no conclusive election, nominations automatically reopen.)

Nominating the secretary. He then continues:

CHAIR: "The next business in order is the election of a secretary [if one is needed]. Nominations are now in order." (The correct and orderly nominating process follows:)

MEMBER A: "Mr. Chairman, I nominate Mr. M." (The Chair repeats each name and uses the same form throughout; thus:)

CHAIR: "Mr. M has been nominated. Are there further nominations for secretary?"

MEMBER B: "I nominate Mrs. L."

CHAIR: "Mrs. L has been nominated. Are there further nominations?"

MEMBER C: "I nominate Miss V."

CHAIR: "Miss V has been nominated. Are there further nominations?" (Silence having followed, D rises.)

MEMBER D: "Mr. Chairman, I move that nominations be closed." (Seconded.)

CHAIR: "It has been moved and seconded to close nominations. Those in favor of closing nominations will say aye; those opposed will say no." (It requires a $\frac{2}{3}$ vote; therefore, the Chair properly describes the action thus:) "There being two-thirds in favor of the motion, the ayes have it; nominations are closed."

Note: Normally, motions requiring a $\frac{2}{3}$ vote are put to vote either by show of hands or by a rising vote. However, if the Chair feels certain that a motion will meet with general approval, as in the above case of closing nominations, a voice vote may be used for the assembly's greater comfort; but the Chair must announce the result to indicate its $\frac{2}{3}$ vote requirement as shown just above. The vote can, of course, be doubted, if need be.

CHAIR (continues): "The three nominees for secretary are Mr. M, Mrs. L and Miss V."

Such candidates are voted on orally in the order in which they were nominated. If there are two or more candidates, the first candidate who receives a majority vote is declared elected, and the election is then automatically ended; thus:

CHAIR: "Those in favor of Mr. M for secretary will say aye; those opposed will say no. The noes have it, and Mr. M is not elected. The next name is Mrs. L. Those in favor of Mrs. L will say aye; those opposed will say no. The ayes have it, and Mrs. L is elected." The office is now filled, and the election automatically ends right there.

Since Mrs. L was the first candidate of the three to receive a majority vote, Miss V is not voted on, because the majority which elected Mrs. L will protect its choice and logically will vote *no* if Miss V's name is put to vote; hence, it would be a waste of time to vote on Miss V. Therefore, after a choice is made by a majority vote, other nominees, if any, are not voted on. If no one of the three is elected, nominations automatically reopen and further names are placed in nomination.

Note: To help your nominee you must vote *no* on all nominees whose name is put to vote ahead of him or her. The vote on such election can be taken by secret ballot, if so desired.

Business of the meeting

CHAIR (continues): "The next business in order is to take appropriate action in regard to the object of the meeting; namely: the persistent failure of our officials to remove the snow from our streets this year. What is the pleasure of the assembly?" Or, "What action shall be taken in this connection?"

At this point, the one previously chosen to do so rises and says:

MEMBER E: "Mr. Chairman, I move the adoption of the following resolution:

"Whereas, We annually appropriate money for snow removal; and Whereas, No attempt has as yet been made this year to remove any snow; be it

"*Resolved,* That we, the residents of the Town of X, do hereby protest the continual failure of Town officials to have the snow removed from our streets; and be it further

"*Resolved,* That a copy of this resolution be immediately forwarded to the Snow Removal Commissioners and the *Town News.*"   (Seconded.)

CHAIR: "It has been moved and seconded to adopt the resolution just read" or, "to adopt the following resolution," (which he repeats or reads as given, after which he asks:) "Is there any debate on the resolution?" After debate and amendments, if any, comes the vote, thus: "The question is on adoption of the resolution. Those in favor of its adoption will say aye; those opposed will say no. The ayes have it; the resolution is adopted." (Then the Chair may add:) "This completes the object of this meeting; a motion to adjourn would be in order, unless further steps are deemed desirable in relation to this question."

MEMBER F: "Mr. Chairman, just in case the action taken here tonight does not have any effect on our officials, I would like to propose a motion. I move that the chairman of this meeting be authorized to call a similar meeting of this group and other citizens again this year when, in his judgment, it is necessary and proper in this same connection."   (Seconded.)

CHAIR: "It has been moved and seconded that the Chair be authorized . . ." etc. (Put to vote and carried.) "Is there any further business to come before this meeting?"

MEMBER G: "Mr. Chairman, I move we adjourn."   (Seconded.)

CHAIR: "It has been moved and seconded to adjourn. Those in favor will say aye; those opposed will say no. The ayes have it, and the meeting is adjourned." Or, "Before voting on the motion to adjourn, the Chair would like to thank the residents for their civic-mindedness in coming to this meeting and also for their cooperation here tonight. And now, those in favor of adjourning will say aye; those opposed will say no. The ayes have it and the meeting is adjourned."

Chapter 25
TOWN AND CITY GOVERNMENT
I. TOWN GOVERNMENT

Origin and history. In the New England states, and in some middle and western states that have derived their institutions from New England, the word town is used to designate a well-known unit of local government. The towns constituted the original units, and formed the constituent elements of the colonies and the states. They have remained unchanged in this essential nature, having undergone only such modifications as have been rendered necessary by time and adaptation to changed conditions.

Creation of towns today. The power to create towns is invested in the legislature, except as state *constitutions* may otherwise specify.

Authority of town government. The legislature usually grants to towns the authority to make laws upon matters of purely local concern. Such grants of authority are strictly construed, so as to confer upon the towns only those powers expressly granted, and such implied powers as are necessary to carry it into execution. The authority to confer powers implies the authority to revoke them.

Town Meetings

Annual town meetings and special town meetings are subject to regulation by statute, not only as to the business to be transacted, but also as to the manner of conducting them.

Hence, towns are subordinate creatures of the state; and they may exercise only such powers as the legislature may grant from time to time.

The warrant. The usual method of calling a town meeting is by a warrant (sometimes it is called a warning). "Warrant" means authorization: that is, the call is issued by authorization of the selectmen of the town (or of the clerk, where he is expressly authorized by law), stating the objects of the meeting, the time and place, and giving proper notice.

The warrant contains the agenda (order of business) of the subjects or propositions scheduled to be acted upon at the town meeting. No proposition or subject may be acted on unless the general subject matter of the business to be transacted is described with reasonable definiteness in order to authorize actions on all subjects that are properly, or even incidentally, embraced by it.

Articles in the warrant are usually inserted either on the selectmen's own initiative, or upon the request of a prescribed or specified minimum number of registered voters of the town concerned (duly filed with the selectmen).

Illustration of a warrant's agenda. The contents, or subjects, of the warrant are normally arranged in article form; thus:

ARTICLE 1. To choose all necessary town officers.

ARTICLE 2. To hear the report of the town officers.

ARTICLE 3. To see if the town will vote to authorize the town treasurer, with the approval of the selectmen, to borrow money in anticipation of the revenue of the current year.

ARTICLE 30. To see if the town will vote to appropriate the sum of $2,000 for defraying the expenses of a proper observance of Memorial Day, or direct how the same shall be raised, or take any action relating thereto.

ARTICLE 40. To see if the town will vote to appropriate the sum of $3,000 to repair or reconstruct the northeast corner of the public library building, or to act in relation thereto.

How transacted. As each article is reached (say, Article 40), under usual town practice, a *motion* is first made by the sponsor of the article, or the chairman of the finance committee, etc., that the meeting take some specified action upon the article (as by moving "to appropriate the sum of three thousand dollars for repairs to the public library," or, if moved by the chairman of the finance committee, by recommending to the meeting "to authorize the appropriation of three thousand dollars for repairs to the public library," or to take any other desired action thereon, if any).

Basic rules. All motions based on articles in the town meeting warrant are subject to the rules of parliamentary law. Motions at a town meeting may be amended, postponed or referred and the motions to end or limit debate thereon are valid. Motions may be laid on the table, reconsidered or rescinded.

The vote required to pass a motion at a town meeting may vary from common parliamentary practice. For instance, in some towns a $\frac{2}{3}$ vote rather than a majority may be required for reconsideration or to table a motion.

Books on town meetings. There are several good books on town meetings exclusively. A fine book is *Town Meeting Time* by Johnson, Trustman and Wadsworth (Little, Brown, 1962). *Town Meeting Time* makes many additions to the views of others, and is an excellent account of comparisons and contrasts in parliamentary practices in town meetings.

Prayer, national anthem, pledge. If a town opens its meetings with religious and patriotic observances, prayer should precede the national anthem, pledge of allegiance to the flag, and other ceremonies. Such observances are not business requiring the presence of a quorum.

The moderator. The presiding officer of a town meeting is known as the moderator. He can also be referred to as the "Chair," as in all other bodies. Hence, say "Mr. Moderator," or "Madam Moderator" if a woman presides (although the derivative word "moderatrix" is perfectly proper).

Moderator's duties and privileges. The moderator is not required to decide any question not directly concerned with the proceedings, and it is not his duty to pass on a hypothetical question.

He may vote on any and every question members can vote on (including appeals), if he is a member either by independent election or an ex officio member. He wisely substains from voting when his vote will not affect the result (thus avoiding show of partisanship), except on ballot voting or unless the statute compels him to vote.

KEY QUIZ

Q. Are motions based on articles in a town meeting warrant subject to the rules of parliamentary law? *A.* Yes.

Q. Can they be amended, postponed or referred, and can the motions to end debate thereon or to limit the debate be made? *A.* Yes.

Q. Can they be laid on the table? *A.* Yes.

Q. Can they be reconsidered or rescinded? *A.* Yes.

Q. What votes are required to adopt motions on pending articles, and on subsidiary, privileged and incidental motions (pp. 47–48) in town meetings, as distinguished from the necessary vote required under general parliamentary practice? *A.* Votes on questions or motions vary with town meetings, as, for instance, under common parliamentary law, only a majority vote is needed to reconsider a motion, even if that motion needs a ⅔ vote for adoption, while in some town meetings a ⅔ vote is required to reconsider; also to table needs only a majority vote, whereas in some town meetings a ⅓ vote is necessary; and many other differences.

Q. Can the result of a vote as declared by the moderator be challenged? *A.* Yes, if it is challenged immediately and the challenge is duly seconded by the required number of voters.

The moderator relinquishes the chair to another if he wishes to engage in debate or to argue with the members on the merits of a question (because he thus becomes partisan), and he does not resume presiding until the question on which he spoke has been disposed of.

The moderator does not relinquish the chair when he gives information or speaks on matters within his knowledge or on questions of fact, as this does not constitute debate.

Appeals from moderator's decisions. The right of members to appeal from wrong, unreasonable or capricious rulings of a moderator insures the meeting against his arbitrary control of the proceedings and cannot be taken away from the members, except where appeals are prohibited by law or a bylaw.

But if the law (statute or bylaw) vests in the moderator the exclusive power to decide the question on which the appeal is based, then there can be no appeal from his decision. Thus, if the law declares that "When two or more members rise at once to claim the floor the moderator shall name the member who is first to speak," then the right to decide is lodged exclusively in the moderator and his decision is never appealable (until the law is amended in due course). The same is true with other appeals in which the moderator is expressly authorized by law to decide.

However, if there is no express law granting to the moderator the exclusive power to decide an appeal, then it is the duty of the moderator to entertain a relevant appeal, such as on amendments to motions, or opinions or judgments on essential proceedings.

Appeals which cannot be entertained. Appeals may not be entertained from the following proceedings: responses to parliamentary inquiries or information; from decisions of recognition; from decisions on dilatoriness of motions; if another appeal is taken on the same motion or question upon which an appeal is already pending; on a question on which an appeal has just been decided; during the call of the yeas and nays; from common facts, known truths, and existing rules or laws.

Appeals from the moderator's ruling must be taken at once. The right of appeal is cut off by the intervention of other business or of any other matter whatsoever.

Who may move reconsideration. The motion to reconsider must be made by one who voted on the prevailing side of the motion to be reconsidered if (a) the town's bylaws so specify, or (b) its parliamentary authority so provides (as do Robert and Demeter). If there is no such bylaw, or the town's parliamentary authority (if any) does not so specify (as in Cushing), then any member can move reconsideration regardless of how he voted on it, or if he voted at all on the motion. (See Reconsider, Key Quiz).

To kill undesirable article. The quickest ways to kill a useless or otherwise undesirable article in the warrant is by a motion to: (1) postpone indefinitely; (2) dismiss the article; or (3) take no action thereon. An affirmative vote on these motions can be reconsidered prior to final adjournment of the meeting, unless prohibited.

Decorum in debate. Members desiring to speak must rise; they must address themselves to "Mr. Moderator" (or "Madam Moderator" or "Moderatrix"); they must confine themselves to the question under debate and avoid personalities, and sit down when they have finished speaking.

Interrupting a member in debate. A member desiring to interrupt another in debate should rise, address the moderator and say: "Mr. Moderator, will the speaker yield the floor?" The speaker then decides whether he will yield the floor.

A member having the floor may not be deprived of the floor by a parliamentary inquiry or question of information unless he yields the floor; nor may he be deprived of the floor by improper points of order.

But a member who yields the floor to another to make a motion, such as an amendment, or who yields the floor without reservation, loses the floor thereby.

Courtesy resolutions. It is not inappropriate for a town meeting, when in session, to act on courtesy motions or resolutions expressing appreciation, compliment or condolence, where need be, provided no one objects. Objection can be made because it is not within the scope of the meeting to act on matters not contained in the warrant. However, a standing bylaw can be enacted in due course authorizing resolutions of appreciation, compliment or condolence.

Adjournment. A town meeting may be adjourned to another time and place by majority vote of the meeting itself, or as may be authorized by statute or a bylaw. A quorum is not necessary to adjournment.

After one motion to adjourn has been disposed of, another motion to adjourn is not in order unless some other matter or question has intervened. But if no one at all objects to renewing the motion to adjourn without the interposition of other business, such renewal is valid.

Adjourned meetings. Members of a town meeting are bound to take notice of any adjourned meetings of a town meeting, and to be present at the time and place of such adjournment without special notice. If special notice is sent, such notice must not contain any indication of favor to or prejudice against any proceeding or action taken at the previous sitting of the meeting. It should simply state the time and place of such adjourned meeting.

Business considered at adjourned meetings. If an annual meeting holds an adjourned meeting, any business which would have been proper to consider at that meeting may be considered and acted on at the adjourned meeting.

And nothing can be considered at an adjourned meeting of a special meeting, unless it could have been considered and acted on at the special meeting.

II. CITY GOVERNMENT

Definition of city. (1) A city is an instrument of the state, created to carry out its will. (2) It is a branch, or a subordinate agent, of the state government. (3) It is a body politic and corporate, with the general powers of a corporation, and the powers specified or necessarily implied therefrom which have been conferred upon it by the state legislature or the city charter.

City government is a term usually meaning the mayor, board of aldermen and common council of a city.

Legislative branch. The legislative branch of a city government usually consists of a board of aldermen and a board of councilmen, except, of course, where either the one or the other has been abolished and only one of the two constitutes the legislative chamber, as is now the case in some cities.

City council; board of aldermen. A city council or a board of aldermen is primarily a legislative and an administrative body; but it is often charged with judicial or quasi-judicial functions. Thus, when the city council or the board is sitting on charges involving the removal of an officer for cause, it acts in a judicial or quasi-judicial capacity. (The term city council hereunder also includes the board of aldermen.)

Basic rules. Motions, orders and resolutions in city councils are subject to the rules of parliamentary law. They are debatable and amendable and may be reconsidered. A majority vote is required for adoption of an order or resolution. A majority vote usually adopts reconsideration, although a $\frac{2}{3}$ vote is required in some city councils. Quorum is a majority of the whole body unless otherwise expressly specified. Laws passed by city councils are called ordinances.

Order of business. The following is a sample of the order of business in city councils (and in boards of aldermen, with some slight variations):
1. Roll call of the members.
2. Reading of journal of the previous meeting.
3. Communications from His Honor the Mayor.
4. Papers from the board of aldermen.
5. Communications and reports of city officers.
6. Presentation of petitions, memorials and remonstrances.
7. Reports of committees.
8. Unfinished business of preceding meeting.
9. Motions, orders and resolutions.

KEY QUIZ

Q. Are motions, orders and resolutions in city councils subject to the rules of parliamentary law? *A.* Yes.

Q. Are they debatable or amendable? *A.* Yes.

Q. What vote adopts an order or resolution? *A.* Majority vote.

Q. Can they be reconsidered? *A.* Yes.

Q. What vote adopts reconsideration therein? *A.* Majority vote in most councils; but a ⅔ vote in some others.

Q. What is the quorum in city councils? *A.* A majority of the whole body, unless otherwise expressly specified.

Q. If a council consists of 25 members (a majority being specified as constituting a legal quorum), what is the legal quorum of the council if one member has died, one has resigned, one was expelled and two refuse to qualify? *A.* In such a case, since the council's membership is now 20 instead of 25, its legal quorum now is 11 members (members dead, resigned, disqualified—or refusing to qualify are not counted as part of the whole number).

Differing rules in city councils. City councils differ in their rules just as other organizations' rules differ. Here are some differences and contrasts.

1. "In the absence of the president, the oldest member in terms of *seniority* shall take the chair." *Contrast:* "In the absence of the president the senior member *by age* present shall preside."

2. "Debate on reconsideration shall be limited to *twenty* minutes, and no member shall occupy more than *four* minutes." *Contrast:* "Debate on motions to reconsider shall be limited to *thirty* minutes, and no member shall speak longer than *five* minutes."

3. "Reconsideration may be moved only by a member who voted on the prevailing side." *Contrast:* "When a vote has been taken, *any* member may move a reconsideration thereof."

4. "No appeal from the decision of the president shall be entertained unless it is seconded, and no other business shall be in order until the appeal has been decided." *Contrast:* "Appeals from the decision of the Chair shall be referred without debate to the committee on rules."

5. And many other differing rules in different city councils.

Common rules in municipal bodies. For persons aspiring for election to city council, the rules stated below (common to all municipal bodies with but slight variation) are important to know.

1. A quorum shall consist of a majority of all the members.

2. The president shall preserve order and decorum. He may speak to points of order, and decide all points of order subject to appeal.

3. The president shall appoint all committees, fill all vacancies and designate the rank of the members thereof.

4. Motions shall be put in writing if the president so directs.

5. No motion or proposition of a subject different from that under consideration shall be admitted under color of amendment.

6. If, within 30 days, a matter referred to a committee is not reported upon (except in committee of the whole) it may be recalled by a standing vote of three members of the council.

7. After a motion has been put, it shall not be withdrawn except by unanimous consent.

8. Main motions shall be subject to subsidiary motions.

9. When a motion to reconsider has been decided, that decision shall not be reconsidered, and no question shall be twice reconsidered unless it has been amended after the reconsideration.

10. Every member when about to speak shall rise, address the Chair, and wait until he is recognized, and, in speaking, shall refrain from mentioning any other member by name, shall confine himself to the question, shall not use unbecoming, abusive, or unparliamentary language, and shall avoid reference to personalities.

11. Any member who, in debate or otherwise, indulges in reference to personalities or makes charges reflecting upon the character of another member shall make an apology in open session at the meeting at which the offense is committed, or at the next succeeding regular meeting, and, failing to do so, shall be named by the president or held in contempt and suspended from further participation in debate until said apology is made.

12. There shall be the following standing committees (for example): Appropriations and Finance, Claims, Confirmations, Hospitals, Inspection of Prisons, Legislative Matters, Licenses, Ordinances, Public Housing, Public Lands, Public Services and Recreation, Rules, Urban Development, Rehabilitation and Renewal.

13. When the Council shall determine to go into committee of the whole, the president shall appoint the member who shall take the chair as presiding officer in such committee.

14. All papers addressed to the Council shall be filed with the clerk of committees by . . . [specify the hour, day, etc.].

15. All ordinances, orders and resolutions shall, unless rejected, have two separate readings, after each of which debate shall be in order, and shall then be put on their passage.

16. In naming sums and fixing times the largest sum and the longest time shall be put to a vote first.

17. When a matter had been especially assigned to be taken up at a fixed time or at a certain stage of the proceedings, such matter shall, at the appointed time or stage, be in order upon the call of any member to the exclusion of all other business.

18. A motion for the yeas and nays on any question shall be taken when requested by one-fifth of the members present.

19. No member shall vote or serve on any committee on any questions where his private right is immediately concerned as distinct from the public interest.

20. When a main question has been voted on, any member who voted on the prevailing side may move reconsideration thereof during the same meeting, or give notice at the meeting to reconsider such motion at the next meeting, or may give notice of such reconsideration to the Clerk before 11 A.M. on . . . [specify day].

21. Seats of members of the Council shall be numbered and shall be determined in the presence of the Council by drawing the names of members and the number of seats simultaneously.

22. In all votes, the form of expression shall be: *"Ordered"* for everything by way of command, and the form shall be *"Resolved"* for everything expressing opinions, principles, facts or purposes.

23. Every member who is present shall vote unless the Council for special reason excuse him, or because of private interest.

24. The order of business may be changed by a $\frac{2}{3}$ vote.

25. When a committee is chosen by the Chair, the first person named shall be chairman.

26. No ordinance shall be amended after its passage to be enrolled, but may be rejected at any stage of its progress.

27. Whenever, on a rising vote or a roll call, a quorum does not vote, the Chair shall ascertain if a quorum is present, and the fact shall be recorded in the journal.

28. The absence of a member from three successive committee meetings shall be deemed a resignation therefrom, and the president shall fill it at the next meeting of the Council.

29. The president may call upon any member to preside. But if the body has a vice president or a vice chairman present, another member may not preside.

30. These rules may be amended at any meeting by a ⅔ vote of all the members of the Council.

Chapter 26
MODEL RULES FOR A POLITICAL CITY COMMITTEE

Rule I. Composition.

Clause 1. The (name of political party) City Committee of (name of city) shall consist of the members of the ward committees of the Party duly elected at the caucuses held for that purpose in the said City.

Clause 2. The officers of the City Committee shall consist of a chairman, a vice chairman, a secretary and a treasurer.

Clause 3. These officers shall be elected binennially at the meeting held for organization. A majority vote of the whole number present shall be necessary for election, provided, however, that no such election shall be held unless a majority of the existing membership of the City Committee shall be present.

Rule II. Vacancy in Office.

Clause 1. Any vacancy occurring in any of the offices of the City Committee shall be filled by the remaining members thereof; any vacancy occurring in the membership of any ward committee shall be filled by the remaining members of such ward committee.

Clause 2. If any such vacancy occurring in a ward committee shall not be filled, as hereinbefore provided, within sixty days of its occurrence, then the executive committee of the City Committee shall fill such vacancy by selecting a duly qualified elector residing in said ward, who shall represent said ward in the City Committee.

Clause 3. Each ward committee shall elect from its own body a chairman, who shall hold said office at the pleasure of said ward committee.

Rule III. Quorum.

Clause 1. A quorum for the transaction of business of the City Committee shall consist of fifty-one members, except as herein otherwise specifically provided.

Rule IV. Executive Committee.

Clause 1. There shall be an executive committee of the City Committee which shall be composed of the city chairman, vice chairman, secretary, and treasurer of the City Committee, together with the chairmen of the various ward committees.

Clause 2. The executive committee shall have all the powers of the City Committee when the latter is not in session, except to levy assessments or to expel or suspend members (both of which are reserved to the City Committee), or except as may herein be otherwise specified.

Clause 3. A majority of the existing membership of the executive committee shall be a quorum for the transaction of any business before it.

Rule V. Chairman.

Clause 1. The city chairman shall preside at all meetings of the City Committee, and in his absence the vice chairman shall so preside. In the absence of both the chairman and vice chairman, the City Committee shall elect a temporary presiding officer from its own body.

Clause 2. The city chairman shall appoint and call together all standing and special committees of the City Committee, and act as chairman of said committee meetings until said committee is organized and its permanent chairman is appointed.

Rule VI. Treasurer.

Clause 1. The treasurer shall receive and account for all monies collected for or by the City Committee and shall deposit the same in some bank or banks designated by the executive committee.

Clause 2. The treasurer shall pay all bills properly audited and approved, and make such other disbursements as are properly ordered by the city chairman or the executive committee.

Clause 3. The treasurer shall at the request of the city chairman or executive committee make a proper report of the financial condition of the City Committee, showing receipts, expenditures and balance on hand; shall submit the books and records of the office to the executive committee for examination whenever so requested, and shall deliver to his successor all moneys and records in his possession.

Clause 4. The treasurer shall give bond to the City Committee in the sum of (naming the sum) in a surety company authorized to do business in this state, said company to be designated by the executive committee, and the expense of said bond shall be paid from the funds of the City Committee.

Rule VII. Secretary.

Clause 1. The secretary shall keep a correct record of all proceedings of the City Committee, shall file all papers, shall notify all committees of their appointments and perform such other services as the committee may require.

Clause 2. The secretary shall deliver to his successor all books, records or other property of the committee in his possession.

Rule VIII. Finance Committee.

Clause 1. There shall be a standing committee on finance, composed of five members to be appointed by the city chairman.

Clause 2. It shall be the duty of this committee to devise ways and means of raising and collecting funds for use of the City Committee, and upon obtaining proper receipts to deposit the same with the treasurer, said committee to act at all times under the supervision and control of the city chairman and executive committee.

Rule IX. Party Policy Committee.

Clause 1. There shall be a standing committee on party policy composed of three members appointed by the city chairman.

Clause 2. It shall be the duty of this committee to confer with the Party members of the city government or any committee they may select for such conferences, and to perform any other services of such nature that the city chairman may call upon it to do, said committee to act at all times under the supervision and control of the city chairman and the executive committee.

Rule X. Election Officials.

Clause 1. The city chairman shall have the power to prepare lists of those to serve as caucus and election officials, said lists to be given by the city chairman to the board of canvassers.

Rule XI. Meetings.

Clause 1. The City Committee shall meet at the call of the city chairman as often as he may deem it necessary and convenient, provided, however, that it shall meet at least twice yearly. Notice in writing of such meetings shall be sent to each member by the secretary at least five days before the date set for said meeting.

Clause 2. The city chairman shall, whenever requested in writing by twenty-six members of the City Committee, call a meeting of said City Committee within three days after his receiving such request.

Clause 3. Should the city chairman neglect or refuse to call a meeting, when requested to do so in compliance with Clause 2 of this rule, then any fourteen members may call a valid meeting, by notifying all members of the City Committee in writing at least five days prior to the date set for such meeting, reciting in such notification the neglect or refusal to call such meeting and appending their names thereto.

Clause 4. The call for any meeting of the City Committee which fails to comply with the requirements set forth in the preceding three clauses of this rule shall be deemed invalidly called, and all proceedings thereof shall be null and void.

Rule XII. Charges.

Clause 1. The City Committee shall have power to remove any of its officers, and/or, to censure or expel any of its officers or members upon charges previously presented to the executive committee, in writing.

Clause 2. Upon receiving written charges against any member, the executive committee shall appoint a time and place for a hearing, and shall notify the accused member of the same, and that member shall have the right to appear and offer any proper defense thereto. The executive committee shall report its finding to the City Committee at a meeting held next after the meeting at which such charges were preferred.

Clause 3. If the report of the executive committee sustains the charges, the question of the removal from office, censure or expulsion of such member shall be voted upon by the City Committee. A majority of the existing membership of the City Committee shall be necessary to remove from office or to censure or expel a member.

Rule XIII. Disloyalty.

Clause 1. Neglect or refusal to support the nominees of the Party in any election, or the refusal to support the nominee of any Party caucus, shall be deemed disloyalty to the Party and shall subject a member guilty of the same to expulsion in the manner hereinbefore provided in Rule XII.

Rule XIV. Caucus.

Clause 1. All caucuses and primary meetings of the Party in any ward, not included within the provision of the Caucus Law of this state, shall be called within such time and after such notice as may be specified by the executive committee.

Clause 2. Should any ward committee neglect or refuse to call a caucus in accordance with a call therefor issued by the City Committee, the city chairman shall issue a call to the Party electors of such ward to meet in caucus for the transaction of such business as may be set forth in such call, and said city chairman shall designate the person who shall preside at such caucus.

Clause 3. Should it properly appear to the executive committee that the ward committee of any ward has failed to maintain a proper organization of the Party within its ward, or has permitted said committee or organization to be used against the interests of the Party, the executive committee may call caucuses in the same manner and with the same effect as though there were no Party organization in said ward.

Clause 4. In all cases of apparent conflict between a ward committee and the City Committee upon any matter pertaining to the interests of the Party, the decision of the City Committee shall be binding upon all members.

Rule XV. Order of Business.

Clause 1. The order of business at all meetings of the City Committee shall be as follows:

ORDER OF BUSINESS.

1. Call to Order by the City Chairman
2. Call of the Roll of Members
3. Reading of the Minutes
4. Bills and Communications
5. Reports of Committees
6. Presentation of Petitions
7. Special Business
8. Unfinished Business
9. New Business
10. Adjournment

Rule XVI. Parliamentary Authority.

Clause 1. Any parliamentary proceeding of the City Committee on matters not within the provisions of these rules shall be governed by (name of parliamentary law manual).

Rule XVII. Amendments to Rules.

Clause 1. Proposals to alter or amend these rules shall be submitted in writing at a regular meeting of the City Committee, and shall be voted upon at the meeting next after the meeting at which they were submitted, provided, however, that no such alteration or amendment shall be effective unless approved by a $\frac{2}{3}$ vote of the existing membership of the City Committee.

Chapter 27

POLITICAL PARTY CONVENTIONS

This chapter consists of the rules and proceedings governing the two great political parties in the United States: the Democratic and Republican.

I. CONVENTION RULES OF THE REPUBLICAN NATIONAL CONVENTION

Courtesy of the Republican National Committee

Rule 1. Agenda.

The Convention shall proceed in the order of business prepared and printed by the Republican National Committee.

Rule 2. Admission.

No person, except members of the several Delegations and Officers of the Convention, shall be admitted to the section of the Convention Hall apportioned to Delegates.

Rule 3. Credentials.

When the Convention shall have assembled and the Committee on Credentials shall have been appointed, the Secretary of the National Committee shall deliver to the said Committee on Credentials all credentials and other papers.

Rule 4. Contested Seats.

No person on the temporary roll of the Convention and whose right to be seated as a Delegate or Alternate is being contested (except those placed on the temporary roll by affirmative vote of at least two-thirds ($\frac{2}{3}$) of the members of the National Committee), shall be entitled to vote in the Convention or in any Committee thereof until by vote of the Convention the contest as to such person has been finally decided and such person has been permanently seated.

Rule 5. Absent Delegates.

In the absence of any Delegate at Large, or Delegate from any Congressional District, the roll of Alternates for the State or District shall be called in the order in which the names are placed upon the roll of the Convention, unless the State or District Convention or the law of the State or District electing the absent Delegate shall otherwise direct, in which event the Alternates from the State or District shall vote in the order established by the State or District Convention or the law of the State.

Rule 6. Each Delegate One Vote.

Each Delegate in the Convention shall be entitled to one (1) vote, which may be cast by his Alternate in the absence of the Delegate.

Rule 7. Parliamentary Authority.

The Rules of the House of Representatives of the United States shall be the Rules of this Convention, so far as they are applicable and not inconsistent with the Rules herein set forth.

Rule 8. Previous Question.

When the previous question shall be demanded by a majority of the Delegates from any State, and the demand is likewise seconded by two (2) or more States, and the call is sustained by a majority of the Delegates of the Convention, the question shall then be proceeded with and disposed of according to the Rules of the House of Representatives of the United States in similar cases.

Rule 9. Suspend Rules.

A motion to suspend the Rules shall be in order only when made by authority of a majority of the Delegates from any State and seconded by a majority of the Delegates from not less than two (2) other States, severally.

Rule 10. Lay on the Table.

It shall be in order to lay on the table a proposed amendment to a pending measure and such motion, if adopted, shall not carry with it or prejudice such original measure.

Rule 11. Debate.

No member shall speak more than once upon the same question or longer than five (5) minutes, unless by leave of the Convention, except in the presentation of the name of a candidate for nomination for President or Vice President.

Rule 12. Roll Call.

Upon all subjects before the Convention the States shall be called in alphabetical order.

Rule 13. Credentials.

The report of the Committee on Credentials shall be disposed of before the report of the Committee on Resolutions is acted upon, and the report of the Committee on Resolutions shall be disposed of before the Convention proceeds to the nomination of candidates for President and Vice President.

Rule 14. Committee Composition.

(a) The Delegates from each State elected to the National Convention shall, immediately after they are elected, select from their members for each Committee of the National Convention one man and one woman to serve thereon and shall file notice of such selection with the Secretary of the National Committee; provided, however, that no Delegate may serve on more than one Committee of the National Convention. Alternates may not serve as members of the Convention Committees.

(b) All resolutions relating to the Platform shall be referred to the Committee on Resolutions without reading and without debate.

Rule 15. Vote Recorded.

When a majority of the Delegates of any six (6) States severally shall demand that a vote be recorded, the same shall be taken by the States in the order hereinbefore established.

Rule 16. Nominating Speeches.

In making the nominations for President and Vice President and voting thereon, in no case shall the Call of the Roll be dispensed with. No nominating speech for any candidate for President or Vice President shall exceed fifteen (15) minutes in length; nor shall there be more than four (4) seconding speeches for any candidate for President or Vice President; and each of said seconding speeches shall not exceed five (5) minutes in length.

Rule 17. Majority Attained.

When it appears at the close of the Roll Call that any candidate for the nomination for President or Vice President has received the majority of the votes entitled to be cast in the Convention, the Chairman of the Convention shall announce the question to be: "Shall the nomination of the candidate be made unanimous?" If no candidate shall have received such majority the Chairman shall direct the vote to be taken again and shall repeat the taking of the vote until some candidate shall have received a majority of votes.

Rule 18. Vote Announcement.

(a) In the balloting, the vote of each State shall be announced by the Chairman of the respective Delegations; and in case the vote of any State shall be divided, the Chairman shall announce the number of votes for each candidate, or for or against any proposition; but if exception is taken by any Delegate to the correctness of such announcement by the Chairman of his Delegation, the Chairman of the Convention shall direct the roll of members of such Delegation to be called and the result shall be recorded in accordance with the vote of the several Delegates in such Delegation.

No Delegate or Alternate shall be bound by any attempt of any State or Congressional District, the District of Columbia, Puerto Rico or the Virgin Islands (etc.) to impose the unit rule.

(b) In the balloting, if any delegation shall pass when its name is called, then at the conclusion of the roll call all Delegations which passed shall be called in alphabetical order; and no Delegation will be allowed to change its votes until all Delegations which passed shall have been given a second opportunity to vote.

II. CONVENTION RULES OF THE
DEMOCRATIC NATIONAL CONVENTION

Courtesy of the Democratic National Committee

Adjournment.

Motion to adjourn may be made at any time recognition is secured for that purpose, but such recognition is not in order during roll call. While motion to adjourn to meet at designated time is not admitted in the House of Representatives, it is in order in the Convention.

Simple motion to adjourn is not debatable and may not be laid on the table; but the qualified motion to adjourn to certain time is debatable, is subject to amendment and may be tabled.

Motion to adjourn to day certain to meet at another place is in order and is decided by a majority vote.

Alternates.

Alternates are seated together on the floor of the Convention but, if possible, not with the delegation.

States are represented by an alternate for each full *vote*, regardless of the number of delegates the State is entitled to send.

In the absence of his delegate, an alternate has all the privileges of voting and debate to which his principal is entitled.

Unless otherwise authorized, the first alternate on the list is alternate for the first delegate on the list and for no other.

Where both the delegate and his alternate are absent, the alternate for another delegate from that State may cast the ballot unless otherwise instructed.

Where an alternate votes in the absence of his principal, the vote automatically can be cancelled on the appearance of the delegate prior to announcement of result and the vote of the delegate can be registered instead.

Where under a State statute delegates and alternates are elected by districts, the alternate receiving the highest number of votes is presumed to fill the first vacancy and the alternate polling the next highest number of votes, the next vacancy.

In the absence of both delegate and alternate the vote cannot be counted unless the unit rule is invoked, but a delegate or alternate absent when their names are called may vote on arrival, if done prior to announcement of result of the ballot.

An alternate may challenge the accuracy of the vote of the delegation in absence of his principal.

Amendments.

Amendments are required to be submitted in writing and must be germane to the proposition to which offered.

Agreement to the motion to lay amendment on the table *carries with it* the proposition to which amendment is offered.

Majority and minority reports from committees are subject to amendment from the floor unless the previous question is operating.

Chairman of Convention.

The Chairman may not appoint to preside temporarily in his stead any one not a member of the Convention.

No appeal from decision of chair is in order on recognition, or when dilatory, in response to parliamentary inquiry or during roll call.

The Chair does not decide hypothetical questions or inquiries not directly raised by the proceedings, and does not pass on disagreements within a delegation. Chairman may direct Sergeant-at-Arms to remove disorderly spectators.

Challenging Vote.

On roll call by States, a delegation is polled on challenge by any member of the delegation.

Demand for poll of delegation, or challenge of accuracy of count, must be made when vote is reported, and comes too late after the next State is called, or after intervening business.

Such demand may not be made by any one not a member of the delegation, and no delegate may request poll of any other delegation than his own.

Demand for poll of vote may not apply to single delegate only but must include entire delegation. Demand for poll may be withdrawn at any time before poll starts.

Chairman of Convention may defer poll until conclusion of roll call.

When a delegation is polled, the delegates in responding to their names are restricted to the bare announcement of their vote, and explanations or comments of any character are not in order.

The Convention Chairman may send a representative to the delegation to conduct the poll.

The determination of the Convention Chairman's representative of the result of the poll so challenged shall be spread upon the records of the Convention and shall be conclusive unless an open poll in the hearing of the entire Convention is demanded by one-third of the delegates of the State involved.

A demand for a poll may be withdrawn at any time.

Committees.

A rule of the Convention customarily provides for the reference of all resolutions and communications, except those relating to rules and order of business, to the committee having jurisdiction, without reading or debate.

When committees are recognized to report, the chairman of the committee may read the report himself or have it read by the reading clerk of the Convention.

At the conclusion of the reading of the report the chairman has thirty minutes in which he may (1) speak to the report, (2) yield time to others to speak, or (3) move the previous question.

When committee reports are submitted, the question on agreeing to the report is considered as pending.

Minority reports from committees are presented and read immediately following majority report and *both* are open to debate, and amendment, unless previous question is ordered; but no minority report shall be entertained unless personally signed by not less than ten percent of the members of the committee, and minority reports can not be considered after the majority report has been adopted.

Where more than one minority report is submitted, all are presented before consideration begins, and are taken up in the order presented. Question comes first on minority reports and then on majority report or majority report as amended.

Contests.

By direction of the Convention, the names of all delegates and alternates are certified to the National Committee not less than thirty days prior to the opening of the Convention.

Within this thirty days the National Committee meets, hears and decides all contests, and compiles the temporary roll.

In hearing contested election cases, each side is given 30 minutes, any part of which may be reserved for rebuttal. Briefs may be filed in advance or at the time.

Under the order of business, contests are referred to the Committee on Credentials without discussion and no motion relating to such contests is in order from the floor until the committee has reported back to the convention.

When the committee report is taken up in the Convention, the report or a motion to seat one of the contesting delegations is subject to amendment but is usually decided without debate.

Delegates on the temporary roll are seated, assigned to committees, recognized for debate, and vote on all questions, pending adjudication of contests by the Convention, but may not vote on questions directly pertaining to contests for their own seats.

In the Convention, all contests for seats are referred without debate to the Committee on Credentials which meets and hears contestants, individually or by counsel, and reports its conclusions to the Convention in the form of a majority report designating the permanent roll.

Following the reading of the majority report, dissenting members of the Committee on Credentials are recognized to submit minority reports proposing the seating of delegations other than those included in the majority report, and debate is in order until closed by the previous question.

Debate having been concluded, either by agreement or operation of the previous question, the vote is taken on the minority reports in the order in which presented and then recurs on the adoption of the majority report establishing the permanent roll.

Note: In lieu of submitting a minority report, a motion is in order to recommit the majority report to the Committee on Credentials with instructions to report it back forthwith with an amendment substituting a contesting delegation for one named in the report. If the motion to recommit is agreed to, the chairman of the committee immediately submits the report as amended without consulting his committee or retiring from the hall and the permanent roll is adopted as amended. Contests are sometimes resolved by seating both contesting delegations with half the State vote to each.

Debate.

Recognition for debate is within discretion of the Chair, but members of committees reporting the proposition under discussion, or entitled to the floor under prevailing orders of business, take precedence. Chairman of a committee is entitled to close debate on report of a committee.

Although recognition in the House of Representatives is for one hour, the established rules of the Convention now provide that no delegate shall occupy the floor in debate for more than ten (10) minutes without the unanimous consent of the Convention, but on occasions the rules are suspended, and time increased by a two-thirds vote.

Nominating and seconding speeches for President shall not exceed a total of fifteen (15) minutes for each candidate, and nominating and seconding speeches for Vice President shall not exceed a total of ten (10) minutes for each candidate.

A delegate desiring to interrupt the speaker shall address the Chair and secure consent of the speaker.

Debate is not in order during roll call, either by States, or in poll of delegation, and no delegate may be recognized to speak or to explain a vote while roll call is pending.

When reports of committees or other warmly contested issues are before the Convention, it is customary to enter into a unanimous consent agreement or to secure an order through suspension of the rules limiting debate and fixing control of time without reference to usual rules of debate.

Decorum.

Delegates and guests are expected to be seated and to refrain from loud conversation during sessions of the Convention.

Admission to floor of Convention is limited to officers of the Convention, delegates, alternates and representatives of press, radio and television. Aisles and platform must be kept clear and smoking is forbidden on the floor or in the galleries. Disorder in the galleries gives rise to a question of privilege, but such questions may not interrupt roll call.

The Sergeant-at-Arms maintains decorum under direction from the Chairman of the Convention. All persons on the platform are required to be seated during proceedings.

Only the speaker entitled to recognition and the Chairman stand. All others who cannot be seated should retire promptly.

Delegates.

Delegates shall be residents of the States, Territories or Districts which they represent.

The Convention accepts the temporary roll of delegates prepared by the National Committee as *prima facie* correct, and contested delegations are accepted, seated, assigned to committees and permitted to vote without restriction until action on contest by the Convention.

A delegate absent when his name is reached in roll call may vote on return before the result is declared, regardless of whether his alternate has voted in his absence.

Those delegates present and voting constitute the delegation, although a majority of the delegation may be absent.

A delegate announcing he would not abide by the decision of the Convention is held not entitled to participate in its deliberations, and delegates failing to observe the rules and orders of the Convention are subject to expulsion by a two-thirds vote.

Division of a Question.

A division of the question, and a separate vote on each substantive proposition contained in a committee report or any pending question, may be requested by any delegate, and such request is in order even after the previous question is demanded.

Instructions.

Where a State convention has instructed its delegation, the Convention will enforce that instruction.

But the Convention takes no cognizance of private agreements among members of a delegation and will not consider propositions to enforce such personal agreements. The burden of proof of instruction rests on proponents, and it is incumbent upon delegates alleging instructions to produce documentary evidence thereof.

Where instructions from States and Congressional districts conflict, the State instructions govern.

Representation in the Convention is from the State and not from sub-divisions thereof, and instructions from the latter are not recognized unless authorized by mandatory statute providing for election of delegates from districts without subjecting them to State authority. Under such statutes, instructions imposed by State authority do not apply.

Qualified Instructions. Under instructions "to vote as a unit on questions as a *majority* may determine," delegates by refusing to vote may not subtract such votes from the total, and the entire vote of the delegation will be recorded as directed by the *majority*.

Note: The Democratic National Convention held in Chicago in 1968 abolished the unit rule provisions hereunder. But as these provisions can be enacted again at any future convention, they are left in here for the delegates' future guidance. See "Unit Rule," page 292.

Instructions to vote for a candidate "until two-thirds determine that he cannot be nominated" are construed literally and a two-thirds vote is required to absolve from instruction, but is construed as meaning two-thirds of those present and voting and not two-thirds of the entire delegation.

Resolutions by State convention "requesting" delegation to vote as a unit are interpreted as if reading "instructed" to vote as a unit; and resolutions "recommending" that the delegation be bound by unit rule are construed as if reading "instructing" that delegation be bound by the unit rule.

Instructions to vote for candidate "as long as there is a reasonable hope of his nomination" are construed as giving majority of delegation right to decide when "reasonable hope" could no longer be entertained.

Instructions to vote for a candidate "until released by him or his authority" are held not to invoke the unit rule, and each member of the delegation is entitled to determine for himself the responsibility to his constituency in casting his vote.

Instructions to vote for a designated candidate are to be distinguished from instructions to vote under the unit rule. Both may be imposed in same instructions, but one does not imply the other, and the Convention will not enforce instructions to vote for certain candidate unless such instructions also invoke the unit rule, although where the unit rule is also imposed the vote of the entire delegation will be recorded in accordance with the vote of the majority.

Where delegations are under the unit rule but are uninstructed as to candidates voted half and half, it is held that the delegation must break the deadlock for itself; and, in event of failure to do so, that rule does not apply and votes are then cast half for one candidate and half for the other.

Instructions to "vote as a unit on all matters pertaining to the business before the convention" are held to apply to balloting for nomination of President as well as to other votes; but where instructions invoked the unit rule "on all questions affecting his nomination," they are held not to apply to questions other than those affecting his nomination; and where a delegation is instructed to vote under the unit rule in "nominating a candidate for President," it is held that the unit rule is not invoked on other propositions.

Instructions to vote as a unit for a candidate for a specific time are held not to continue the unit rule in support of another candidate subsequent to expiration of such time; and where instructions are imposed in behalf of one candidate, it is held that, when ineffective with reference to that candidate, they cannot be transferred to another candidate.

Instructions to vote for a candidate "until released by him," once released, although merely for purpose of casting complimentary vote, are thereby vitiated and may not be invoked again.

The Convention, by suspension of the rules, may release all delegates "from all pledges or instructions of any kind whatsoever relating to any candidate for the nomination for President," but such action is held not to abrogate the unit rule where in operation in any delegation.

Motions and Resolutions.

Delegates must secure recognition from the Chair in order to offer a motion, and the Chair may inquire for what purpose the delegate rises and, after hearing the motion, may decline recognition.

After an order of business is adopted, no motions are admissible unless they are in order under the pending item of business or at that particular stage of the proceedings.

Under the rules of the House of Representatives adopted by the Convention, a second is not required, and motions decided adversely may not be renewed before other business has intervened.

Motions or resolutions may be withdrawn at any time before action by the Convention, even after order for yeas and nays, providing the roll call has not begun.

A rule of the Convention provides for reference to appropriate committees without reading or debate, of all resolutions, petitions and communications introduced, except those pertaining to the rules and order of business, and such reference is in order even before committees have been appointed.

Nominations.

A delegation when reached in the call of States for nomination of President or Vice President has choice of four options: (1) to pass; (2) to nominate a candidate; (3) to second the nomination of a candidate; or (4) to yield to another State.

Delegates may vote for any person whether placed in nomination or not.

States or candidates may withdraw nominations at any time before announcement of the vote.

The roll call is by States. However, any delegate is entitled to recognition in order to nominate or second a nomination and the call by States is merely a convenient and orderly method of procedure.

The Convention enforces instructions, and instructions which precluded voting for another candidate preclude nominating another candidate.

But where a delegation is uninstructed, any member of the delegation may nominate or second a nomination when his State is reached in the call.

When one State yields to another, it is called subsequently when the State to which it yielded would have been called. A delegate instructed for one candidate, or a member of a State delegation instructed under the unit rule for a certain candidate, is not precluded from nominating, or seconding the nomination of another candidate.

Time for Nominating Speeches. The total time for *both* nominating and seconding speeches for *each* candidate for President is limited to fifteen (15) minutes.

The total time for both nominating and seconding speeches for each candidate for Vice President is limited to ten (10) minutes.

In nominating or seconding the nomination of a candidate, delegates may address the Convention from the floor or from the platform as preferred.

It is not in order in nominating a candidate to attack another candidate.

A State failing to respond when called in its turn may be recognized subsequently if it asks recognition before balloting begins.

The call of the States for nominations when reached in the order of business is the only business in order and may not be interrupted by motions to recess, adjourn, fix the time at which to adjourn or other motions, until the call has been completed; but a motion to suspend the rules and recess or adjourn is admissible, and, if carried, the call of States comes up as the unfinished business at the next session of the Convention.

The call of States for nominations having been concluded, a roll call can be dispensed with only by unanimous consent or on motion to suspend the rules.

Acclamation.

Acclamation is a unanimous *viva voce* vote and any objector may raise a point of order; but by long custom the Chairman puts the question "to suspend the rules and declare (*name*) nominated for President of the United States by acclamation."

The motion to nominate by acclamation is sometimes made before roll call starts, and sometimes after roll call in which a candidate has secured a nominating majority; but the roll call having been started, it may not be interrupted by motion to suspend the rules and elect by acclamation. The Chair declines to recognize for that purpose.

Order of Business.

As soon as the permanent organization is completed, the Convention adopts an order of business, which, once agreed to, fixes permanently the parliamentary program of the Convention and may be amended or dispensed with only (a) by unanimous consent, (b) by adoption of a report from the Committee on Rules, or (c) by agreeing to a motion to suspend the rules. Under such order of business, a resolution offered between ballots for President that the Convention remain in session until nomination be made is held not to be in order.

Points of Order.

Points of order against a proceeding come too late after debate has begun or other business has intervened.

Debate on questions of order is within discretion of the Chair.

Points of order arising during a roll call are decided peremptorily and are not subject to appeal.

Previous Question.

Previous question when ordered prevents both debate and amendment.

Committeemen presenting a report may move the previous question; but if it is ordered before any debate is had on the question at any time, forty (40) minutes debate is allowed, twenty (20) minutes on each side.

Proxies.

Neither delegates nor alternates may vote by proxy, unless deputation of proxy is specifically authorized by State convention or other authority selecting the delegates; and, even where duly authorized, persons holding proxies though entitled to *vote* are not entitled to *recognition* for debate.

Quorum.

A quorum is necessary to the transaction of any business either in the Convention or its Committees and is *always* presumed to be present *unless* otherwise determined.

A quorum consists of a majority of the elected and qualified delegates, as required by the Constitution for the transaction of the business of the House of Representatives.

As in the House, any delegate may raise the question of a quorum and a point of no quorum is in order *at any time*.

In the absence of a quorum, the motion to adjourn has precedence over the motion to secure a quorum.

Recess.

The motion to recess while not admitted in the House of Representatives is by long custom held in order in the Convention, but is not debatable.

Reconsideration.

When a motion is carried or lost, any member of the *majority* may move reconsideration on the same or following day.

The majority is construed to mean the *prevailing side*, or, in case of a *tie* vote, the *negative* side.

Suspension of the Rules.

Motion to suspend the rules interrupts the regular order of business and is in order at any time except during roll call; but recognition to move suspension is within discretion of the Chair, and requires a two-thirds vote.

Motion to suspend the rules may not be amended; may not be reconsidered; and may not be laid on the table.

Motion to go into executive session in balloting on nomination of President is not in order, but the motion to suspend the rules and go into executive session is in order.

Motion to drop lowest candidate is not admitted; but the motion to suspend the rules and drop the candidate receiving the lowest vote is admitted between roll calls on nominations.

However, adoption of such motion has no binding effect, as delegates may vote for any person whether placed in nomination or not. Motion to suspend the rules and nominate by acclamation is invoked in most conventions, but is not in order during roll call.

Lay on the Table.

The motion to lay on the table is used for final summary disposition without debate; and a matter once laid on the table cannot be taken up again except by unanimous consent, and the motion to suspend the rules may not be laid on the table. However, the qualified motion to adjourn to a day certain is subject to the motion to lay on the table.

An amendment laid on the table carries with it the proposition to which the amendment was offered.

Two-Thirds Rule.

Note: The two-thirds rule in Democratic National Conventions was formally abolished at Philadelphia in 1936; but as it is subject to adoption by *any* Convention, it is included in the Convention procedure.

Beginning with the Convention of 1832, the Democratic National Convention required a two-thirds ($\frac{2}{3}$) vote for the nomination of President and Vice President.

The two-thirds vote required was not two-thirds of the number of votes in the Convention, but two-thirds of the votes cast, a quorum being present.

Unanimous Consent.

Any action may be taken and any proceeding had by *unanimous* consent, regardless of the rules or the pending business.

But recognition to move unanimous consent is within the discretion of the Chair, and may not be granted except for routine matters or under exceptional circumstances.

Unit Rule.

Note: The unit rule in Democratic national conventions was formally abolished at Chicago in 1968; but as it can be adopted again by any future convention, the unit rule provision is included in the convention procedure hereunder, for the information of the delegates of future Democratic national conventions.

The Democratic National Convention recognizes the unit rule under which a majority of the delegates from a State may cast the entire vote of the State regardless of the preference of the minority.

Where a State convention has instructed its delegation to observe the unit rule, the Convention will enforce it.

Delegations cannot disregard the action of State conventions in their adoption of the unit rule.

Note: Michigan delegation voted 25 to 7 to discard the unit rule adopted by Michigan State Convention in 1952; but the National Convention held that the unit rule adopted by the State convention was in effect.

Delegates are held bound by the unit rule whether they are selected by district caucus or elected by vote of convention.

However, the unit rule may not apply to those States in which delegates are selected at the primaries, the delegates so elected being responsible to their constituents only.

Under the unit rule a majority of the delegates from a State cast the entire vote of the State regardless of the number of delegates absent or the number refusing to vote; but where a majority vote of the delegation has not been cast for any one candidate the unit rule does not apply.

Voting.

On a call of the States, the vote of the State is announced by the chairman of the delegation, or, in his absence, by the vice chairman.

Delegations not prepared to announce their vote may be passed and called at the end of the roll.

Where the majority of the members of a delegation present concur, the entire vote of the delegation is cast although members may be absent.

In order to vote, a delegate must sit with his delegation and may not vote from another part of the hall and may not deputize another to cast his vote for him.

A delegate may decline to vote and may change his vote at any time after call of States has been concluded and prior to final announcement of the result of the ballot.

A delegate proposing to change his vote must rise in his place and personally request the change. It is not sufficient for the chairman of the delegation to submit the request.

A delegate may secure a poll of his own delegation, but of no other delegation, by challenging the accuracy of the count or report; but the vote cannot be challenged until announced at the desk.

Requests for a poll or to change a vote come too late after the next State has been called.

On such poll, delegates are restricted to bare announcement of their vote, and explanation or comment is not admissible.

Polls of delegations are deferred to the end of the roll call.

On roll call by States, a delegation shall be polled on challenge by any member of the delegation.

The Convention Chairman may send a representative to the delegation to conduct the poll; and, in the discretion of the Convention Chairman, the roll call may continue instead of awaiting the result of the polling.

Division of a Question. Any delegate may demand a division of a question containing more than one substantive proposition and a separate vote on any or all of the proposition included.

Roll Call. A roll call for the yeas and nays is ordered upon the demand of a majority of any eight delegations.

A roll call may not be interrupted by debate, or to permit a delegate to explain his vote, or by parliamentary inquiry, or by motion for recess, or by a motion to adjourn, or by a motion to make the vote unanimous.

A motion on which the vote is being taken may not be withdrawn after the roll call begins.

Error in Announcement of the Vote. Error in announcement of a vote is corrected by subsequent announcement.

States which pass are called at the end of the roll.

[1] 17 Pa. Dist. 301, 304.
[2] 41 Fed. 371; 126 Cal. 355.
[3] 7 N.Y. Supp. 135; 17 R.I. 586.
[4] 146 Cal. 699, 81 Pac. 17.
[5] 64 N.H. 213, 9 Atl. 98.
[6] 53 Minn. 371; 67 N.H. 119; 107 N.Y. Supp. 886; Ohio St. 10.
[7] 31 Me. 34; 42 Mo. App. 474; 61 Wash. 79, 111 Pac. 1055.
[8] 78 Ill. 96; 89 Iowa 521.
[9] 61 Wash. 79, 111 Pac. 1055.
[10] 127 U.S. 579; 84 Ala. 613; 113 Ind. 79; 50 Kan. 155; 161 N.Y. 353, 55 N.E. 919; 20 Ohio St. 288; 87 N.J.L. 410; Wend. (N.Y.) 394.
[11] U.S. House Rules and Manual, Rule 1.
[12] 134 U.S. 317; 99 Me. 426.
[13] 22 Hawaii 604; 28 N.Y. Super. 649, memo.
[14] 99 Me. 426, 59 Atl. 529; 52 N.Y. Supp. 1147.
[15] 4 Whart. (Pa.) 603.
[16] 23 Nev. 437, 49 Pac. 41.
[17] 71 Conn. 540, 42 Atl. 636; 161 N.Y. 353, 55 N.E. 919.
[18] 202 Ill. 312, 67 N.E. 17; 23 Nev. 437, 49 Pac. 41.
[19] 45 N.Y. Supp. 852; 20 Misc. 17; 161 N.Y. 353, 55 N.E. 919.
[20] 232 Pa. 53, 81 Atl. 153.
[21] 158 Pa. 476; 48 N.W. 347.
[22] 118 Cal. 618; 88 Conn. 676; 195 Mass. 470.
[23] 195 Mass. 470; 155 Pa. 239.
[24] 14 Neb. 24, 14 N.W. 660; 161 N.Y. 353, 45 N.Y. Supp. 852, 20 Misc. 1147; 44 N.H. 465; 7 Phila. (Pa.) 350.
[25] 50 Mont. 322.
[26] 109 Pac. 915; 79 S 875.
[27] 104 Minn. 252.
[28] 172 Ind. 1; 41 R.I. 79.
[29] 146 Ky. 798, 143 S.W. 369.
[30] 172 Ind. 1; 100 Kan. 101, 193 Pac. 719; 137 N.Y. 346.
[31] 60 Ala. 86; 64 Mo. 139.
[32] 172 Ind. 1, 87 N.E. 141.
[33] 30 Nev. 409, 95 Pac. 391.
[34] 137 N.Y. 346; 30 Nev. 409.
[35] 30 Nev. 409, 97 Pac. 391; 24 Nev. 92; 137 N.Y. 346.
[36] 93 U.S. 599; 137 N.Y. 346, 129 N.Y. Supp. 365; 141 Tenn. 229.
[37] 212 Mass. 23, 98 N.E. 614; 87 N.Y. Supp. 153, 43 Misc. 338.
[38] 93 U.S. 599; 121 Tenn. 229.
[39] 49 Ala. 402.
[40] 12 Iowa 405; 57 Minn. 261.
[41] 53 Fed. 769; 178 Wis. 656.
[42] 62 Me. 296; 107 Mo. 603; 140 N.C. 332; 50 Wis. 178.
[43] 76 Conn. 648; 12 Ont. L. 13.
[44] 54 Kan. 63; 131 Minn. 401.
[45] 227 U.S. 71.
[46] 252 N.Y. Supp. 141 Misc. 7.
[47] 70 L.R.A. 188; 40 N.Y. Supp. 1141.
[48] 265 N.Y. 112, 191 N.E. 854.

[49] 215 Pac. 673; 207 Pac. 829.
[50] 129 Ill. 298; 111 Ky. 598; 195 Mass. 470; 100 Miss. 467; 118 N.Y. 101; 50 Wash. 95.
[51] 114 N.Y. 626, 21 N.E. 420.
[52] 58 N.H. 187.
[53] 144 U.S. 1; 78 Cal. 289; 84 Md. 304; 239 Mo. 303.
[54] 60 Iowa 391, 14 N.W. 775.
[55] 258 Mass. 139, 154 N.E. 555.
[56] 114 U.S. 1; 34 Minn. 135.
[57] 113 Ill. 137; 131 Ind. 338; 32 N.J. Eq. 341.
[58] 98 Ala. 629; 42 Conn. 32; 106 Iowa 673; 69 Mich. 189.
[59] 74 Mich. 269, 41 N.W. 921; 33 S.C.L. 457.
[60] 69 N.H. 606, 45 Atl. 562.
[61] 23 Cal. 314; 160 Mo. App. 682; 68 Tex. 30; 125 N.Y. Supp. 613.
[62] 14 Ariz. 278; 267 Ill. 439; 125 N.W. (S.D.) 122.
[63] 28 Cal. App. 478; 132 La. 435; 125 Minn. 407; 108 Miss. 242; 87 N.J.L. 410; 144 N.Y. 66; 33 N.Y. 493; 131 Wis. 198.
[64] 96 Cal. 371; 168 Ill. 369; 82 Mich. 532; 133 N.Y. 493.
[65] 175 Ky. 123, 194 S.W. 122.
[66] 28 Colo. 60, 62 Pac. 856.
[67] 155 Ky. 72, 159 S.W. 646; 131 La. 439, 59 So. 866; 58 Okla. 672.
[68] 96 W.Va. 716 at 723.
[69] 235 Ill. 326; 177 Ind. 178; 64 Kan. 216; 108 Me. 161; 79 W.Va. 432.
[70] 57 Cal. 148; 259 Ill. 496; 114 Me. 35; 127 Minn. 33.
[71] 106 Cal. 500; 138 Ky. 277.
[72] 165 Ala. 619, 51 So. 719.
[73] 177 Ind. 78, 97 N.E. 534.
[74] 108 Me. 177, 79 Atl. 532.
[75] 282 Ill. 122; 95 Md. 703.
[76] 19 Ariz. 254, 169 Pac. 596.
[77] 250 Ill. 521, 95 N.E. 484.
[78] 229 Ill. 198, 82 N.E. 215.
[79] 158 Ill. 609; 177 Mass. 518.
[80] 72 Kan. 701; 132 La. 424; 15 N.Y. 750; 32 Ont. L. 1.
[81] 216 N.Y. 732, 110 N.E. 776; 29 R.I. 239, 69 Atl. 851.
[82] 159 Ky. 568, 167 S.W. 893; 216 N.Y. 732, 110 N.E. 776.
[83] 132 La. 545; 89 Neb. 65.
[84] 172 Cal. 137; 25 Nev. 131; 34 Ore. 462; 7 S.D. 343; 14 Ont. L. 253; 42 N.S. 282.
[85] 143 Cal. 104; 21 Colo. 460.
[86] 106 N.Y. Supp. 205, 55 Misc. 5.
[87] 287 Ill. 382, 122 N.E. 611.
[88] 14 N.D. 311.
[89] 72 Kan. 247.
[90] 114 Me. 443, 96 Atl. 769.
[91] 79 W.Va. 425, 95 S.E. 99.
[92] 194 Mich. 399.
[93] 106 Atl. (N.H.) 483.
[94] 176 Cal. 218; 78 N.H. 358.
[95] 252 Ill. 340; 113 Me. 485.
[96] 23 Colo. 65, 46 Pac. 120; 78 N.H. 358, 101 Atl. 31; 52 AmS.R. 254.
[97] 113 Me. 485, 94 Atl. 943.
[98] 23 Colo. 65, 46 Pac. 120.
[99] 141 Cal. 412; 72 Conn. 99; 18 Hawaii 167; 95 Md. 703; 156 N.Y. 36; 111 N.C. 124.
[100] 288 Ill. 315, 177 Ind. 178; 177 Iowa 64; 72 Kan. 701; 113 Me. 485; 38 Mont. 590; 83 Neb. 64; 35 Nev. 300.
[101] 253 Ill. 326; 98 Ky. 596; 113 Me. 485; N.Y. Supp. 232.
[102] 29 Ill. 54; 125 Ky. 750; 46 Minn. 274, 48 N.W. 112.

[103] 125 Ky. 750, 102 S.W. 263.
[104] 115 La. 1019, 40 So. 443.
[105] 69 N.H. 556, 45 Atl. 410.
[106] 130 Mo. 621, 32 S.W. 1127.
[107] 131 Ala. 387, 31 So. 93.
[108] 231 Ill. 42, 83 N.E. 87.
[109] 189 S.W. 960 (Tex. Civ. App.).
[110] 194 N.Y. 99, 66 N.E. 818.
[111] 31 S.W. 653.
[112] 139 U.S. 278; 135 Ill. 591.
[113] 259 Ill. 436, 102 N.E. 810.
[114] 68 Kan. 776, 75 Pac. 1031.
[115] 26 Cal. App. 108, 146 Pac. 79.
[116] 155 N.Y. 545, 42 N.Y. Supp. 957.
[117] 170 Ill. 630; 188 N.Y. 266.
[118] 135 La. 92, 64 So. 993.
[119] 180 Ky. 526; 110 Me. 204.
[120] 128 Ga. 483; 170 Ind. 704.
[121] 121 Ky. 548; 47 Miss. 266; 13 Puerto Rico 96.
[122] 119 N.Y. 91; 11 Wash. 423.
[123] 27 Mo. App. 633.
[124] 23 Ill. 456.
[125] 23 Ill. 456; 110 N.Y. 33.
[126] 3 W. & S. (Pa.) 45.
[127] 13 Pa. 288.
[128] 53 N.H. 9; 24 Am. Dec. 223.
[129] 108 S.W. 421.
[130] 55 Fed. 839; 22 Neb. 375.
[131] 118 Mass. 78; 91 Tenn. 303.
[132] 77 Pa. 397.
[133] 51 Cal. 155
[134] 43 Md. 1, 20 Pa. 484.
[135] 5 Rob. (N.Y.) 649.
[136] 41 How. Pr. (N.Y.) 302.
[137] 69 Conn. 286.
[138] 76 Wis. 464.
[139] 69 Ill. 27; 73 Wis. 257.
[140] 187 Mass. 40, 72 N.E. 253.
[141] 187 Mass. 40, 72 N.E. 253; 63 Neb. 792, 111 S.W. 699.
[142] 68 N.H. 333, 44 Atl. 485.
[143] 18 Vt. 266.
[144] 31 Ill. 25; 97 Ind. 421.
[145] 233 Ill. 73; 53 N.H. 9.
[146] 108 S.W. 421; 528 S.W. 247.
[147] 219 Ill. 503; 24 Pick (Mass.) 211.
[148] 108 Tenn. 173; 80 Ky. 443; 25 Kan. 177.
[149] 2 W.Va. 310.
[150] 36 Me. 36 at 47.
[151] 54 Ala. 599.
[152] 41 Mo. 41; 97 N.Y. 271.
[153] 77 Va. 300; 71 Atl. 139.
[154] 136 Ga. 376; 296 Ill. 494.
[155] 63 Okla. 42, 168 Pac. 780.
[156] 32 Ky. L. Rep. 979, 107 S.W. 751.
[157] 109 Minn. 18, 122 N.W. 462.
[158] 198 Ill. 340, 200 Mass. 152.
[159] 3 S. & R. (Pa.) 145.
[160] 133 Cal. 196; 64 Mo. 89.
[161] 93 U.S. 599; 178 Wis. 656.

[162] 194 Iowa 28; 12 La. 655.
[163] 67 Fla. 423; 113 Ind. 434; 81 N.C. 394; 98 N.J.L. 417.
[164] 159 Ark. 438; 85 Md. 252; 4 Wyo. 535.
[165] 136 Ga. 405; 21 Wis. 496.
[166] 175 Ark. 86; 107 Cal. 285; 204 Ky. 260; 98 Mich. 360.
[167] 24 N.Y. Supp. 629; 70 Hun. 87.
[168] 105 Ill. 240; 230 Mo. 408.
[169] 149 Wis. 488, 137 N.W. 20.
[170] 179 Ill. 340; 117 Ind. 496.
[171] 121 Ala. 379; 87 Md. 59.
[172] 34 Wis. 21.
[173] 143 U.S. 18; 82 Ark. 302; 126 Cal. 130; 34 Fla. 530; 186 Ill. 209; 170 Ind. 325; 3 Me. 22; 39 Md. 164; 12 Mass. 537; 64 Miss. 534; 10 Nev. 319; 37 N.H. 295; 183 N.Y. 51; 41 Ore. 509; 12 S.D. 1; 118 Tenn. 390; 21 Tex. 734; 72 Vt. 33; 120 Ohio St. 263.
[174] 34 Fla. 530, 16 So. 413.
[175] 80 Ill. 134; 157 Mass. 128.
[176] 22 Wend. (N.Y.) 9.
[177] 117 Cal. 157; 148 N.Y. 281; 235 Pa. 601; 89 Tex. 69.
[178] 161 Cal. 106; 171 Ill. 417; 51 Ind. 4; 17 Mass. 1; 95 Tenn. 157; 103 Wis. 492.
[179] 165 Ill. App. 368.
[180] 119 Wis. 392; 96 N.W. 783.
[181] 205 Fed. 643, 656.
[182] 131 Iowa 232, 108 N.W. 313; 7 Cow. (N.Y.) 402.
[183] 79 Fed. 10; 111 Ga. 266; 180 Mass. 321; 169 N.Y. 34.
[184] 159 Fed. 564; 166 Ill. 595; 150 Mich. 215; 31 Ont. 154.
[185] 86 Md. 668; 201 Pa. 78.
[186] 99 Me. 253; 75 Miss. 466; 102 N.Y. Supp. 406; 95 Tenn. 157.
[187] 86 Kan. 45; 39 Me. 35; 221 Mass. 38; 118 Mo. 437; 189 N.Y. 294; 21 R.I. 9; 10 Que. K.B. 324
[188] 31 Mich. 458; 120 S.W. 719.
[189] 179 Ill. 524; 111 Minn. 207.
[190] 60 Iowa 493, 15 N.W. 282; 73 Ore. 605; 2 Ore. 246; 87 Tex. 125; 47 Wis. 208.
[191] 101 N.Y. 82, 4 N.E. 348.
[192] 12 Mass. 504; 7 N.Y. Supp. 406.
[193] 4 Wheat. (U.S.) 518, 636; 5 Ga. 535; 122 Ill. 293; 8 Ohio 257, 286.
[194] 1 Blackstone Comm. 468; 2 Kent. Comm. 268.
[195] 1 Minor Inst. 499; 2 Kent Comm. 268.
[196] 1 Kent Comm. 268.
[197] 10 Wall. (U.S.) 566; 196 Fed. 832; 86 Fed. 585.
[198] 208 U.S. 267; 203 Mass. 159; 22 Wend. (N.Y.) 9, 70.
[199] 70 Conn. 590; 131 Pa. 614.
[200] 67 Fed. 816; 41 N.Y. 384.
[201] 109 Pa. 560, 563.
[202] 77 Minn. 498; 75 N.W. 692.
[203] 173 Fed. 601; 129 Ga. 734.
[204] 84 Ala. 613, 4 So. 763.
[205] 161 Cal. 621, 120 Pac. 15.
[206] 75 Conn. 669, 55 Atl. 175.
[207] 172 Cal. 366.
[208] 176 Ind. 682; 162 Iowa 525.
[209] 67 N.Y. Supp. 10; 165 Wis. 548.
[210] 57 Atl. 417; 193 S.W. 400.
[211] 62 Ill. 493; 158 Wis. 649.
[212] 22 Conn. 435; 55 N.H. 415.
[213] 107 Iowa 196; 48 Me. 269.
[214] 21 Cal. App. 95; 93 Mo. 485.
[215] 170 Ky. 748; 209 N.Y. 265.
[216] 227 Pa. 410, 417.

[217] 149 Pa. 84, 29 Atl. 88.
[218] Ky. L. Rep. 204; 103 Wash. 254.
[219] 98 Ala. 92; 12 So. 723.
[220] 122 Mo. App. 437, 99 S.W. 902.
[221] 13 Pa. County Ct. 576.
[222] 181 Iowa 1013, 165 N.W. 854.
[223] 112 Ala. 228, 20 So. 744.
[224] 150 N.C. 216, 63 S.E. 892.
[225] 109 Cal. 571, 42 Pac. 225.
[226] 30 Fed. 91; 207 Ill. 107; 101 Ky. 570; 61 N.J. Eq. 5.
[227] 89 Fed. 397.
[228] 78 N.J. Eq. 484; 10 Md. 468.
[229] 181 Iowa 1013, 165 N.W. 254.
[230] 122 Fed. 115; 270 Ill. 170; 123 N.Y. 91; 181 Pa. 361.
[231] 251 Fed. 937; 160 Ala. 497.
[232] 172 Mich. 650; 244 Pa. 373.
[233] 107 Ill. App. 369; 96 N.Y. 444.
[234] 131 Ga. 329; 49 Wash. 496; 72 W.Va. 221; 21 Wyo. 62.

Addenda

SOME RULES OF LAW PERTAINING TO OFFICE

Consolidation of office. The authority in the organization which possesses the power to create an office has, in the absence of a higher law to the contrary, the implied power to abolish the office it created, or to consolidate two or more offices it has created.

Fixed and unfixed term of office. The phrase "term of office" means a fixed period of time for which the office may be held — as for one year, or two, or three, etc. But if the term is not fixed (as in a newly formed group or organization), the officer is regarded as holding office at the will of the body.

Holding office during good behavior. If a bylaw creates an office which fixes one's term to be "during good behavior," the officer holds only so long as that bylaw remains in force.

Reduction of number of directors. When a bylaw is duly passed reducing the number of directors (as from 15 to 7), all the directors are affected. The body has then the right to provide that those already chosen cast lots to determine whose term of office shall be discontinued, unless prior resignations make this step unnecessary.

Election of ineligible person to office. The election or appointment of an ineligible person is an absolute nullity — except that his legal official acts, while in office, are regarded as the acts of an officer *de facto* (or, in effect, as good as legal).

Misconduct in office. If the cause for removal of an officer is "misconduct *in office*," the phrase "misconduct in office" is broad enough to embrace any willful malfeasance, misfeasance, or nonfeasance in office. If, however, the cause is simply "misconduct," the cause is then for misconduct not connected with the office.

Right to nominate one's self. A member who is eligible to hold office in the organization has the right to nominate himself thereto, if the bylaws do not prohibit it.

Right to appoint one's self. The regular presiding officer (whatever his title) who has unrestricted authority by rule, bylaw or by a motion of the body to *appoint* a committee, has the implied right to appoint himself thereon if he so chooses (although it is rarely done), provided he is eligible as appointee and the bylaws do not expressly prevent it.

And a person or public official who has absolute power by law to *name* any person to fill a vacancy in office or position may name himself if he so chooses, provided he is eligible thereto under the laws governing such appointment.

When an office may be declared vacant without recourse to charges or trial. If an officer (president, treasurer, etc.) is incompetent, tyrannical, contumacious or otherwise seriously obnoxious, his tenure of office may under certain circumstances be declared vacant by the body *without* instituting charges or trial. Two illustrations:

(1) It can be declared vacant when his term of office is *not fixed* (as for one year, two, etc.), in which case the officer holds office merely at the will of the body. (See second paragraph of this section.)

(2) It can be declared vacant even if his term of office *is* fixed by a bylaw, provided the bylaw gives the body an alternative for his removal before the tenure ends. For example: If the bylaw states that the term shall be "for one year [or two, or three] *or* until a successor is elected," then the body (by virtue of the alternative *or*) has the right and the choice to either proceed immediately to elect a successor or wait out the completion of the term.

When an office may not be declared vacant. If, however, the bylaw fixing the term of office states that it shall be "for one year [or two, or three] *and* until a successor is elected," the office cannot be declared vacant because the conjunctive *and* restrains the body from doing so before completion of the tenure of office, *except* upon written charges against him, trial with due notice, etc.

However, if the body wishes to avoid charges and trial thereon, it may amend the bylaw and abolish the office. (See pp. 257, 264.)

Due process of parliamentary law. All attempts to declare a term of office vacant, to abolish the office, or to bring to trial, must be done under due process of parliamentary law with due notice thereof, requisite vote, etc.

————————

Reproduction of page 375. The entire contents of page 375 may be reproduced or published in your organization's publication, or in your local club, school or newspaper without the permission in writing from the publisher, by crediting the title of this manual.

INDEX

THE GREATEST CONVENTION EVER HELD

Resolved under the Omniscient Direction and Orderly Guidance of the Supreme Parliamentarian of the Universe. A Six-Day Divine Convention, Held in Eden (400 miles eastward of Canaan), in the Month of Harvest, in the Beginning of Time and Life.

AGENDA OF THE CONVENTION
Holy Bible, Genesis 1:1–31, and 2:2.

Acts of the First Day
Resolved, That there be light.
"And God said, Let there be light."
Thus on the first day, the Convention "divided the light from the darkness," and it called the light Day and the darkness Night.

Acts of the Second Day
Resolved, That there be a firmanent.
"And God said, Let there be a firmanent."
Thus on the second day, the Convention created not only the sun, moon, stars and comets, but also the atmosphere. It also separated the water which is in the clouds from that which is in the seas and rivers; and it called the firmanent Heaven.

Acts of the Third Day
Resolved, That there be earth and seas.
"And God said, Let the waters under the heaven be gathered together unto one place, and let the dry land appear." He called the dry land Earth, and the gathering together of the waters Seas.
Thus on the third day, the Convention created the earth and seas.

Acts of the Fourth Day
Resolved, That there be sun, moon and the seasons of the year.
"And God said, Let there be lights in the firmament of the heaven to divide the day from the night; and let them be for signs, and for seasons, and for days, and years."
Thus on the fourth day, the Convention provided the sun, the moon, and the seasons of the year.

Acts of the Fifth Day
Resolved, That there be every form of animal life.
"And God said, Let the waters bring forth abundantly the moving creature that hath life, and fowl that may fly above the earth."
Thus on the fifth day, the Convention created all animal life.

Acts of the Sixth Day
Resolved, That there be human life.
"And God said, Let us make man in our image, after our likeness."
Thus on the sixth and last day, the Convention created human life and provided the human race.

The Seventh Day
"And on the seventh day God ended His work." Genesis 2:2.

To Presiding Officers:
(Read also pp. 7, 10, 11, 39–46, 250–252)

The presiding officer is the servant of the organization.

All his acts at meetings and conventions must have the body's approval, unless a bylaw makes them independent.

Presiding officers who are ignorant of parliamentary law or who defy the body's will or deny to the members the proper exercise of their rights are a sad spectacle before intelligent assemblies and frequently cause discontent and disunity.

Capable presiding officers make good meetings.

Incompetent, abusive or obnoxious presiding officers can be censured (see p. 260); and their tenure of office can be shortened or abolished altogether by a $\frac{2}{3}$ vote, and thus they may be legislated out of office at any meeting with prior notice.

You are not expected to know all the law. No one is. But you are expected to be able to at least match the members' combined basic knowledge of it.

Handy Phrases for Members

Mr. Chairman, or, Mr. President, or, Madam Chairman, etc.

I doubt the quorum.

I doubt the vote.

I move that we . . .

I rise to a point of order.

I move that we adopt this resolution: *Resolved*, That . . .

A parliamentary inquiry.

I move to amend the motion.

Mr. Chairman, will the member yield the floor to me?

I do not yield, or, I yield to a *question* only, or, I yield.

Handy Phrases
For Presiding Officers

The meeting will be in order.

The secretary will read the . . .

The first [or, the next] business in order is . . .

The Chair requests order.

The Chair requests quiet.

The Chair can recognize only one member at a time; all other members will be seated.

The Chair now recognizes . . .

For what purpose does the member [delegate] rise?

State your name, city, etc.

The motion is [or, is not] in order.

Do you yield the floor?

The member will refrain from . . .

The Chair wishes to state . . .

Please repeat your motion.

It is moved and seconded that we . . .

It is moved and seconded to amend the motion by . . .

The ayes have it; the amendment is carried. Now, the vote is on the motion as amended.

Those in favor will say aye. Those opposed will say no. The ayes [or, noes] have it.

If there is no objection, the Chair will . . .

Basic Knowledge

You can master basic parliamentary law within six weeks at only *one* hour a day.

Read pages: 7–8, 10, 11, 25–32, 33–34, 37–38, 40–46, 50–62, 66, 68–69, 82–83, 88, 90–91, 92–93, 98, 106–107, 112, 113–114, 119, 120–121, 124, 125, 126–127, 152–153, 165, 168, 169, 177–190.

C